MADARA

Vol. 1

Created & Illustrated by
Sho-u Tajima

Created & Written by
Eiji Otsuka

cmx

Jim Lee
  Editorial Director
John Nee
  VP—Business Development
Jonathan Tarbox
  Group Editor
Paul Levitz
  President & Publisher
Georg Brewer
  VP—Design & Retail Product Development
Richard Bruning
  Senior VP—Creative Director
Patrick Caldon
  Senior VP—Finance & Operations
Chris Caramalis
  VP—Finance
Terri Cunningham
  VP—Managing Editor
Dan DiDio
  VP—Editorial
Alison Gill
  VP—Manufacturing
Rich Johnson
  VP—Book Trade Sales
Hank Kanalz
  VP—General Manager, WildStorm
Lillian Laserson
  Senior VP & General Counsel
David McKillips
  VP—Advertising & Custom Publishing
Gregory Noveck
  Senior VP—Creative Affairs
Cheryl Rubin
  Senior VP—Brand Management
Bob Wayne
  VP—Sales & Marketing

Michael Niyama
Translation and Adaptation
Michael Heisler
Lettering
John J. Hill
CMX Logo & Publication Design
Ed Roeder
Additional Design

ISBN: 1-4012-0529-1

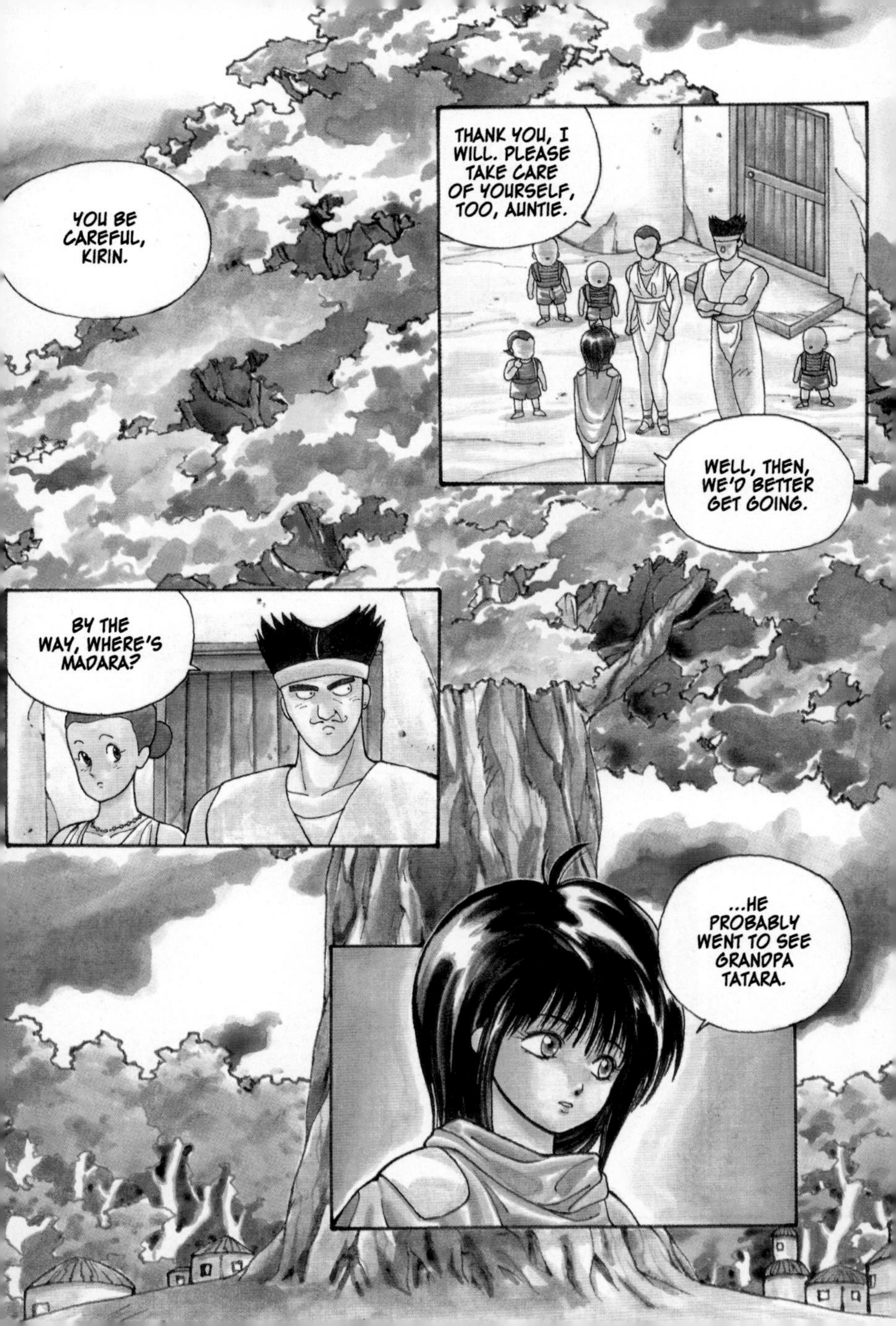
THANK YOU, I WILL. PLEASE TAKE CARE OF YOURSELF, TOO, AUNTIE.
YOU BE CAREFUL, KIRIN.
WELL, THEN, WE'D BETTER GET GOING.
BY THE WAY, WHERE'S MADARA?
...HE PROBABLY WENT TO SEE GRANDPA TATARA.

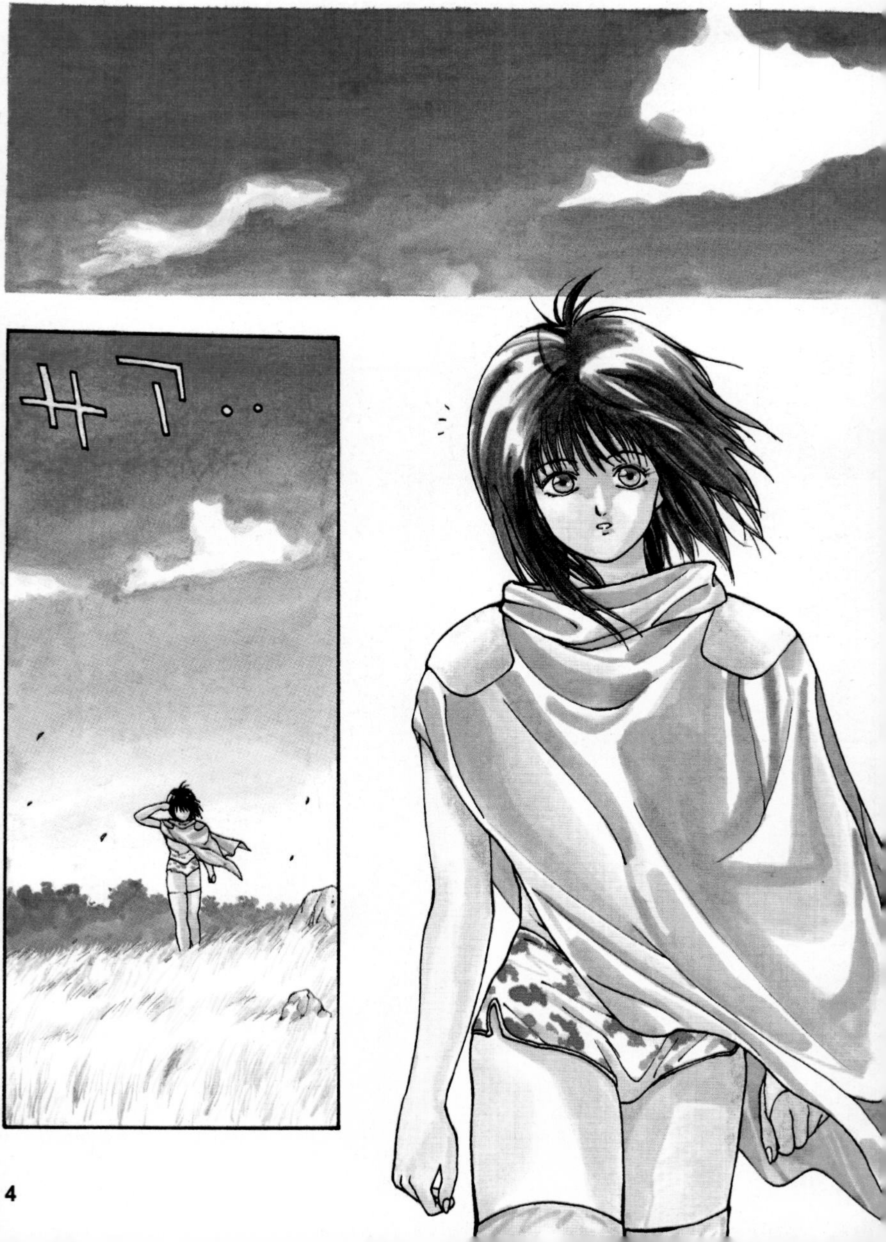
サア..

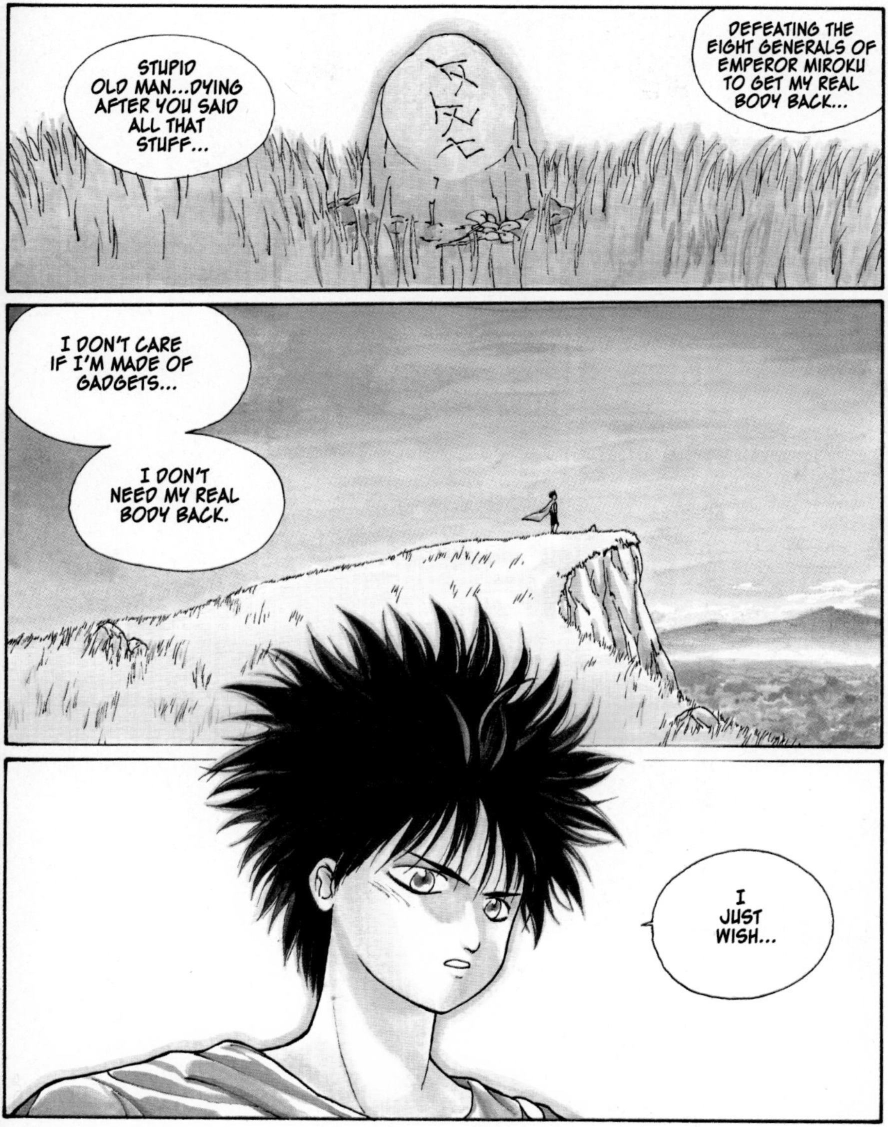
DEFEATING THE EIGHT GENERALS OF EMPEROR MIROKU TO GET MY REAL BODY BACK...
STUPID OLD MAN...DYING AFTER YOU SAID ALL THAT STUFF...
I DON'T CARE IF I'M MADE OF GADGETS...
I DON'T NEED MY REAL BODY BACK.
I JUST WISH...

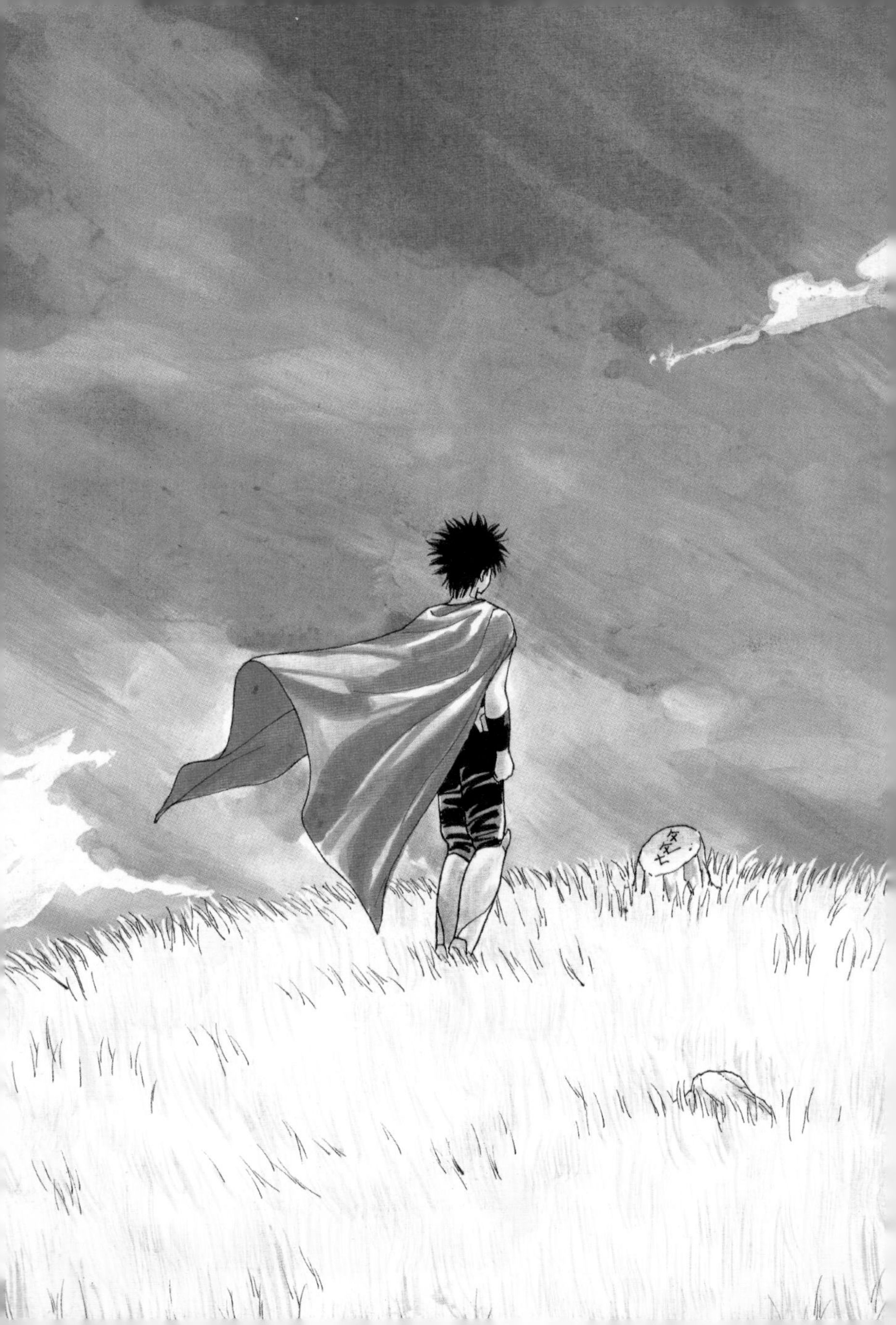

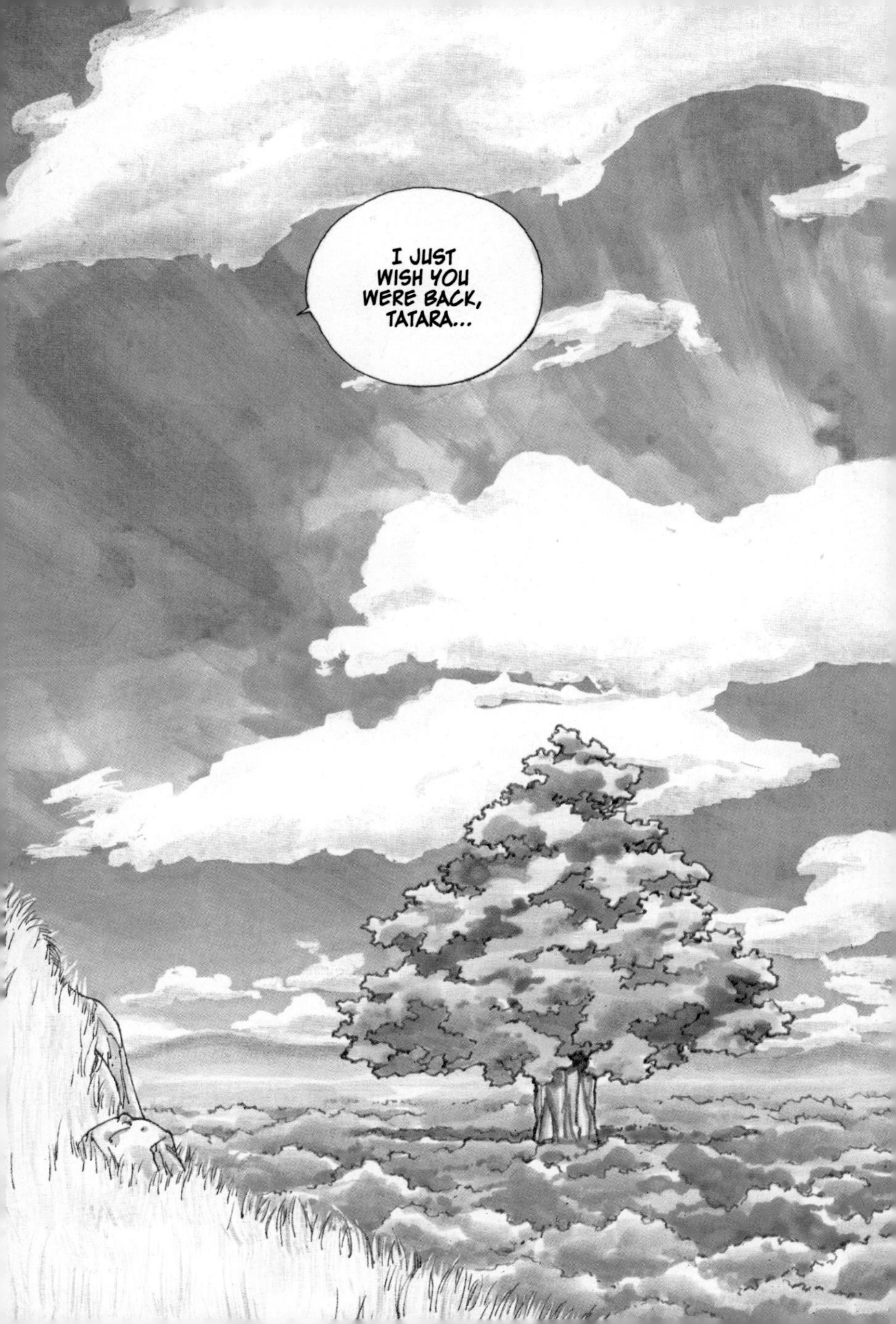
I JUST WISH YOU WERE BACK, TATARA...

序章 **流離譚**

Prologue: The Tale of the Wanderer

"In the year 3499 of the Ugaya Dynasty, a clan claiming to be descendants of the gods came from the eastern islands and invaded this land. The head of the clan was named Miroku, and he had control over demons named *moki*. Following the slaughter and conquest, *moki* ruled the entire land. Miroku erected a massive empire, the Diamond Kingdom, with his royal palace on Mt. Shumi, a holy place said to be the entrance to the Holy Land of Agartha. And it is from this royal palace that the legend of the true king begins, as a child floats downstream on a lotus flower…"

– From the oral tradition, "Account of the Kingdom of a Thousand Years," the Madara Legend, as recorded in the *Nisshu Rajin Jofuku*

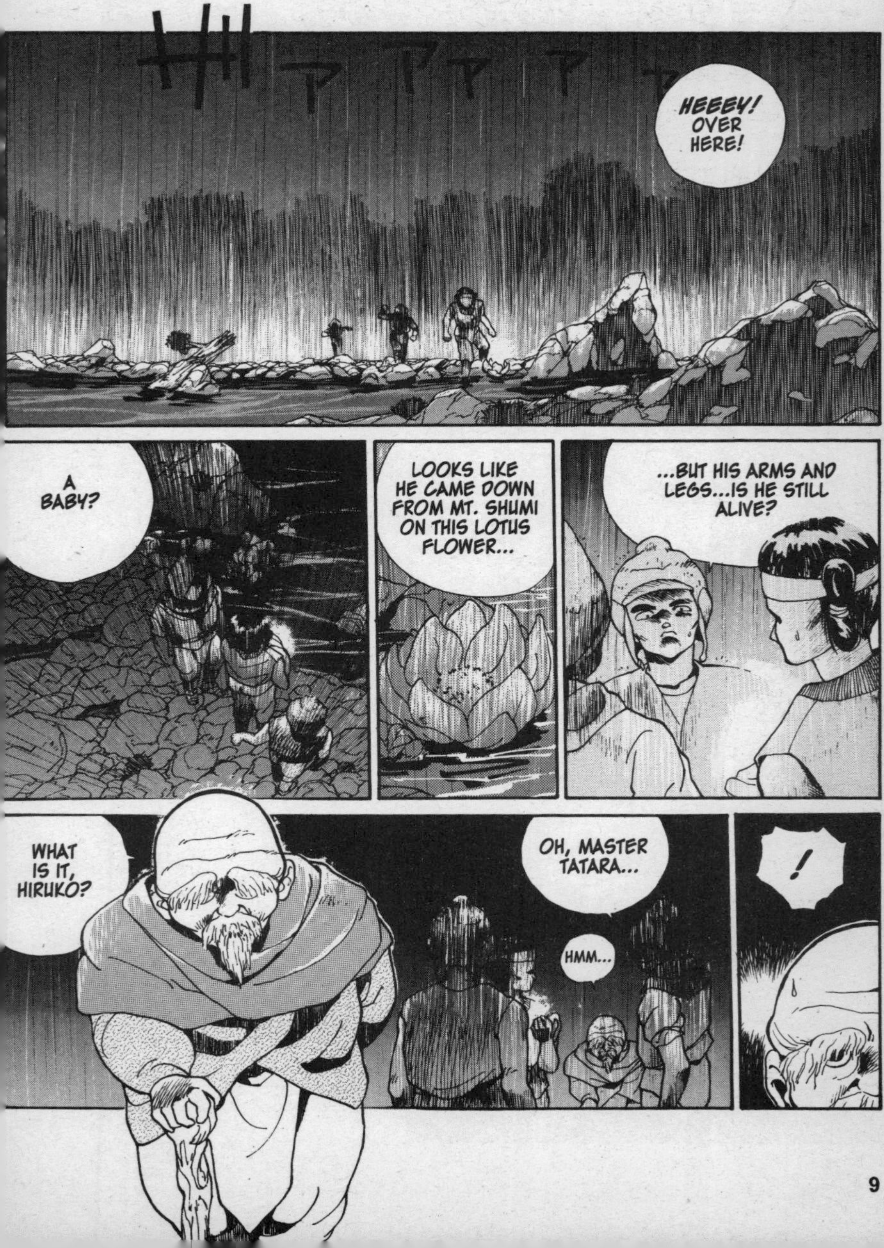
HEEEY! OVER HERE!
A BABY?
LOOKS LIKE HE CAME DOWN FROM MT. SHUMI ON THIS LOTUS FLOWER...
...BUT HIS ARMS AND LEGS...IS HE STILL ALIVE?
WHAT IS IT, HIRUKO?
OH, MASTER TATARA...
HMM...
!

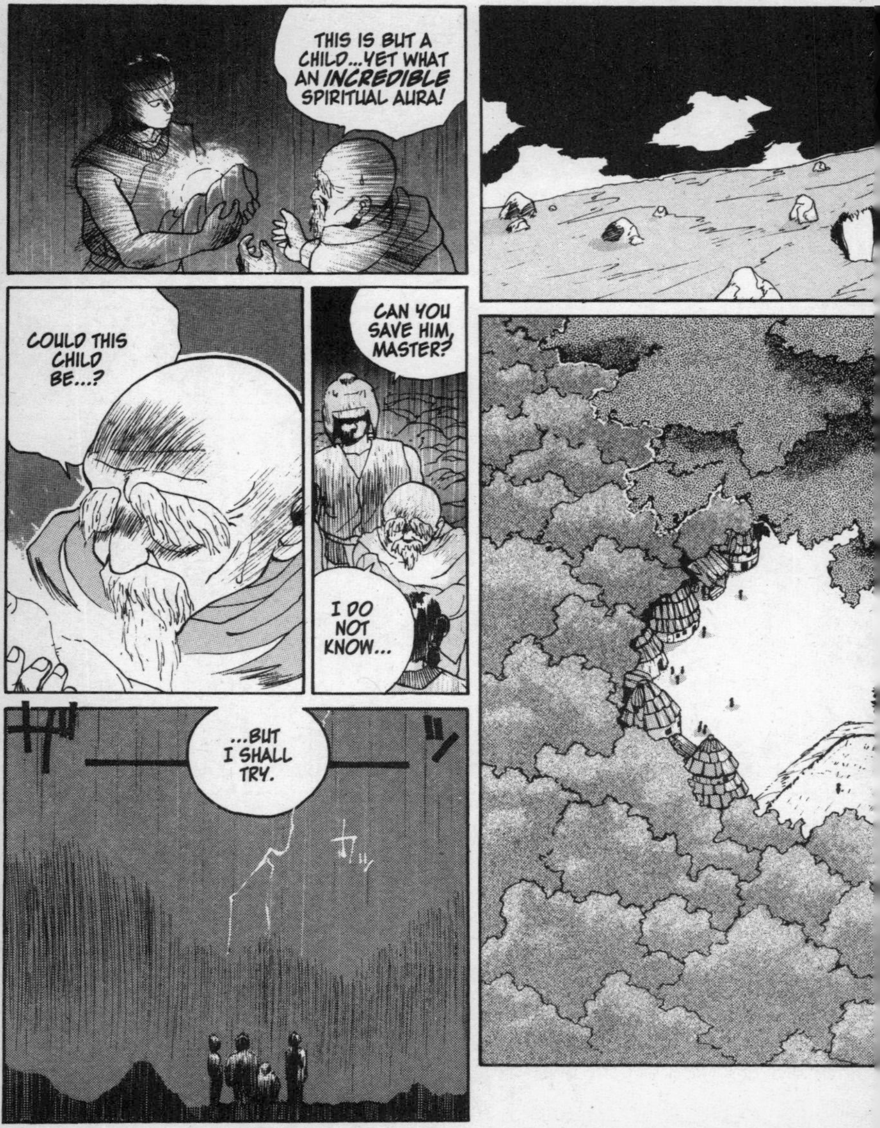
THIS IS BUT A CHILD...YET WHAT AN INCREDIBLE SPIRITUAL AURA!
COULD THIS CHILD BE...?
CAN YOU SAVE HIM, MASTER?
I DO NOT KNOW...
...BUT I SHALL TRY.

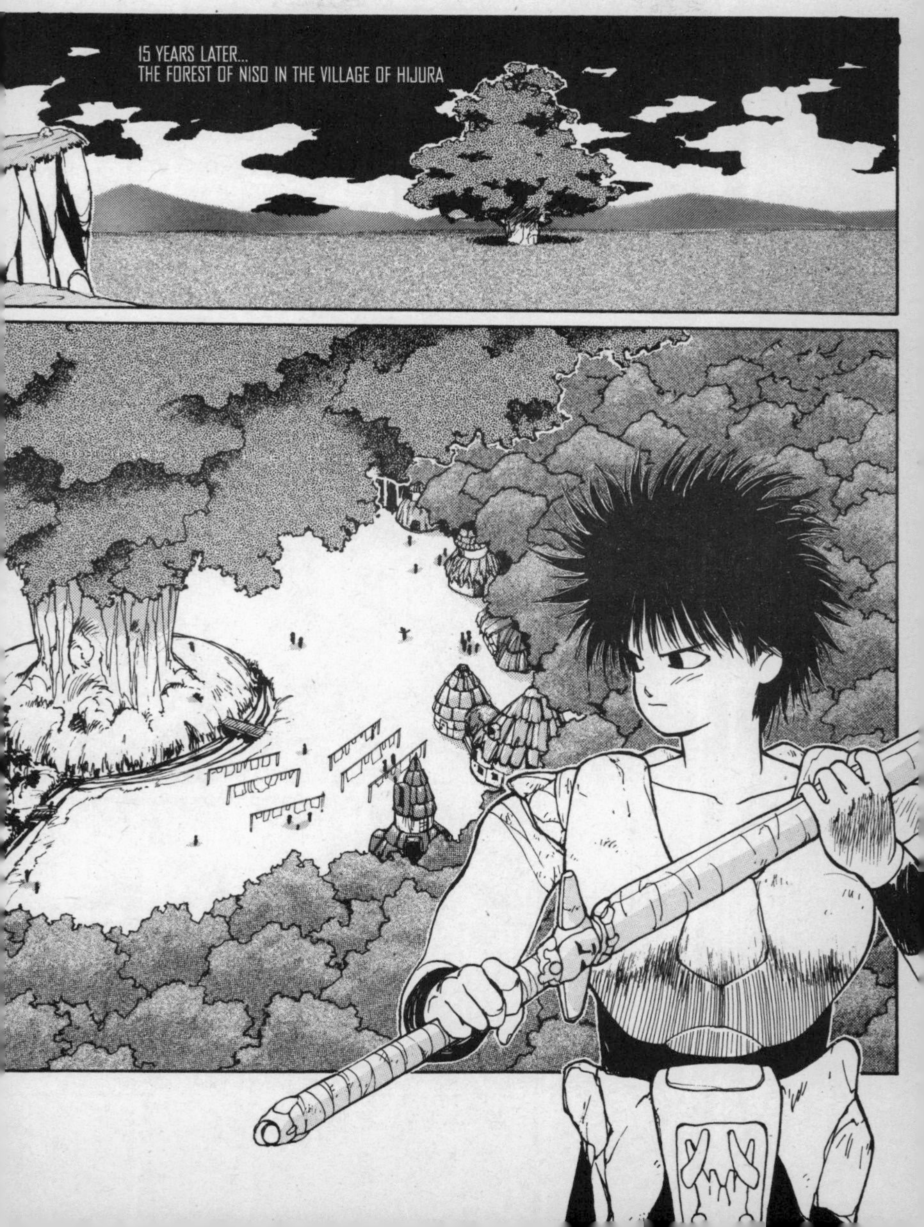
15 YEARS LATER...
THE FOREST OF NISO IN THE VILLAGE OF HIJURA

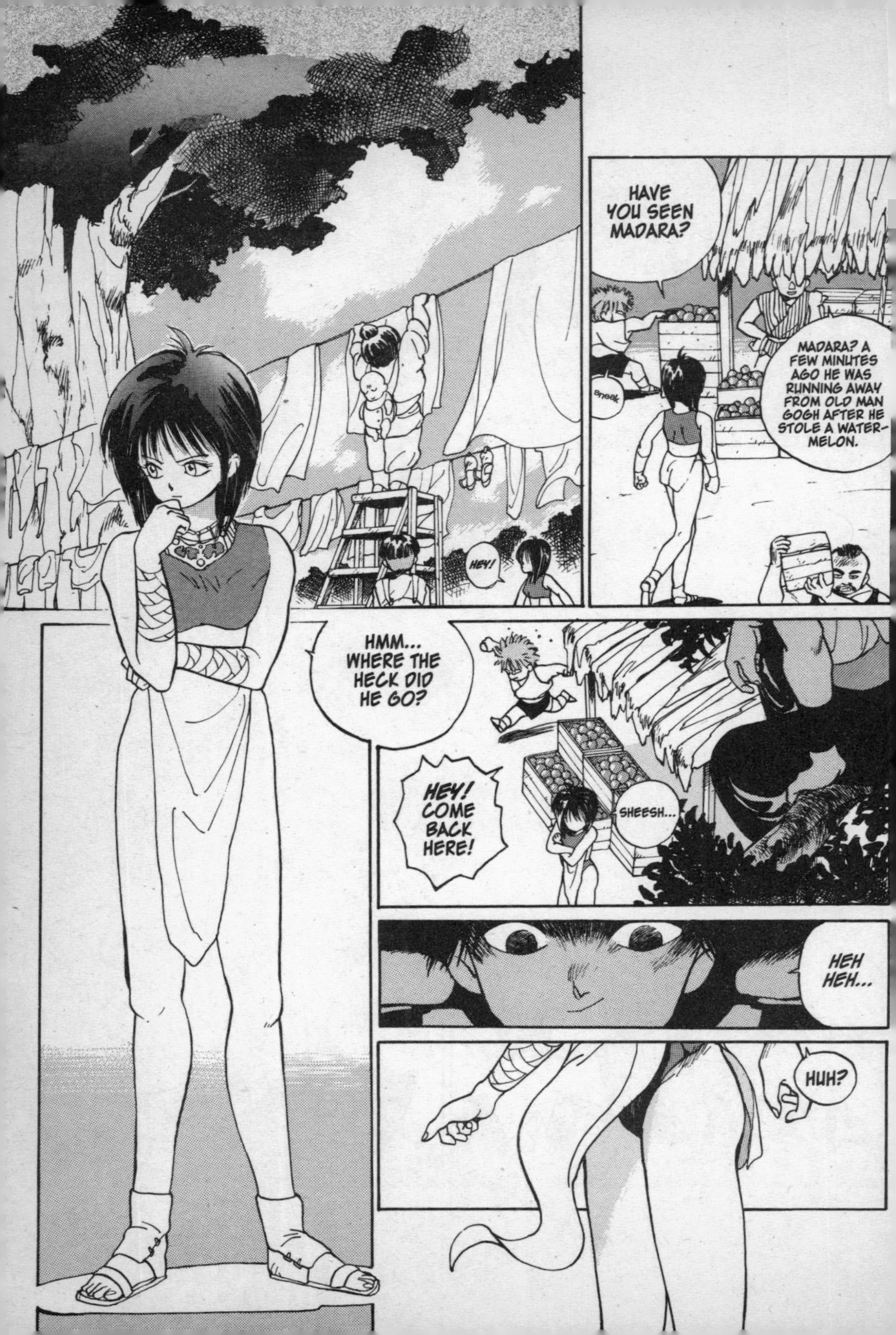
HAVE YOU SEEN MADARA?
MADARA? A FEW MINUTES AGO HE WAS RUNNING AWAY FROM OLD MAN GOGH AFTER HE STOLE A WATER-MELON.
sneak
HEY!
HMM... WHERE THE HECK DID HE GO?
HEY! COME BACK HERE!
SHEESH...
HEH HEH...
HUH?

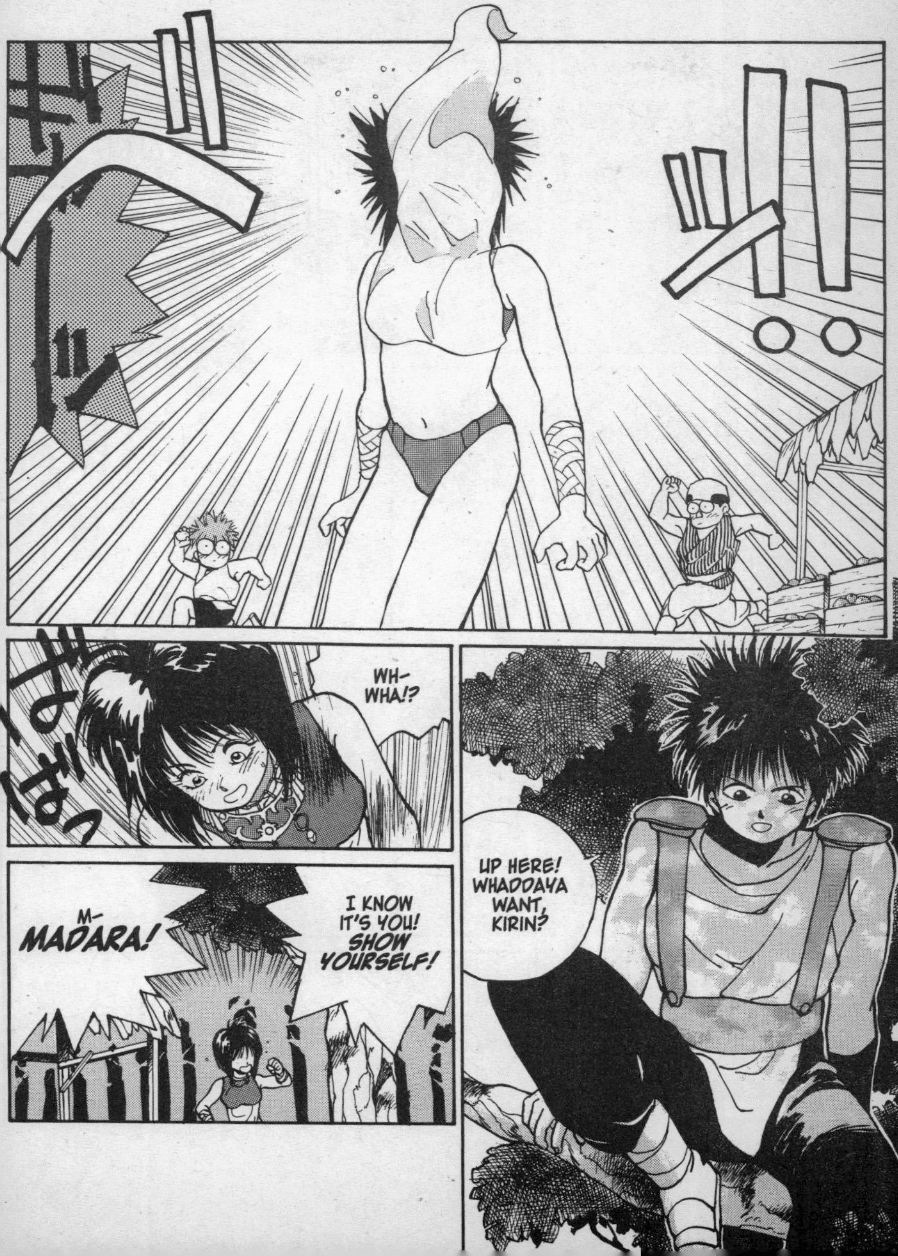

WH- WHA!?
I KNOW IT'S YOU! SHOW YOURSELF!
M- MADARA!
UP HERE! WHADDAYA WANT, KIRIN?

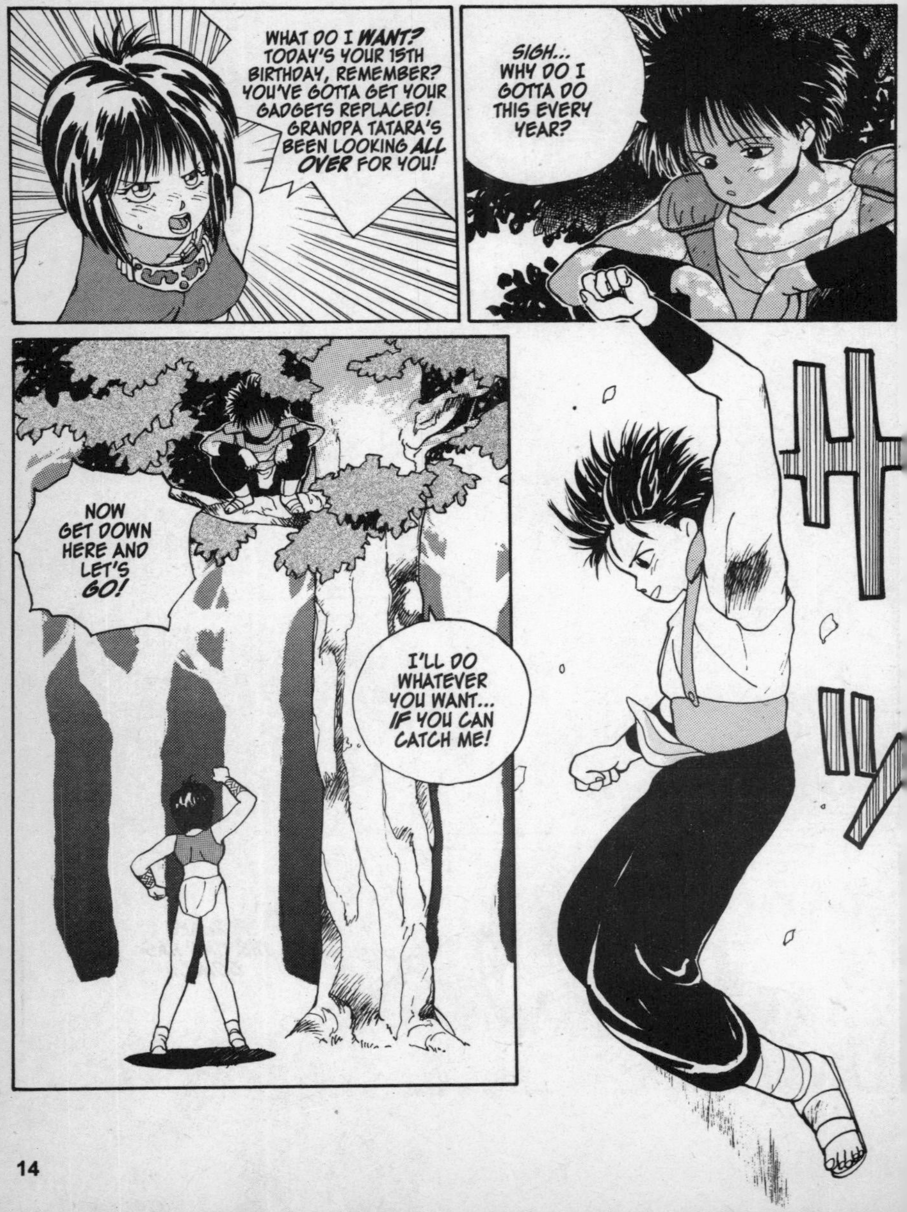
SIGH... WHY DO I GOTTA DO THIS EVERY YEAR?
WHAT DO I WANT? TODAY'S YOUR 15TH BIRTHDAY, REMEMBER? YOU'VE GOTTA GET YOUR GADGETS REPLACED! GRANDPA TATARA'S BEEN LOOKING ALL OVER FOR YOU!
NOW GET DOWN HERE AND LET'S GO!
I'LL DO WHATEVER YOU WANT... IF YOU CAN CATCH ME!

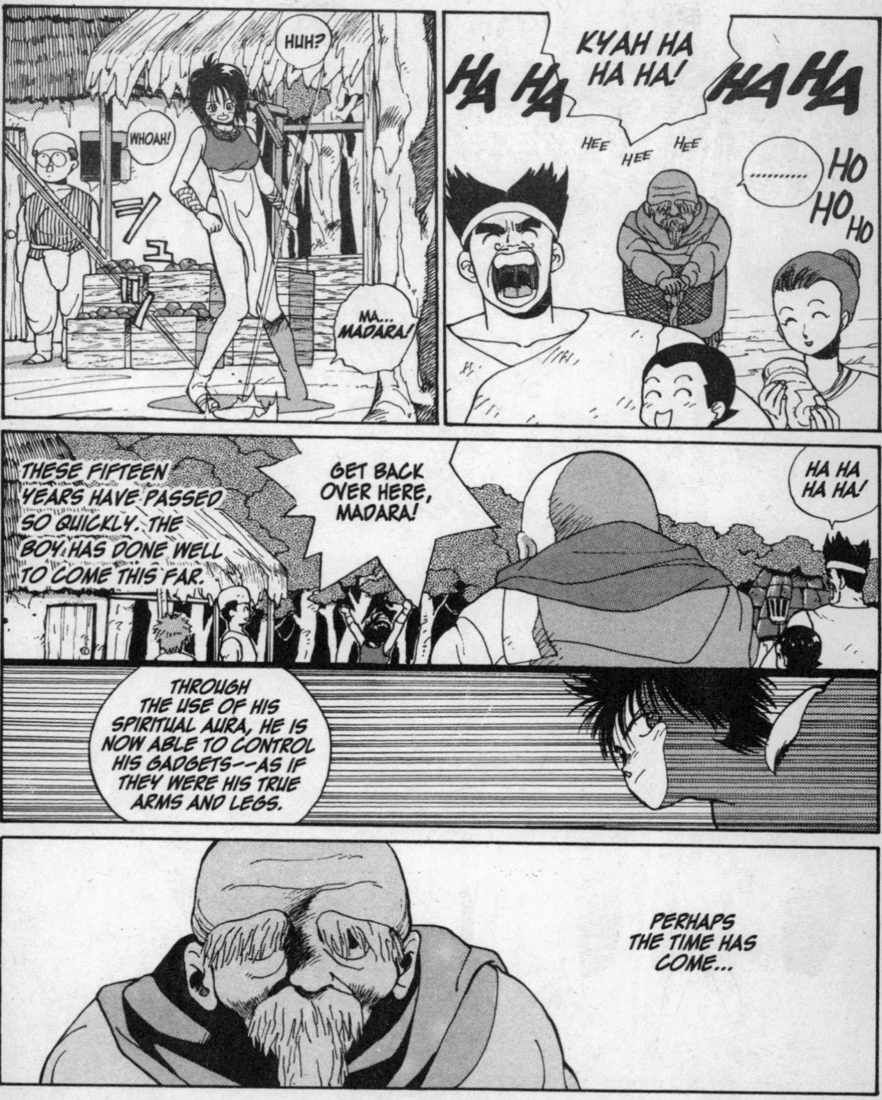
HUH?
WHOAH!
MA... MADARA!
KYAH HA HA HA!
HA HA
HA HA
HEE HEE HEE
....
HO HO HO
THESE FIFTEEN YEARS HAVE PASSED SO QUICKLY. THE BOY HAS DONE WELL TO COME THIS FAR.
GET BACK OVER HERE, MADARA!
HA HA HA HA!
THROUGH THE USE OF HIS SPIRITUAL AURA, HE IS NOW ABLE TO CONTROL HIS GADGETS--AS IF THEY WERE HIS TRUE ARMS AND LEGS.
PERHAPS THE TIME HAS COME...

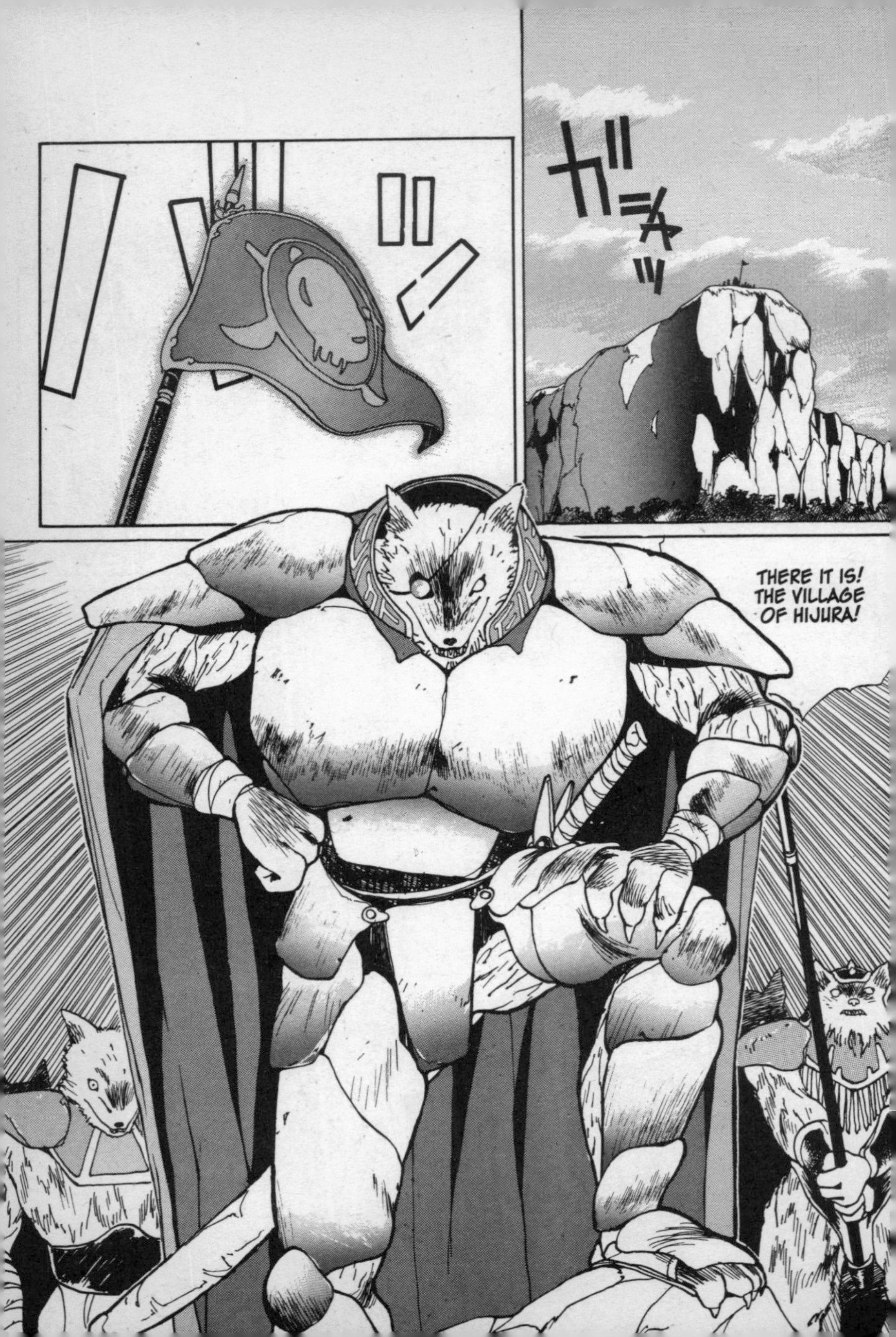
THERE IT IS! THE VILLAGE OF HIJURA!

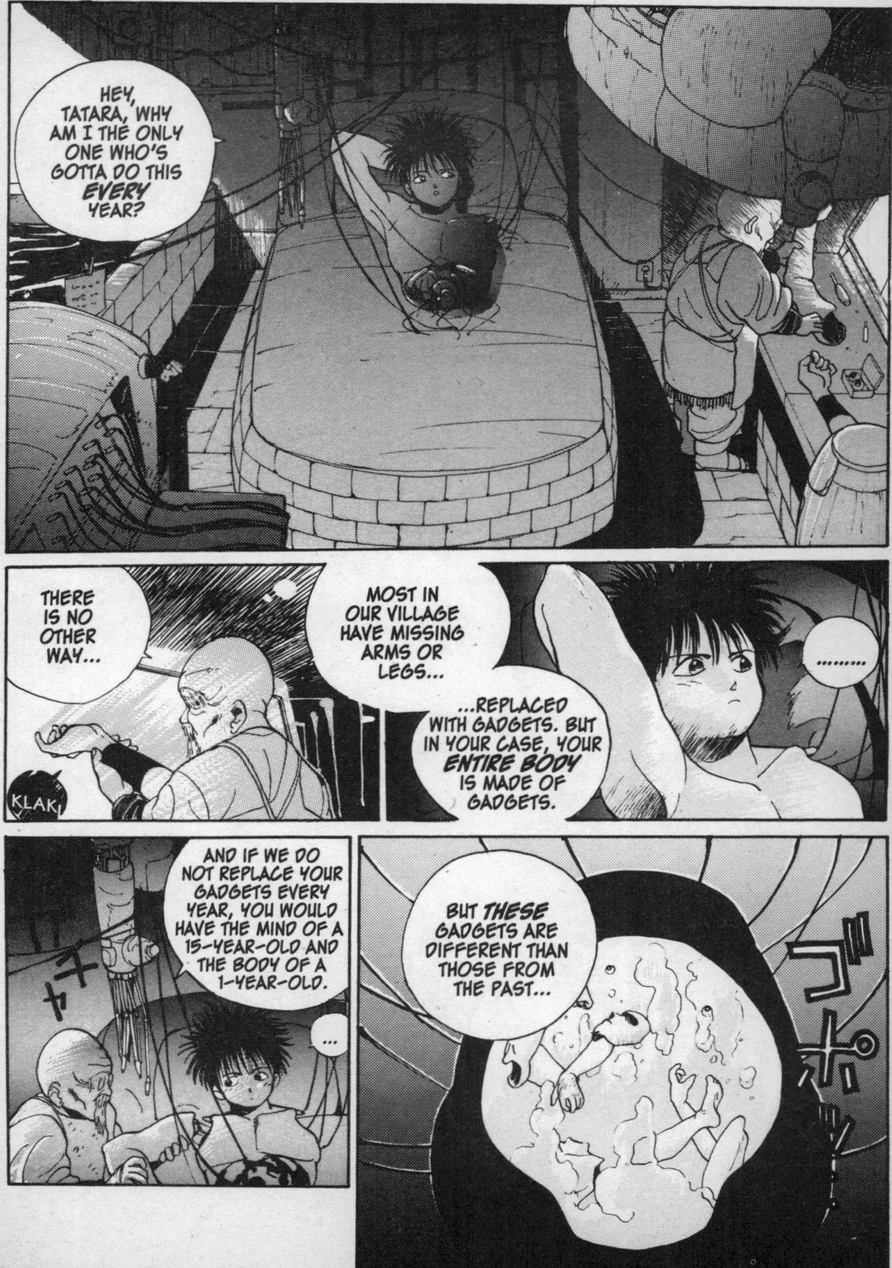
HEY, TATARA, WHY AM I THE ONLY ONE WHO'S GOTTA DO THIS *EVERY* YEAR?
THERE IS NO OTHER WAY...
KLAK
MOST IN OUR VILLAGE HAVE MISSING ARMS OR LEGS...
...REPLACED WITH GADGETS. BUT IN YOUR CASE, YOUR *ENTIRE BODY* IS MADE OF GADGETS.
....
AND IF WE DO NOT REPLACE YOUR GADGETS EVERY YEAR, YOU WOULD HAVE THE MIND OF A 15-YEAR-OLD AND THE BODY OF A 1-YEAR-OLD.
...
BUT *THESE* GADGETS ARE DIFFERENT THAN THOSE FROM THE PAST...

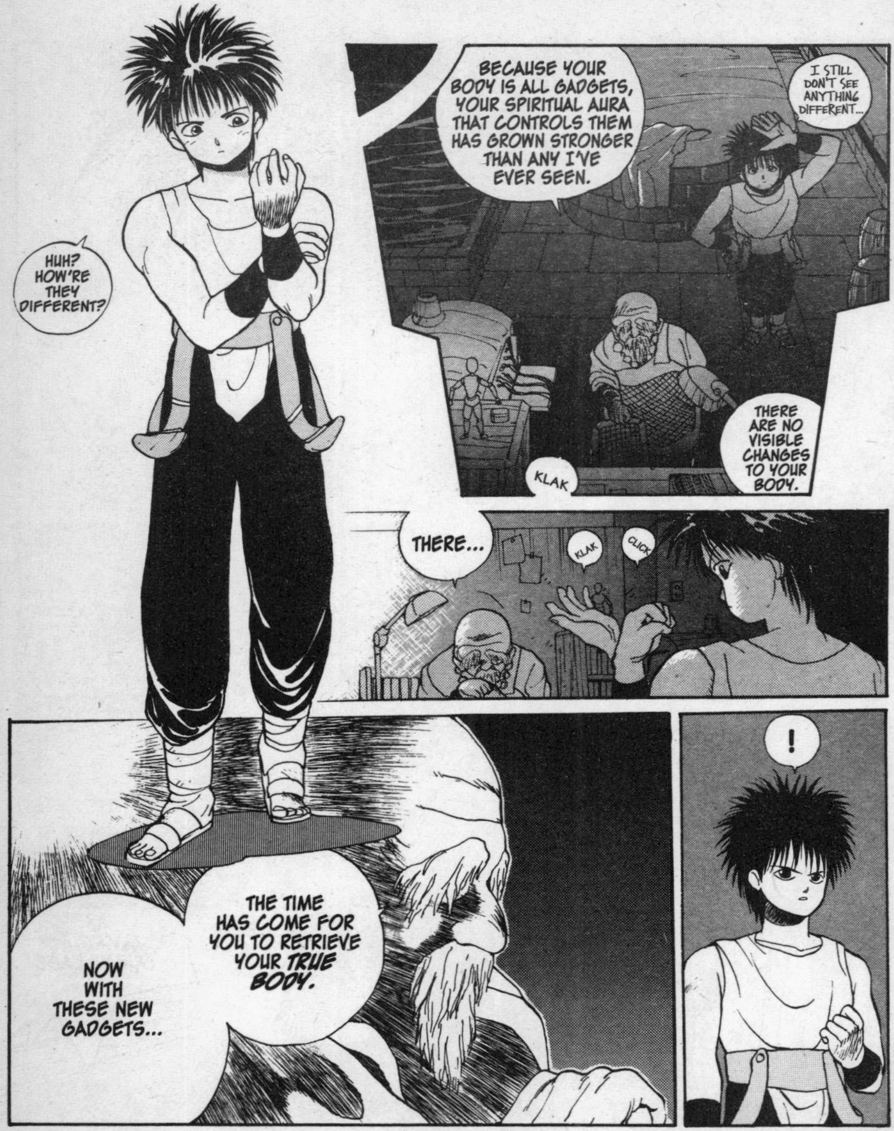
BECAUSE YOUR BODY IS ALL GADGETS, YOUR SPIRITUAL AURA THAT CONTROLS THEM HAS GROWN STRONGER THAN ANY I'VE EVER SEEN.
I STILL DON'T SEE ANYTHING DIFFERENT...
THERE ARE NO VISIBLE CHANGES TO YOUR BODY.
KLAK
THERE...
KLAK
CLICK
HUH? HOW'RE THEY DIFFERENT?
!
NOW WITH THESE NEW GADGETS...
THE TIME HAS COME FOR YOU TO RETRIEVE YOUR *TRUE BODY*.

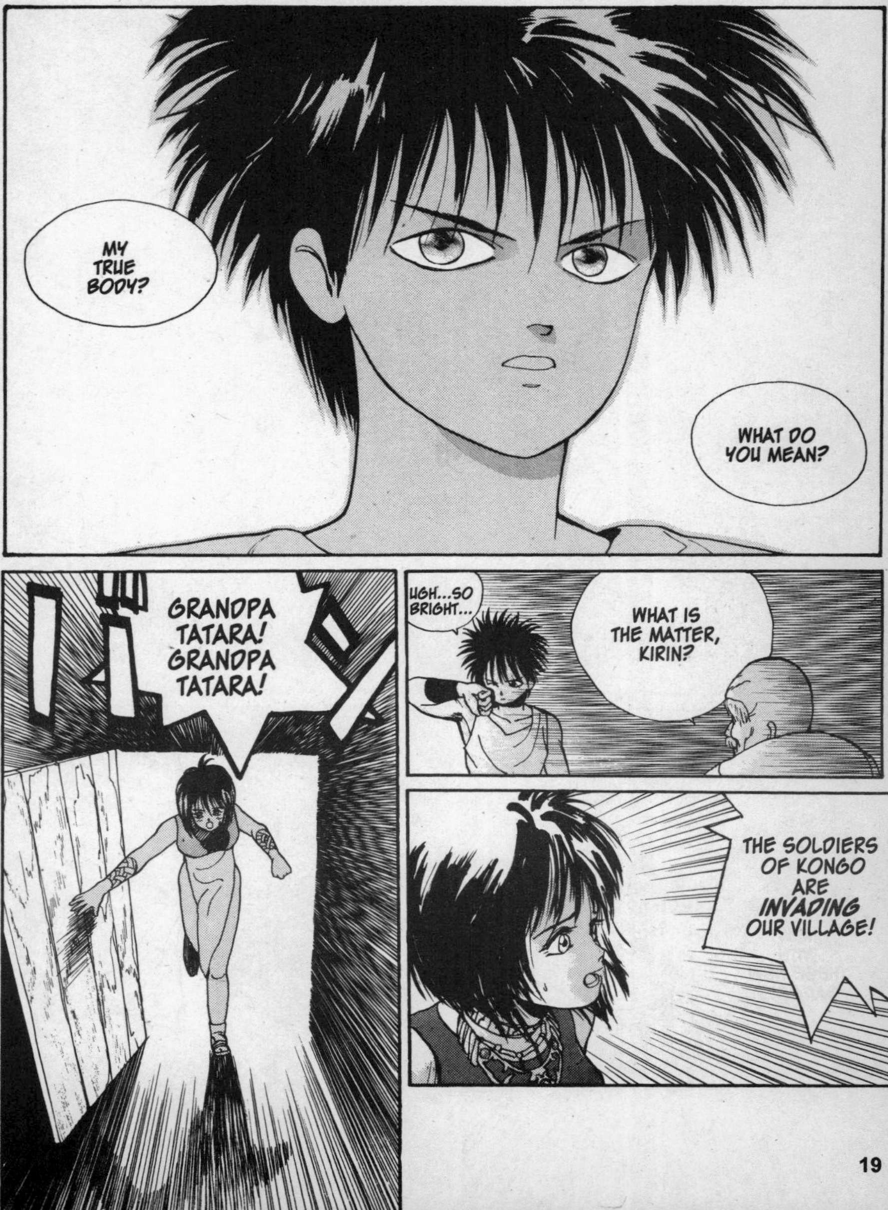
MY TRUE BODY?
WHAT DO YOU MEAN?
GRANDPA TATARA! GRANDPA TATARA!
UGH...SO BRIGHT...
WHAT IS THE MATTER, KIRIN?
THE SOLDIERS OF KONGO ARE *INVADING* OUR VILLAGE!

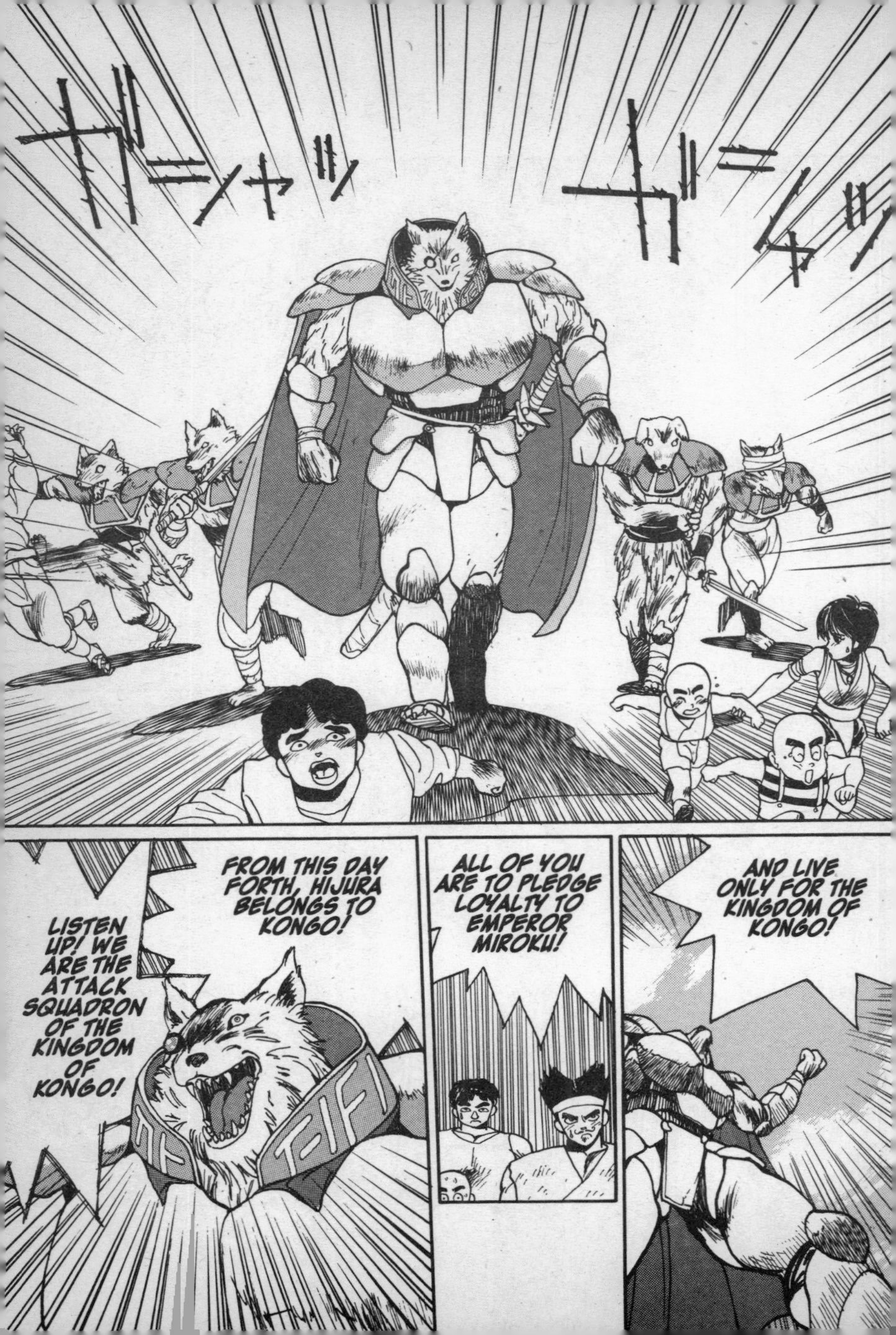

LISTEN UP! WE ARE THE ATTACK SQUADRON OF THE KINGDOM OF KONGO!
FROM THIS DAY FORTH, HIJURA BELONGS TO KONGO!
ALL OF YOU ARE TO PLEDGE LOYALTY TO EMPEROR MIROKU!
AND LIVE ONLY FOR THE KINGDOM OF KONGO!

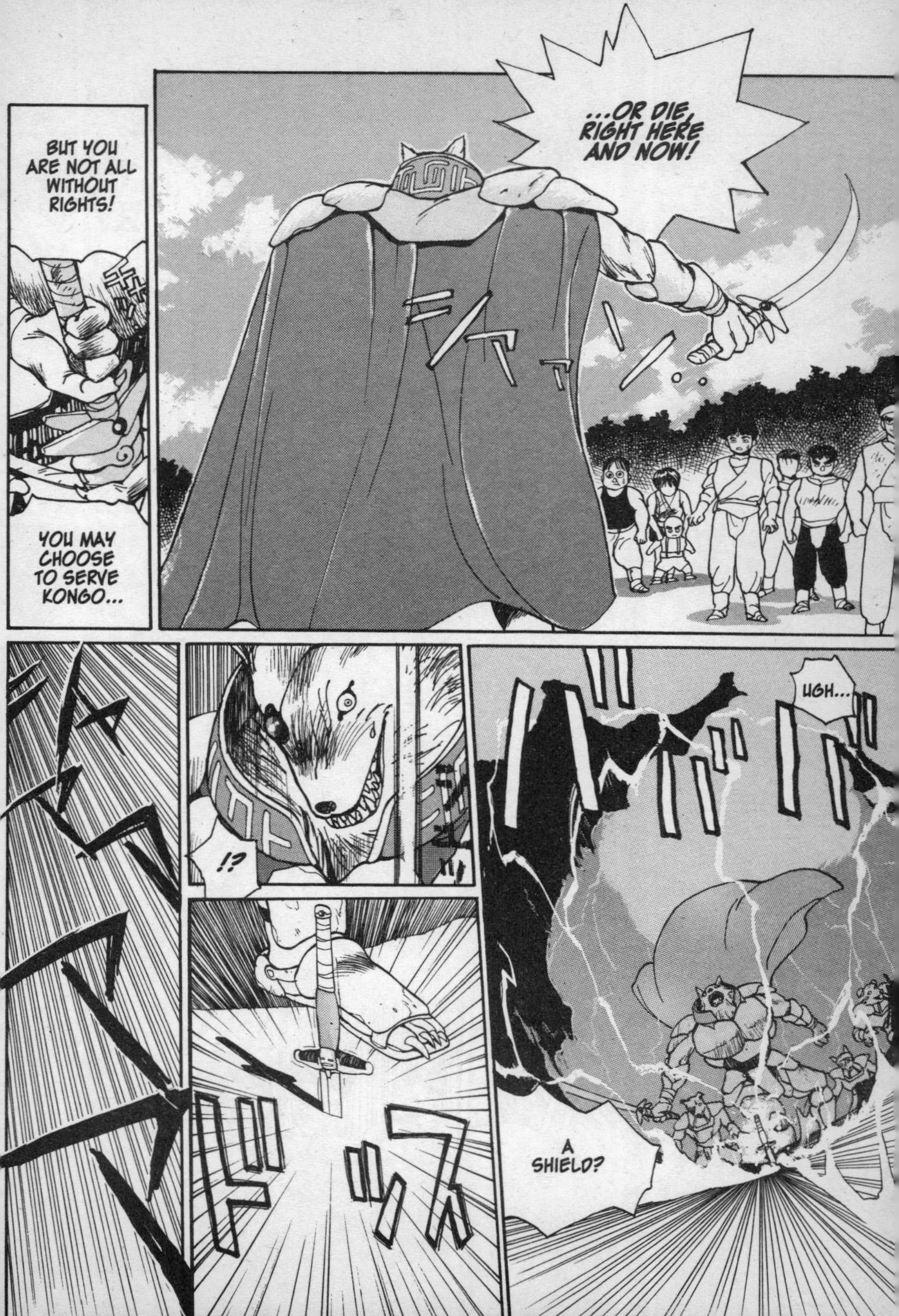
...OR DIE, RIGHT HERE AND NOW!
BUT YOU ARE NOT ALL WITHOUT RIGHTS!
YOU MAY CHOOSE TO SERVE KONGO...
!?
UGH...
A SHIELD?

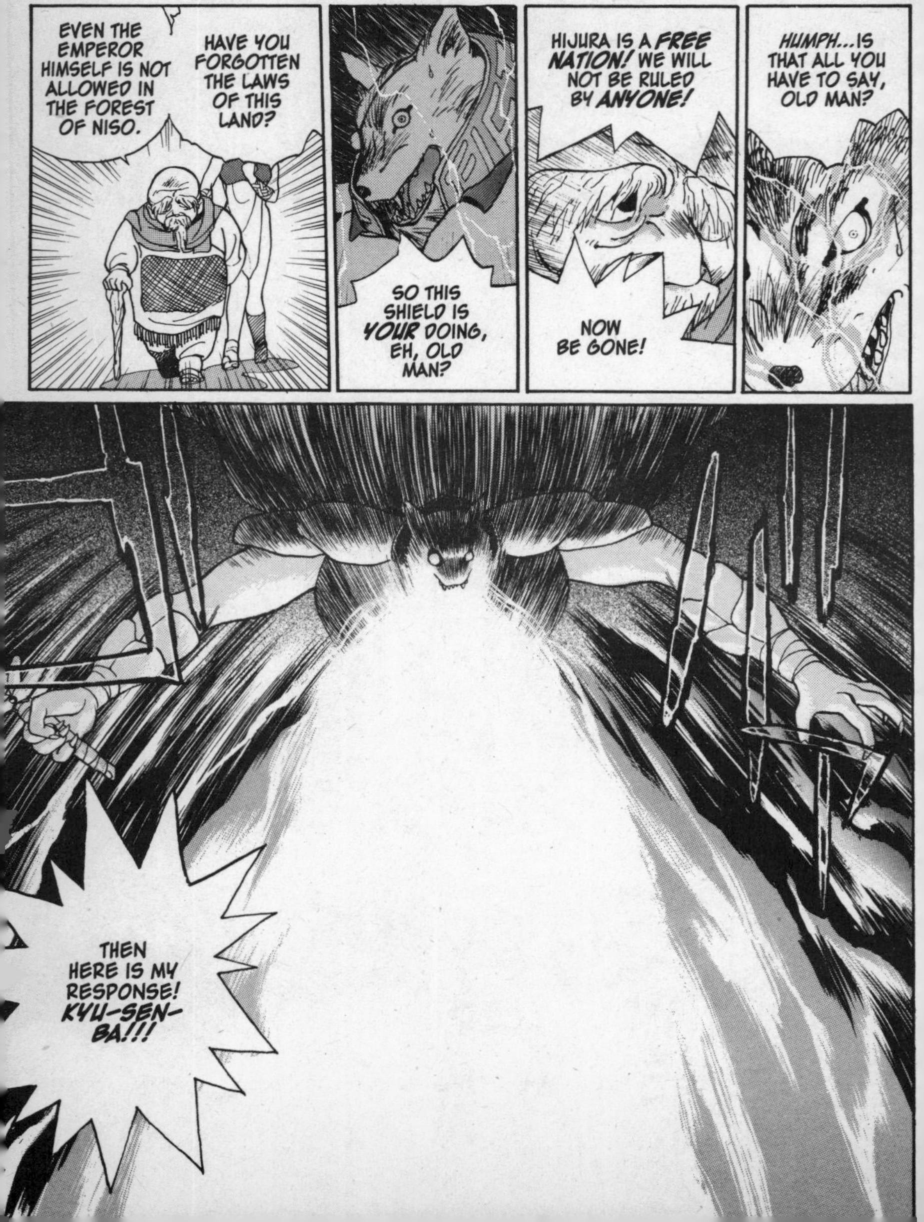

EVEN THE EMPEROR HIMSELF IS NOT ALLOWED IN THE FOREST OF NISO.
HAVE YOU FORGOTTEN THE LAWS OF THIS LAND?
SO THIS SHIELD IS YOUR DOING, EH, OLD MAN?
HIJURA IS A FREE NATION! WE WILL NOT BE RULED BY ANYONE!
NOW BE GONE!
HUMPH...IS THAT ALL YOU HAVE TO SAY, OLD MAN?
THEN HERE IS MY RESPONSE! KYU-SEN-BA!!!

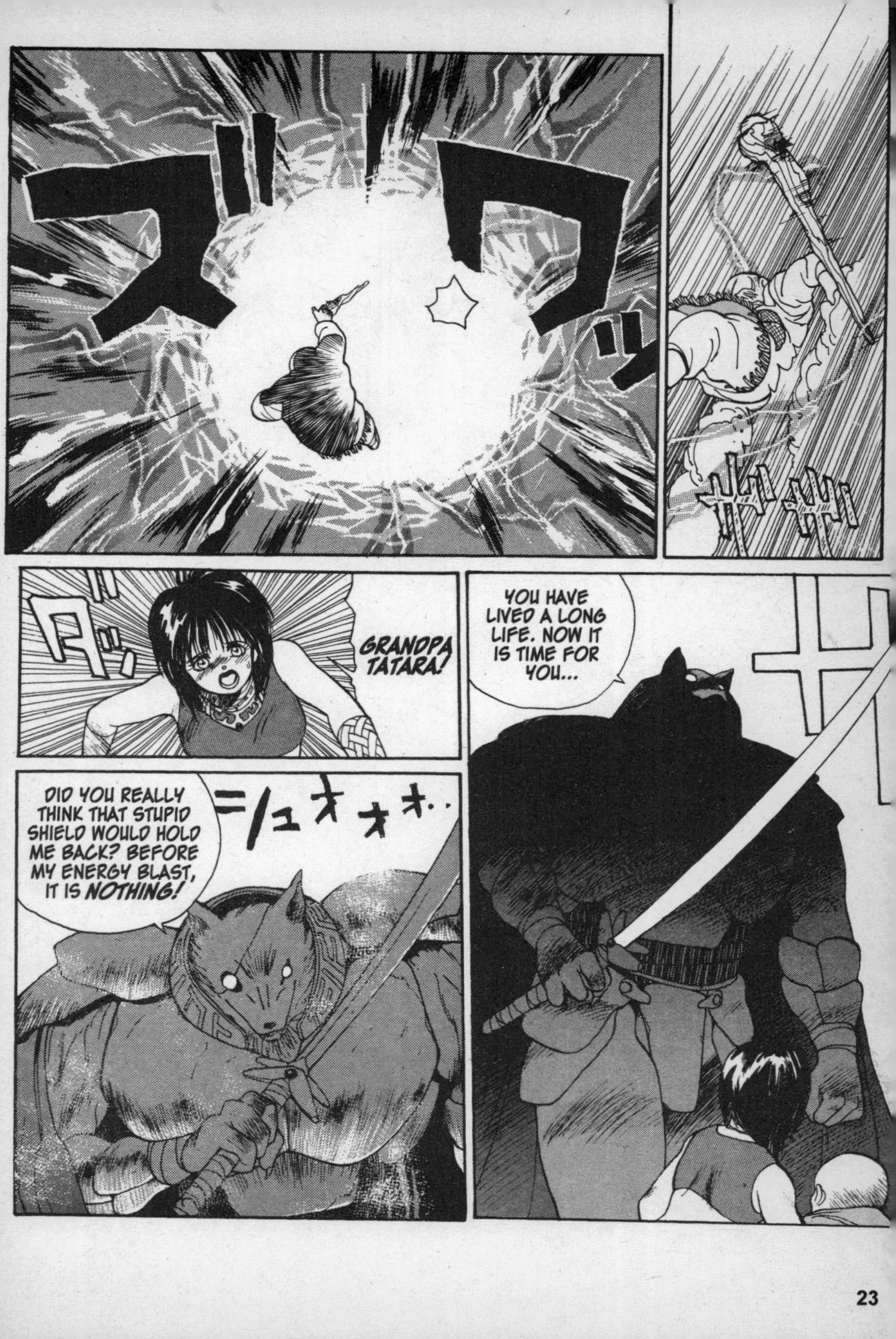
GRANDPA TATARA!
DID YOU REALLY THINK THAT STUPID SHIELD WOULD HOLD ME BACK? BEFORE MY ENERGY BLAST, IT IS *NOTHING!*
YOU HAVE LIVED A LONG LIFE. NOW IT IS TIME FOR YOU...

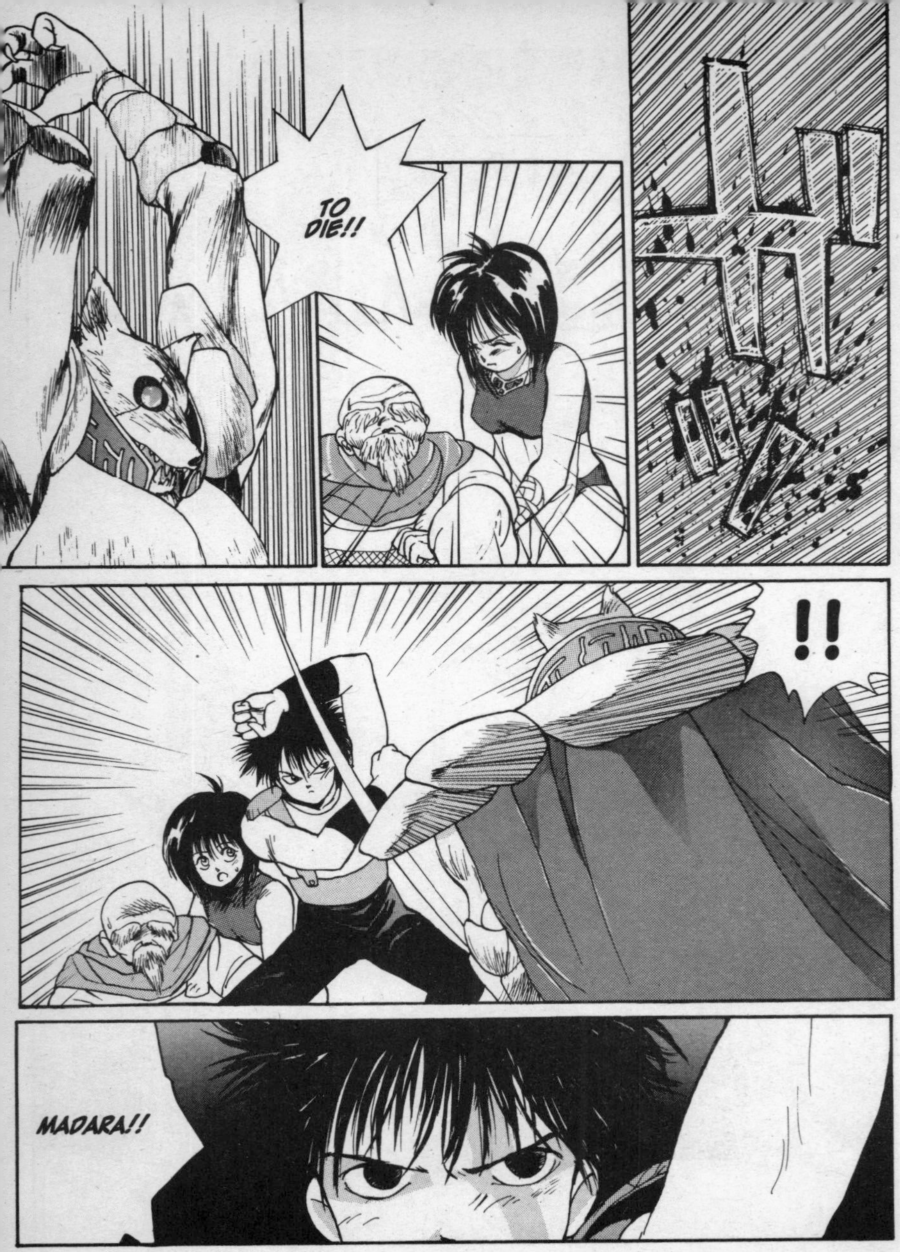
TO DIE!!
!!
MADARA!!

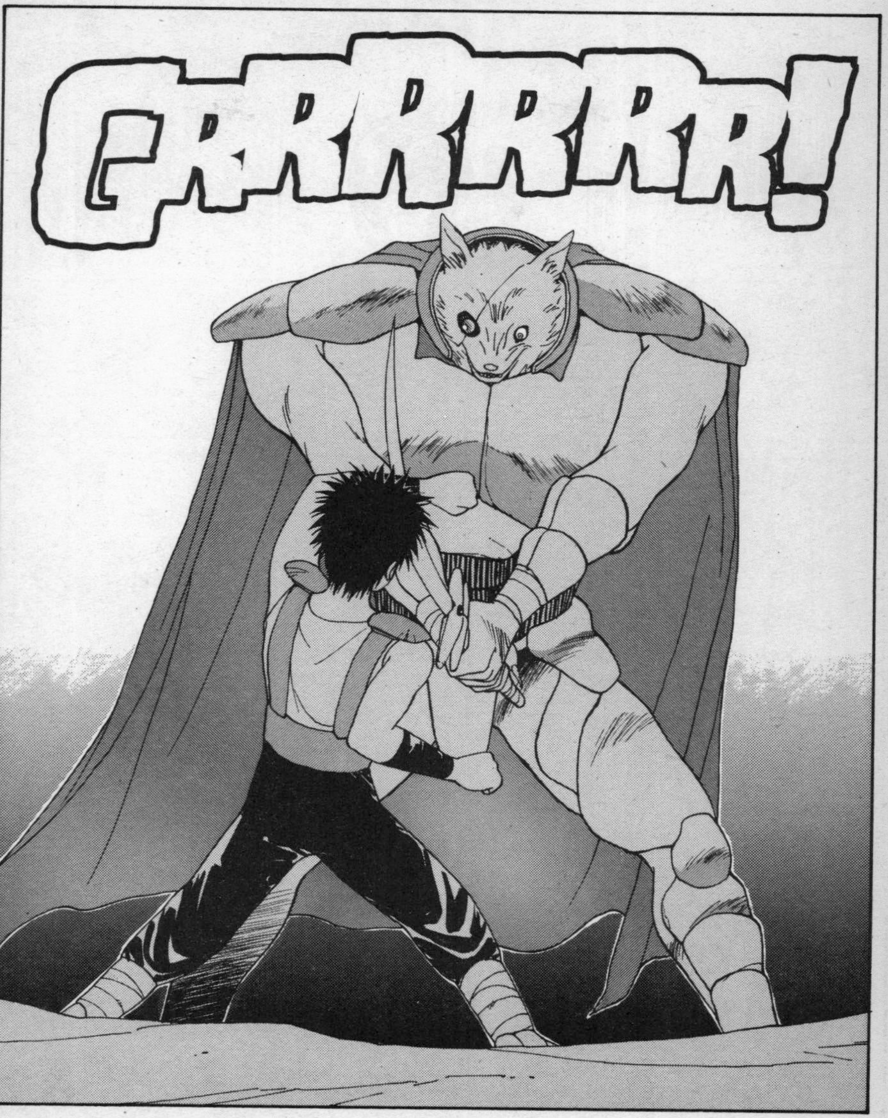
GRRRRRRR!

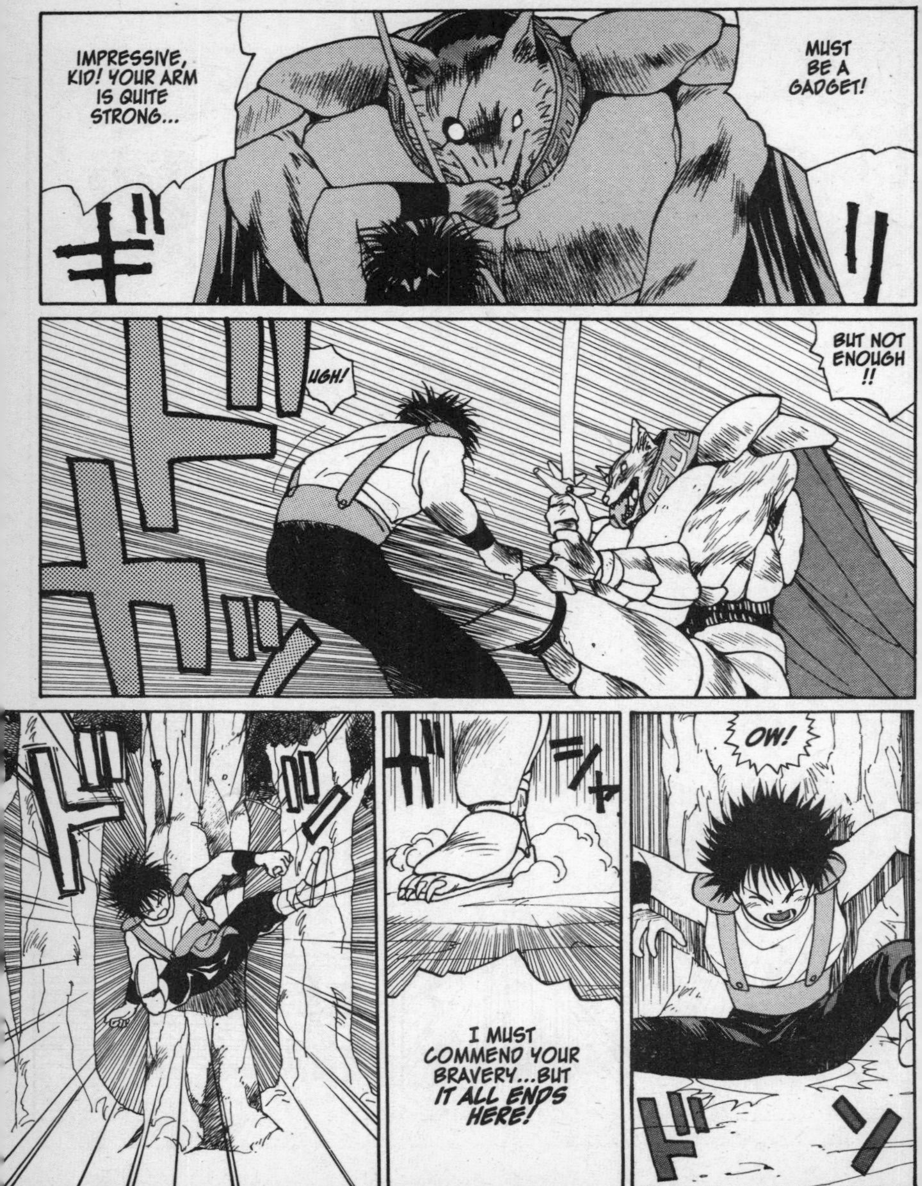
MUST BE A GADGET!
IMPRESSIVE, KID! YOUR ARM IS QUITE STRONG...
BUT NOT ENOUGH !!
UGH!
OW!
I MUST COMMEND YOUR BRAVERY...BUT IT ALL ENDS HERE!

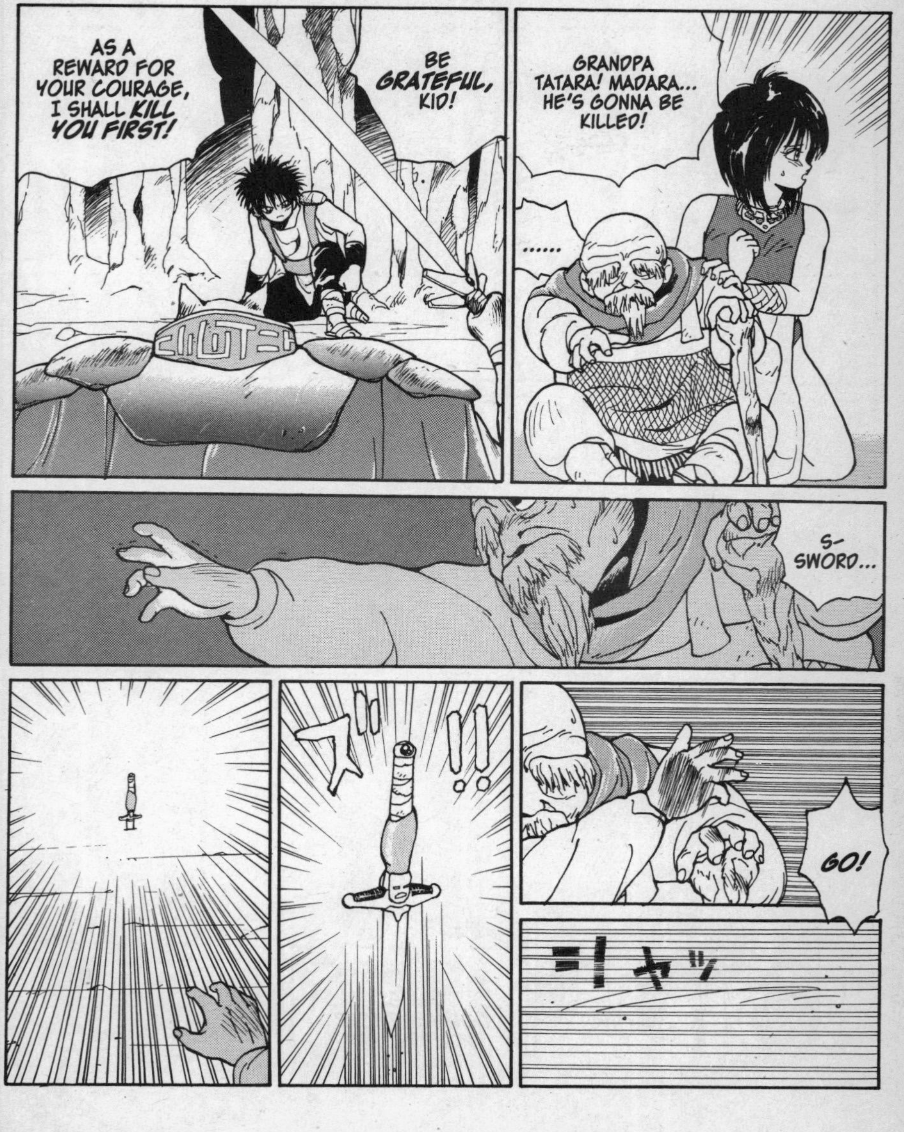
AS A REWARD FOR YOUR COURAGE, I SHALL KILL YOU FIRST!
BE GRATEFUL, KID!
GRANDPA TATARA! MADARA... HE'S GONNA BE KILLED!
......
S-SWORD...
GO!

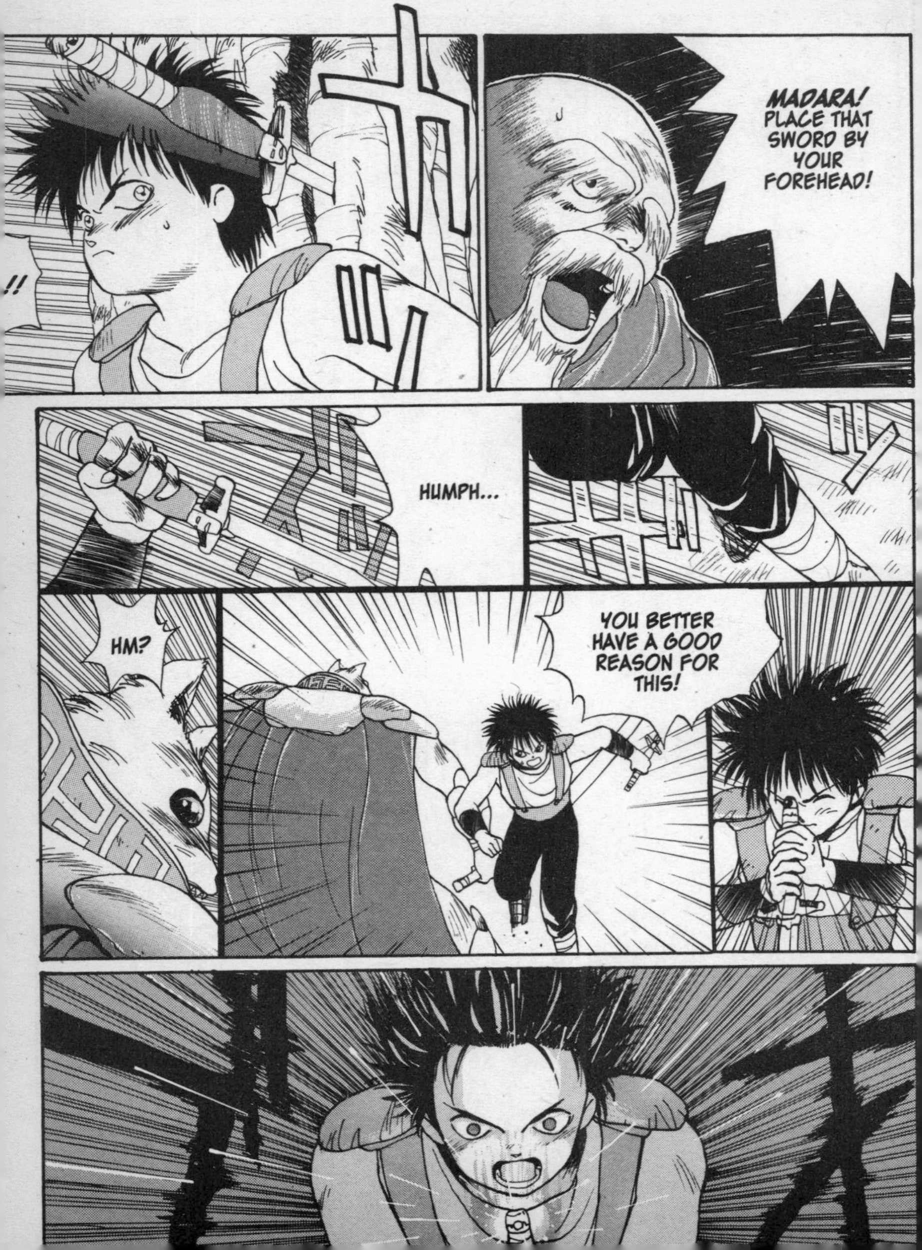
!!
MADARA! PLACE THAT SWORD BY YOUR FOREHEAD!
HUMPH...
HM?
YOU BETTER HAVE A GOOD REASON FOR THIS!

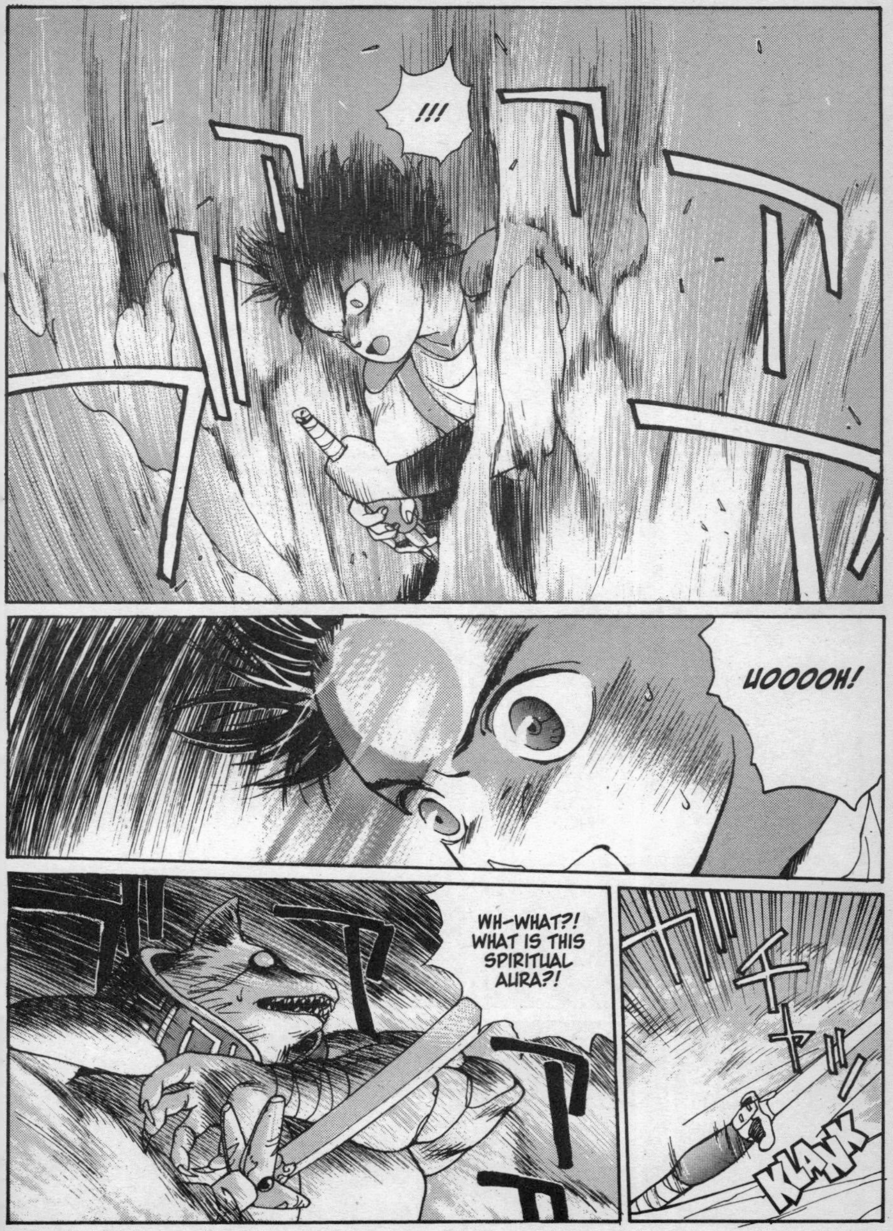
!!!
UOOOOH!
WH-WHAT?! WHAT IS THIS SPIRITUAL AURA?!
KLANK

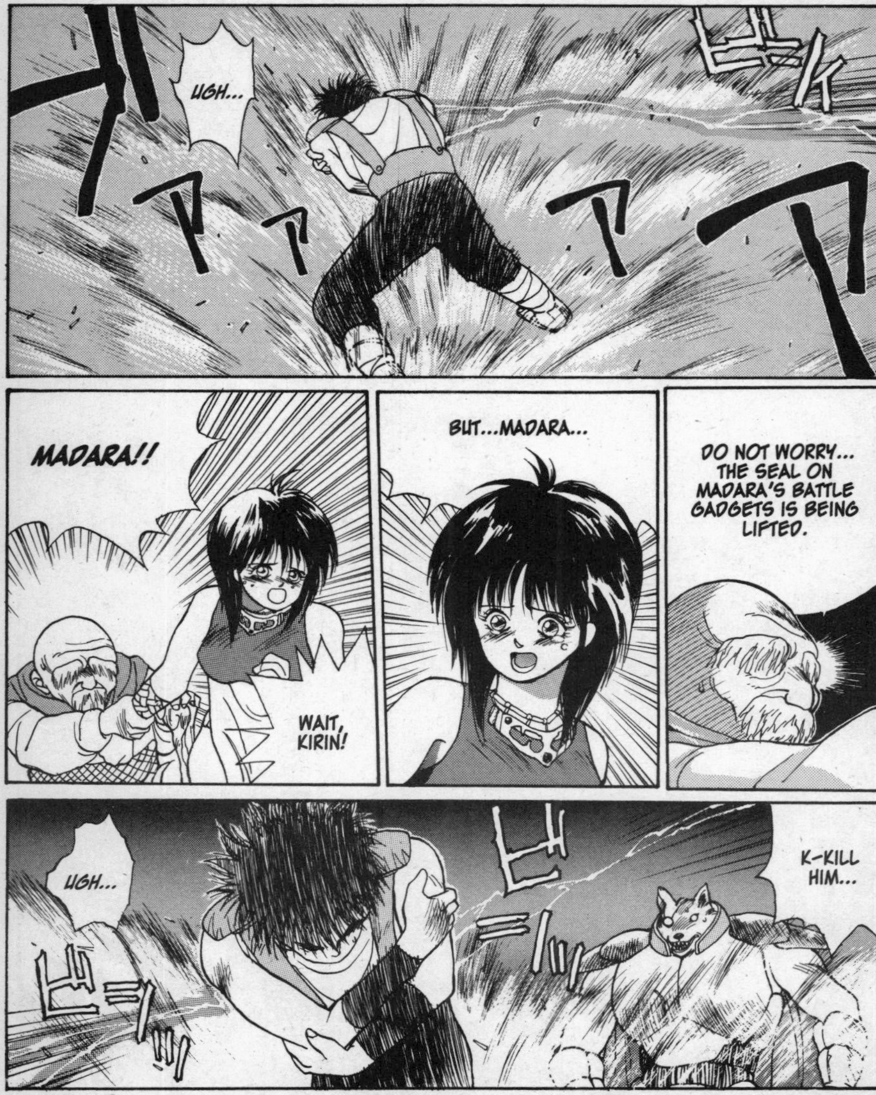
UGH...
MADARA!!
WAIT, KIRIN!
BUT...MADARA...
DO NOT WORRY... THE SEAL ON MADARA'S BATTLE GADGETS IS BEING LIFTED.
UGH...
K-KILL HIM...

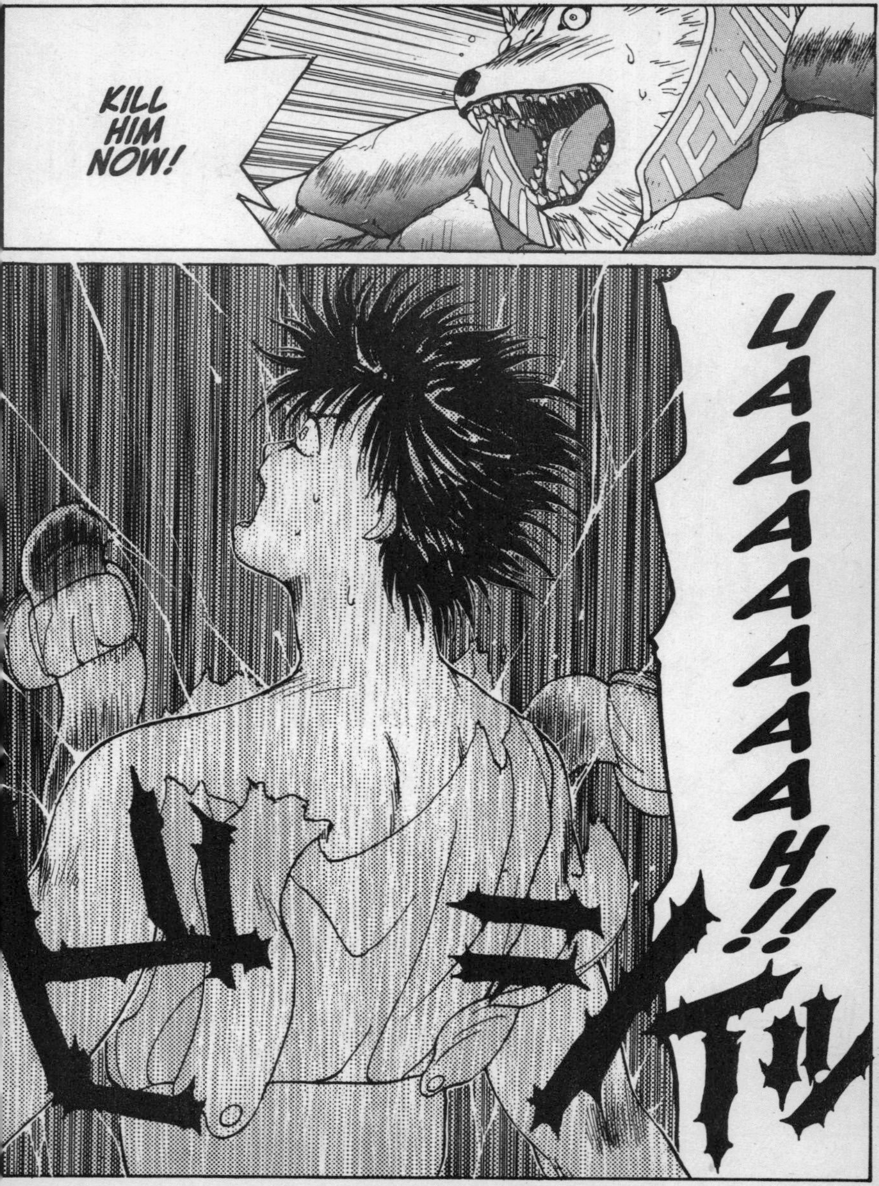
KILL HIM NOW!
UAAAAAAAH!!

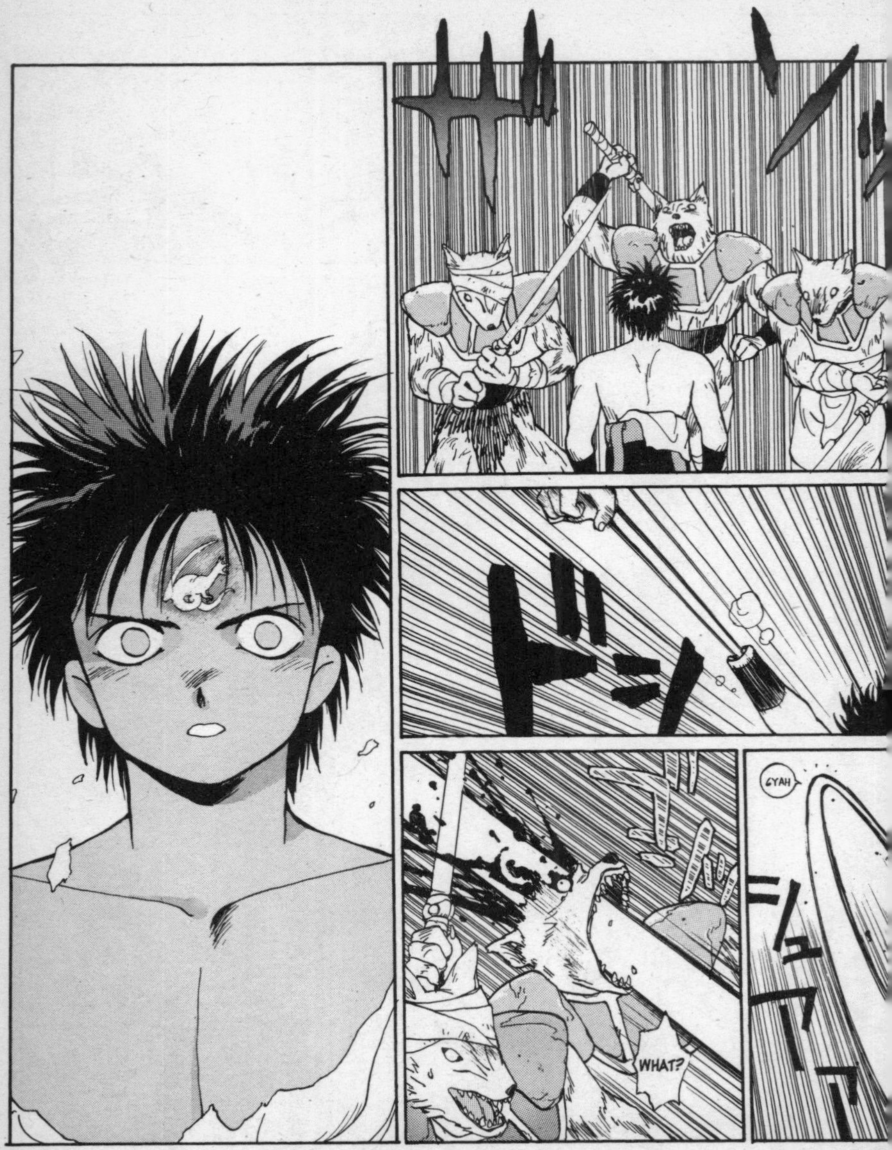
GYAH
WHAT?

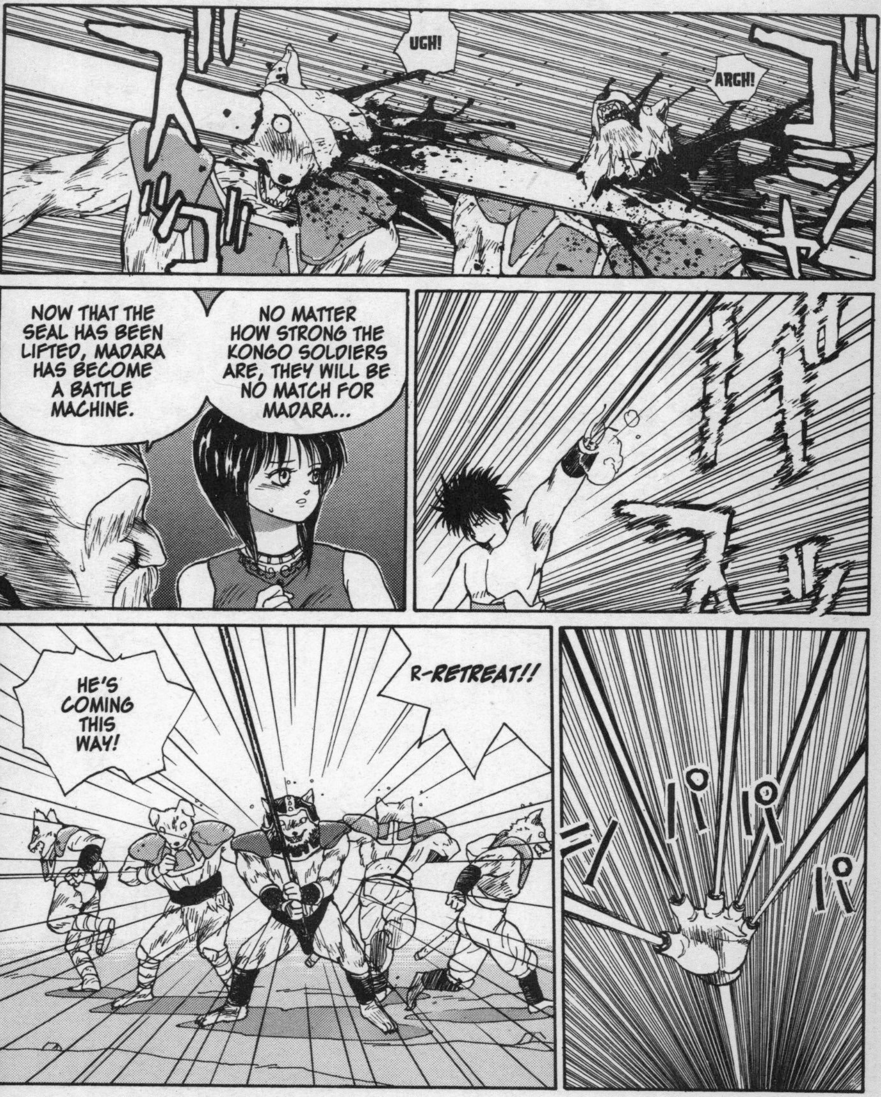
UGH!
ARGH!
NOW THAT THE SEAL HAS BEEN LIFTED, MADARA HAS BECOME A BATTLE MACHINE.
NO MATTER HOW STRONG THE KONGO SOLDIERS ARE, THEY WILL BE NO MATCH FOR MADARA...
HE'S COMING THIS WAY!
R-RETREAT!!

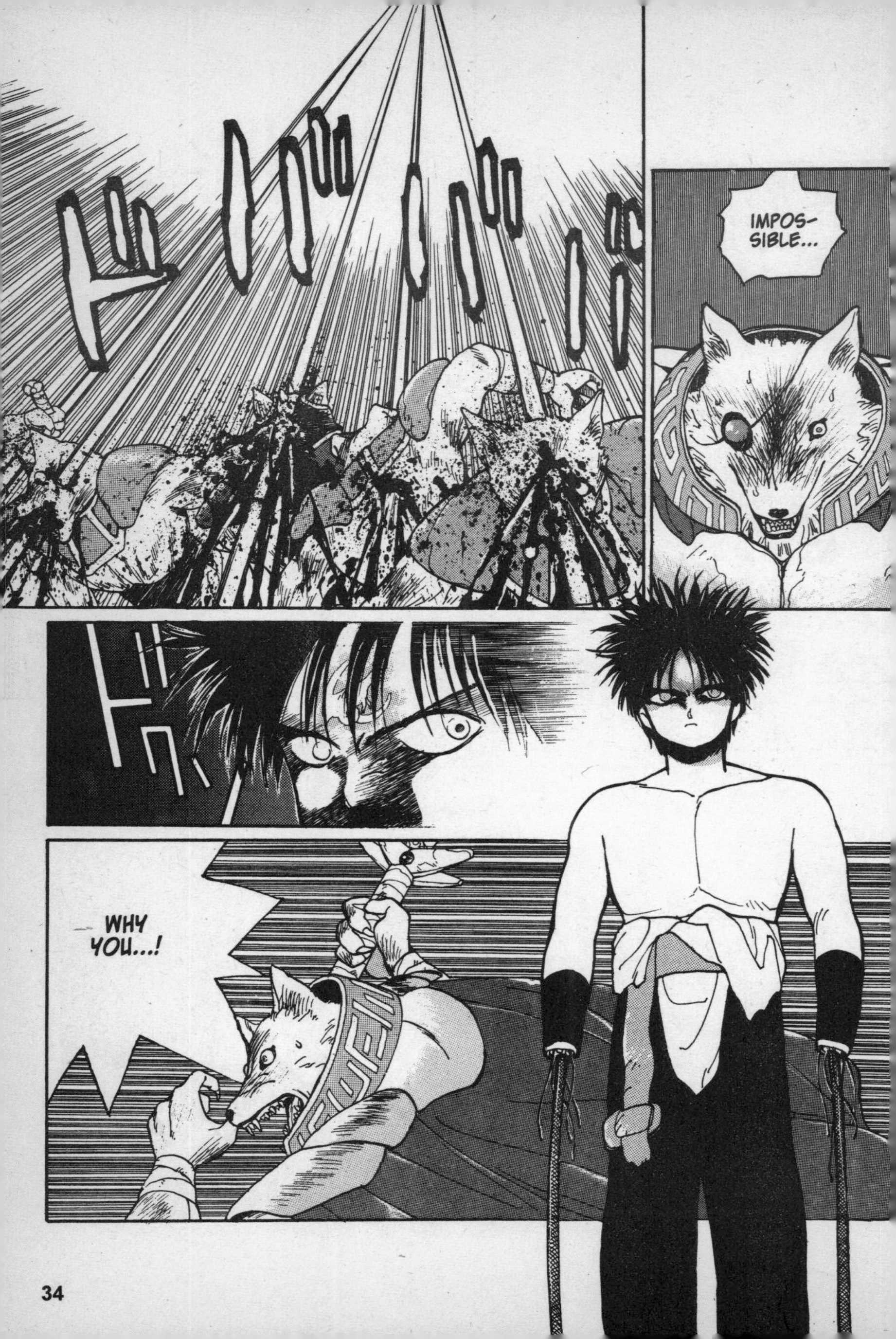
IMPOS-
SIBLE...
WHY
YOU...!

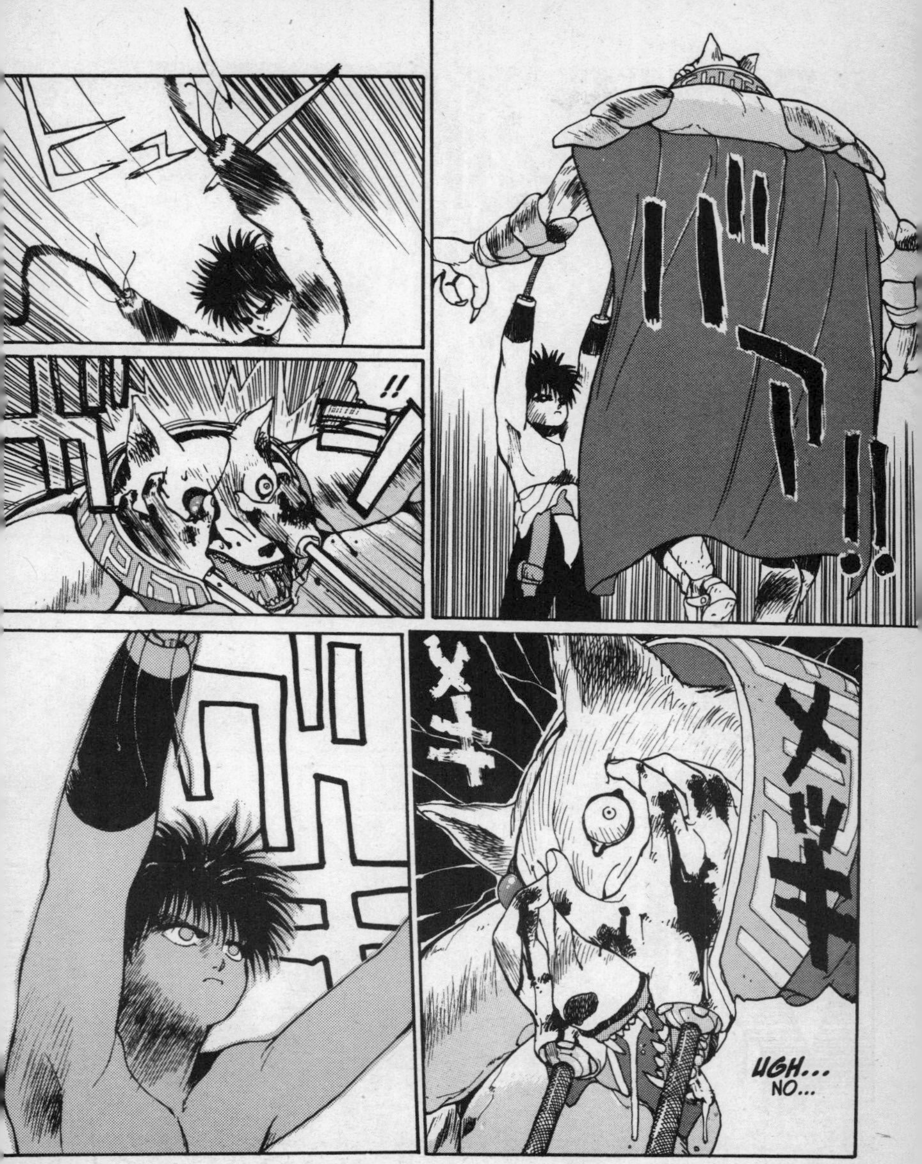
!!
UGH...
NO...

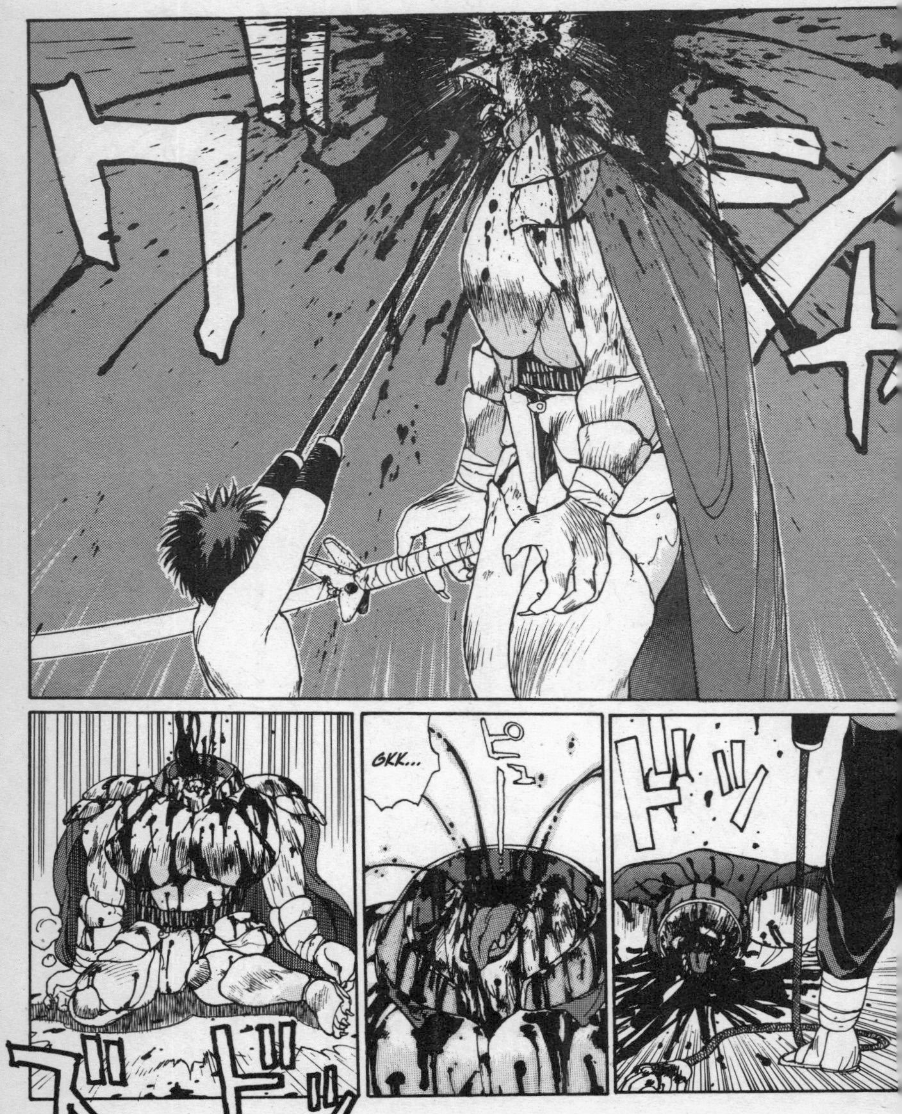
GKK...

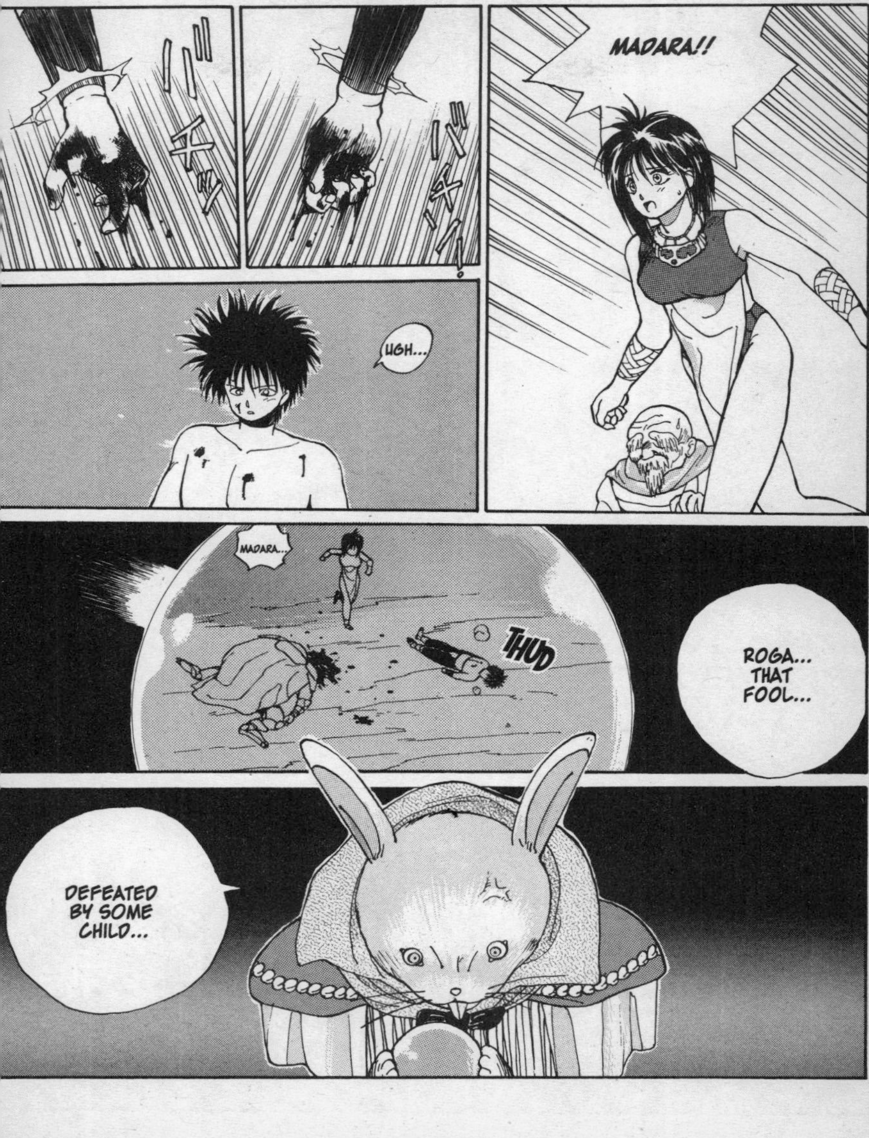
MADARA!!
UGH...
MADARA...
THUD
ROGA... THAT FOOL...
DEFEATED BY SOME CHILD...

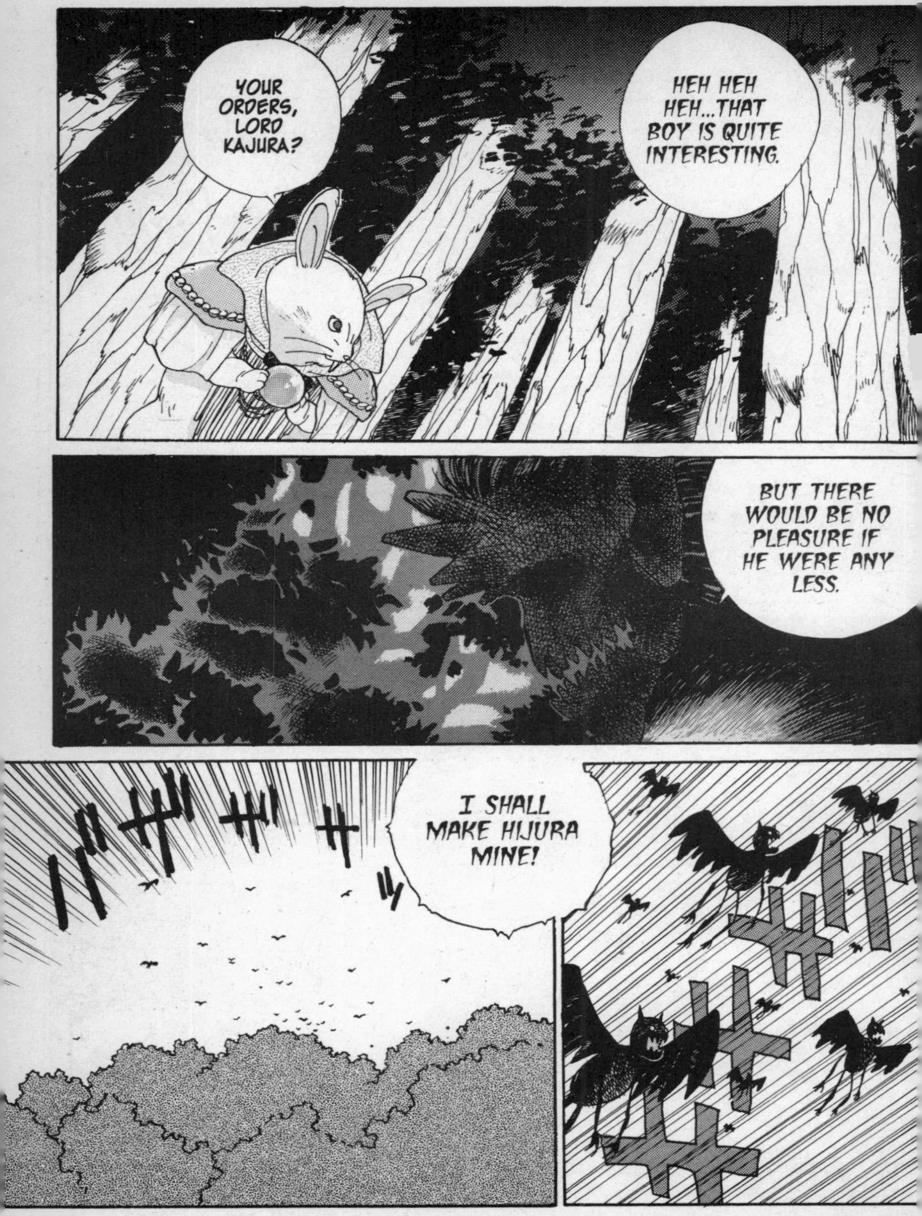

HEH HEH HEH...THAT BOY IS QUITE INTERESTING.
YOUR ORDERS, LORD KAJURA?
BUT THERE WOULD BE NO PLEASURE IF HE WERE ANY LESS.
I SHALL MAKE HIJURA MINE!

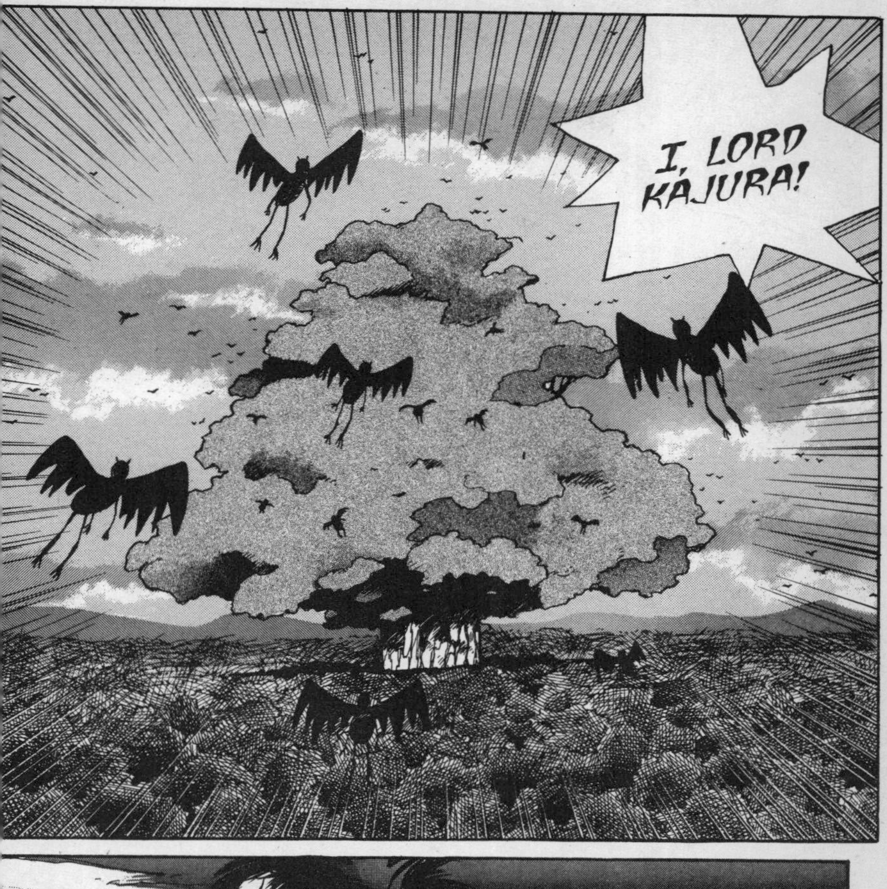
I, LORD KÁJURA!
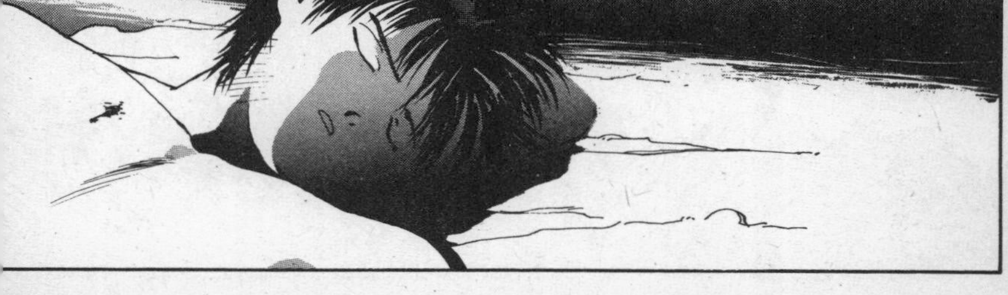

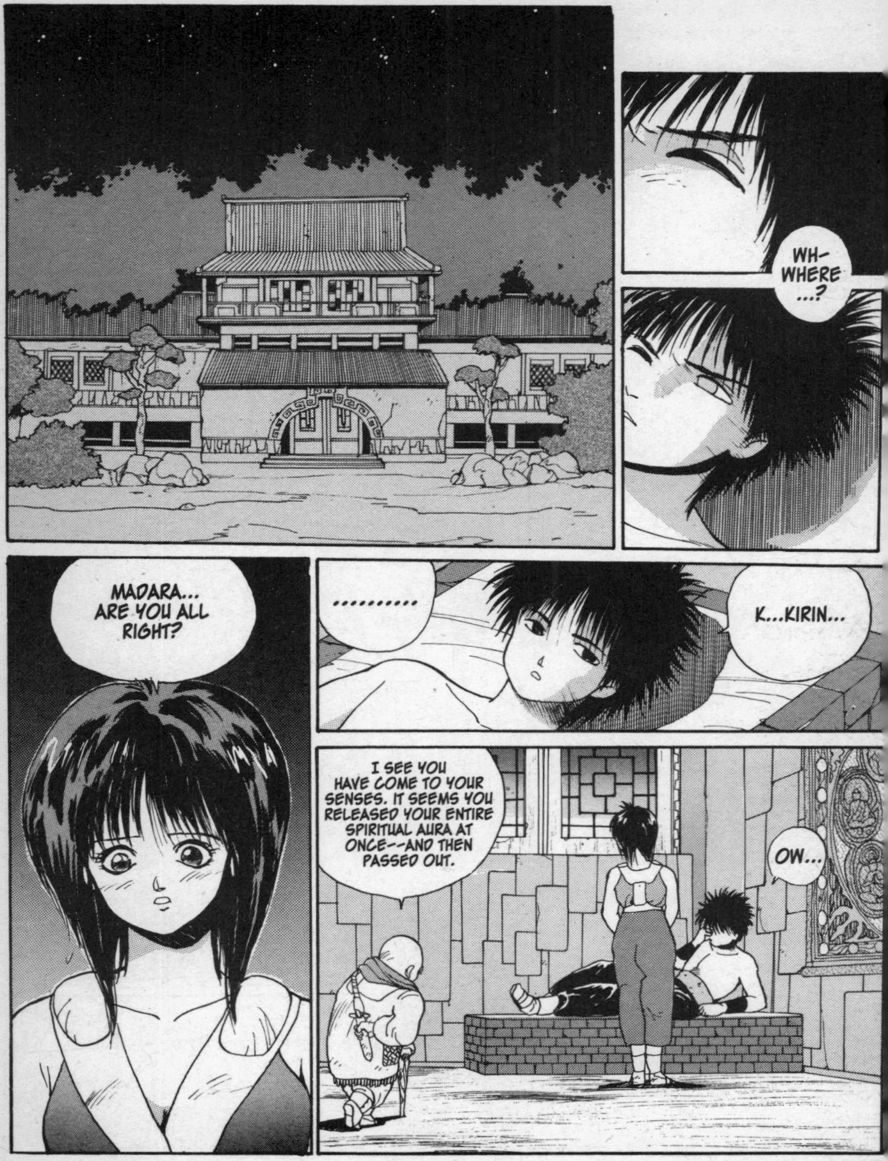
WH- WHERE ...?
MADARA... ARE YOU ALL RIGHT?
....
K...KIRIN...
I SEE YOU HAVE COME TO YOUR SENSES. IT SEEMS YOU RELEASED YOUR ENTIRE SPIRITUAL AURA AT ONCE--AND THEN PASSED OUT.
OW...

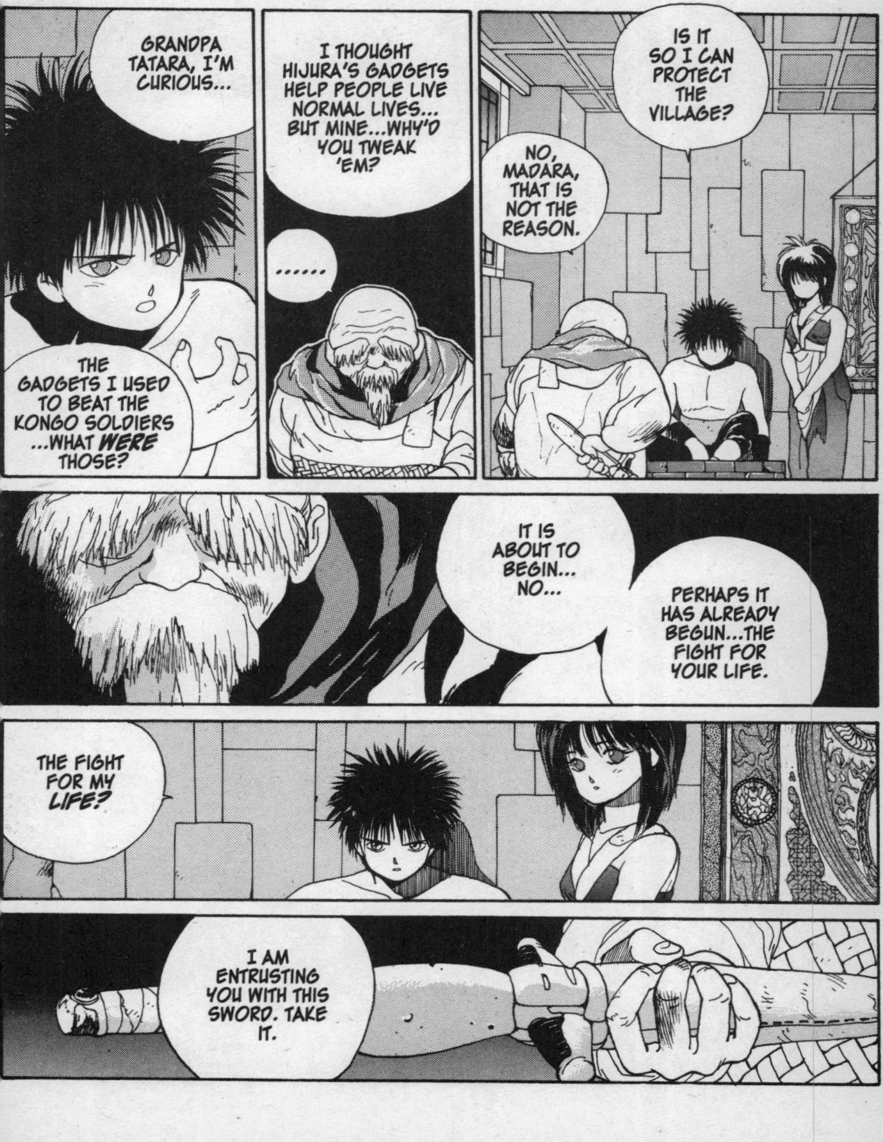

GRANDPA TATARA, I'M CURIOUS...
THE GADGETS I USED TO BEAT THE KONGO SOLDIERS ...WHAT *WERE* THOSE?
I THOUGHT HIJURA'S GADGETS HELP PEOPLE LIVE NORMAL LIVES... BUT MINE...WHY'D YOU TWEAK 'EM?
......
IS IT SO I CAN PROTECT THE VILLAGE?
NO, MADARA, THAT IS NOT THE REASON.
IT IS ABOUT TO BEGIN... NO...
PERHAPS IT HAS ALREADY BEGUN...THE FIGHT FOR YOUR LIFE.
THE FIGHT FOR MY *LIFE?*
I AM ENTRUSTING YOU WITH THIS SWORD. TAKE IT.

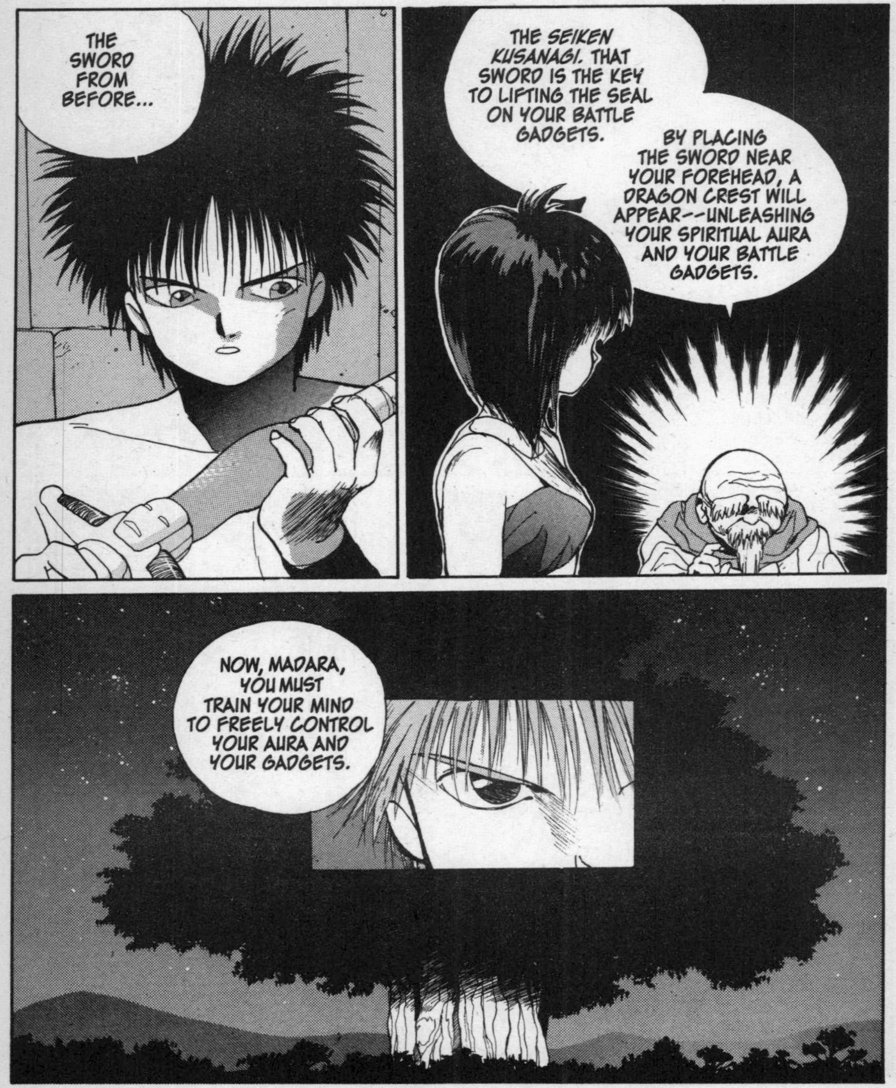

THE SWORD FROM BEFORE...
THE SEIKEN KUSANAGI. THAT SWORD IS THE KEY TO LIFTING THE SEAL ON YOUR BATTLE GADGETS.
BY PLACING THE SWORD NEAR YOUR FOREHEAD, A DRAGON CREST WILL APPEAR--UNLEASHING YOUR SPIRITUAL AURA AND YOUR BATTLE GADGETS.
NOW, MADARA, YOU MUST TRAIN YOUR MIND TO FREELY CONTROL YOUR AURA AND YOUR GADGETS.

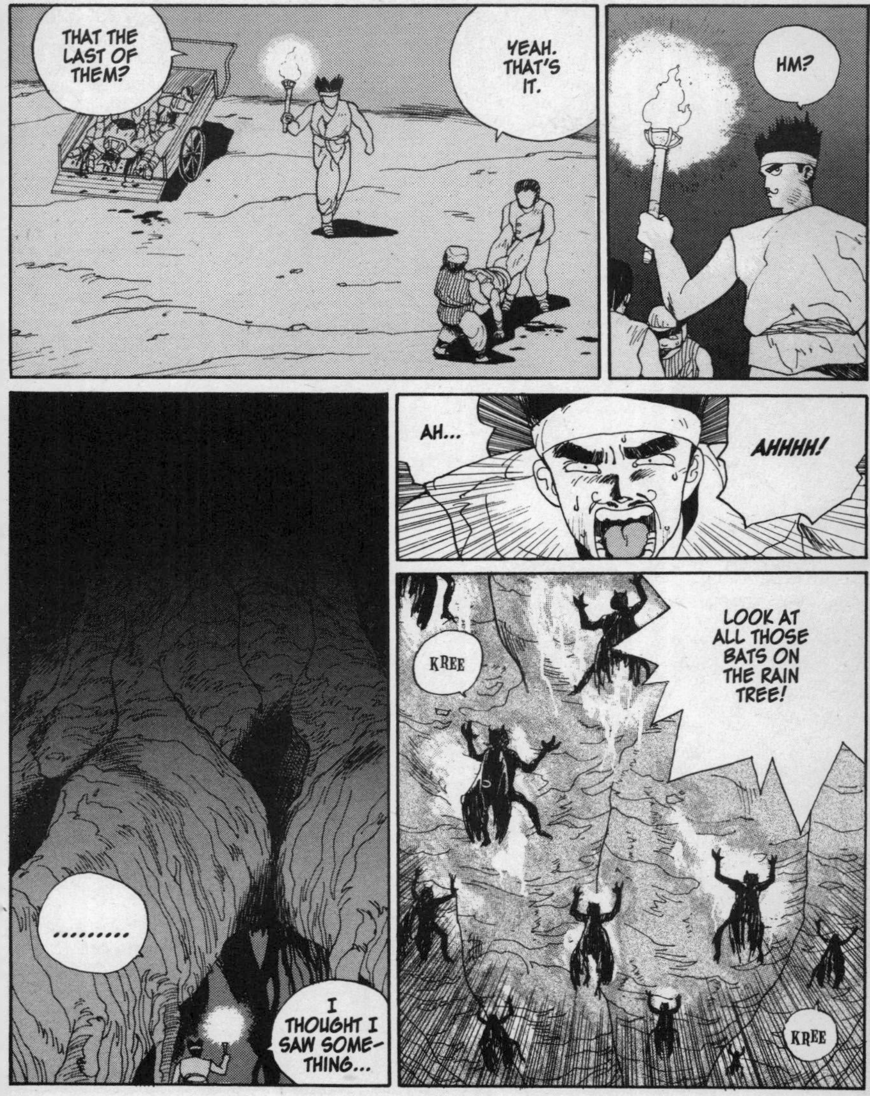

THAT THE LAST OF THEM?
YEAH. THAT'S IT.
HM?
AH...
AHHHH!
KREE
LOOK AT ALL THOSE BATS ON THE RAIN TREE!
KREE
....
I THOUGHT I SAW SOME-THING...

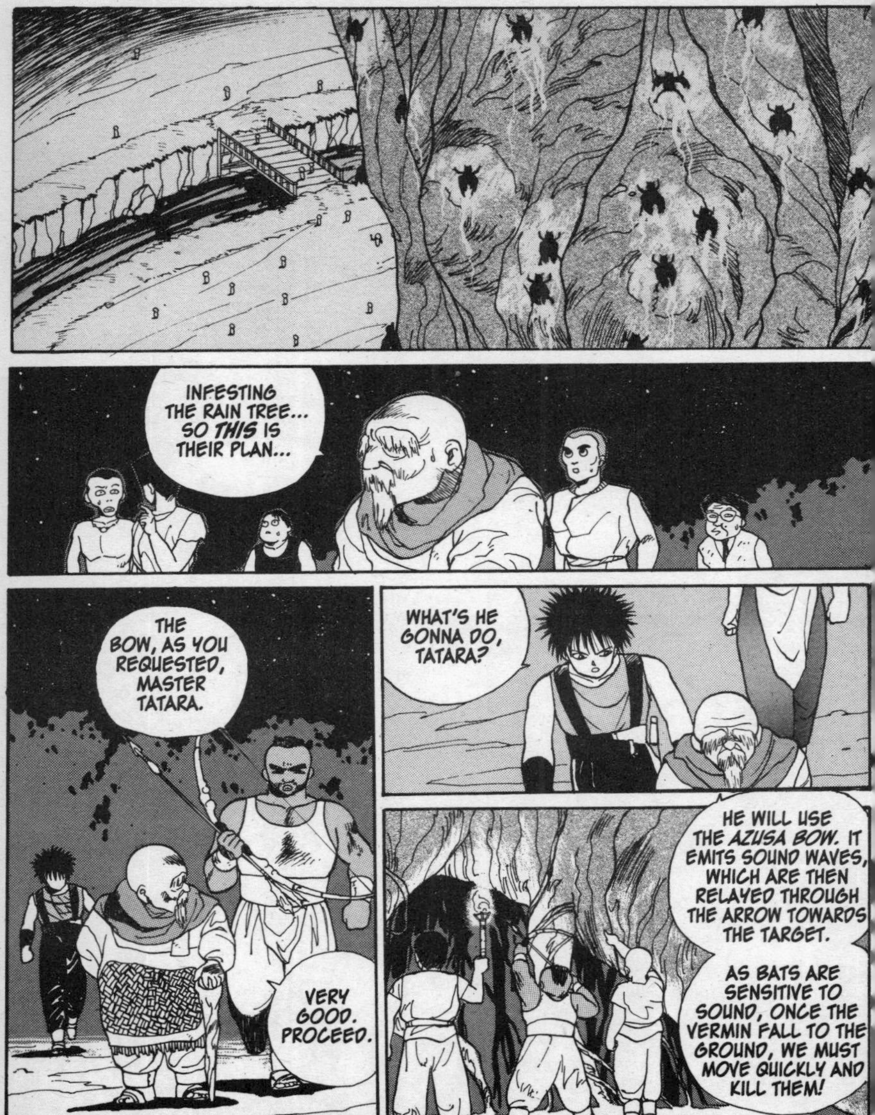
INFESTING THE RAIN TREE... SO *THIS* IS THEIR PLAN...
THE BOW, AS YOU REQUESTED, MASTER TATARA.
VERY GOOD. PROCEED.
WHAT'S HE GONNA DO, TATARA?
HE WILL USE THE *AZUSA BOW*. IT EMITS SOUND WAVES, WHICH ARE THEN RELAYED THROUGH THE ARROW TOWARDS THE TARGET.
AS BATS ARE SENSITIVE TO SOUND, ONCE THE VERMIN FALL TO THE GROUND, WE MUST MOVE QUICKLY AND KILL THEM!

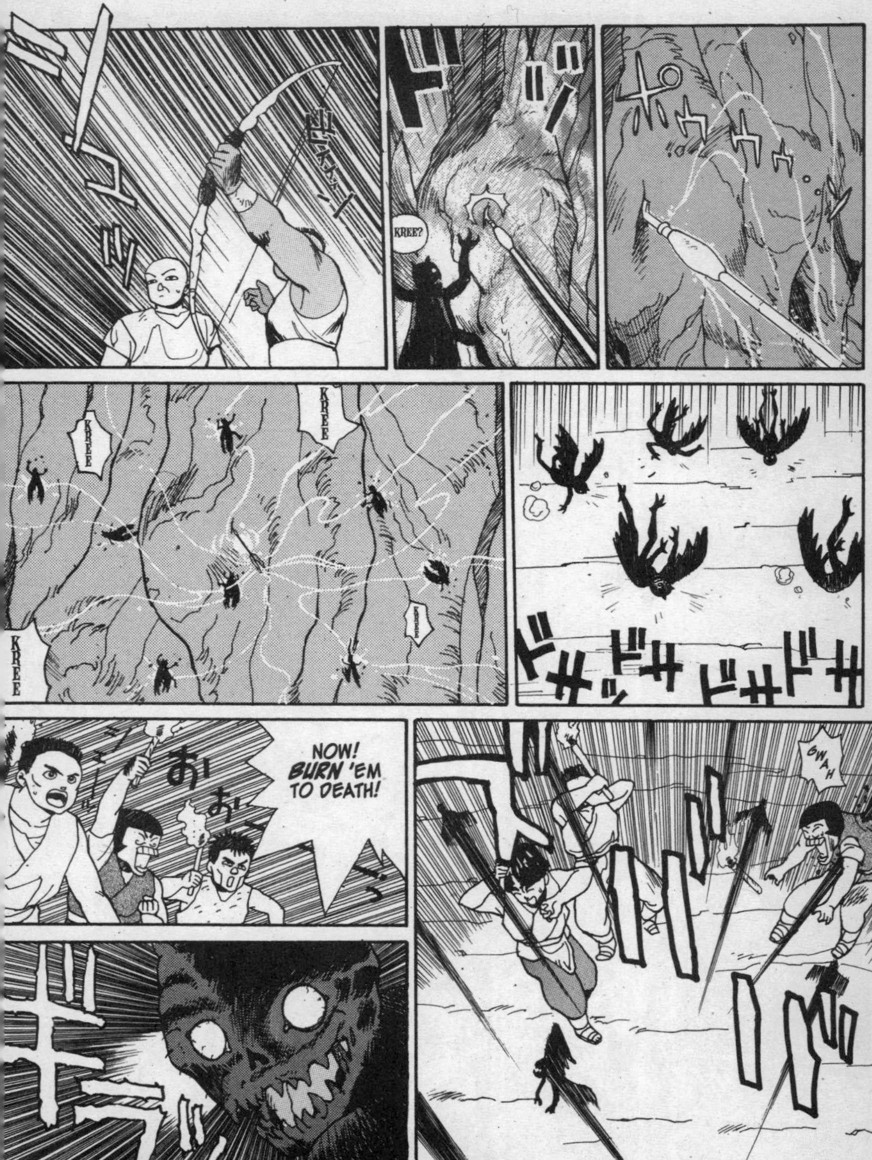
KREE?
KREE
KREE
KREE
KREE
NOW! BURN 'EM TO DEATH!
GWAH

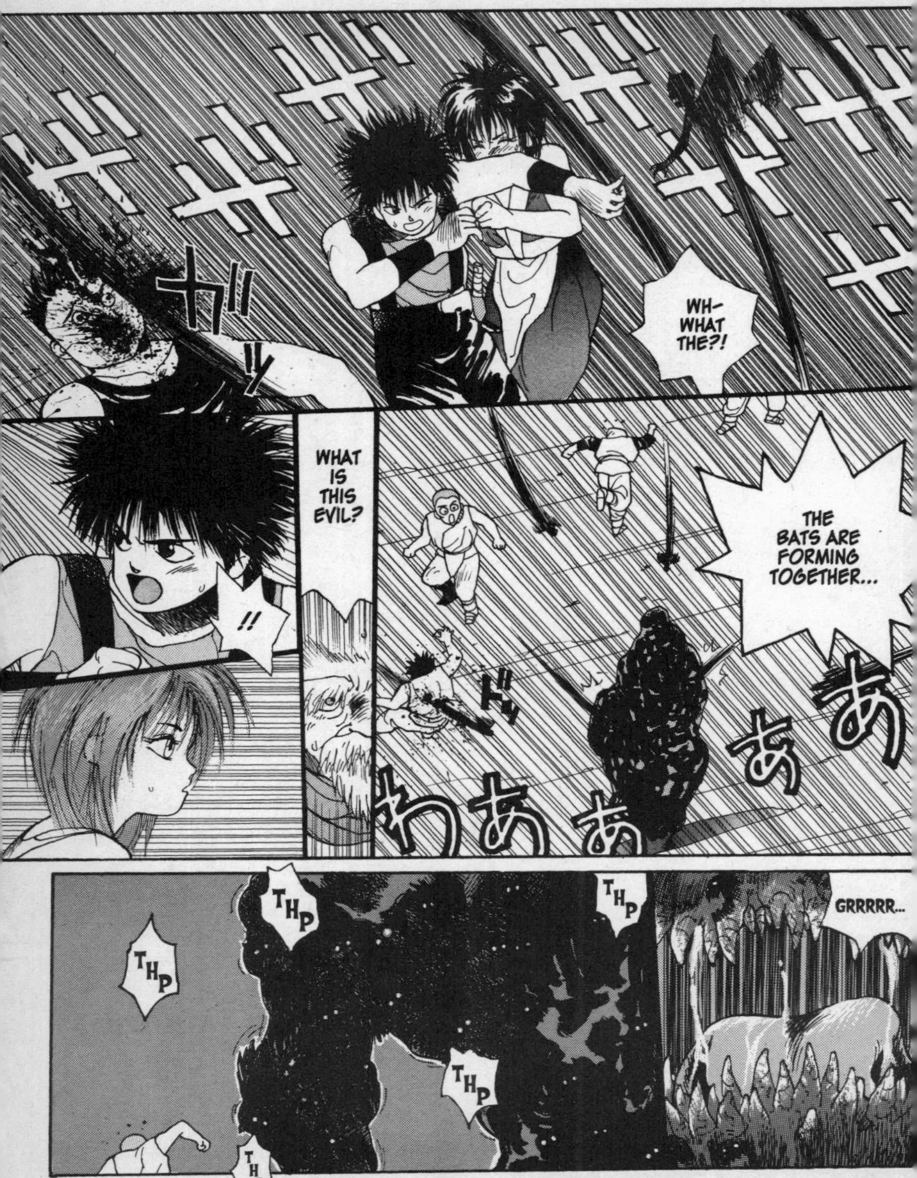
WH-
WHAT
THE?!
THE
BATS ARE
FORMING
TOGETHER...
WHAT
IS
THIS
EVIL?
!!
GRRRRR...
THP
THP
THP
THP
THP

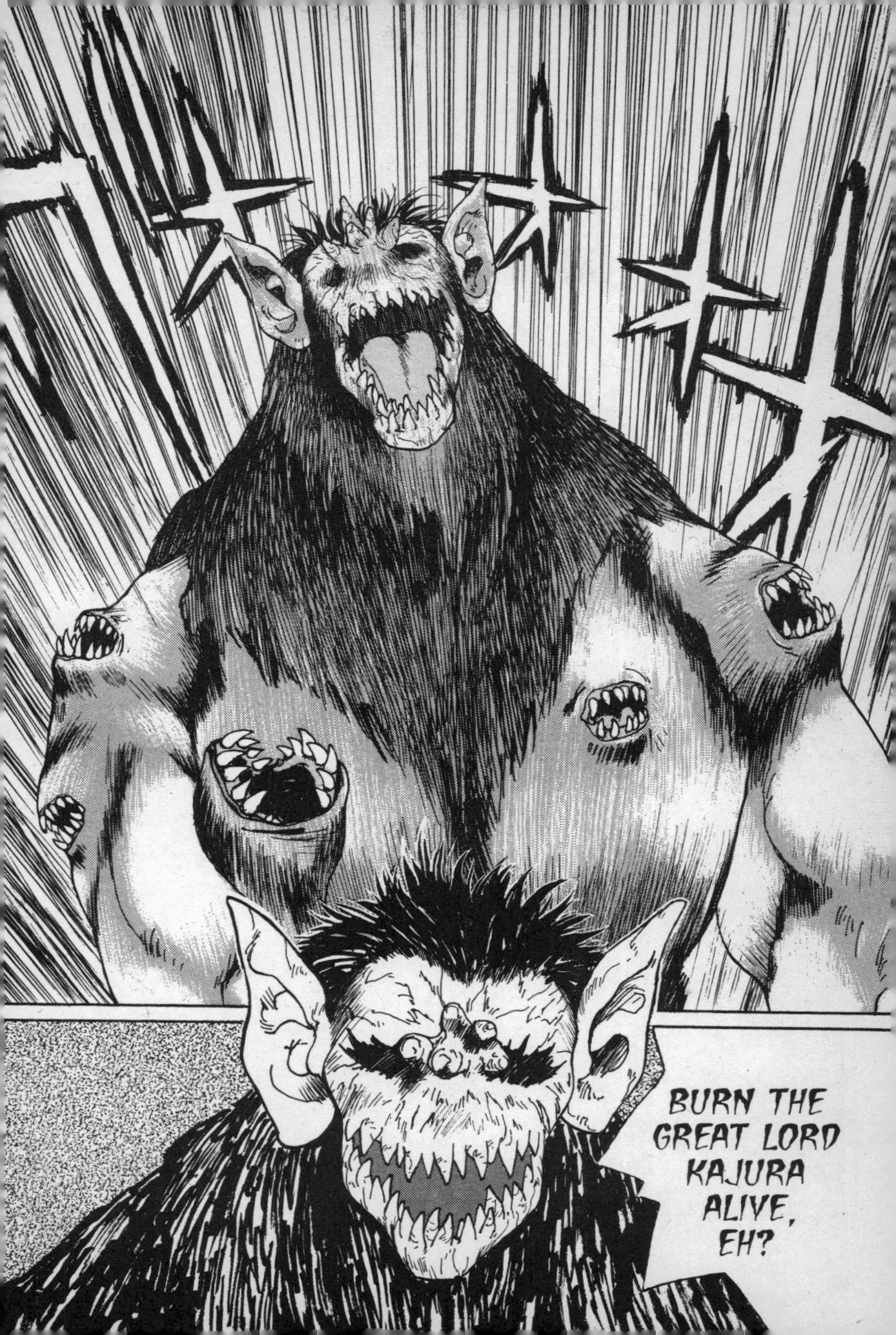
BURN THE GREAT LORD KAJURA ALIVE, EH?

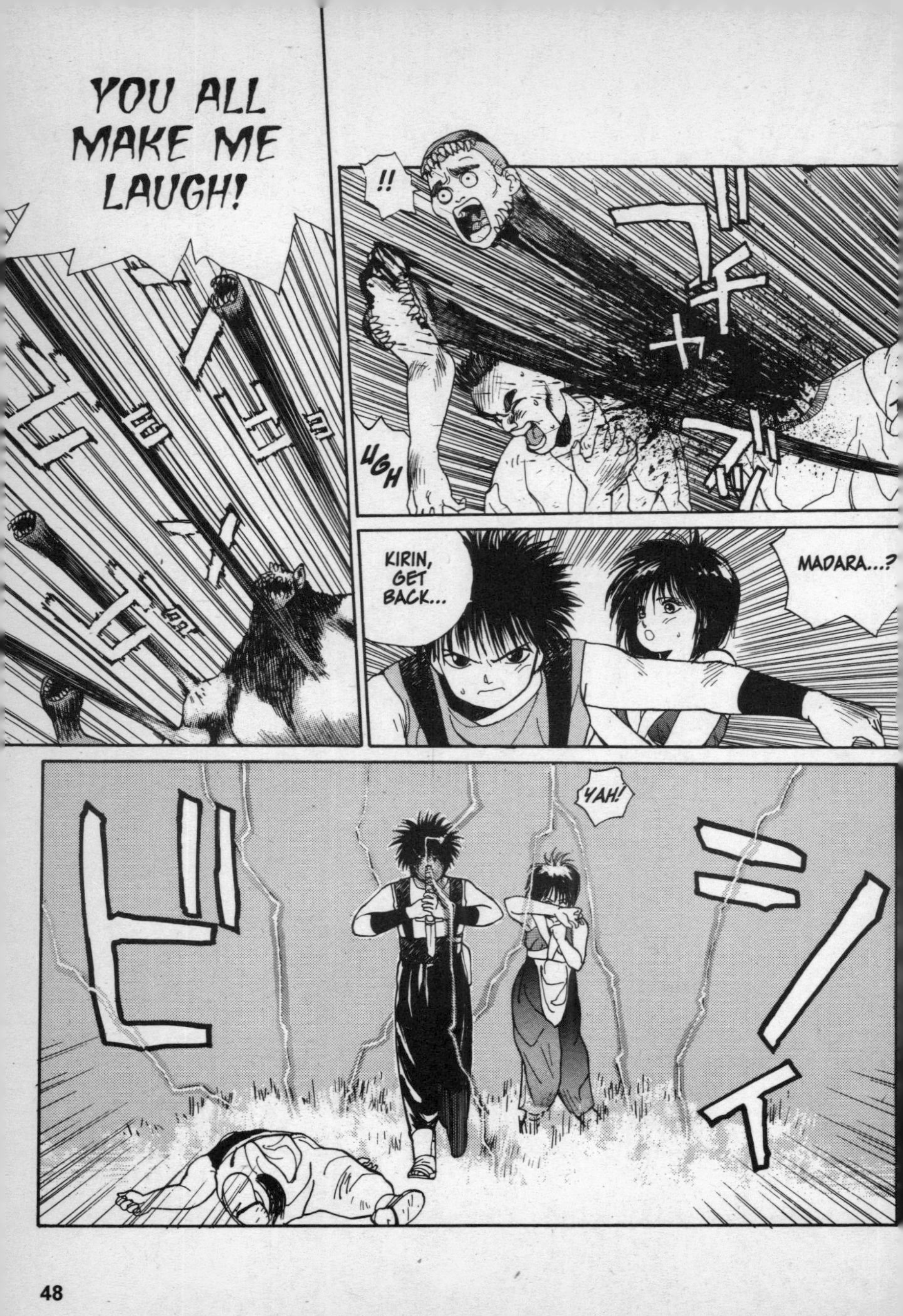
YOU ALL MAKE ME LAUGH!
!!
UGH
MADARA...?
KIRIN, GET BACK...
YAH!

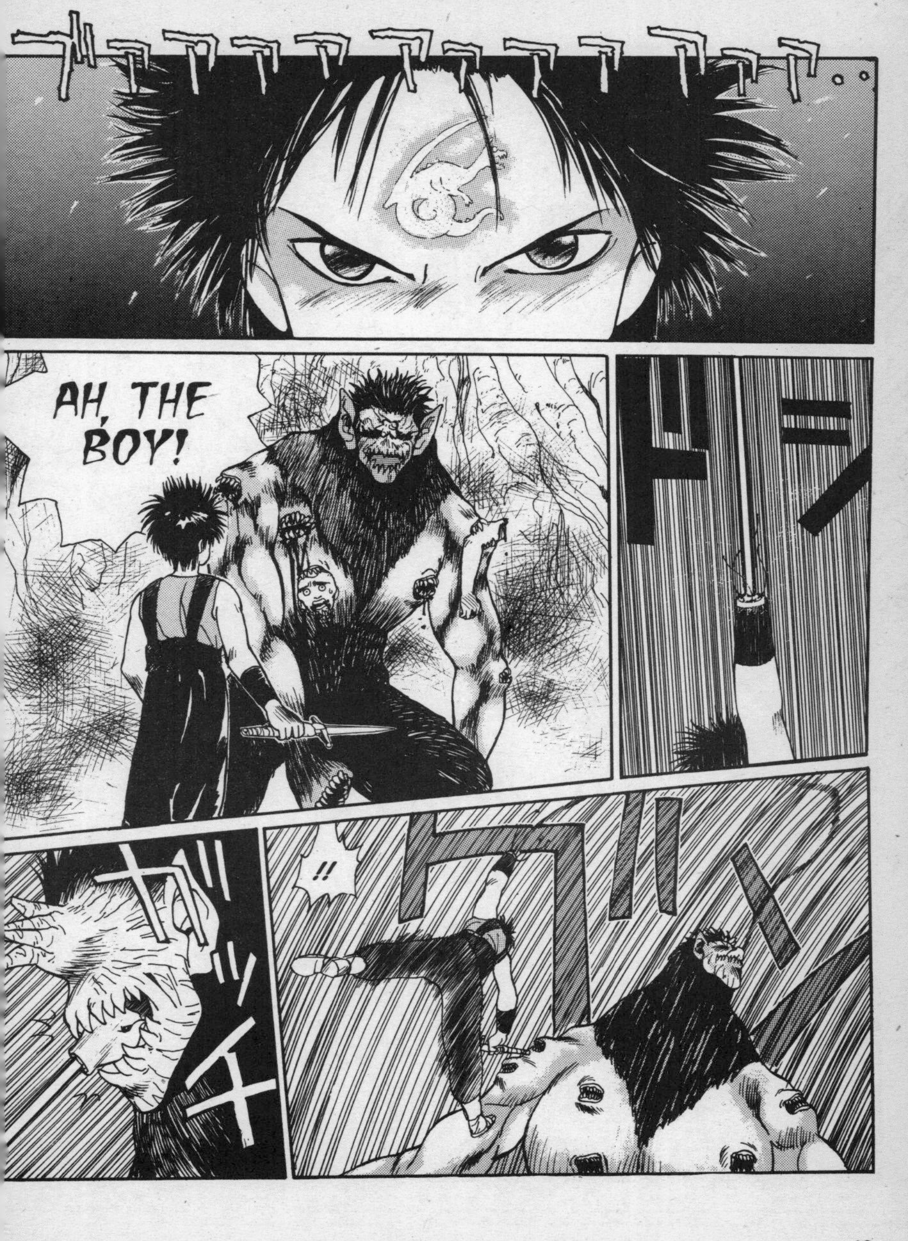
AH, THE BOY!
!!

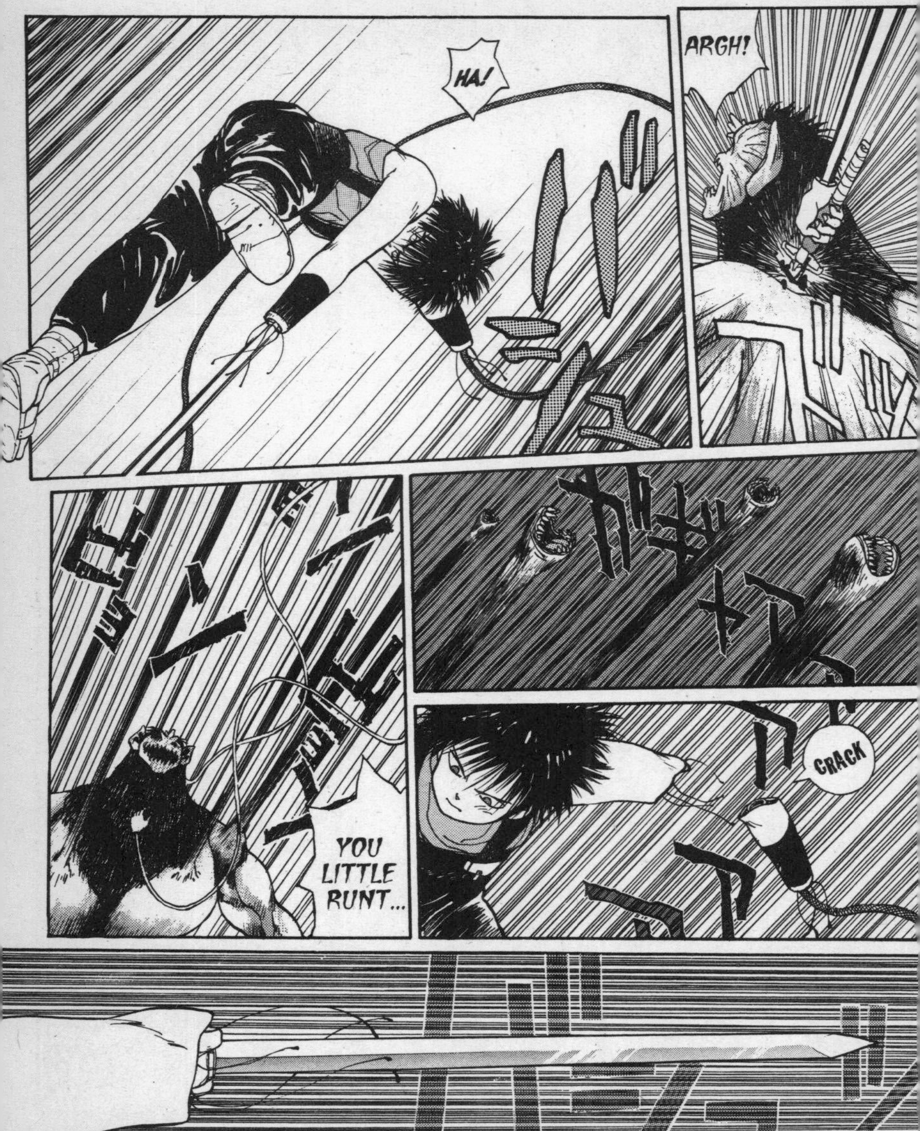
ARGH!
HA!
YOU LITTLE RUNT...
CRACK

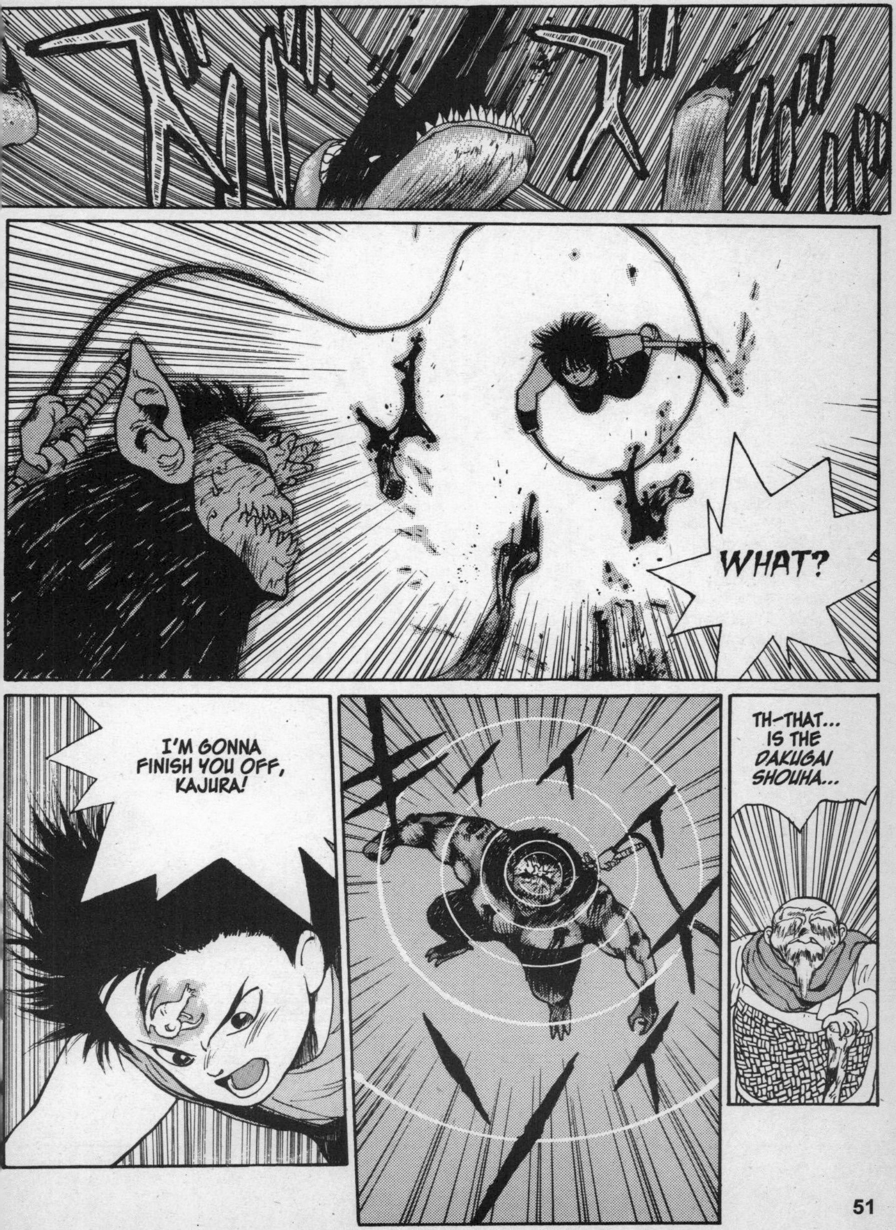
WHAT?
TH-THAT... IS THE DAKUGAI SHOUHA...
I'M GONNA FINISH YOU OFF, KAJURA!

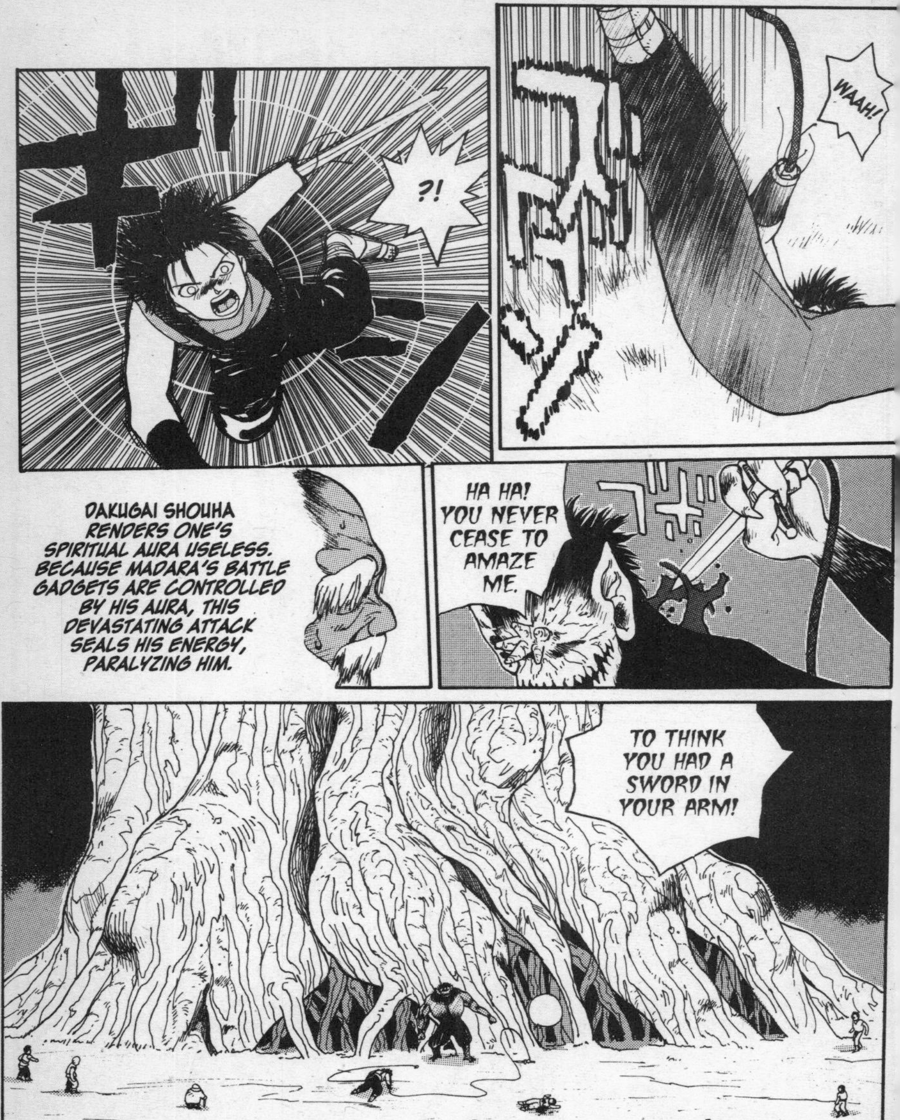
?!
WAAH!
DAKUGAI SHOUHA RENDERS ONE'S SPIRITUAL AURA USELESS. BECAUSE MADARA'S BATTLE GADGETS ARE CONTROLLED BY HIS AURA, THIS DEVASTATING ATTACK SEALS HIS ENERGY, PARALYZING HIM.
HA HA! YOU NEVER CEASE TO AMAZE ME.
TO THINK YOU HAD A SWORD IN YOUR ARM!

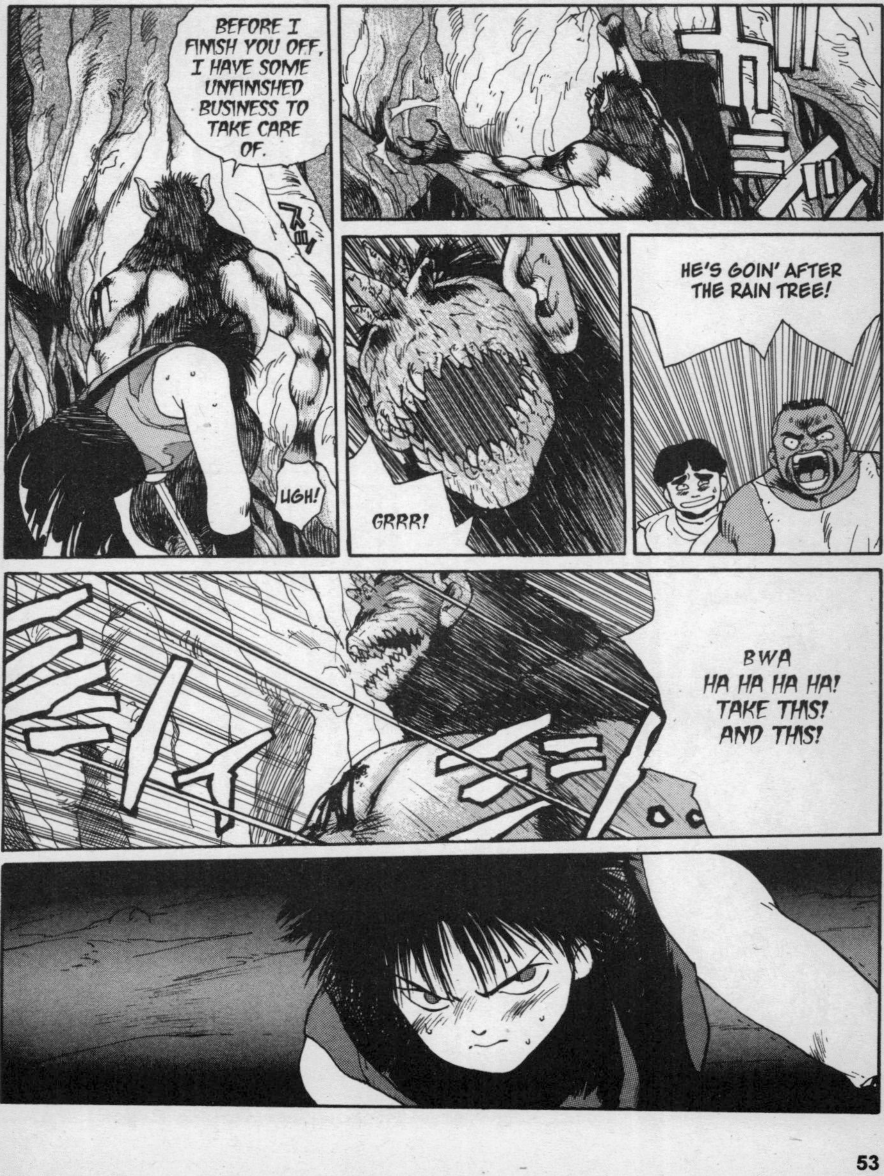
BEFORE I FINISH YOU OFF, I HAVE SOME UNFINISHED BUSINESS TO TAKE CARE OF.
UGH!
HE'S GOIN' AFTER THE RAIN TREE!
GRRR!
BWA HA HA HA HA! TAKE THIS! AND THIS!

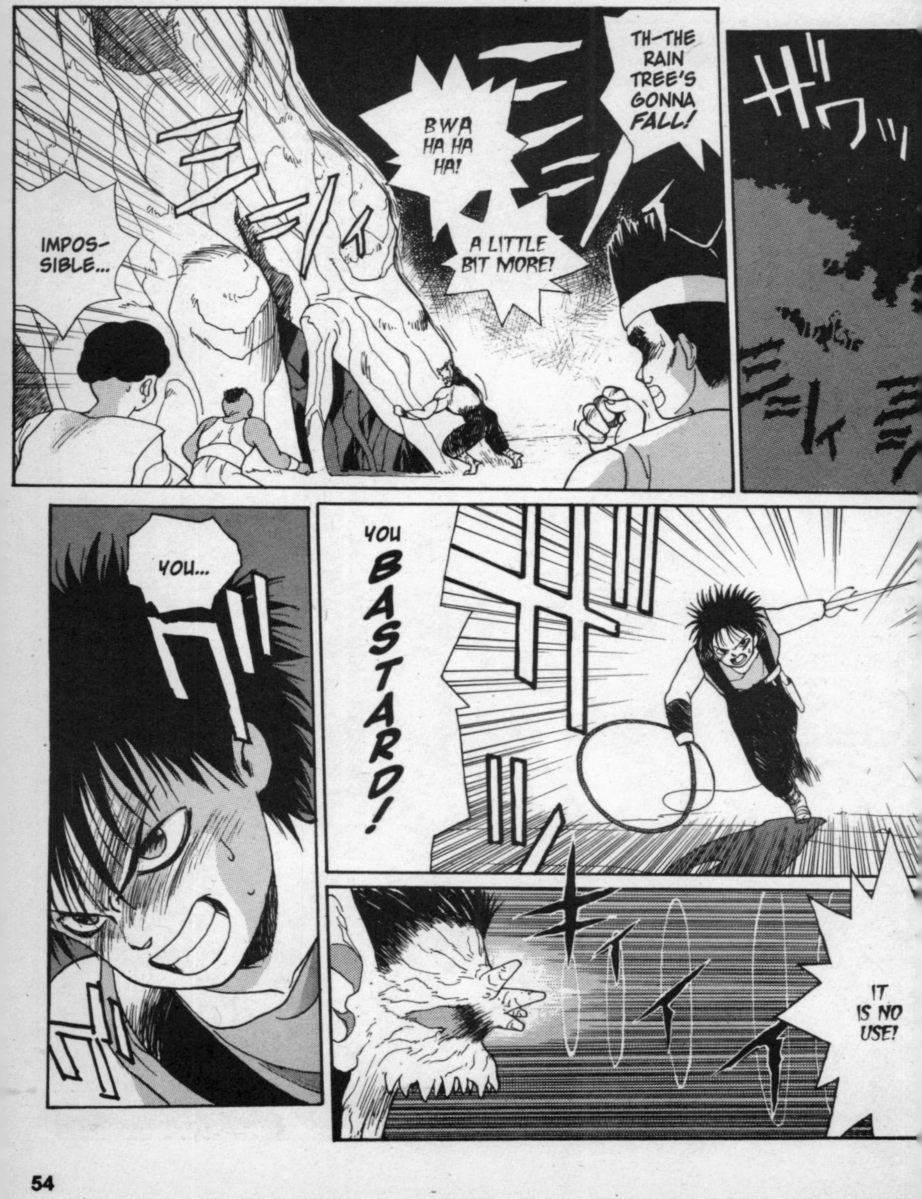
ザワッ
TH-THE RAIN TREE'S GONNA FALL!
BWA HA HA HA!
A LITTLE BIT MORE!
IMPOSSIBLE...
YOU BASTARD!
IT IS NO USE!
YOU...

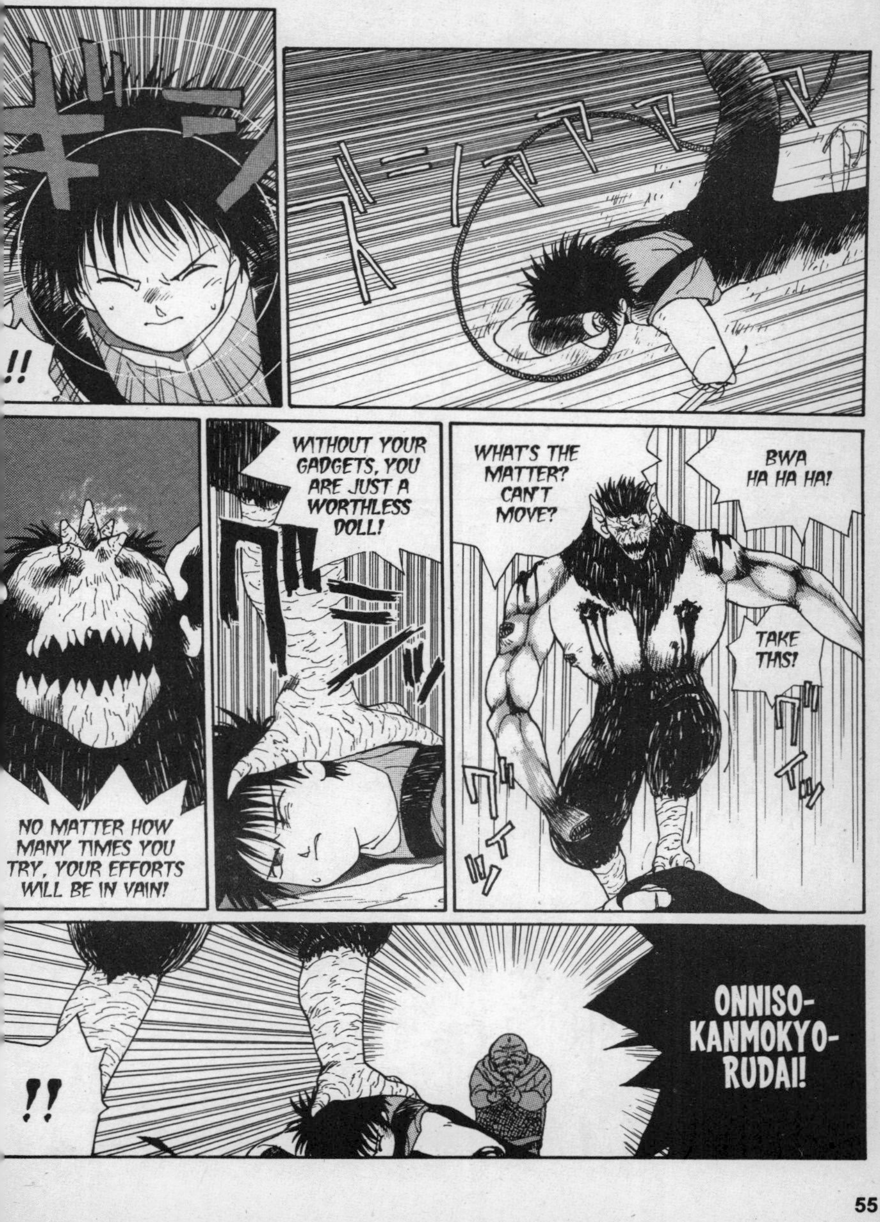
!!
BWA HA HA HA!
WHAT'S THE MATTER? CAN'T MOVE?
TAKE THIS!
WITHOUT YOUR GADGETS, YOU ARE JUST A WORTHLESS DOLL!
NO MATTER HOW MANY TIMES YOU TRY, YOUR EFFORTS WILL BE IN VAIN!
ONNISO-KANMOKYO-RUDAI!
!!

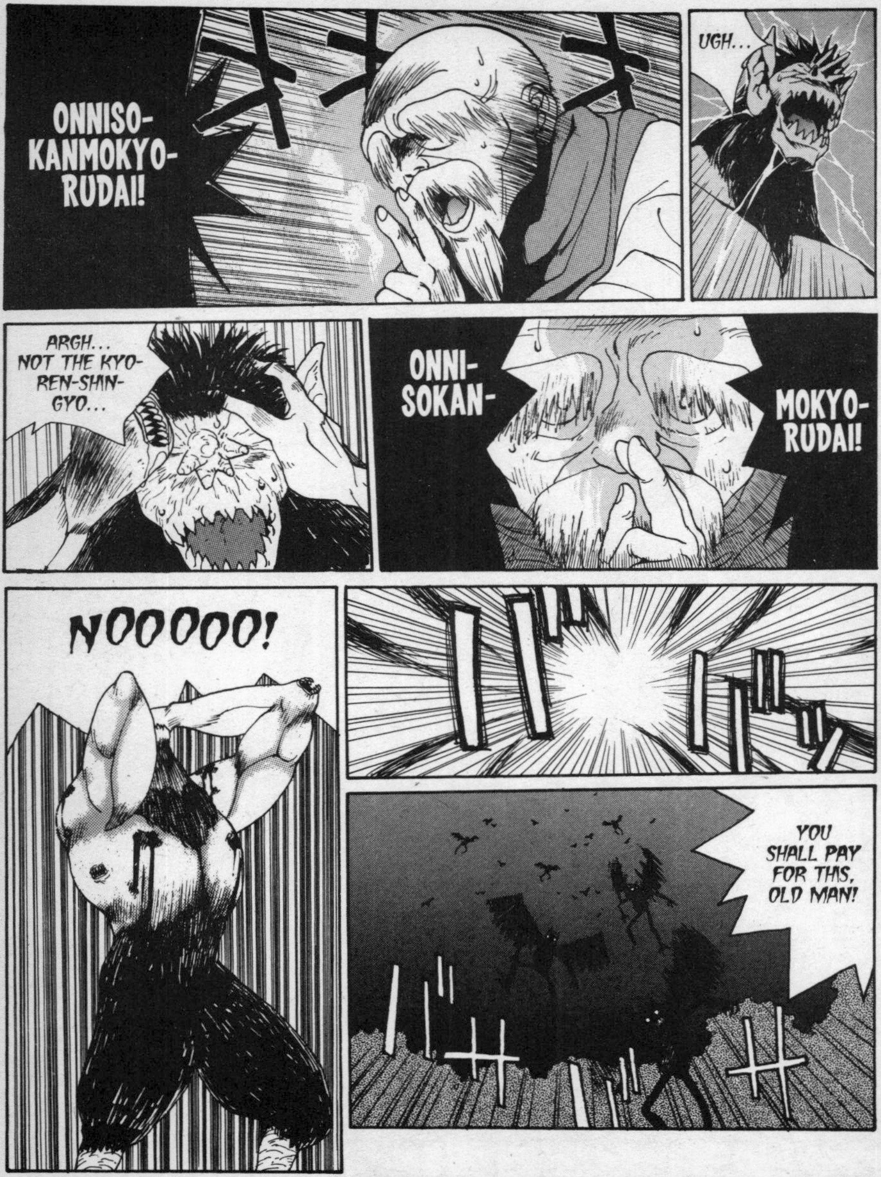
ONNISO-
KANMOKYO-
RUDAI!
UGH...
ARGH... NOT THE KYO-REN-SHIN-GYO...
ONNI-
SOKAN-
MOKYO-
RUDAI!
NOOOOO!
YOU SHALL PAY FOR THIS, OLD MAN!

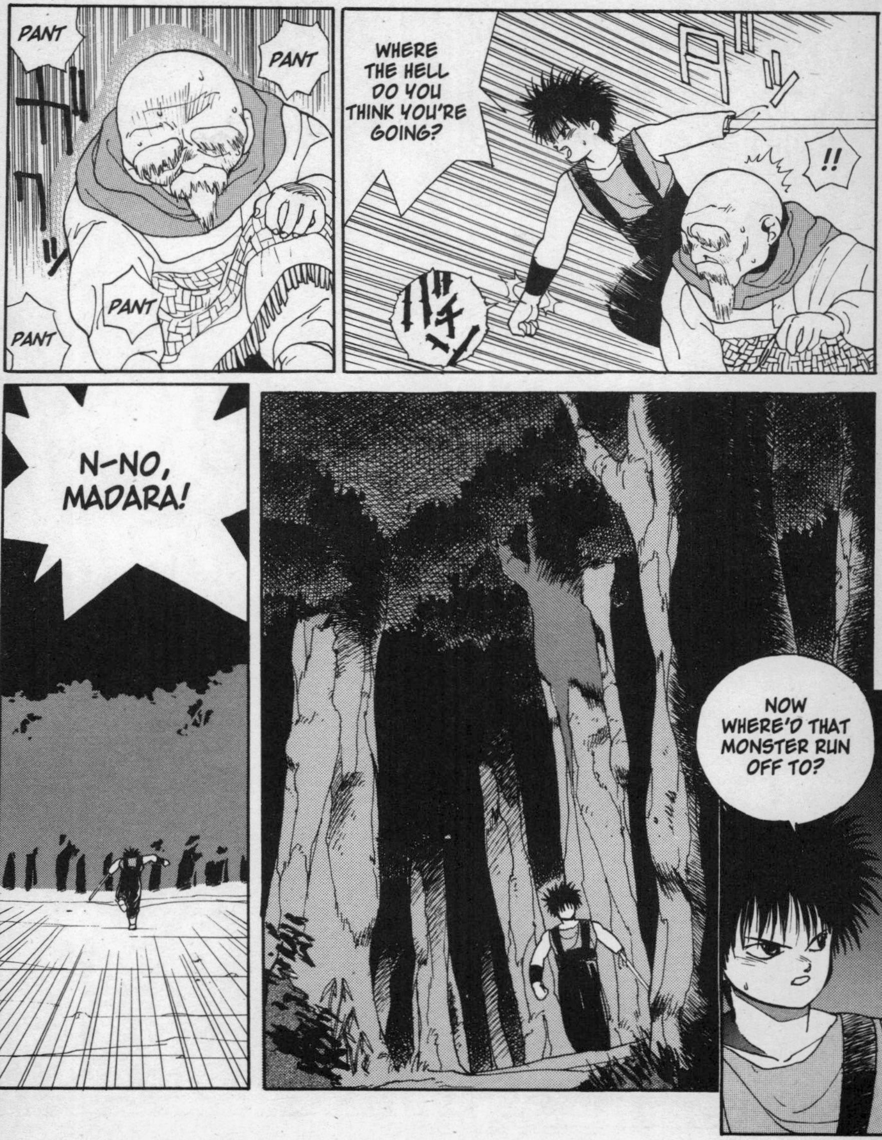

PANT
PANT
PANT
PANT
WHERE THE HELL DO YOU THINK YOU'RE GOING?
!!
N-NO, MADARA!
NOW WHERE'D THAT MONSTER RUN OFF TO?

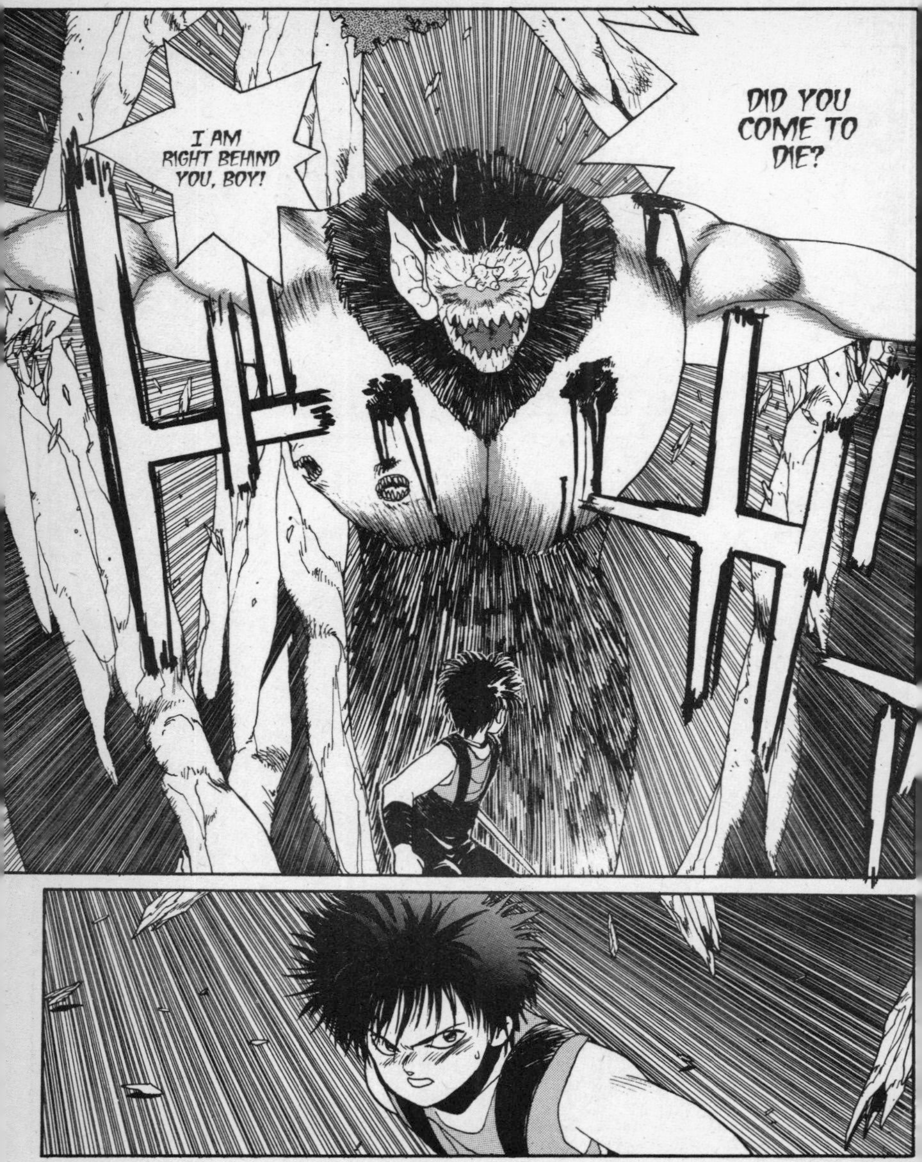
DID YOU COME TO DIE?
I AM RIGHT BEHIND YOU, BOY!

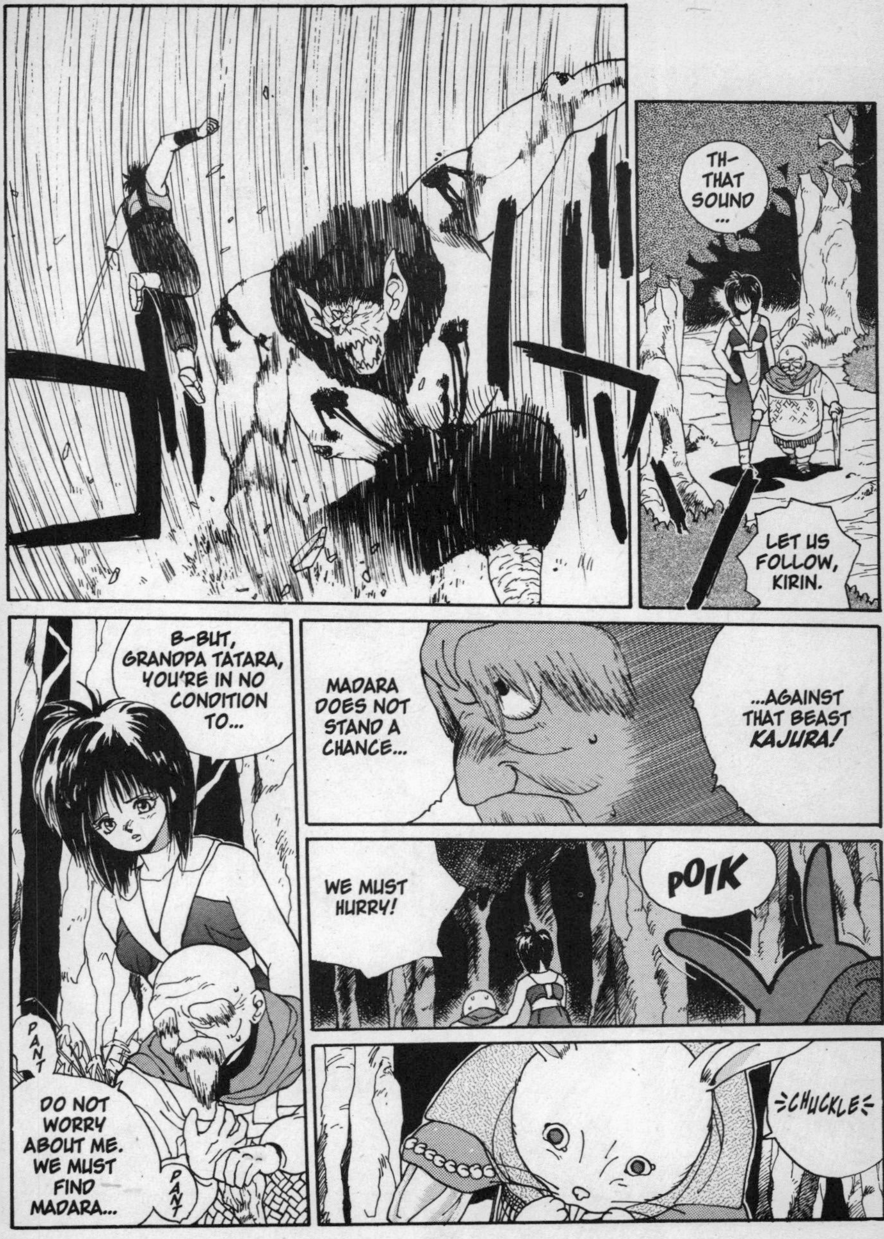

TH-THAT SOUND ...
LET US FOLLOW, KIRIN.
B-BUT, GRANDPA TATARA, YOU'RE IN NO CONDITION TO...
PANT
PANT
DO NOT WORRY ABOUT ME. WE MUST FIND MADARA...
MADARA DOES NOT STAND A CHANCE...
...AGAINST THAT BEAST KAJURA!
WE MUST HURRY!
POIK
CHUCKLE

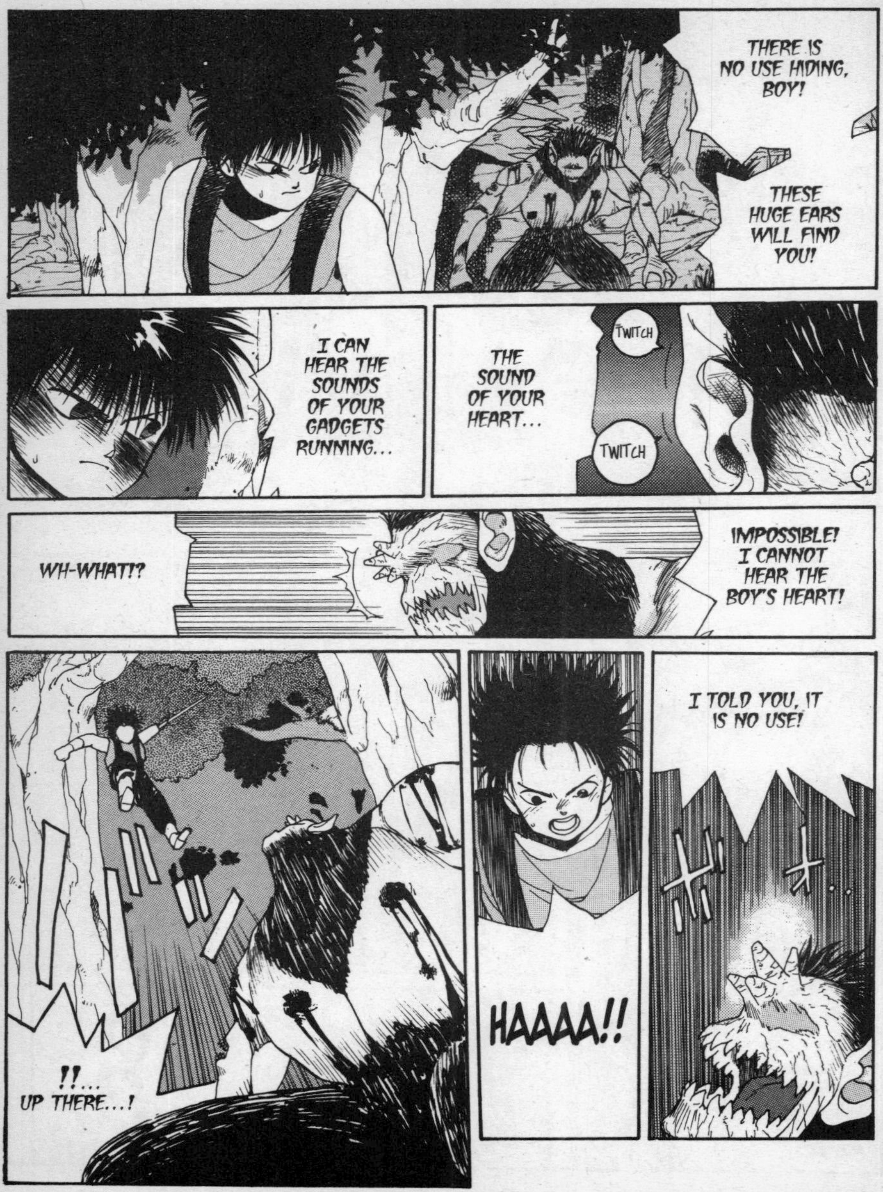
THERE IS NO USE HIDING, BOY!
THESE HUGE EARS WILL FIND YOU!
I CAN HEAR THE SOUNDS OF YOUR GADGETS RUNNING...
THE SOUND OF YOUR HEART...
TWITCH
TWITCH
WH-WHAT!?
IMPOSSIBLE! I CANNOT HEAR THE BOY'S HEART!
!!... UP THERE...!
HAAAA!!
I TOLD YOU, IT IS NO USE!

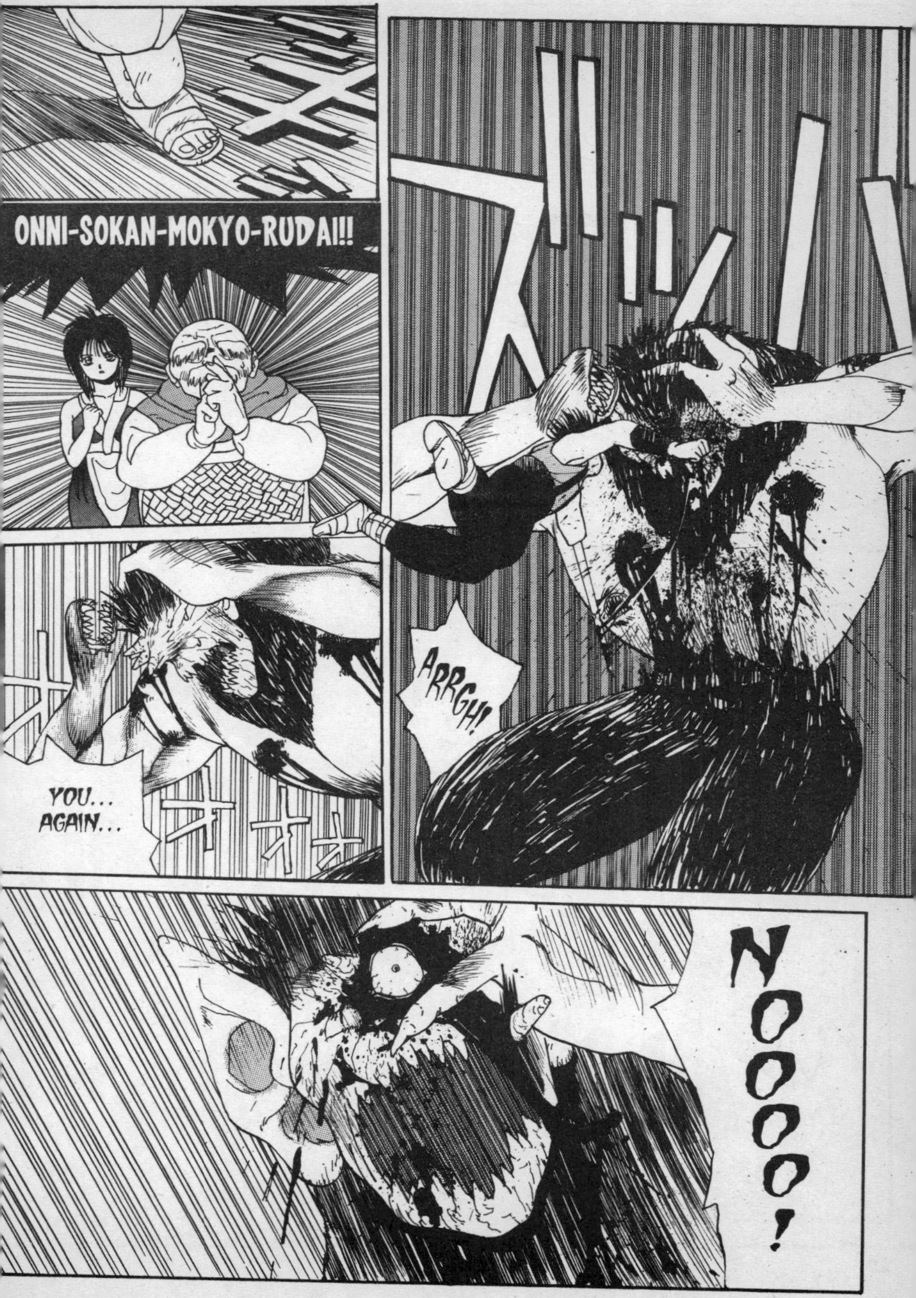
ONNI-SOKAN-MOKYO-RUDAI!!
ARRGH!
YOU... AGAIN...
NOOOO!

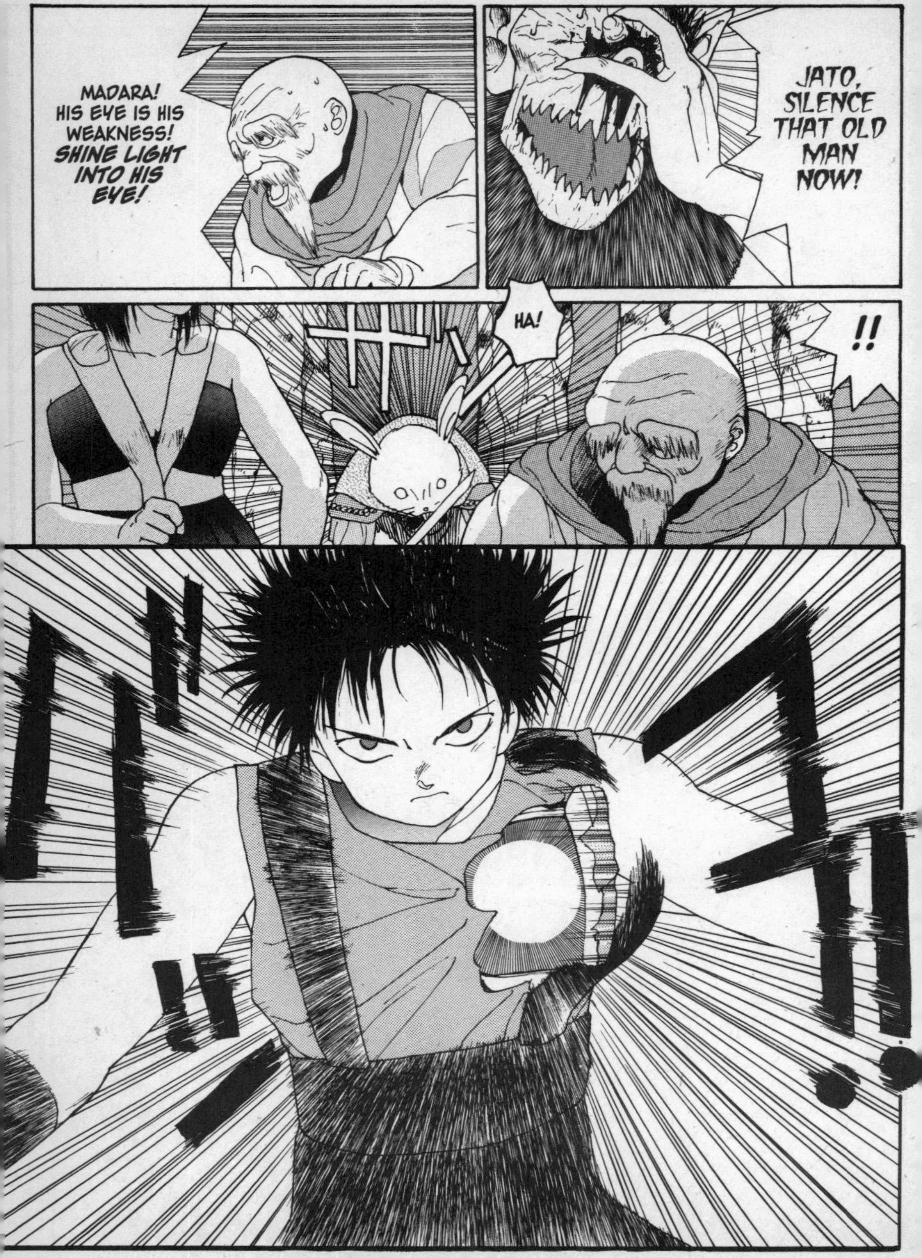
JATO, SILENCE THAT OLD MAN NOW!
MADARA! HIS EYE IS HIS WEAKNESS! SHINE LIGHT INTO HIS EYE!
!!
HA!

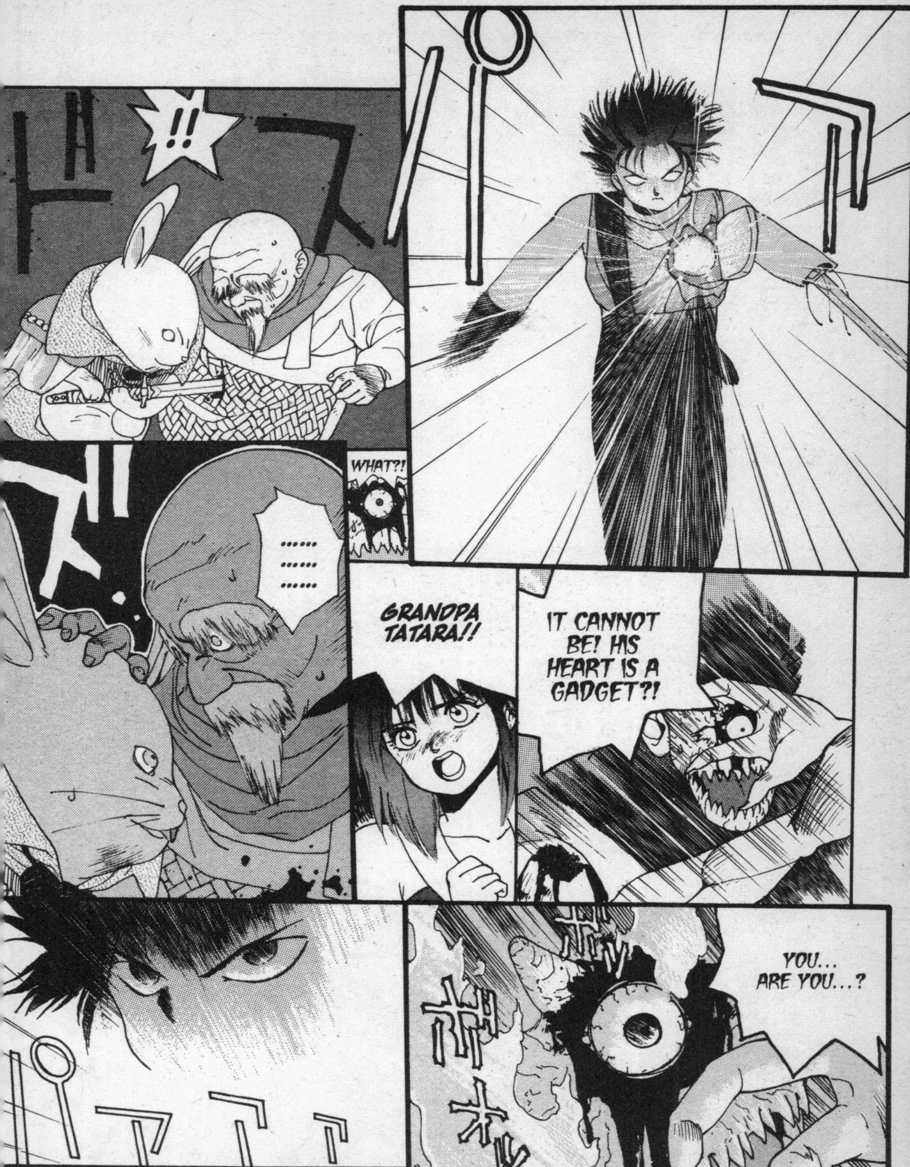
!!
WHAT?!
......
......
......
IT CANNOT BE! HIS HEART IS A GADGET?!
GRANDPA TATARA!!
YOU... ARE YOU...?

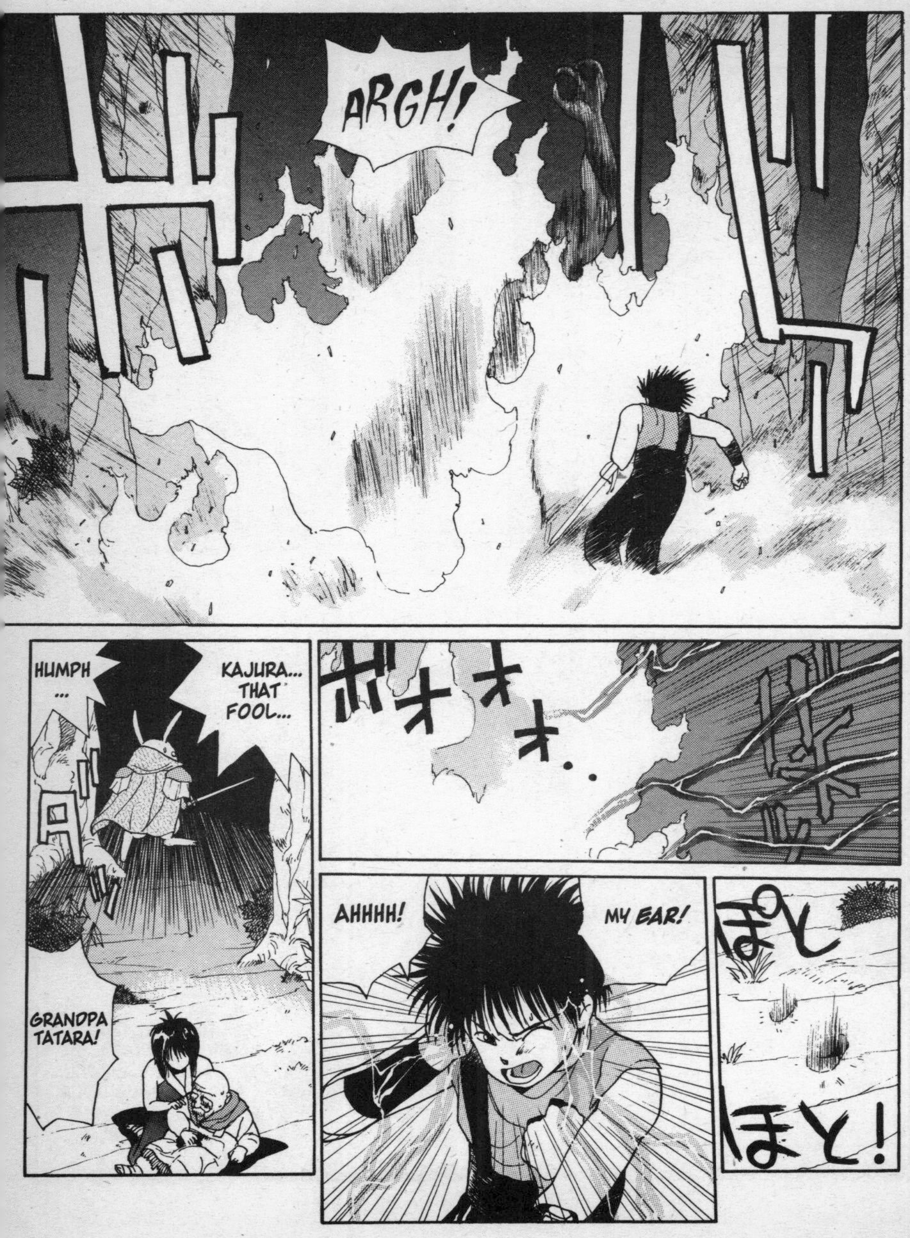

ARGH!
ボオオオ..
ぽと
ぽと!
MY EAR!
AHHHH!
KAJURA... THAT FOOL...
HUMPH...
GRANDPA TATARA!

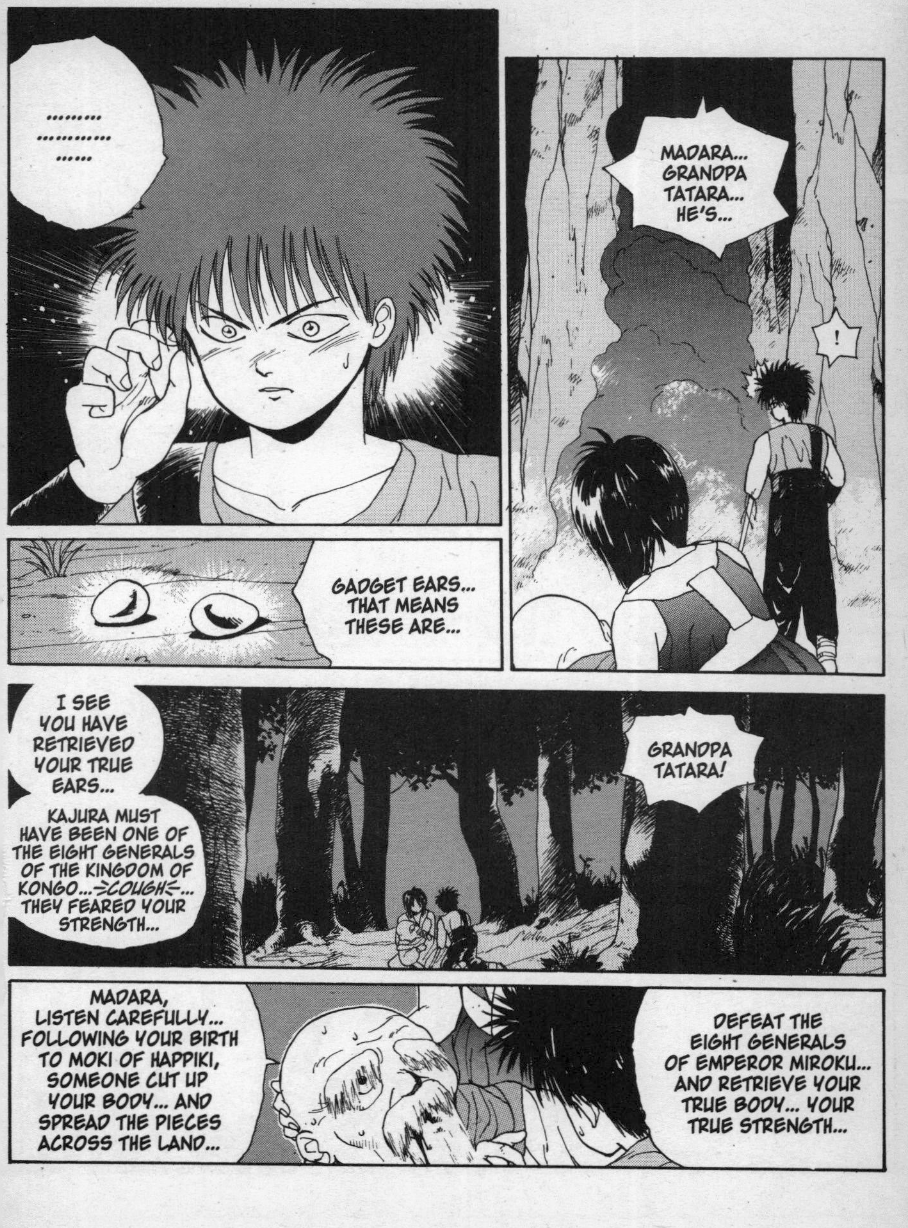

....
....
....
GADGET EARS... THAT MEANS THESE ARE...
MADARA... GRANDPA TATARA... HE'S...
!
I SEE YOU HAVE RETRIEVED YOUR TRUE EARS...
KAJURA MUST HAVE BEEN ONE OF THE EIGHT GENERALS OF THE KINGDOM OF KONGO...⇒COUGH⇐... THEY FEARED YOUR STRENGTH...
GRANDPA TATARA!
MADARA, LISTEN CAREFULLY... FOLLOWING YOUR BIRTH TO MOKI OF HAPPIKI, SOMEONE CUT UP YOUR BODY... AND SPREAD THE PIECES ACROSS THE LAND...
DEFEAT THE EIGHT GENERALS OF EMPEROR MIROKU... AND RETRIEVE YOUR TRUE BODY... YOUR TRUE STRENGTH...

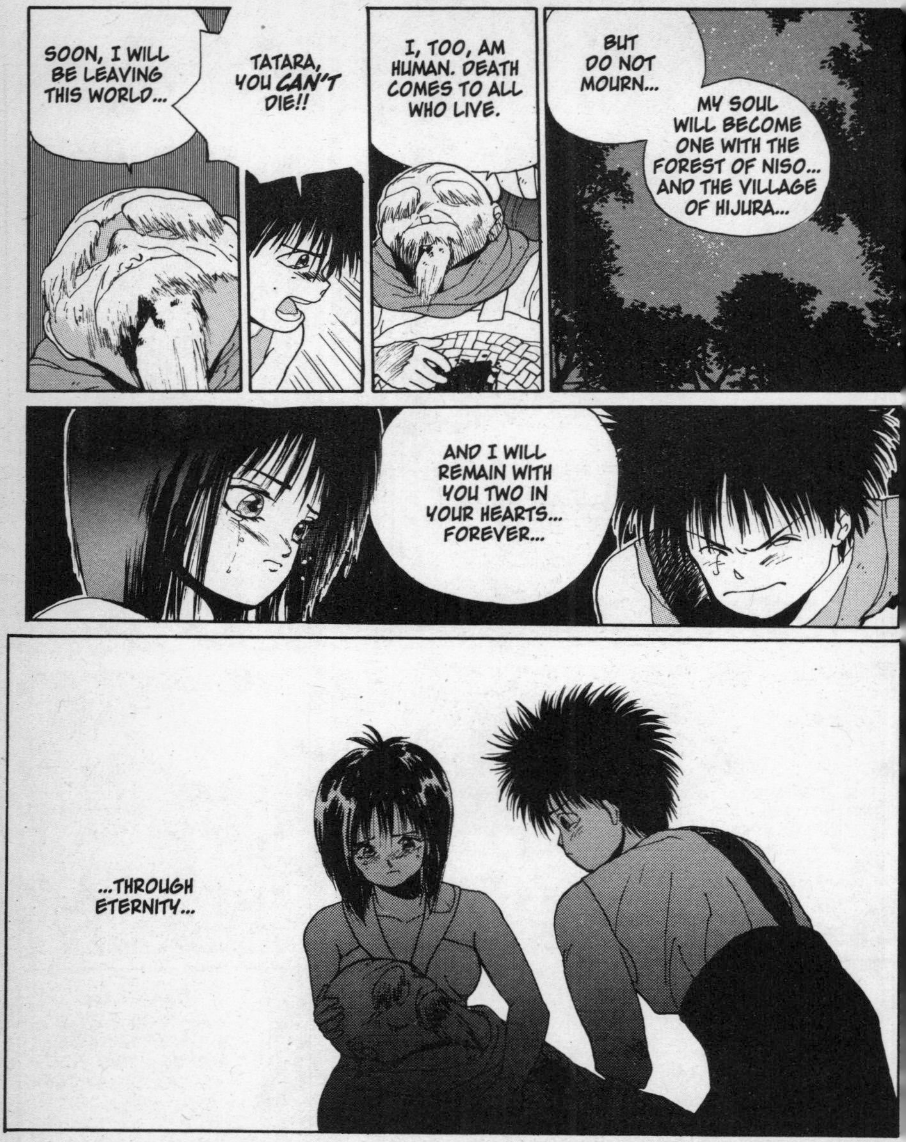
SOON, I WILL BE LEAVING THIS WORLD...
TATARA, YOU CAN'T DIE!!
I, TOO, AM HUMAN. DEATH COMES TO ALL WHO LIVE.
BUT DO NOT MOURN...
MY SOUL WILL BECOME ONE WITH THE FOREST OF NISO... AND THE VILLAGE OF HIJURA...
AND I WILL REMAIN WITH YOU TWO IN YOUR HEARTS... FOREVER...
...THROUGH ETERNITY...

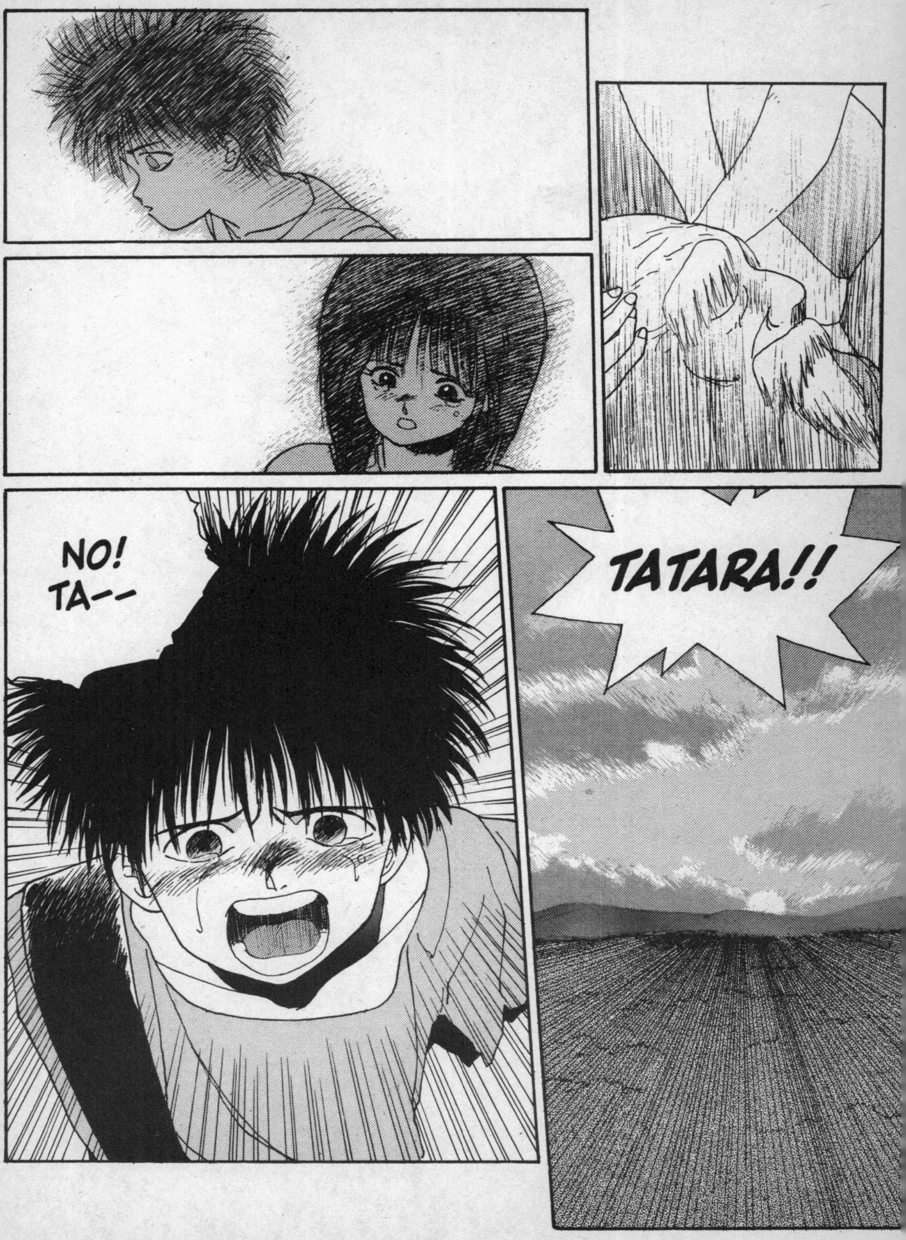
TATARA!!
NO! TA--

第一章 風姫譚

Chapter 1: The Tale of the Wind Princess

"A boy with the dragon's crest
etched on his forehead will one day
come forth from the east. He will
journey to the Holy Land of Agartha
and lead mankind to heaven…"

-- From the oral tradition of the Wind Tribe

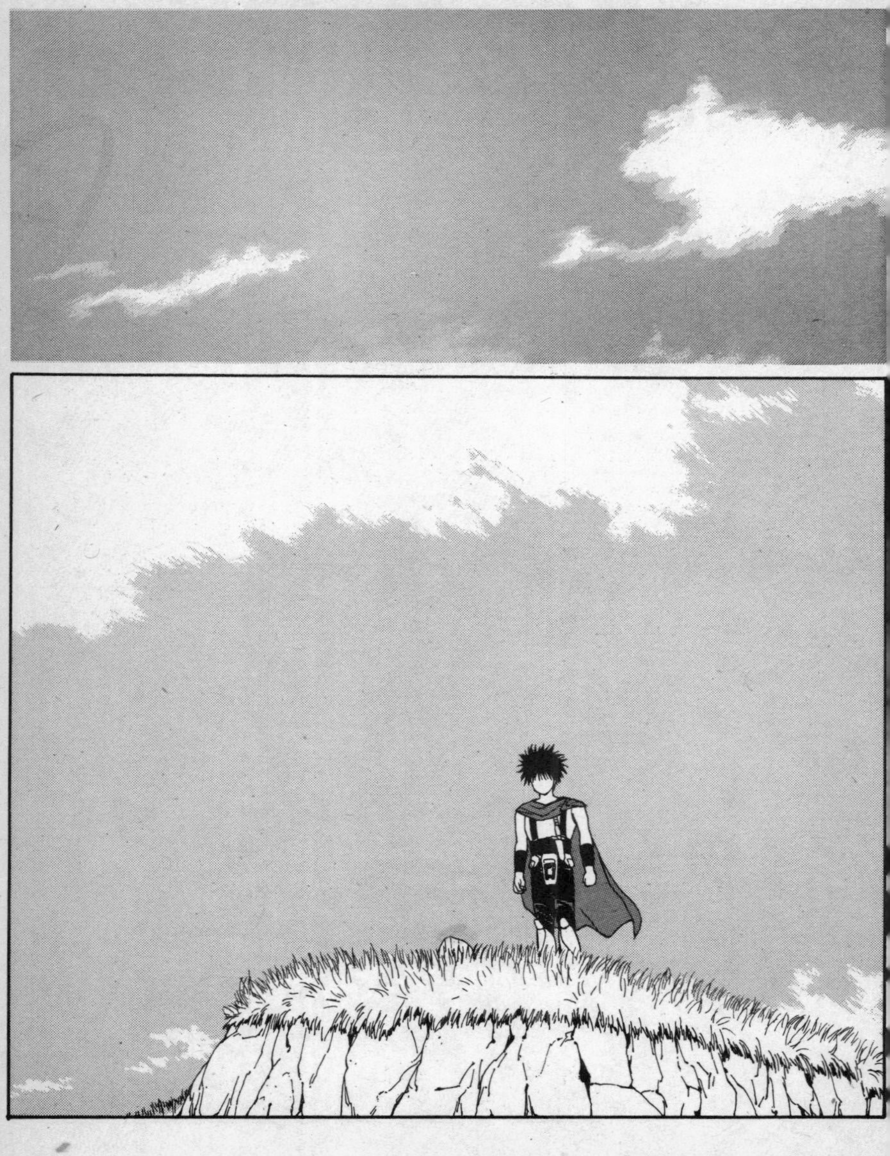

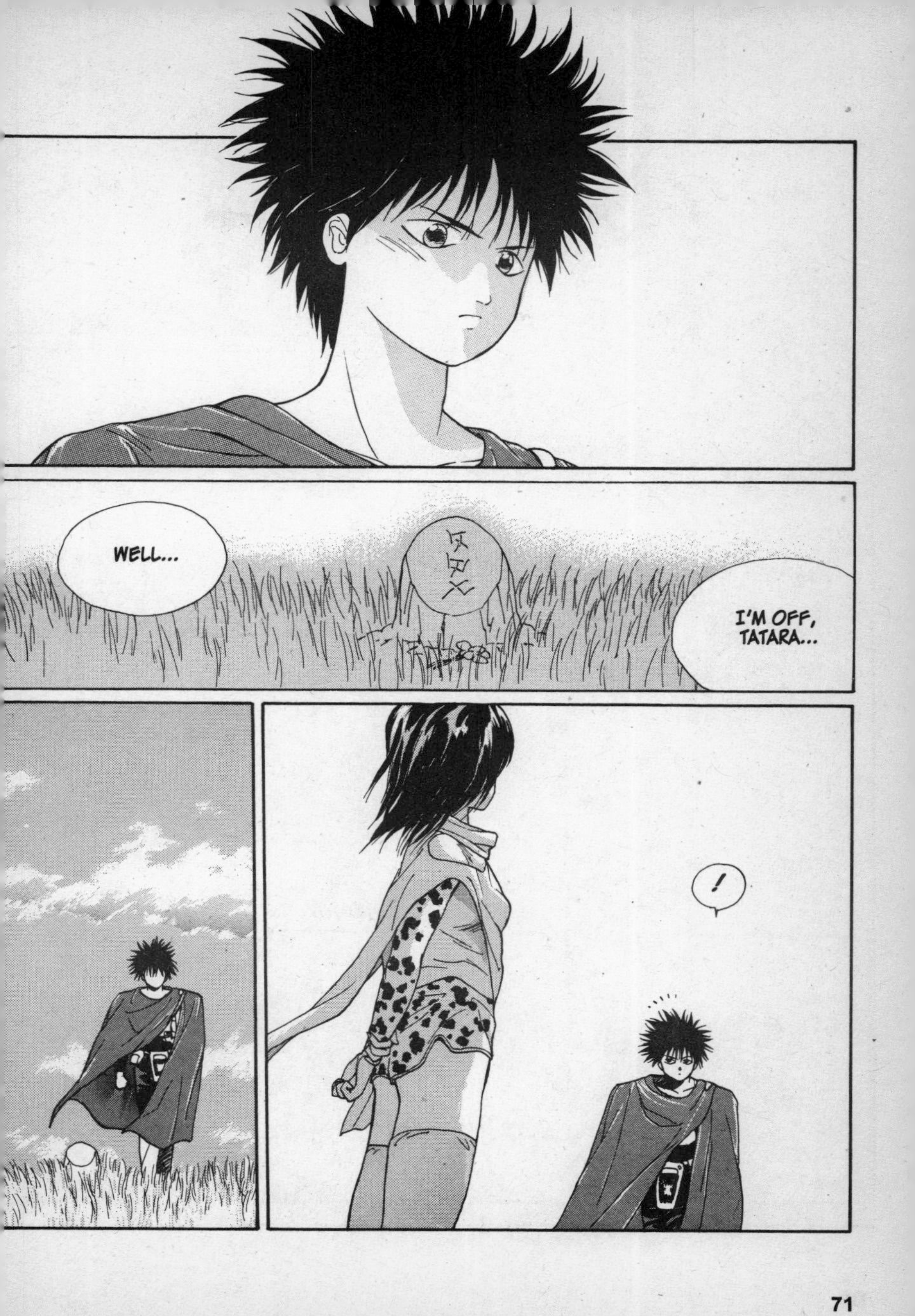
WELL...
I'M OFF, TATARA...
!

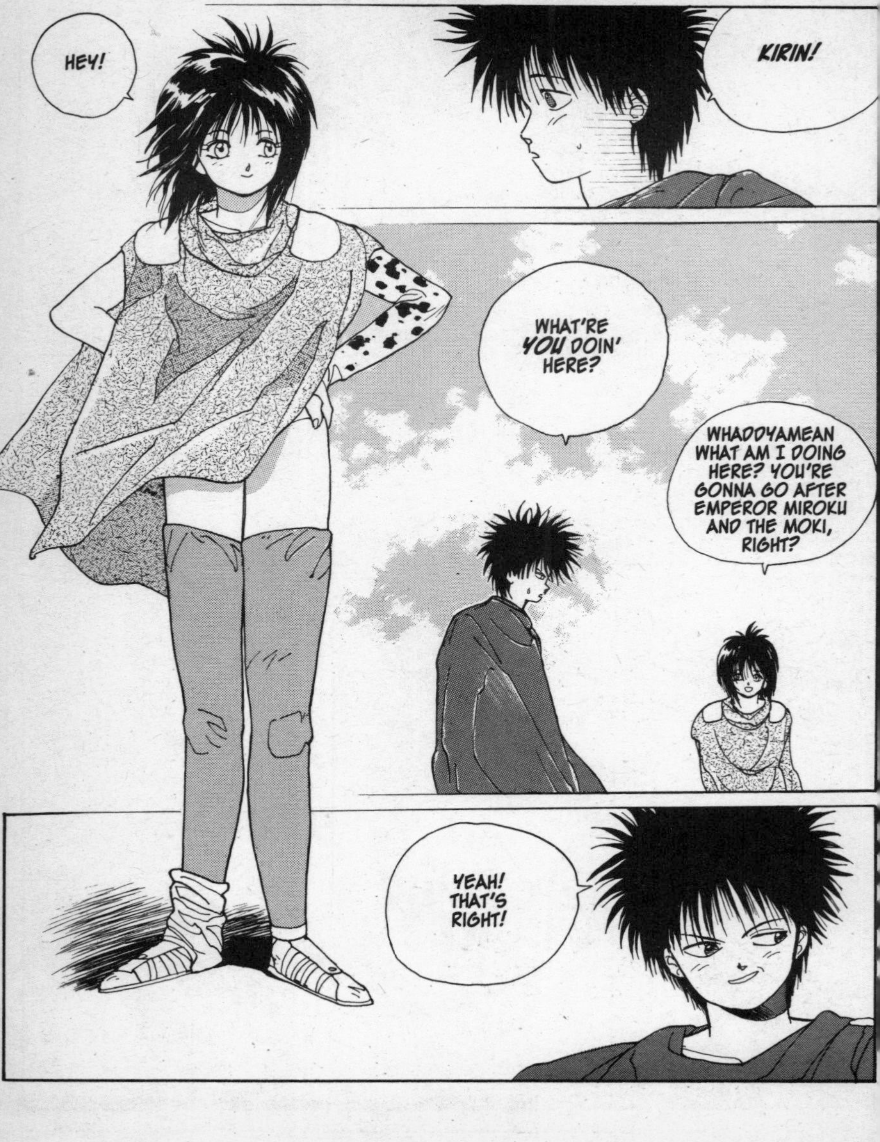
HEY!
KIRIN!
WHAT'RE *YOU* DOIN' HERE?
WHADDYAMEAN WHAT AM I DOING HERE? YOU'RE GONNA GO AFTER EMPEROR MIROKU AND THE MOKI, RIGHT?
YEAH! THAT'S RIGHT!

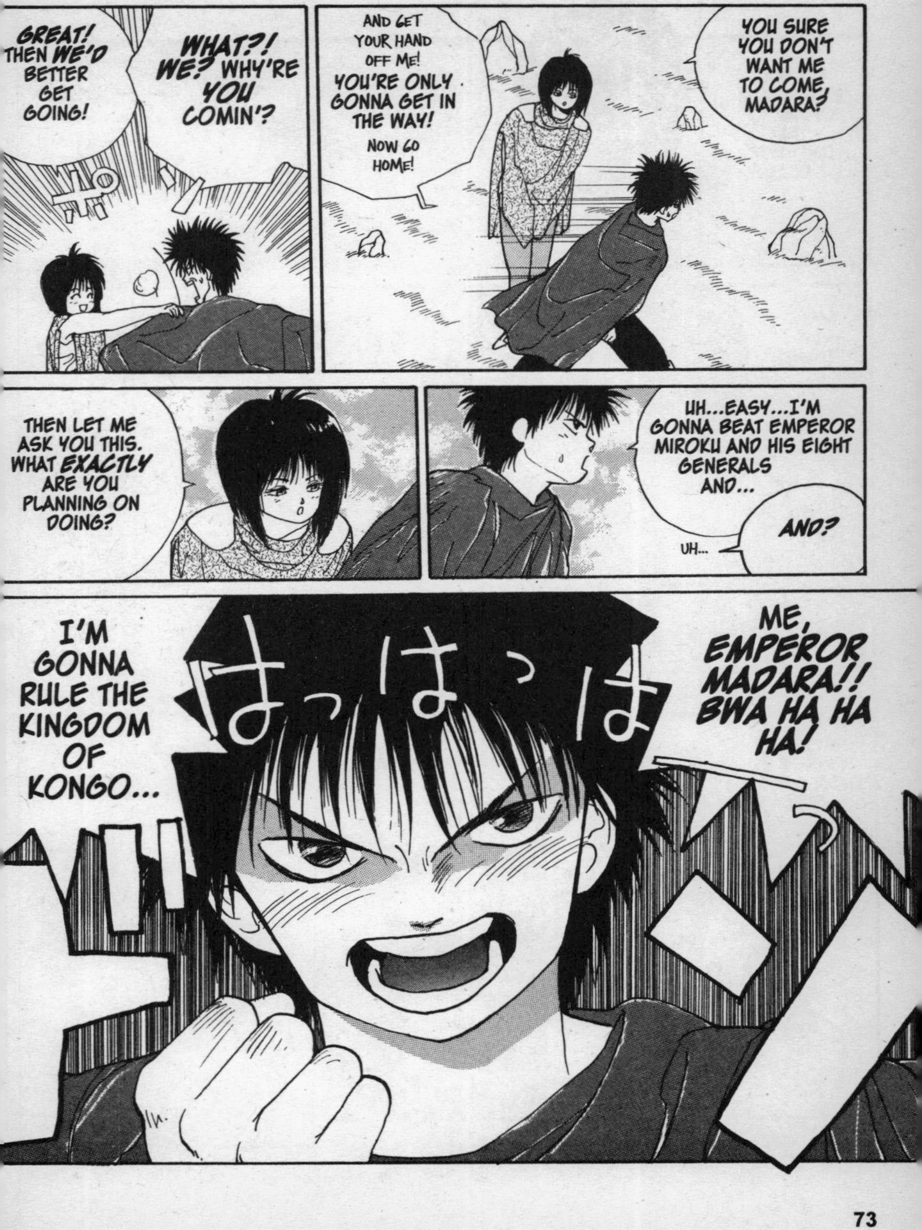
GREAT! THEN WE'D BETTER GET GOING!
WHAT?! WE? WHY'RE YOU COMIN'?
AND GET YOUR HAND OFF ME! YOU'RE ONLY GONNA GET IN THE WAY! NOW GO HOME!
YOU SURE YOU DON'T WANT ME TO COME, MADARA?
THEN LET ME ASK YOU THIS. WHAT EXACTLY ARE YOU PLANNING ON DOING?
UH...EASY...I'M GONNA BEAT EMPEROR MIROKU AND HIS EIGHT GENERALS AND...
AND?
UH...
I'M GONNA RULE THE KINGDOM OF KONGO...
はっはっは
ME, EMPEROR MADARA!! BWA HA HA HA!

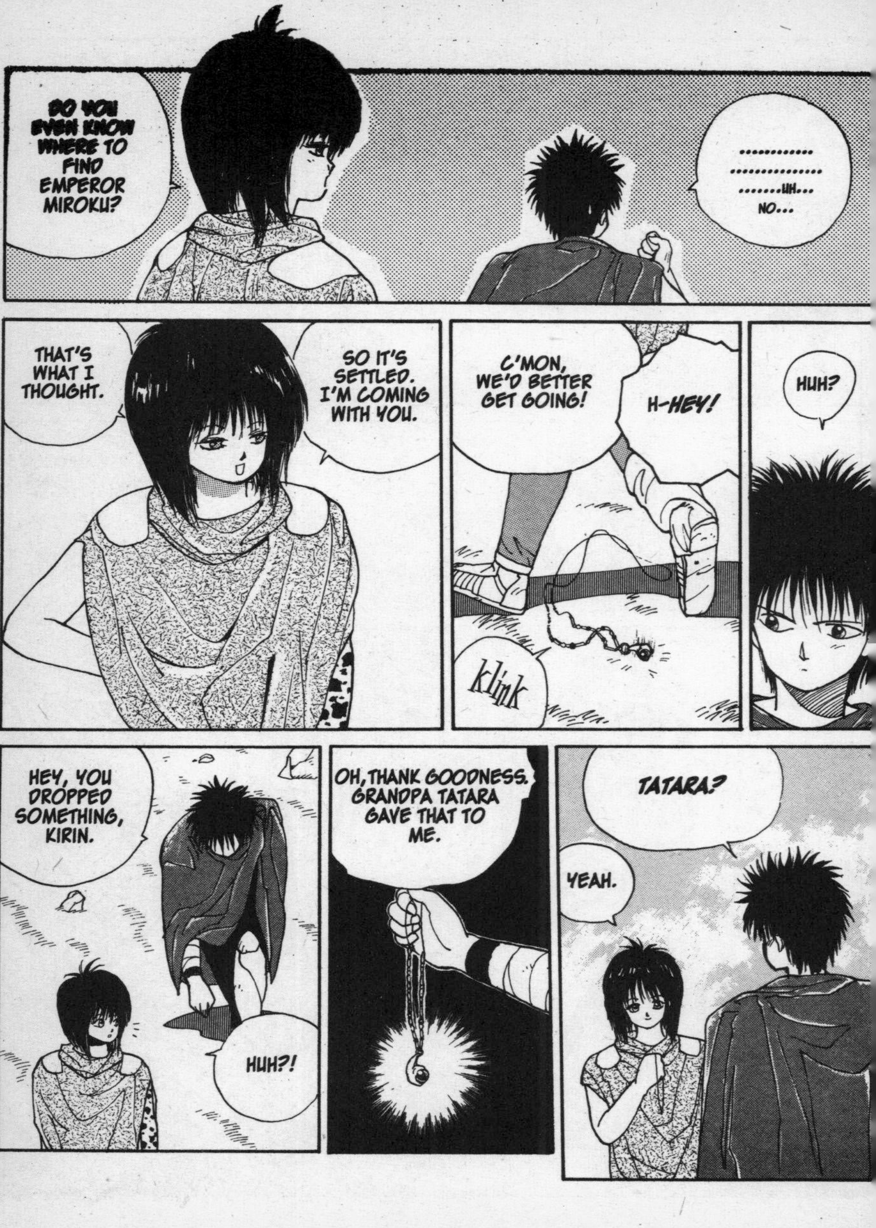
DO YOU EVEN KNOW WHERE TO FIND EMPEROR MIROKU?
....UH... NO...
THAT'S WHAT I THOUGHT.
SO IT'S SETTLED. I'M COMING WITH YOU.
C'MON, WE'D BETTER GET GOING!
H-HEY!
klink
HUH?
HEY, YOU DROPPED SOMETHING, KIRIN.
HUH?!
OH, THANK GOODNESS. GRANDPA TATARA GAVE THAT TO ME.
TATARA?
YEAH.

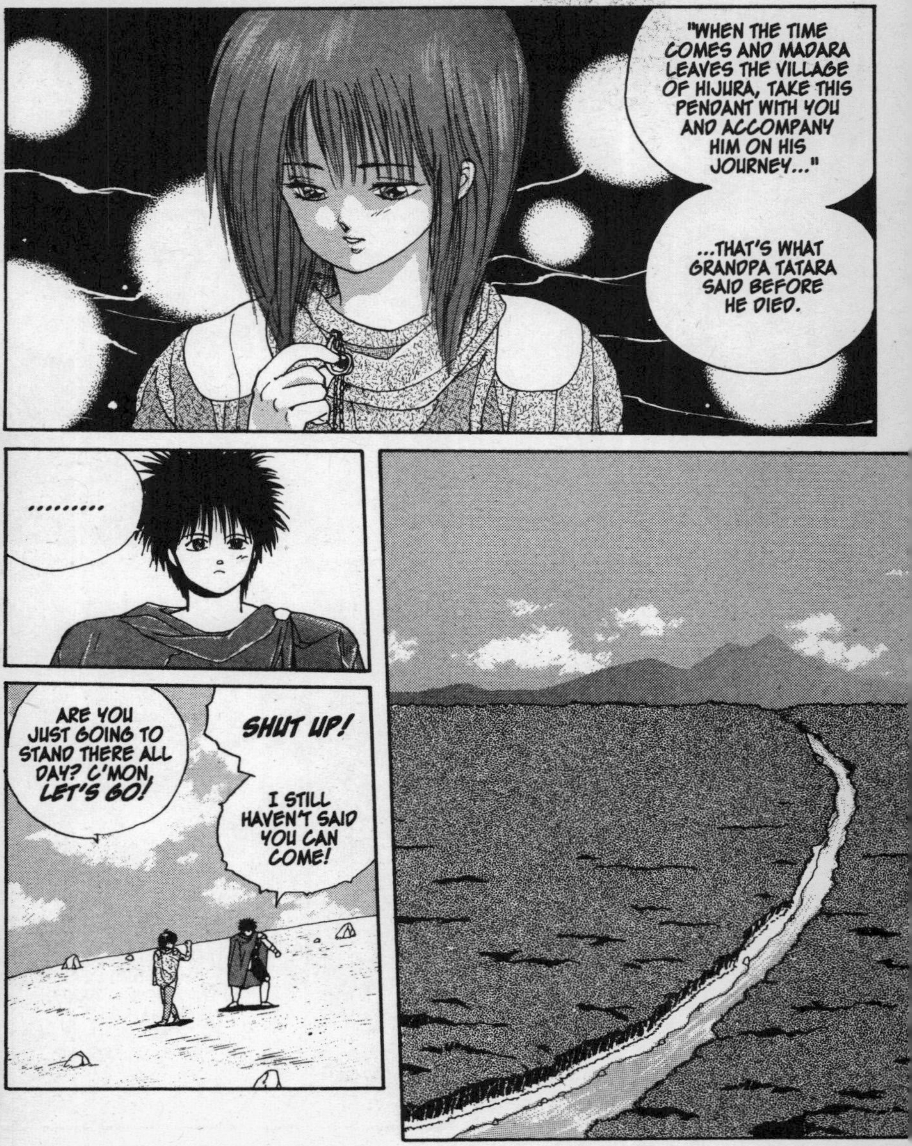
"WHEN THE TIME COMES AND MADARA LEAVES THE VILLAGE OF HIJURA, TAKE THIS PENDANT WITH YOU AND ACCOMPANY HIM ON HIS JOURNEY..."
...THAT'S WHAT GRANDPA TATARA SAID BEFORE HE DIED.
....
ARE YOU JUST GOING TO STAND THERE ALL DAY? C'MON, LET'S GO!
SHUT UP!
I STILL HAVEN'T SAID YOU CAN COME!

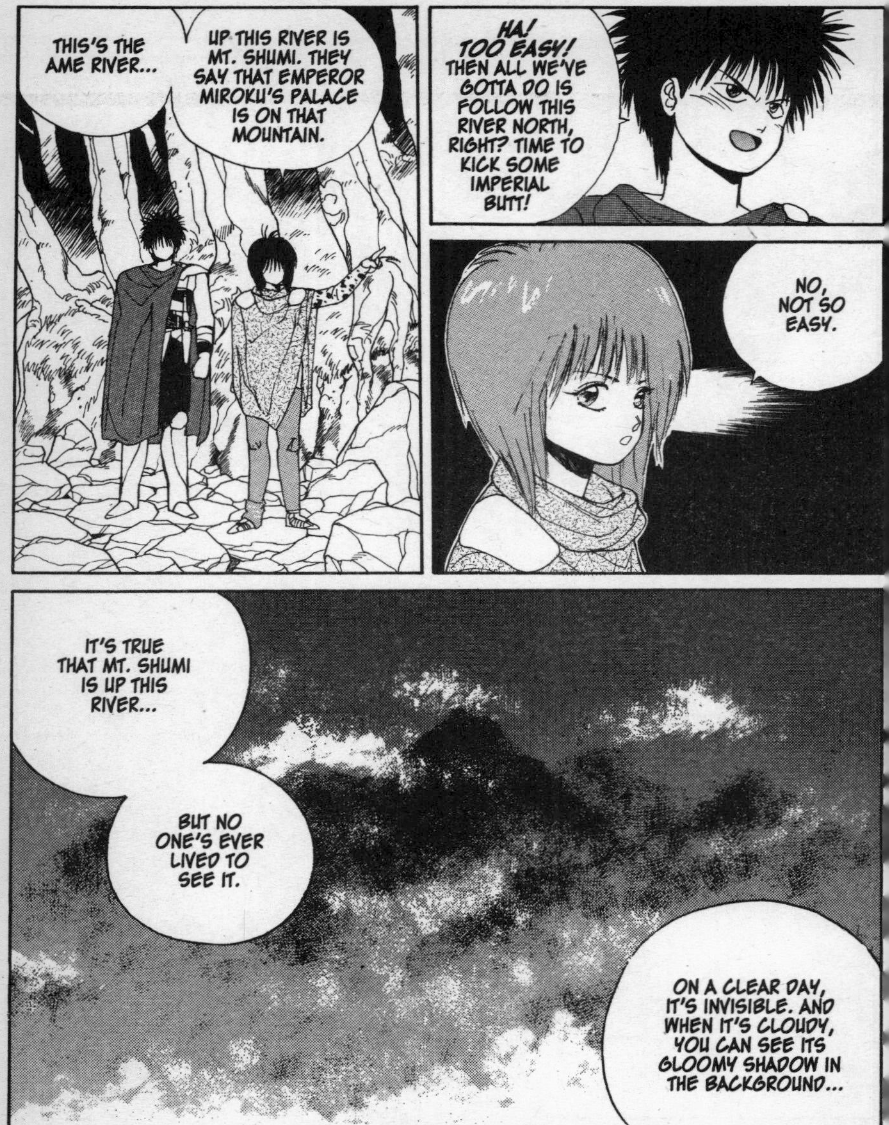
THIS'S THE AME RIVER...
UP THIS RIVER IS MT. SHUMI. THEY SAY THAT EMPEROR MIROKU'S PALACE IS ON THAT MOUNTAIN.
HA! TOO EASY! THEN ALL WE'VE GOTTA DO IS FOLLOW THIS RIVER NORTH, RIGHT? TIME TO KICK SOME IMPERIAL BUTT!
NO, NOT SO EASY.
IT'S TRUE THAT MT. SHUMI IS UP THIS RIVER...
BUT NO ONE'S EVER LIVED TO SEE IT.
ON A CLEAR DAY, IT'S INVISIBLE. AND WHEN IT'S CLOUDY, YOU CAN SEE ITS GLOOMY SHADOW IN THE BACKGROUND...

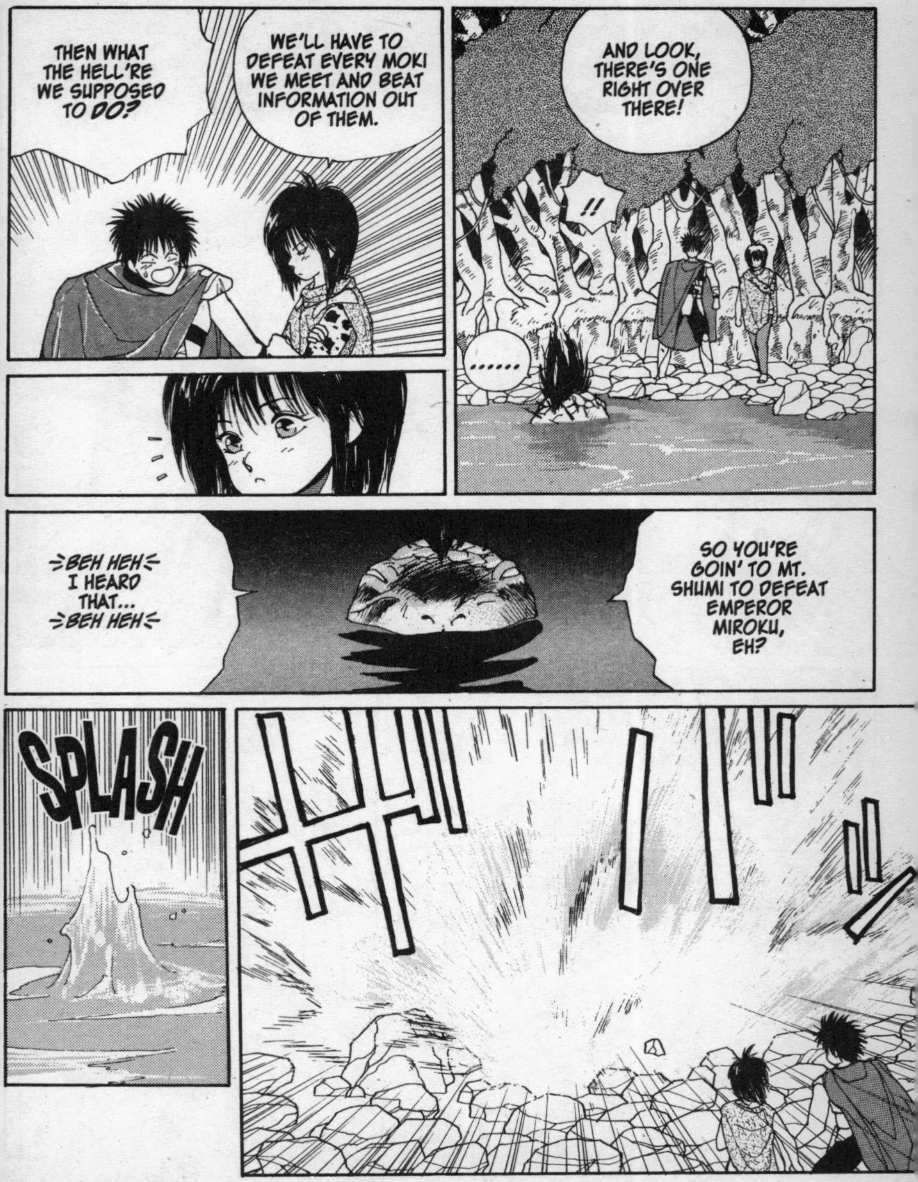

THEN WHAT THE HELL'RE WE SUPPOSED TO *DO?*
WE'LL HAVE TO DEFEAT EVERY MOKI WE MEET AND BEAT INFORMATION OUT OF THEM.
AND LOOK, THERE'S ONE RIGHT OVER THERE!
!!
......
SO YOU'RE GOIN' TO MT. SHUMI TO DEFEAT EMPEROR MIROKU, EH?
=BEH HEH= I HEARD THAT... =BEH HEH=
SPLASH

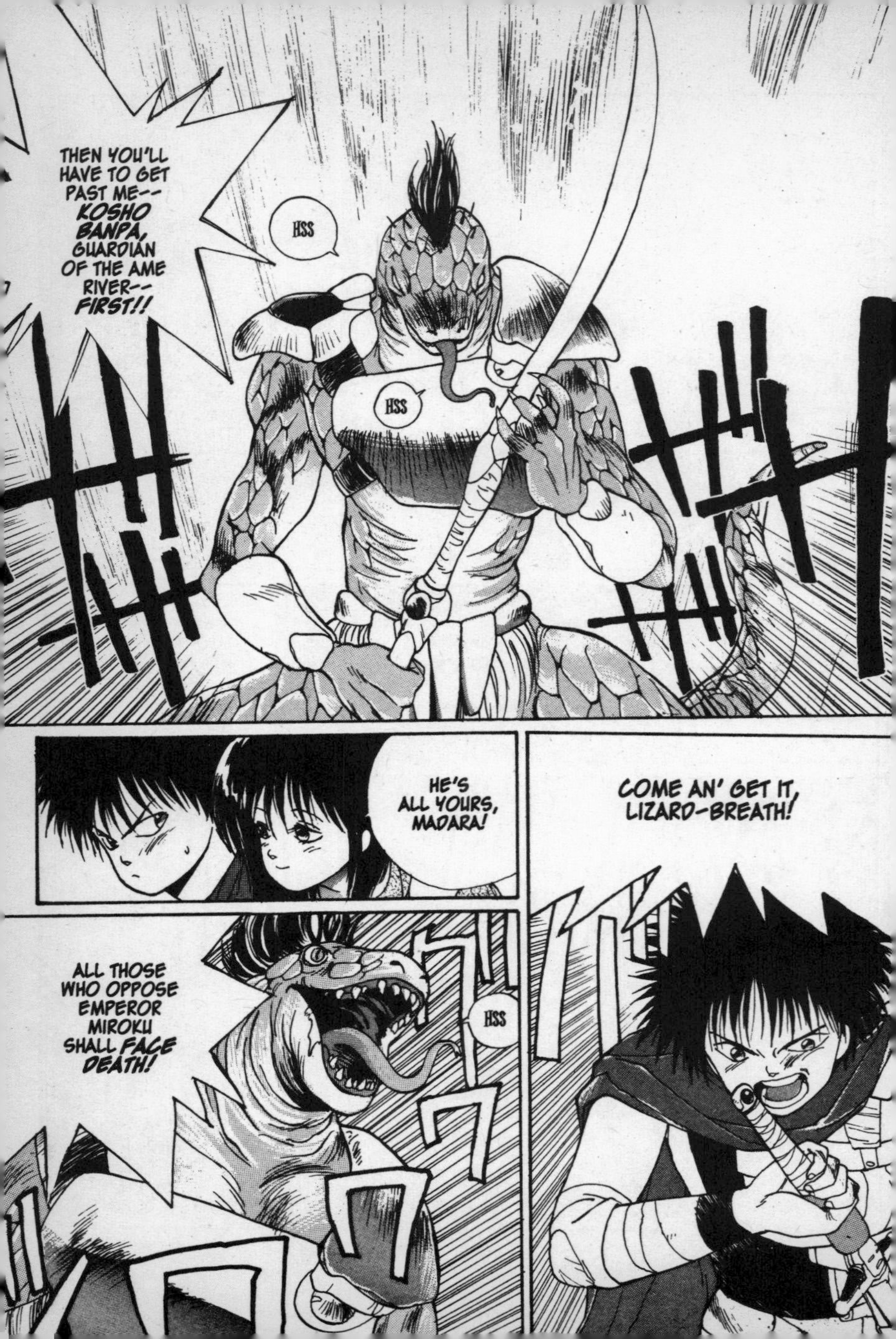
THEN YOU'LL HAVE TO GET PAST ME-- KOSHO BANPA, GUARDIAN OF THE AME RIVER-- FIRST!!
HSS
HSS
HE'S ALL YOURS, MADARA!
COME AN' GET IT, LIZARD-BREATH!
ALL THOSE WHO OPPOSE EMPEROR MIROKU SHALL FACE DEATH!
HSS

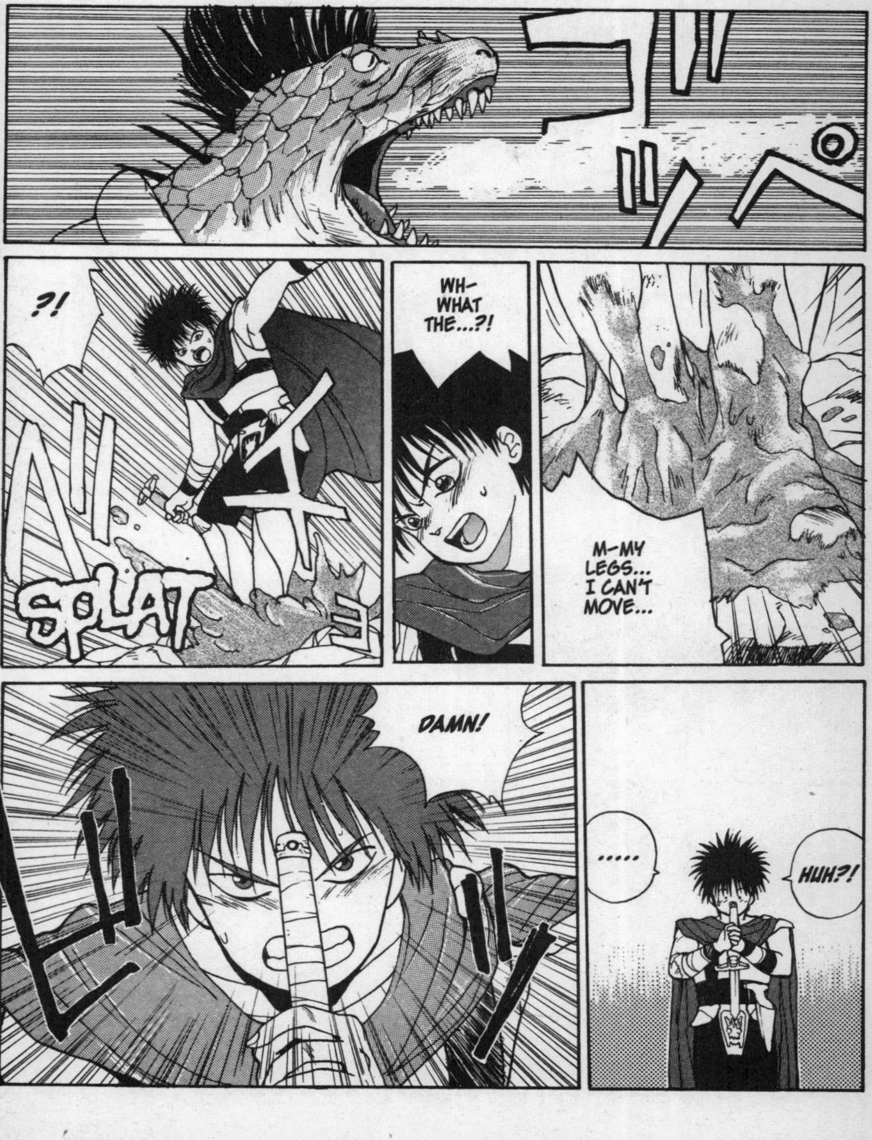
?!
SPLAT
WH- WHAT THE...?!
M-MY LEGS... I CAN'T MOVE...
DAMN!
.....
HUH?!

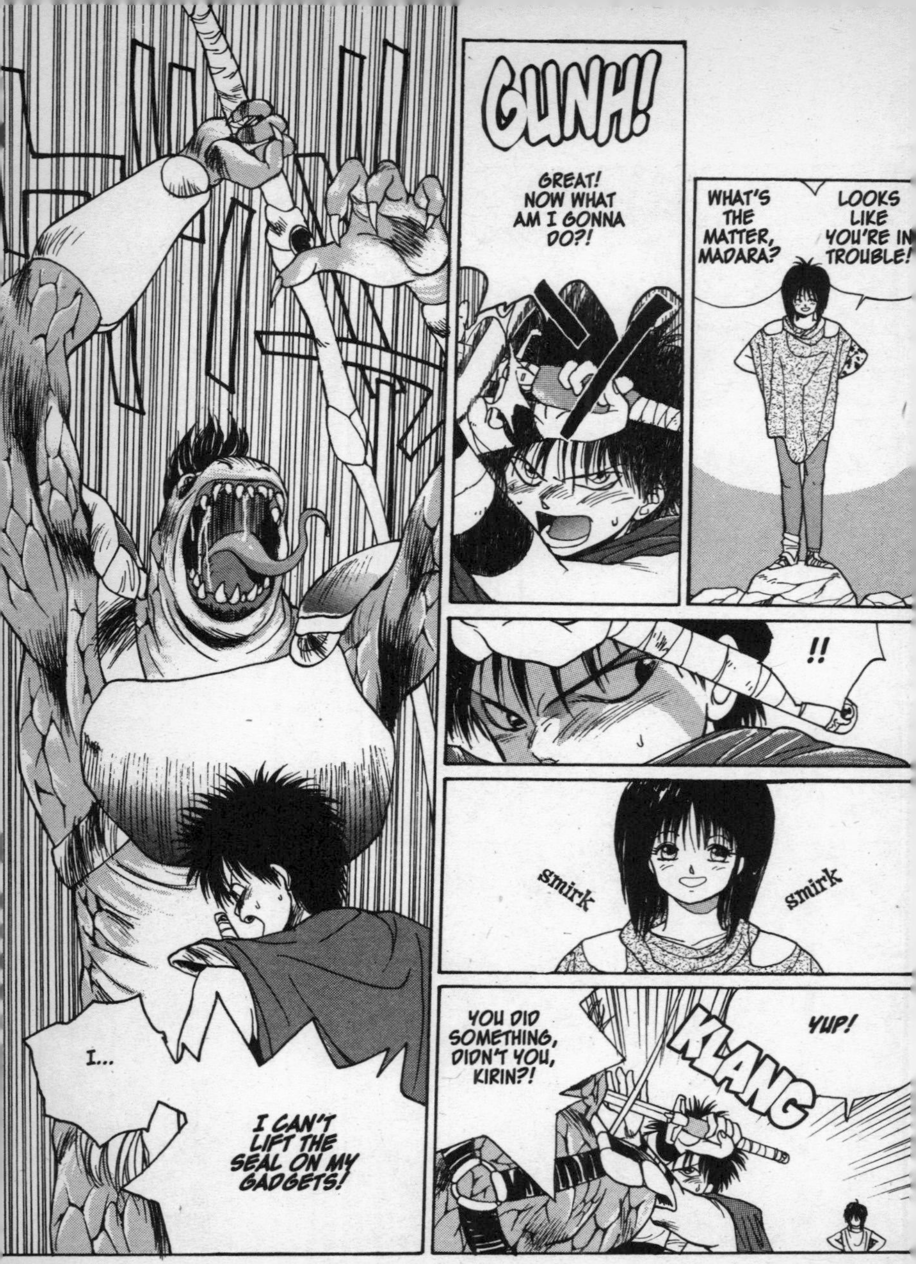
I...
I CAN'T LIFT THE SEAL ON MY GADGETS!
GUNH!
GREAT! NOW WHAT AM I GONNA DO?!
WHAT'S THE MATTER, MADARA?
LOOKS LIKE YOU'RE IN TROUBLE!
!!
smirk
smirk
YOU DID SOMETHING, DIDN'T YOU, KIRIN?!
KLANG
YUP!

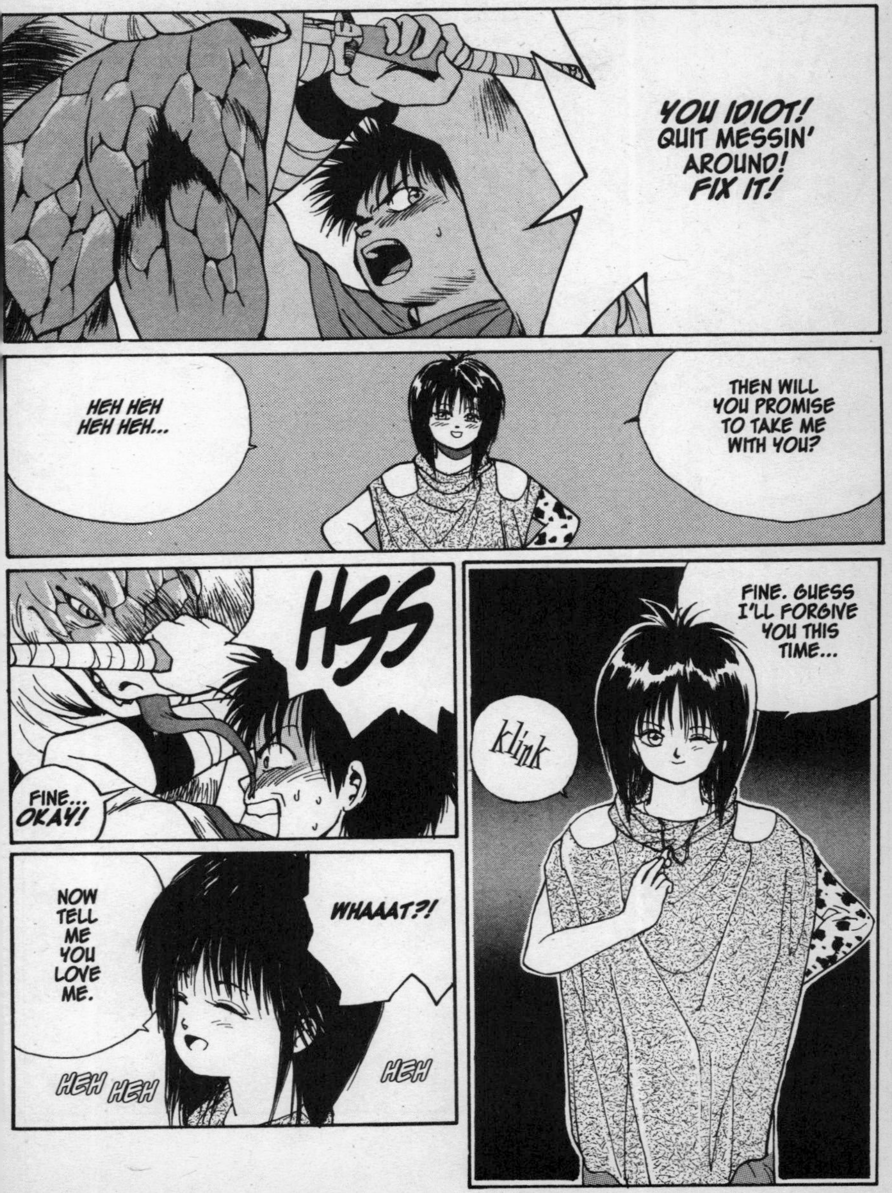

YOU IDIOT! QUIT MESSIN' AROUND! FIX IT!
HEH HEH HEH HEH...
THEN WILL YOU PROMISE TO TAKE ME WITH YOU?
HSS
FINE... OKAY!
FINE. GUESS I'LL FORGIVE YOU THIS TIME...
klink
NOW TELL ME YOU LOVE ME.
WHAAAT?!
HEH HEH
HEH

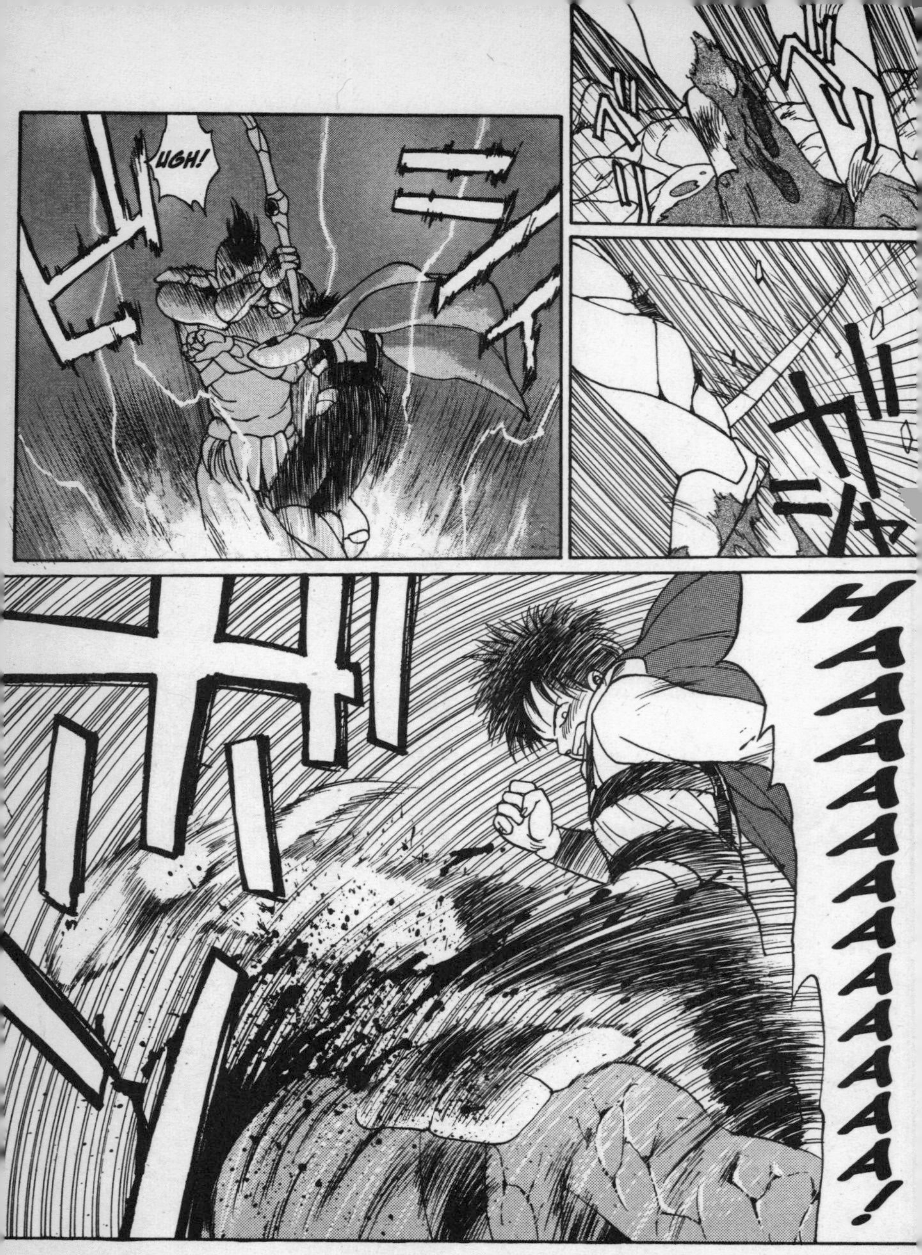
UGH!
HAAAAAAAAAAAAAAA!

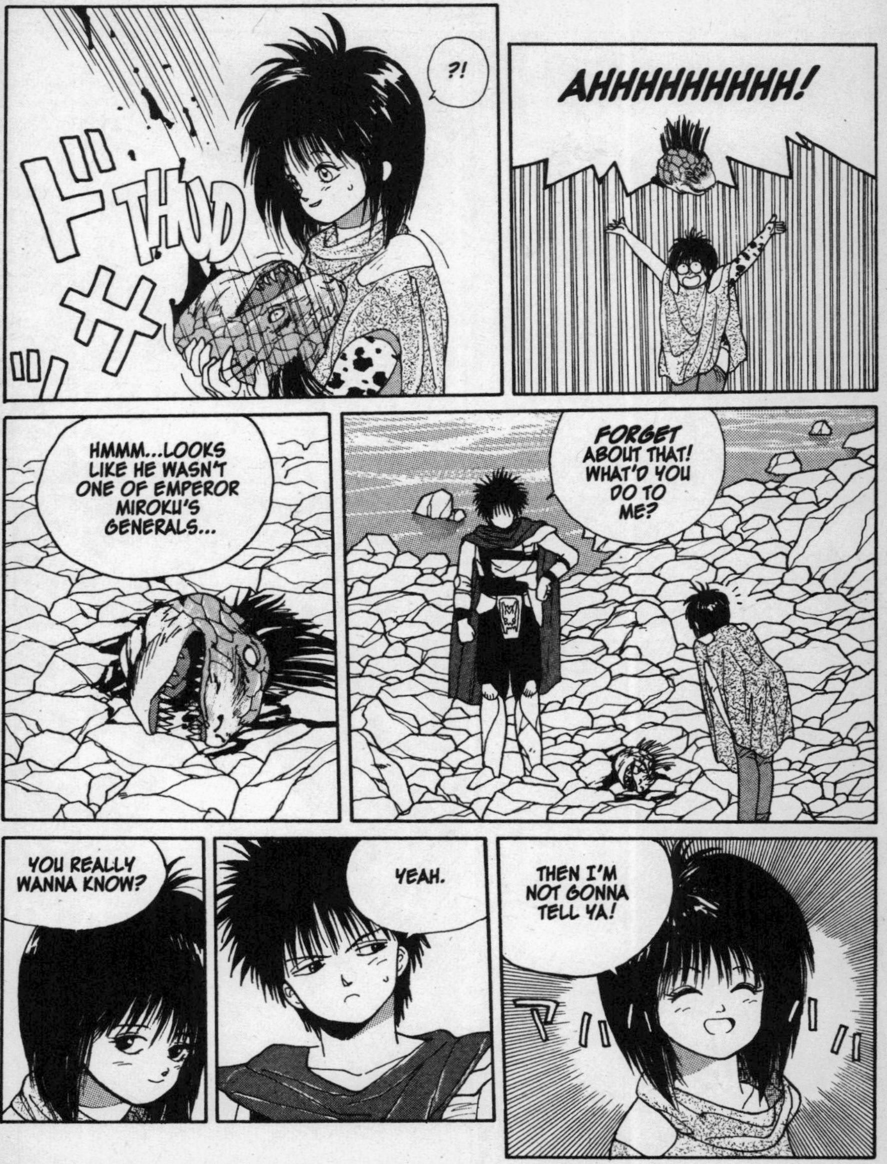

THUD
?!
AHHHHHHHHH!
HMMM...LOOKS LIKE HE WASN'T ONE OF EMPEROR MIROKU'S GENERALS...
FORGET ABOUT THAT! WHAT'D YOU DO TO ME?
YOU REALLY WANNA KNOW?
YEAH.
THEN I'M NOT GONNA TELL YA!

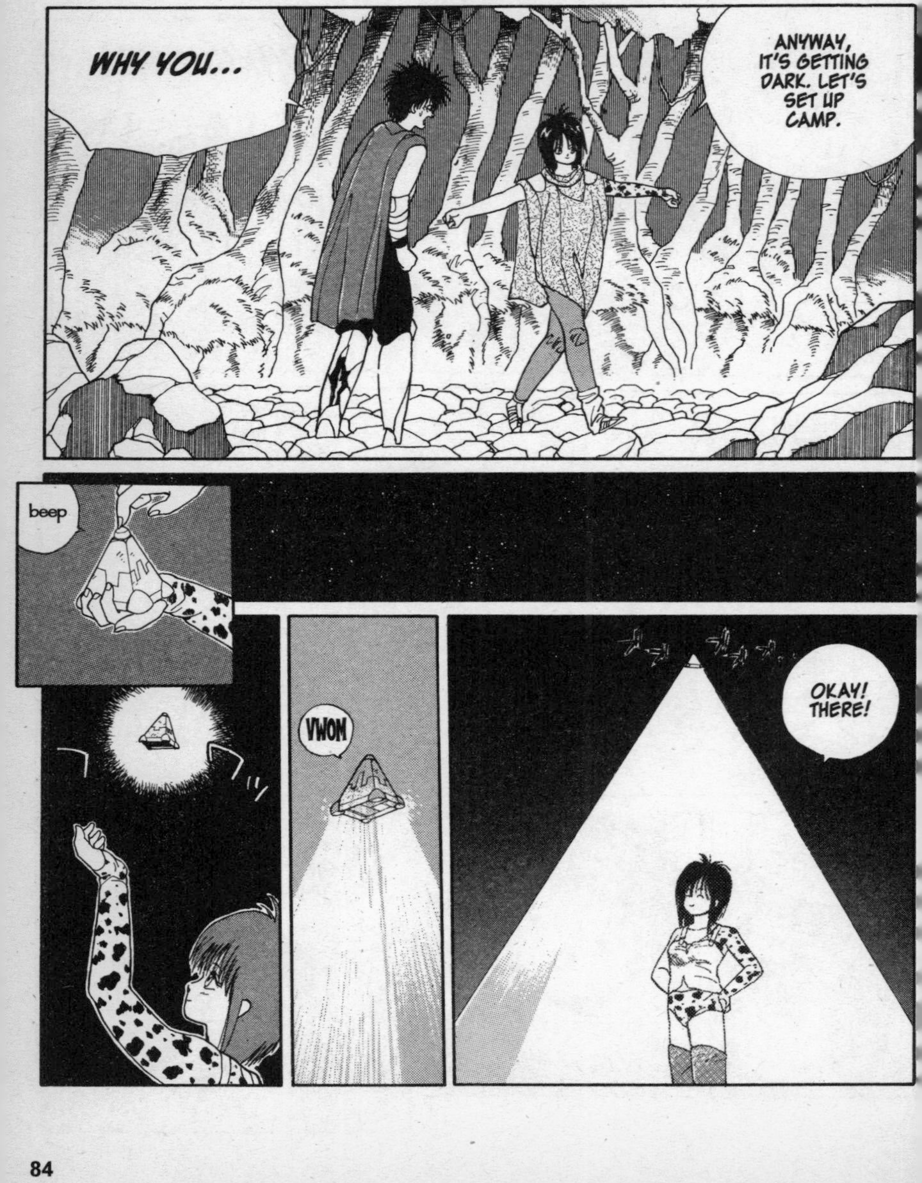
WHY YOU...
ANYWAY, IT'S GETTING DARK. LET'S SET UP CAMP.
beep
VWOM
OKAY! THERE!

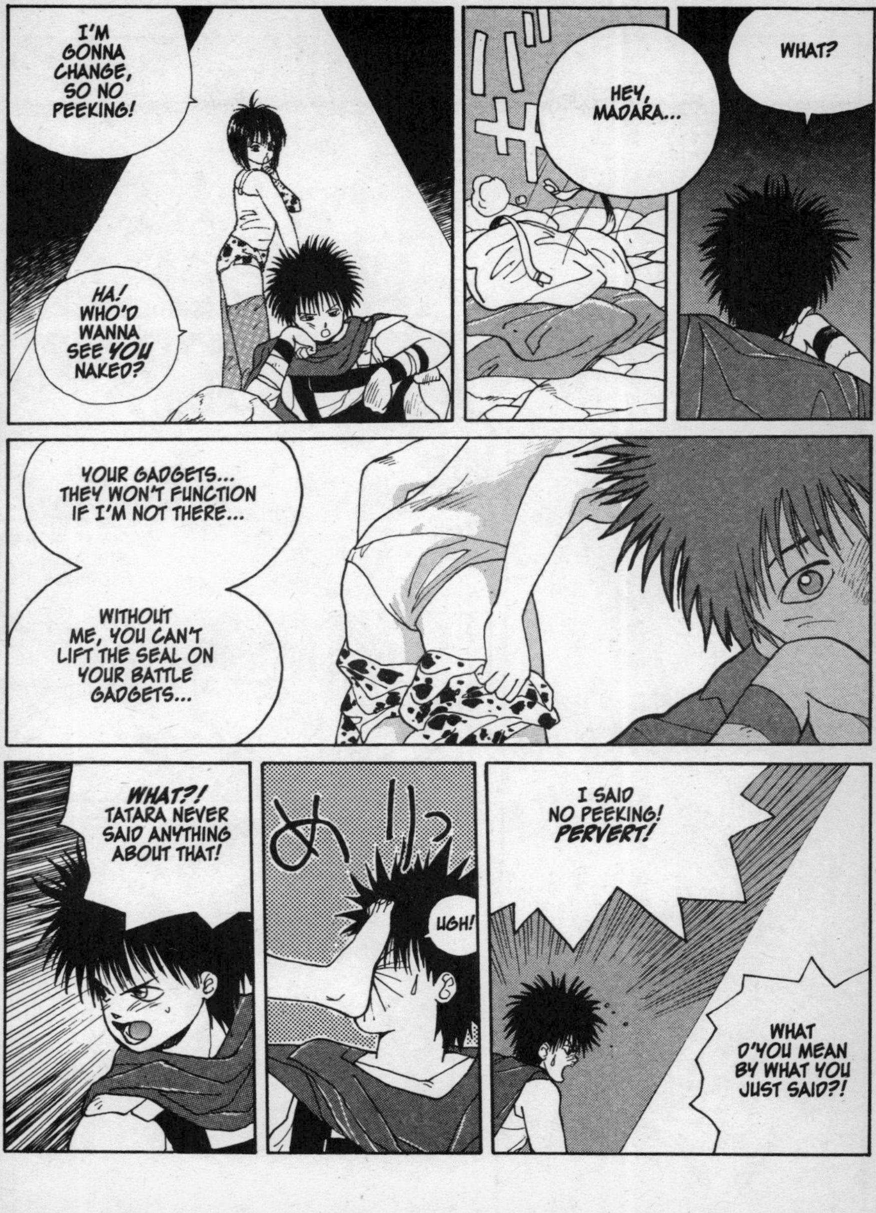
I'M GONNA CHANGE, SO NO PEEKING!
HA! WHO'D WANNA SEE YOU NAKED?
HEY, MADARA...
WHAT?
YOUR GADGETS... THEY WON'T FUNCTION IF I'M NOT THERE...
WITHOUT ME, YOU CAN'T LIFT THE SEAL ON YOUR BATTLE GADGETS...
WHAT?! TATARA NEVER SAID ANYTHING ABOUT THAT!
UGH!
I SAID NO PEEKING! PERVERT!
WHAT D'YOU MEAN BY WHAT YOU JUST SAID?!

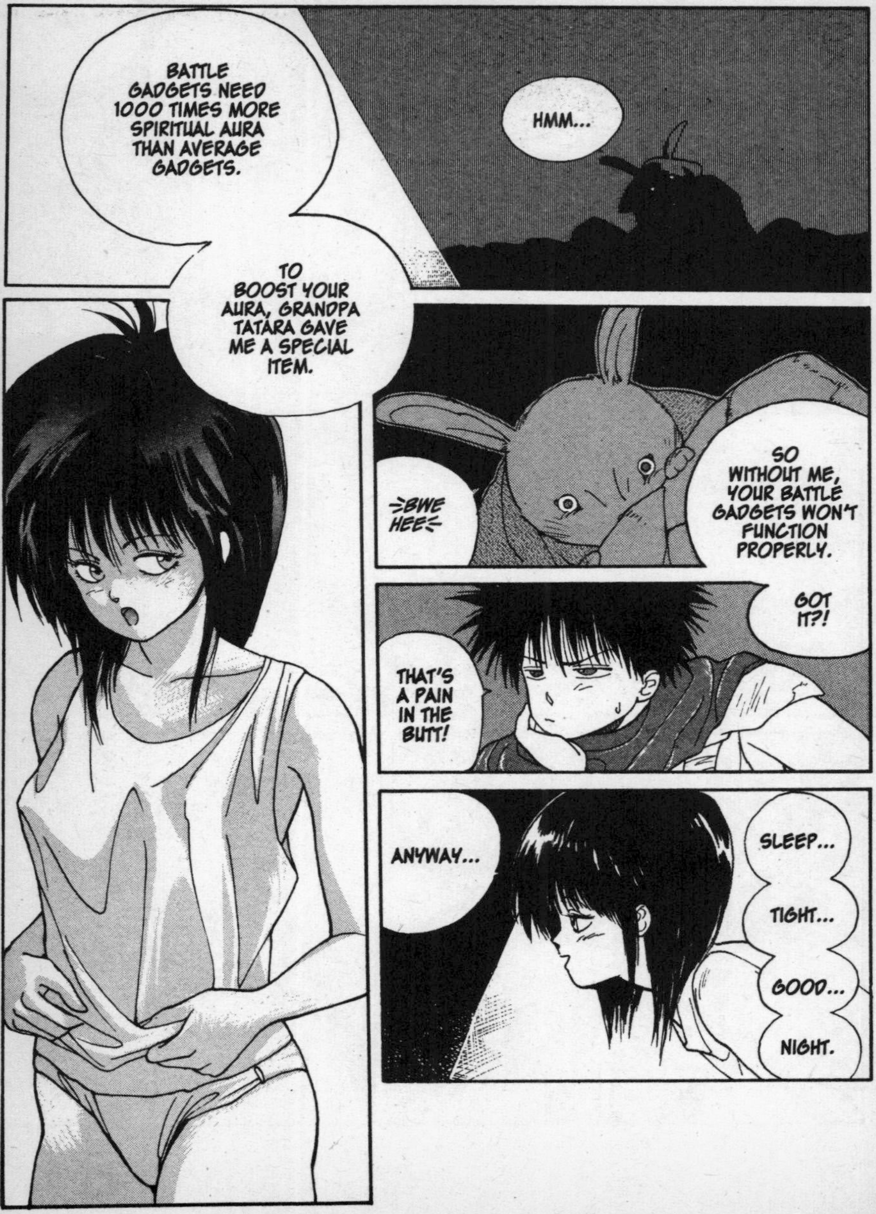
BATTLE GADGETS NEED 1000 TIMES MORE SPIRITUAL AURA THAN AVERAGE GADGETS.
HMM...
TO BOOST YOUR AURA, GRANDPA TATARA GAVE ME A SPECIAL ITEM.
SO WITHOUT ME, YOUR BATTLE GADGETS WON'T FUNCTION PROPERLY.
BWE HEE
GOT IT?!
THAT'S A PAIN IN THE BUTT!
ANYWAY...
SLEEP...
TIGHT...
GOOD...
NIGHT.

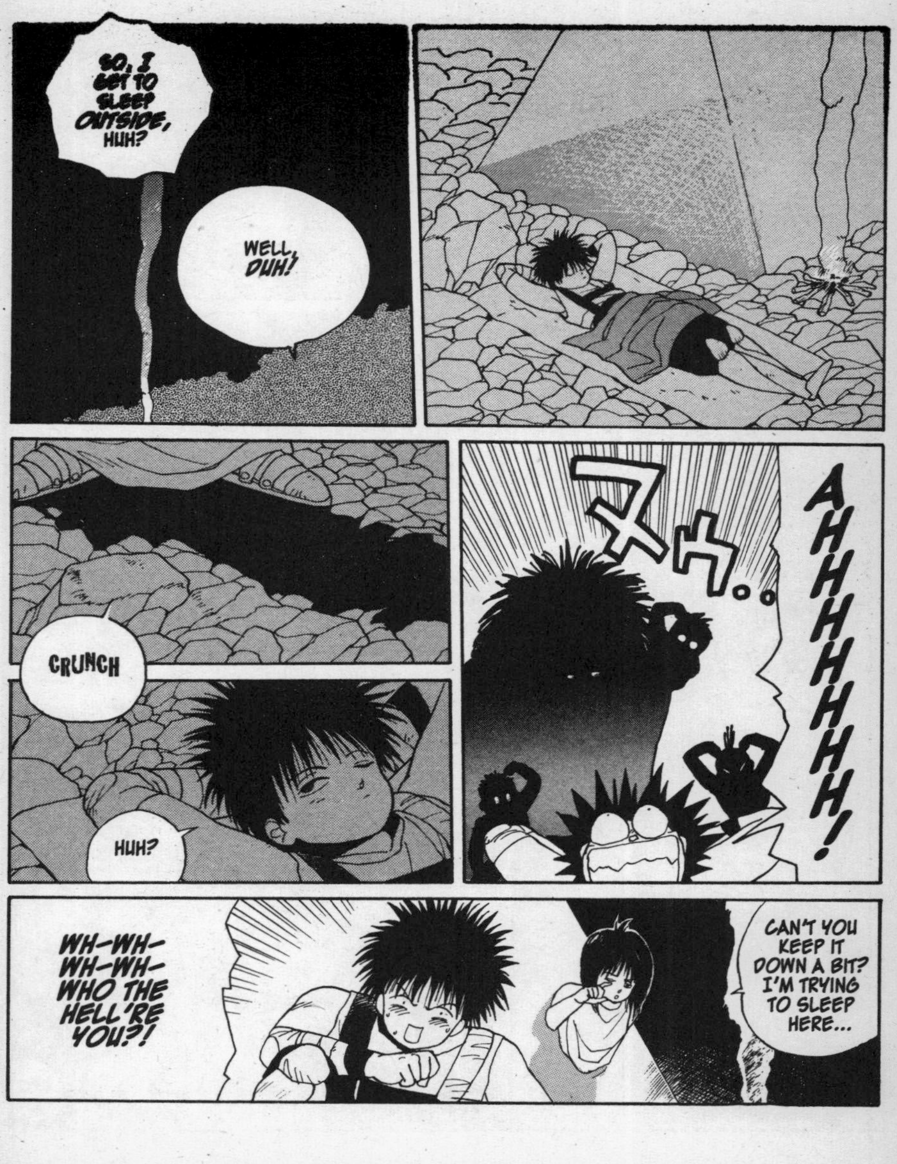
SO, I GET TO SLEEP OUTSIDE, HUH?
WELL, DUH!
CRUNCH
HUH?
ヌゥ..
AHHHHHHHHH!
WH-WH-WH-WH-WHO THE HELL'RE YOU?!
CAN'T YOU KEEP IT DOWN A BIT? I'M TRYING TO SLEEP HERE...

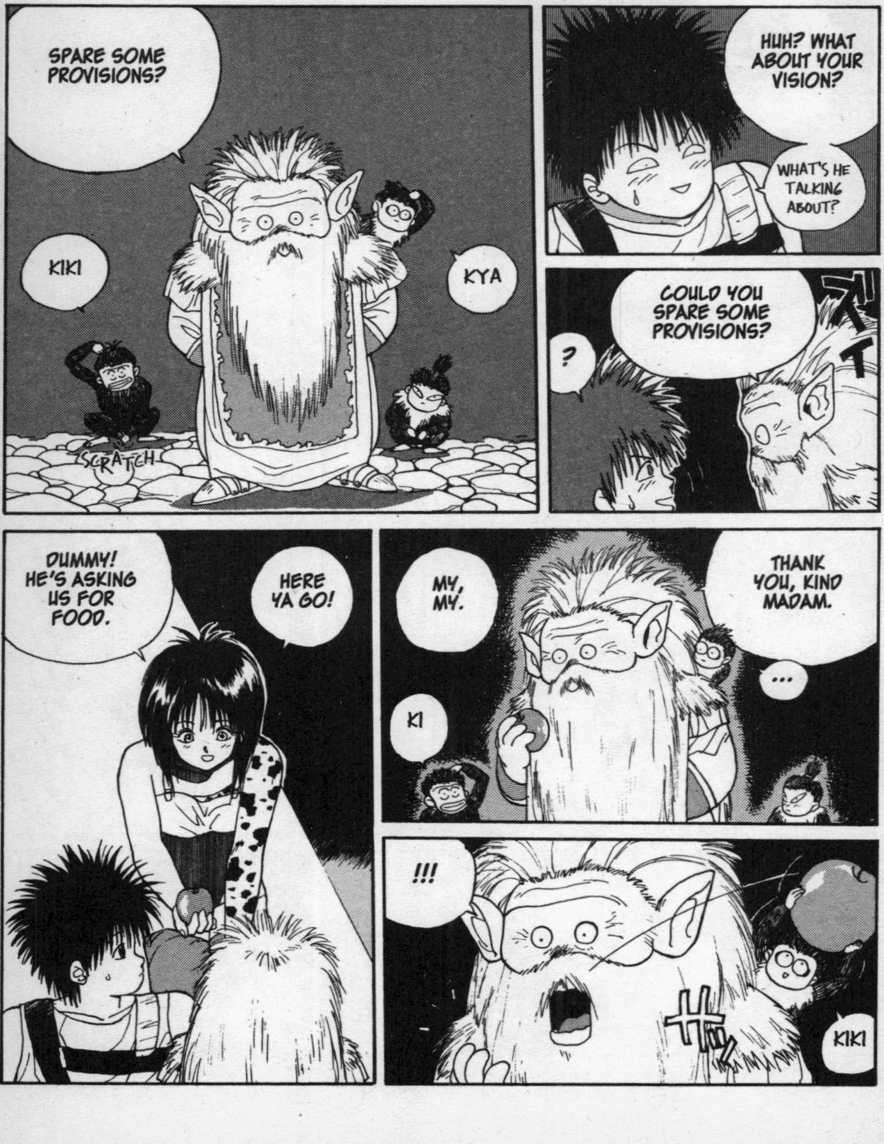
SPARE SOME PROVISIONS?
KIKI
KYA
SCRATCH
HUH? WHAT ABOUT YOUR VISION?
WHAT'S HE TALKING ABOUT?
COULD YOU SPARE SOME PROVISIONS?
?
DUMMY! HE'S ASKING US FOR FOOD.
HERE YA GO!
MY, MY.
THANK YOU, KIND MADAM.
...
KI
!!!
KIKI

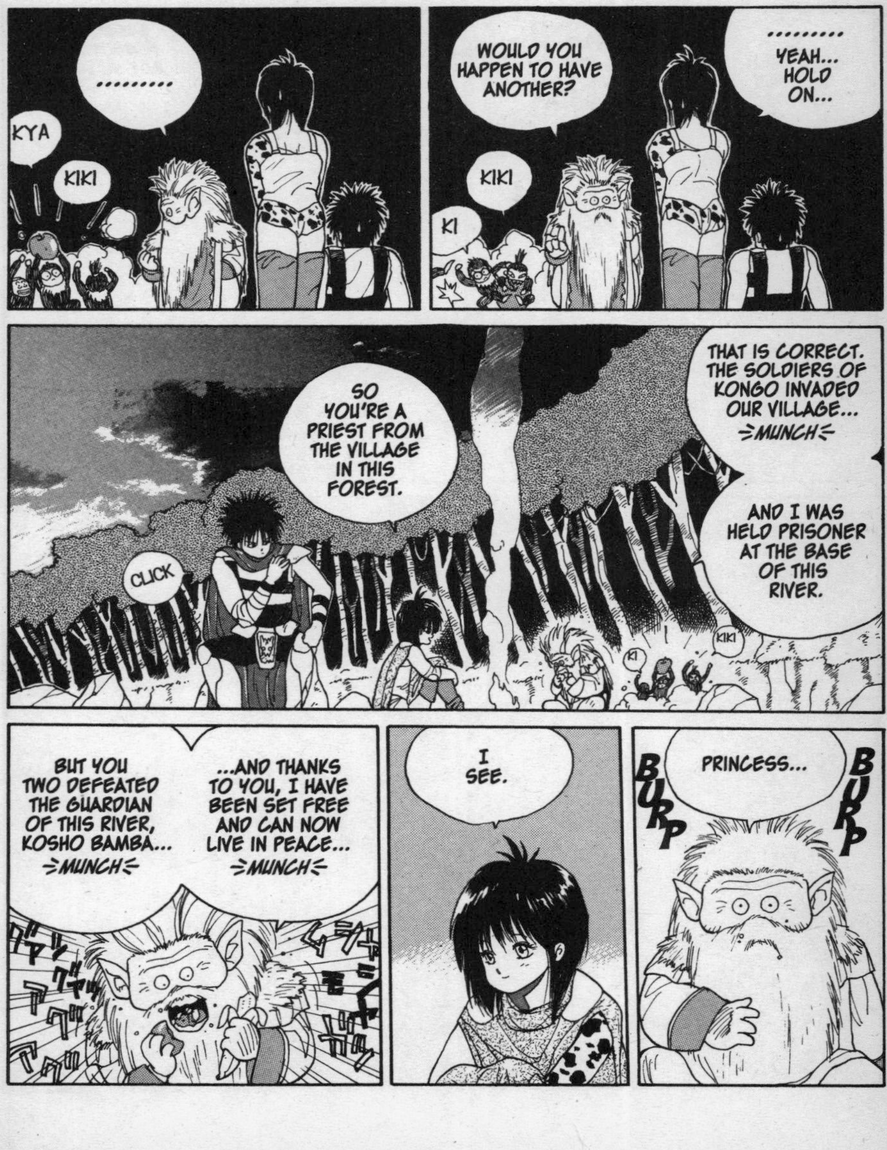
....
KYA
KIKI
WOULD YOU HAPPEN TO HAVE ANOTHER?
....
YEAH... HOLD ON...
KIKI
KI
SO YOU'RE A PRIEST FROM THE VILLAGE IN THIS FOREST.
CLICK
THAT IS CORRECT. THE SOLDIERS OF KONGO INVADED OUR VILLAGE... MUNCH
AND I WAS HELD PRISONER AT THE BASE OF THIS RIVER.
KIKI
KI
BUT YOU TWO DEFEATED THE GUARDIAN OF THIS RIVER, KOSHO BAMBA... MUNCH
...AND THANKS TO YOU, I HAVE BEEN SET FREE AND CAN NOW LIVE IN PEACE... MUNCH
I SEE.
PRINCESS...
BURP
BURP

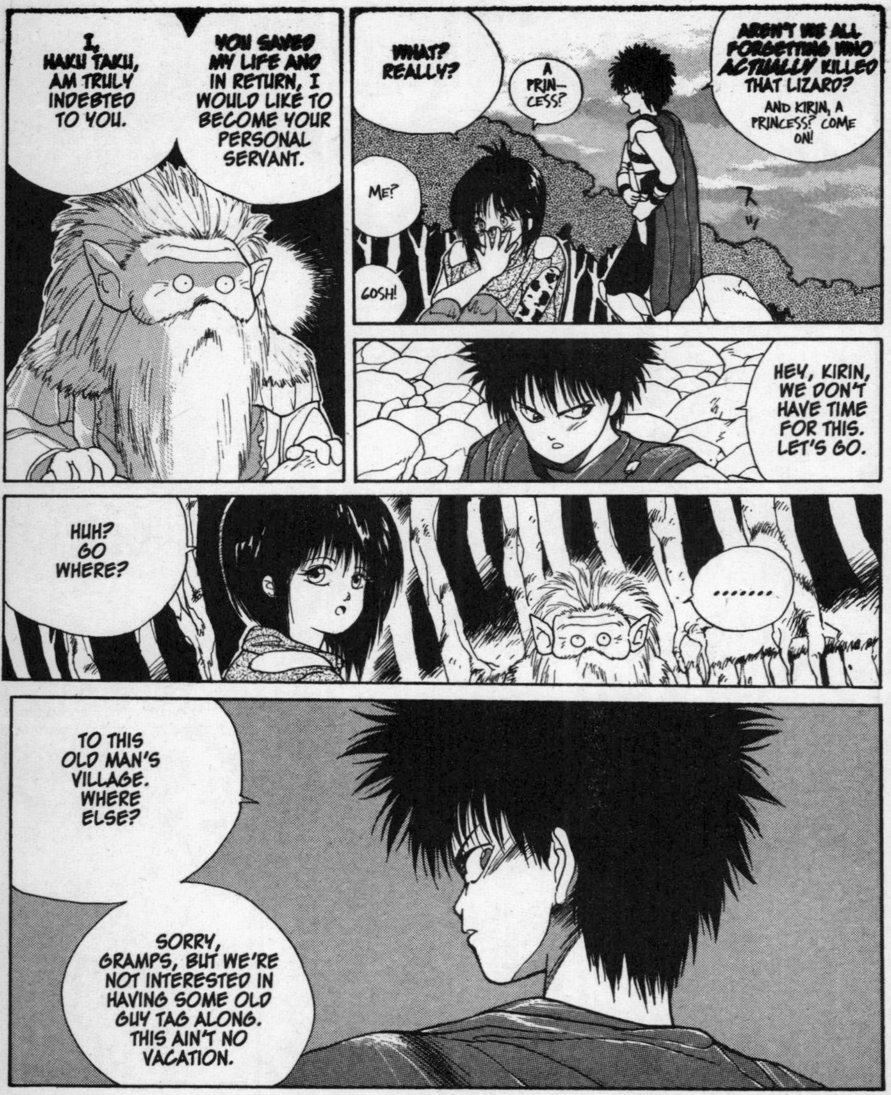

YOU SAVED MY LIFE AND IN RETURN, I WOULD LIKE TO BECOME YOUR PERSONAL SERVANT.
I, HAKU TAKU, AM TRULY INDEBTED TO YOU.
AREN'T WE ALL FORGETTING WHO ACTUALLY KILLED THAT LIZARD?
AND KIRIN, A PRINCESS? COME ON!
A PRIN-CESS?
WHAT? REALLY?
ME?
GOSH!
HEY, KIRIN, WE DON'T HAVE TIME FOR THIS. LET'S GO.
....
HUH? GO WHERE?
TO THIS OLD MAN'S VILLAGE. WHERE ELSE?
SORRY, GRAMPS, BUT WE'RE NOT INTERESTED IN HAVING SOME OLD GUY TAG ALONG. THIS AIN'T NO VACATION.

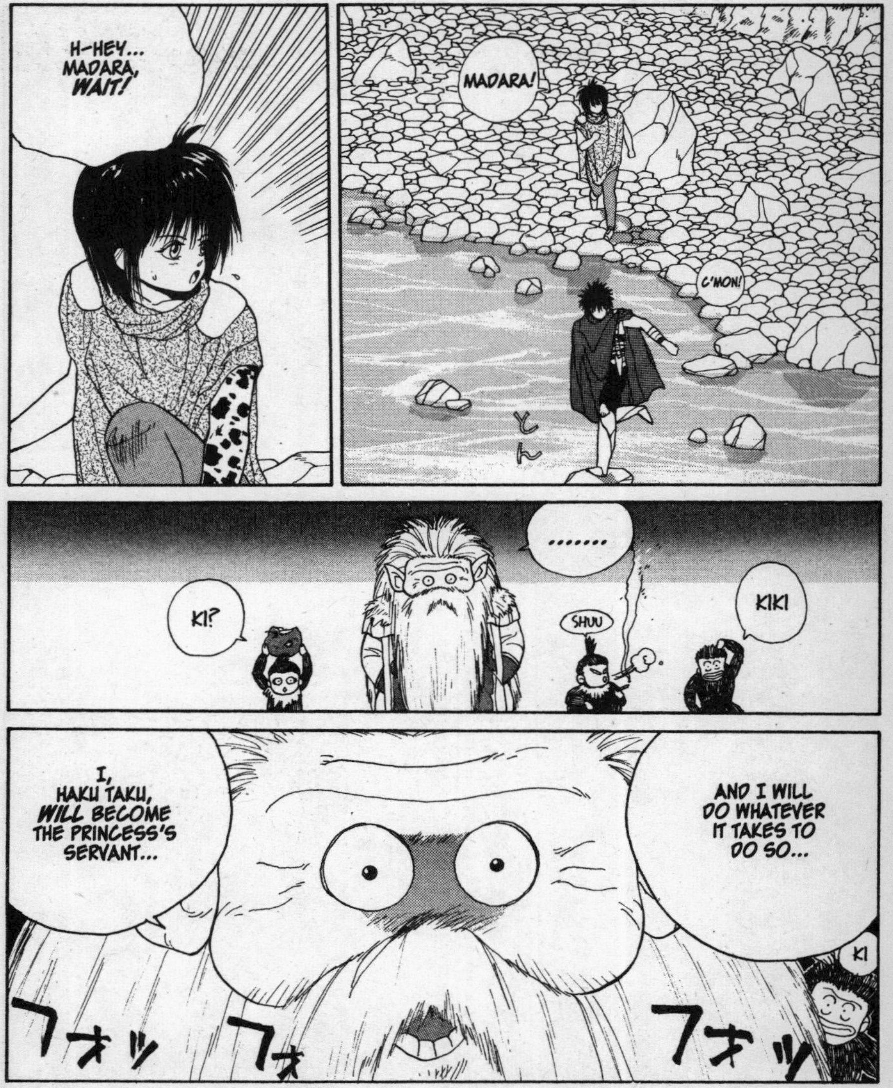

H-HEY... MADARA, WAIT!
MADARA!
C'MON!
とん
....
KI?
SHUU
KIKI
I, HAKU TAKU, WILL BECOME THE PRINCESS'S SERVANT...
AND I WILL DO WHATEVER IT TAKES TO DO SO...
KI
フォッ フォ フォッ

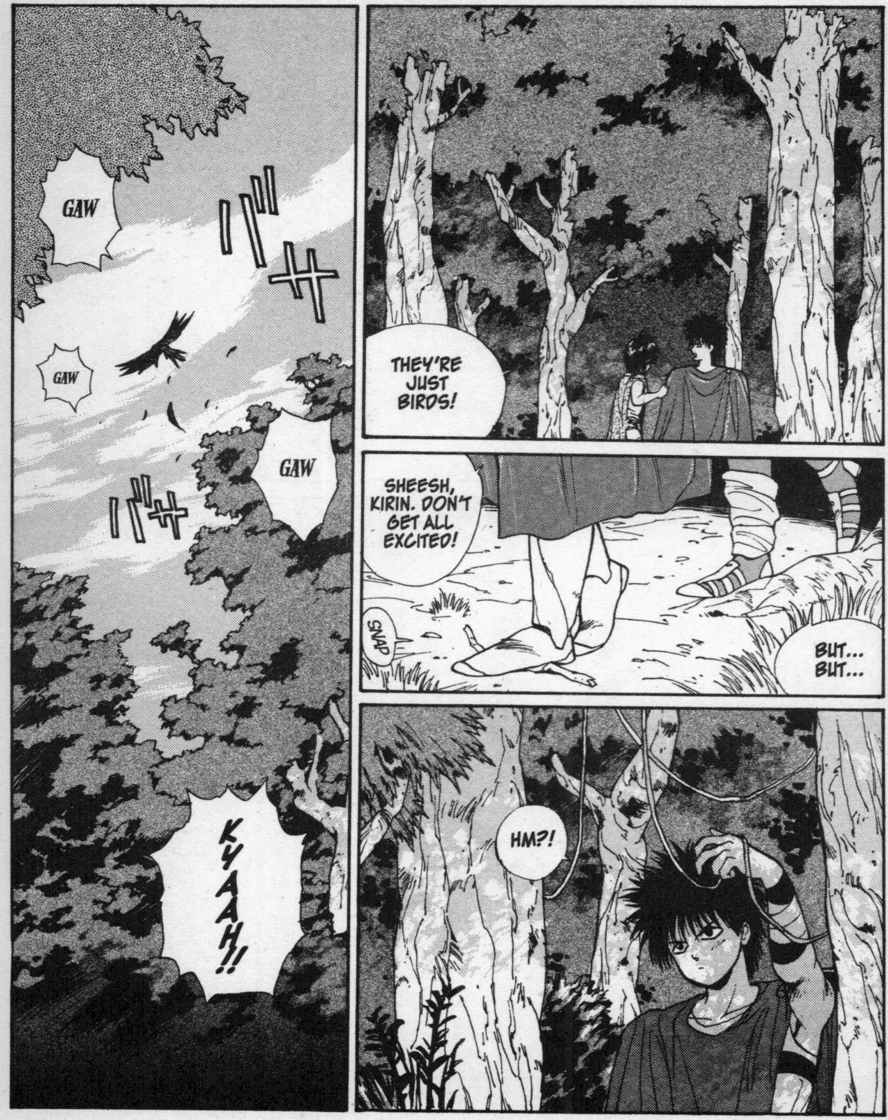
GAW
GAW
GAW
KYAAAH!!
THEY'RE JUST BIRDS!
SHEESH, KIRIN. DON'T GET ALL EXCITED!
SNAP
BUT... BUT...
HM?!

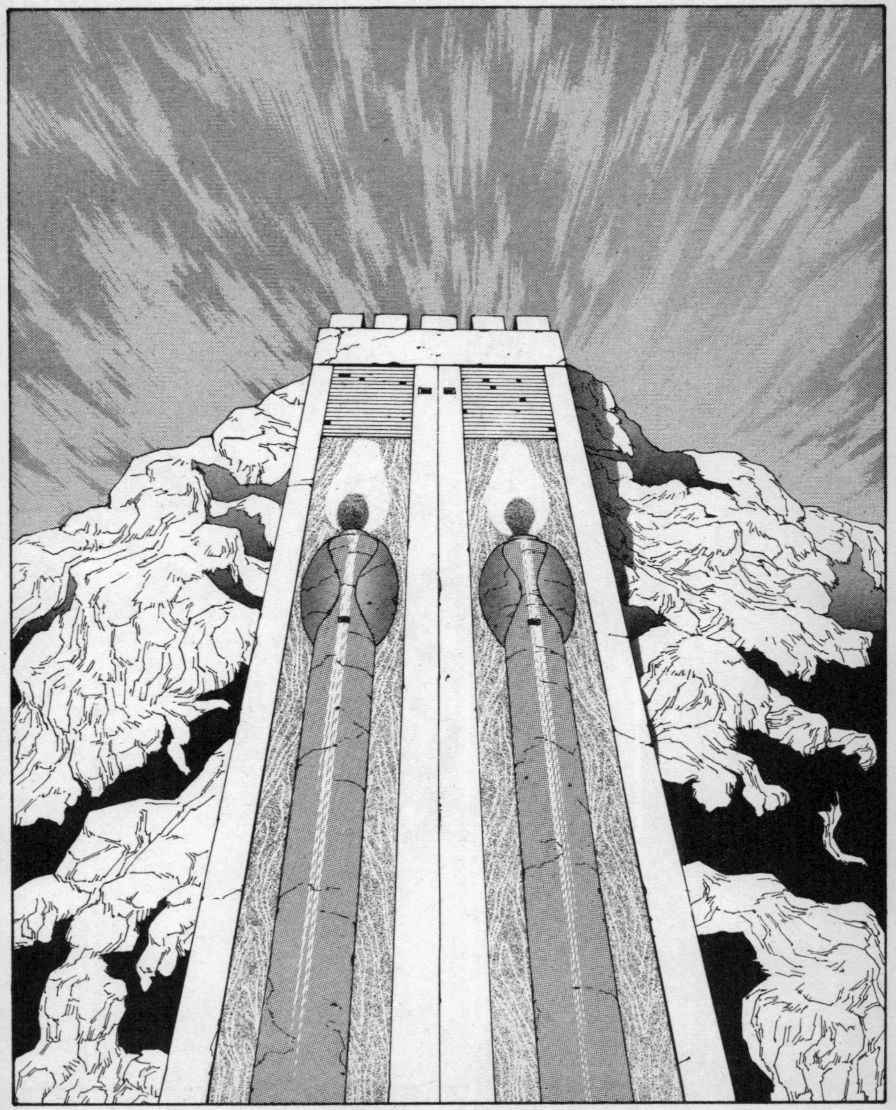

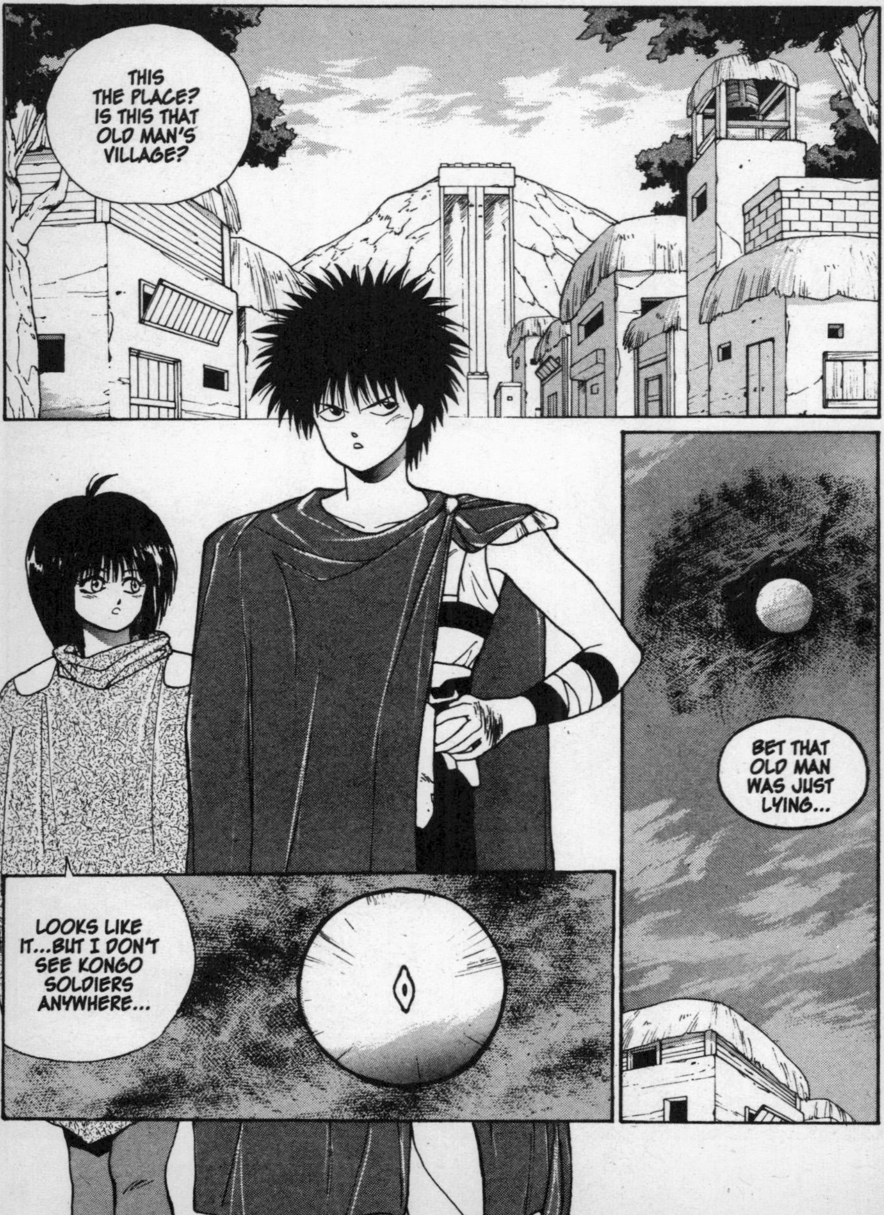
THIS THE PLACE? IS THIS THAT OLD MAN'S VILLAGE?
BET THAT OLD MAN WAS JUST LYING...
LOOKS LIKE IT...BUT I DON'T SEE KONGO SOLDIERS ANYWHERE...

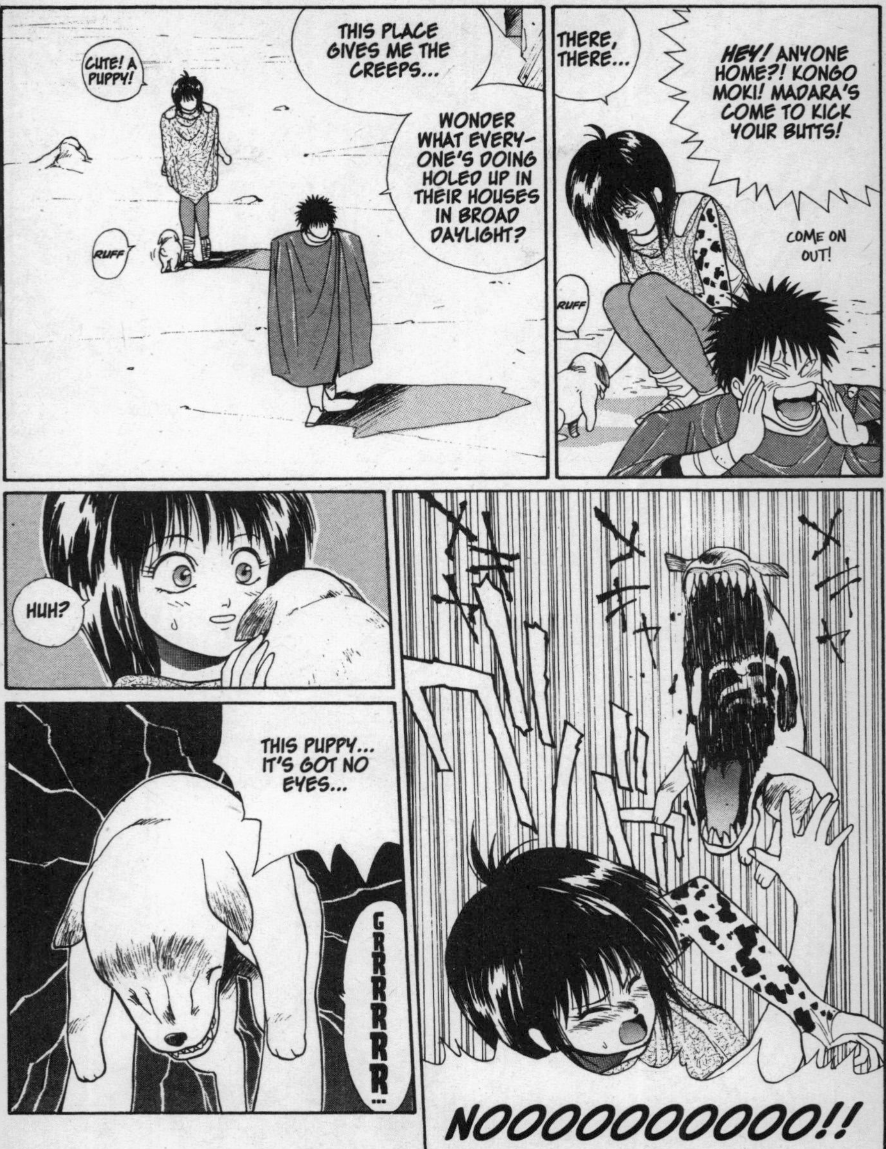

CUTE! A PUPPY!
RUFF
THIS PLACE GIVES ME THE CREEPS...
WONDER WHAT EVERY-ONE'S DOING HOLED UP IN THEIR HOUSES IN BROAD DAYLIGHT?
THERE, THERE...
HEY! ANYONE HOME?! KONGO MOKI! MADARA'S COME TO KICK YOUR BUTTS!
COME ON OUT!
RUFF
HUH?
THIS PUPPY... IT'S GOT NO EYES...
GRRRRRR...
NOOOOOOOOOO!!

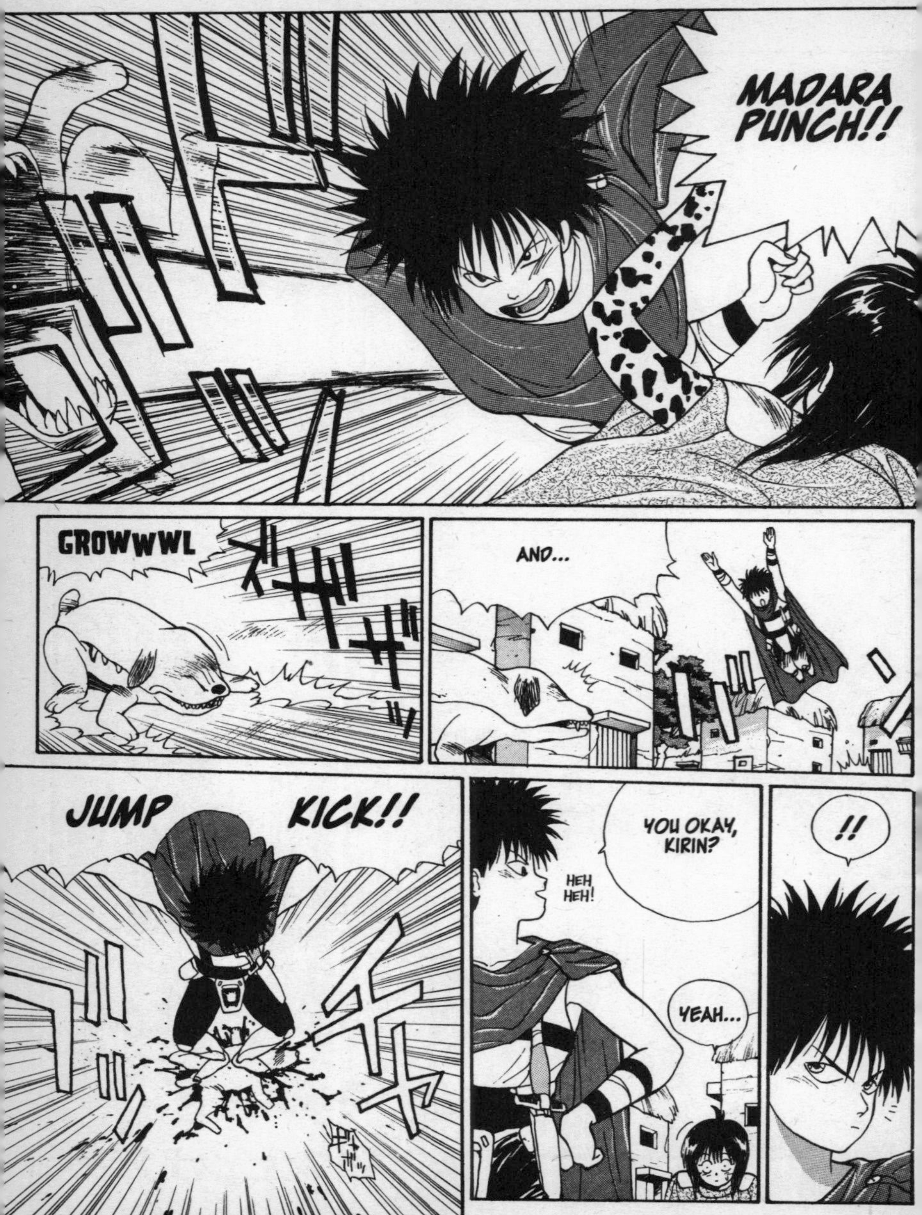
MADARA PUNCH!!
GROWWWL
AND...
JUMP KICK!!
YOU OKAY, KIRIN?
HEH HEH!
YEAH...
!!

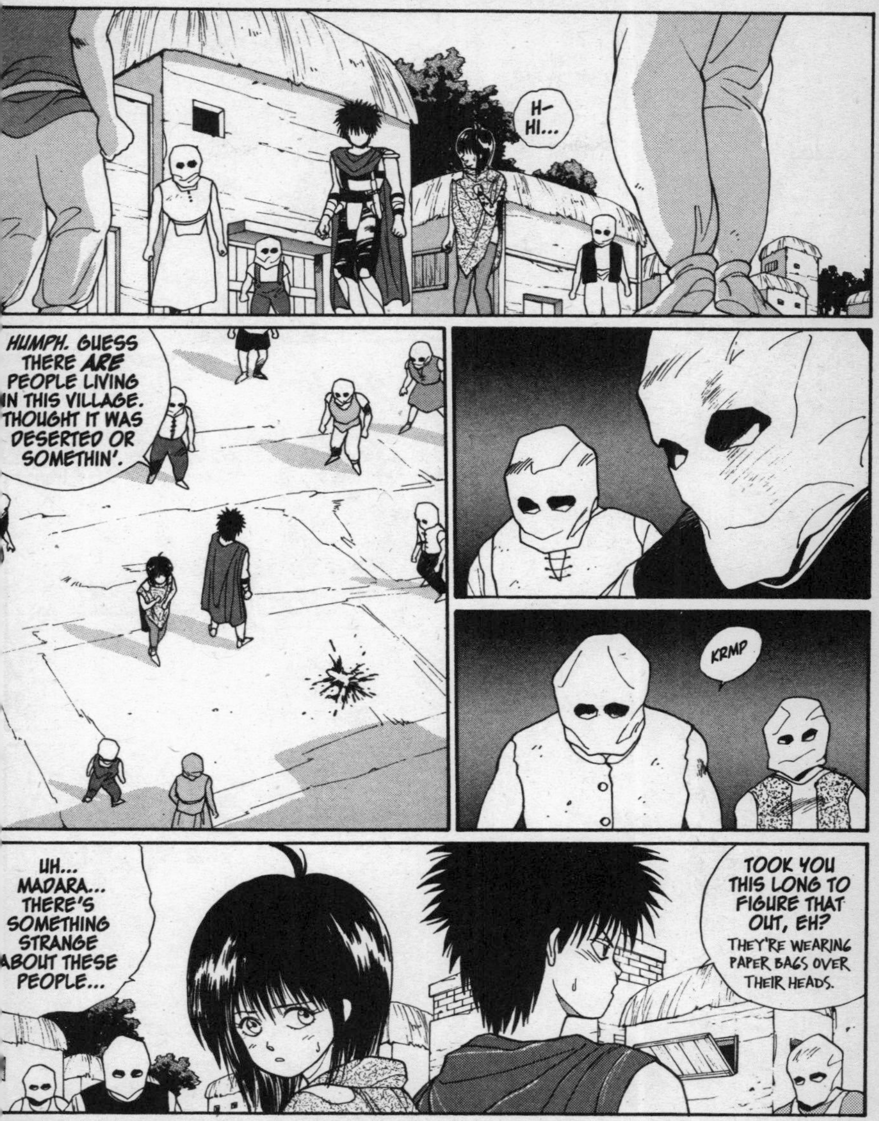

H-HI...
HUMPH. GUESS THERE ARE PEOPLE LIVING IN THIS VILLAGE. THOUGHT IT WAS DESERTED OR SOMETHIN'.
KRMP
UH... MADARA... THERE'S SOMETHING STRANGE ABOUT THESE PEOPLE...
TOOK YOU THIS LONG TO FIGURE THAT OUT, EH? THEY'RE WEARING PAPER BAGS OVER THEIR HEADS.

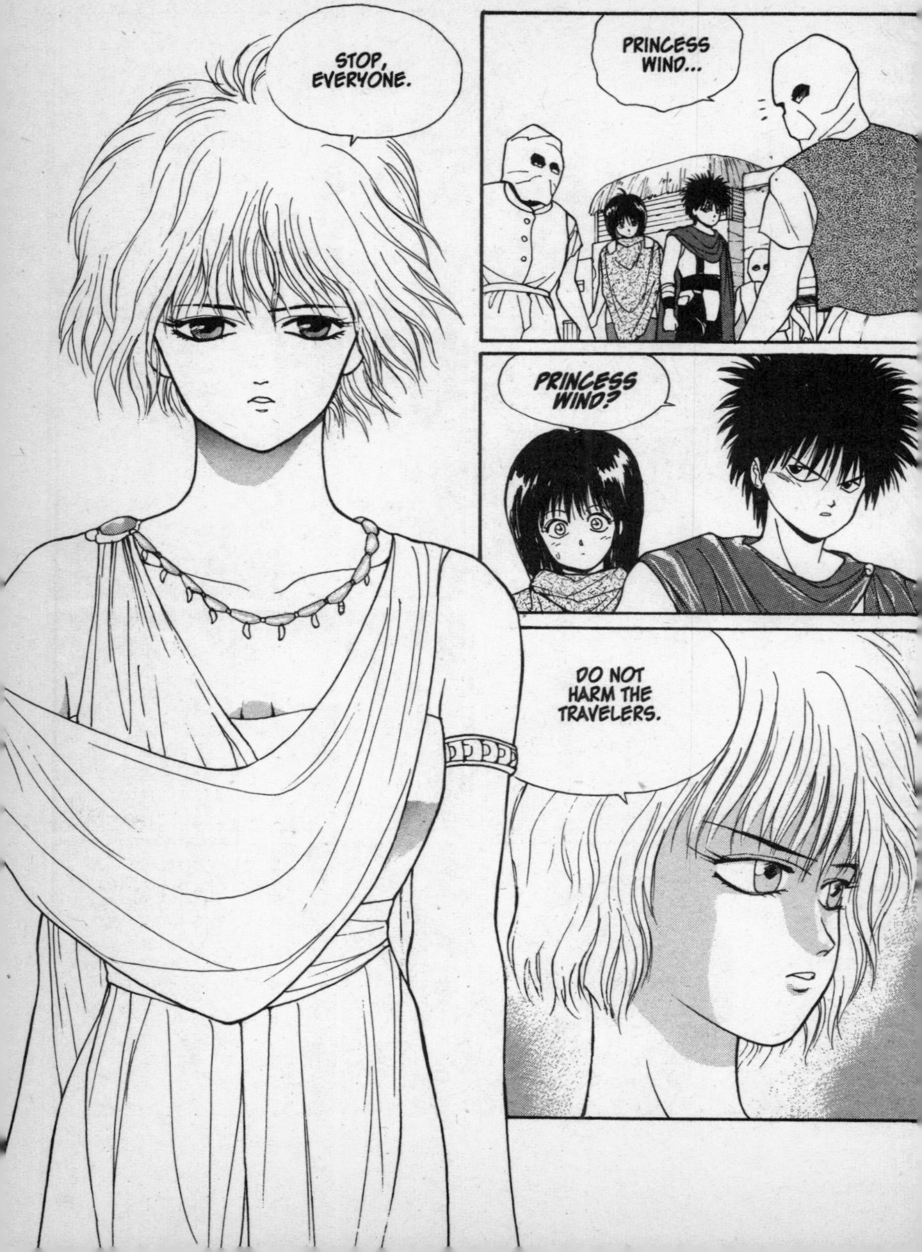
STOP, EVERYONE.
PRINCESS WIND...
PRINCESS WIND?
DO NOT HARM THE TRAVELERS.

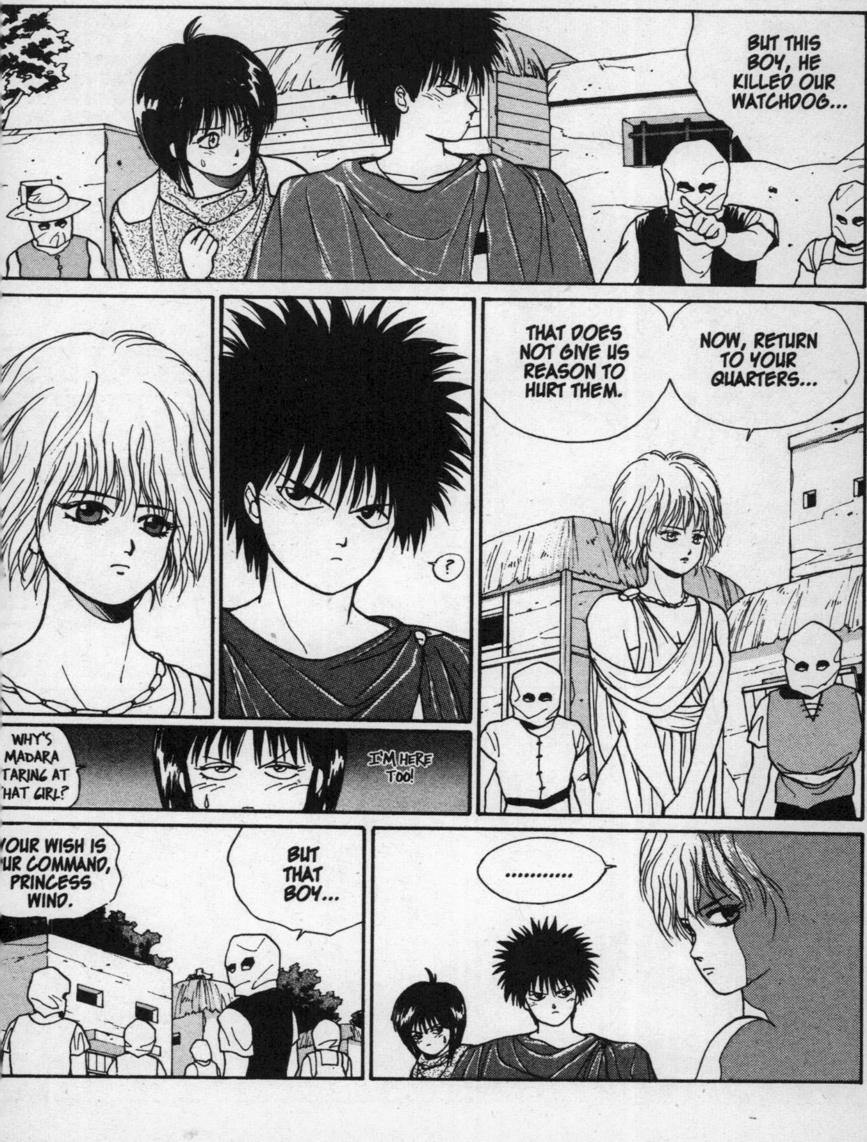

BUT THIS BOY, HE KILLED OUR WATCHDOG...
?
THAT DOES NOT GIVE US REASON TO HURT THEM.
NOW, RETURN TO YOUR QUARTERS...
WHY'S MADARA TARING AT HAT GIRL?
I'M HERE TOO!
OUR WISH IS UR COMMAND, PRINCESS WIND.
BUT THAT BOY...
....

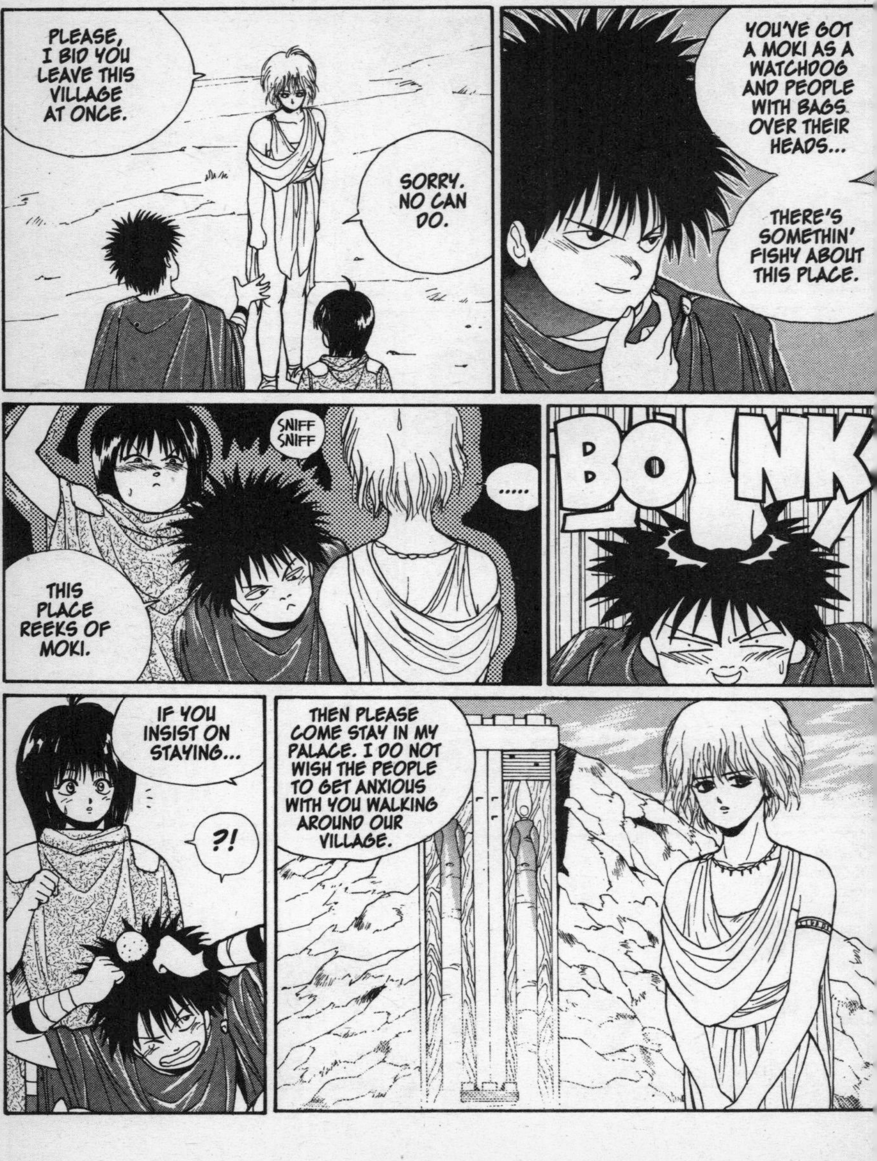
PLEASE, I BID YOU LEAVE THIS VILLAGE AT ONCE.
SORRY. NO CAN DO.
YOU'VE GOT A MOKI AS A WATCHDOG AND PEOPLE WITH BAGS OVER THEIR HEADS...
THERE'S SOMETHIN' FISHY ABOUT THIS PLACE.
SNIFF SNIFF
THIS PLACE REEKS OF MOKI.
.....
BONK
IF YOU INSIST ON STAYING...
?!
THEN PLEASE COME STAY IN MY PALACE. I DO NOT WISH THE PEOPLE TO GET ANXIOUS WITH YOU WALKING AROUND OUR VILLAGE.

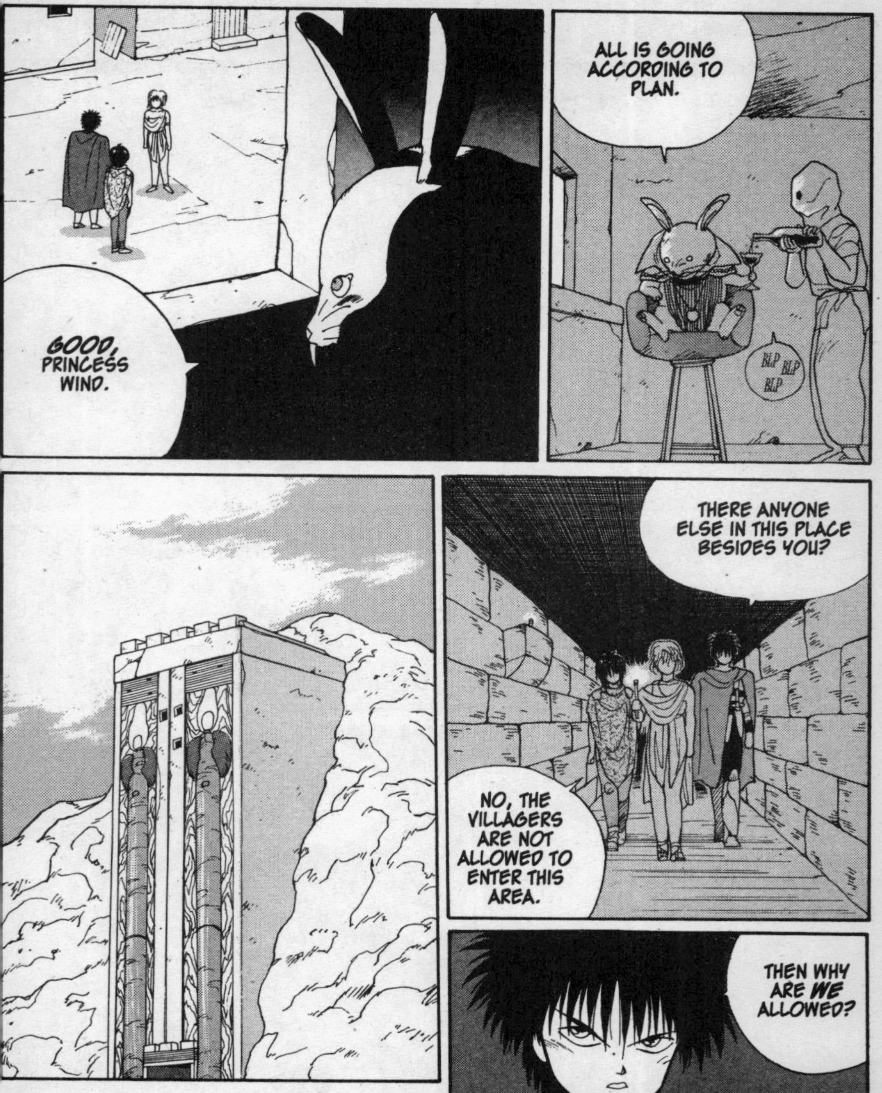
GOOD, PRINCESS WIND.
ALL IS GOING ACCORDING TO PLAN.
BLP BLP BLP
THERE ANYONE ELSE IN THIS PLACE BESIDES YOU?
NO, THE VILLAGERS ARE NOT ALLOWED TO ENTER THIS AREA.
THEN WHY ARE WE ALLOWED?

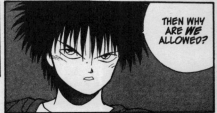

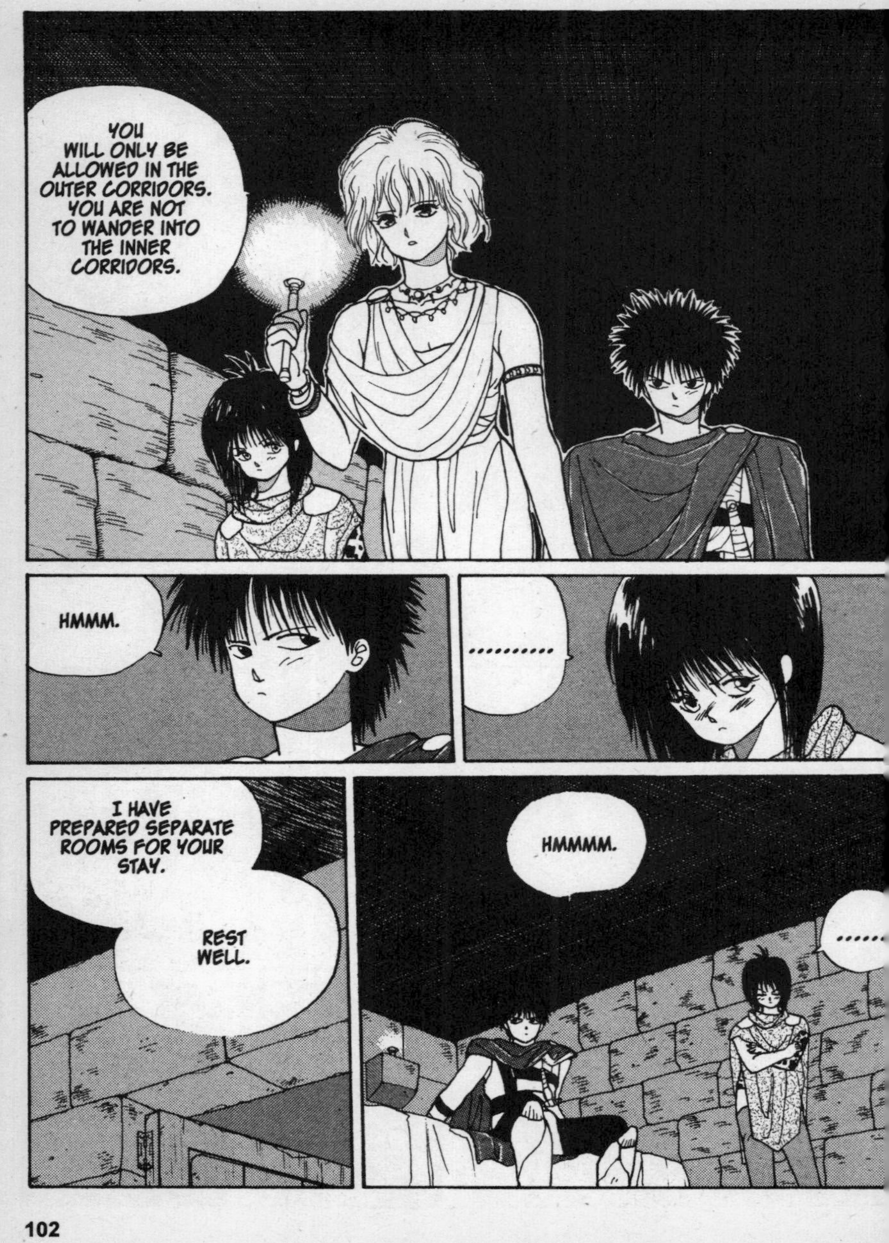
YOU WILL ONLY BE ALLOWED IN THE OUTER CORRIDORS. YOU ARE NOT TO WANDER INTO THE INNER CORRIDORS.
HMMM.
....
I HAVE PREPARED SEPARATE ROOMS FOR YOUR STAY.
REST WELL.
HMMMM.
......

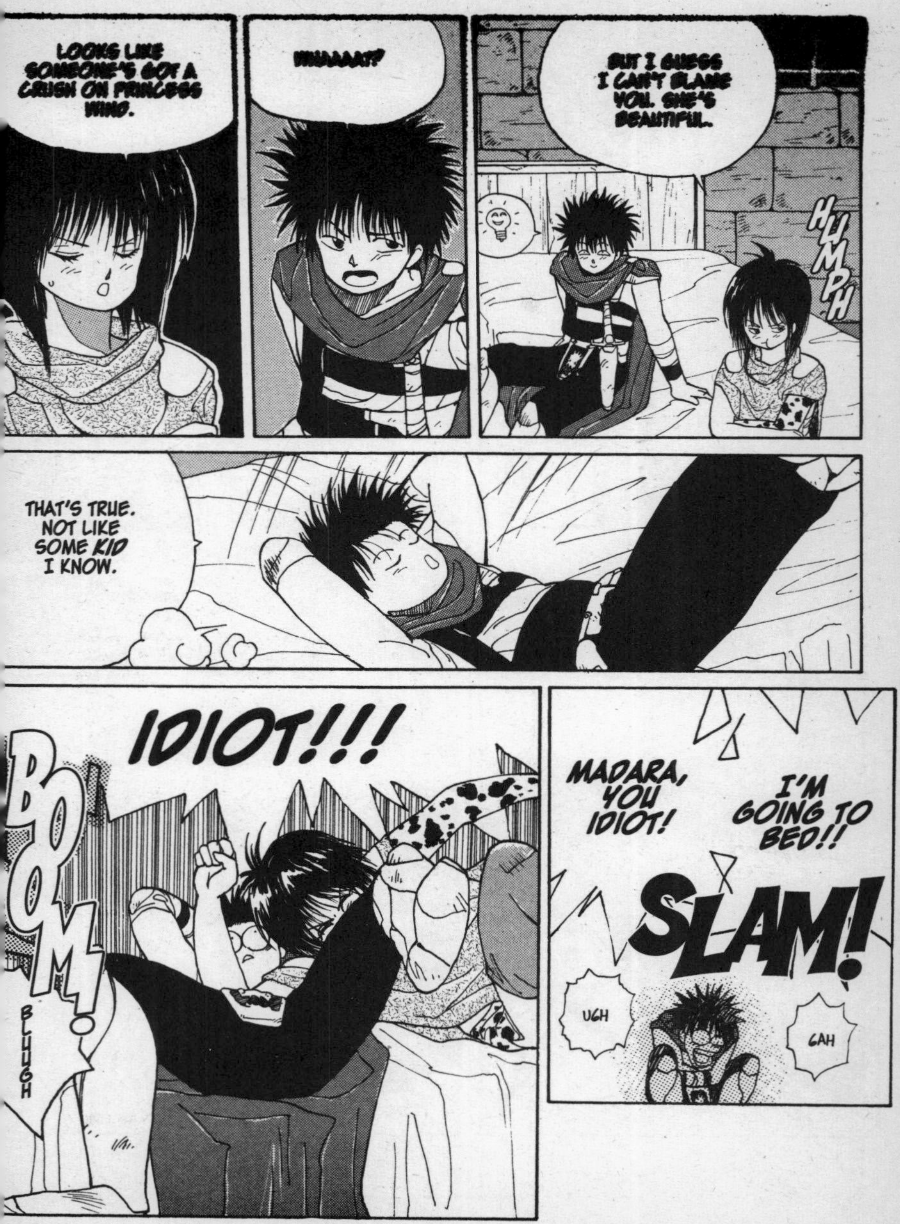
LOOKS LIKE SOMEONE'S GOT A CRUSH ON PRINCESS WIND.
WHAAAAT?
BUT I GUESS I CAN'T BLAME YOU. SHE'S BEAUTIFUL.
HUMPH
THAT'S TRUE. NOT LIKE SOME *KID* I KNOW.
IDIOT!!!
BOOM!
BLUUGH
MADARA, YOU IDIOT!
I'M GOING TO BED!!
SLAM!
UGH
GAH

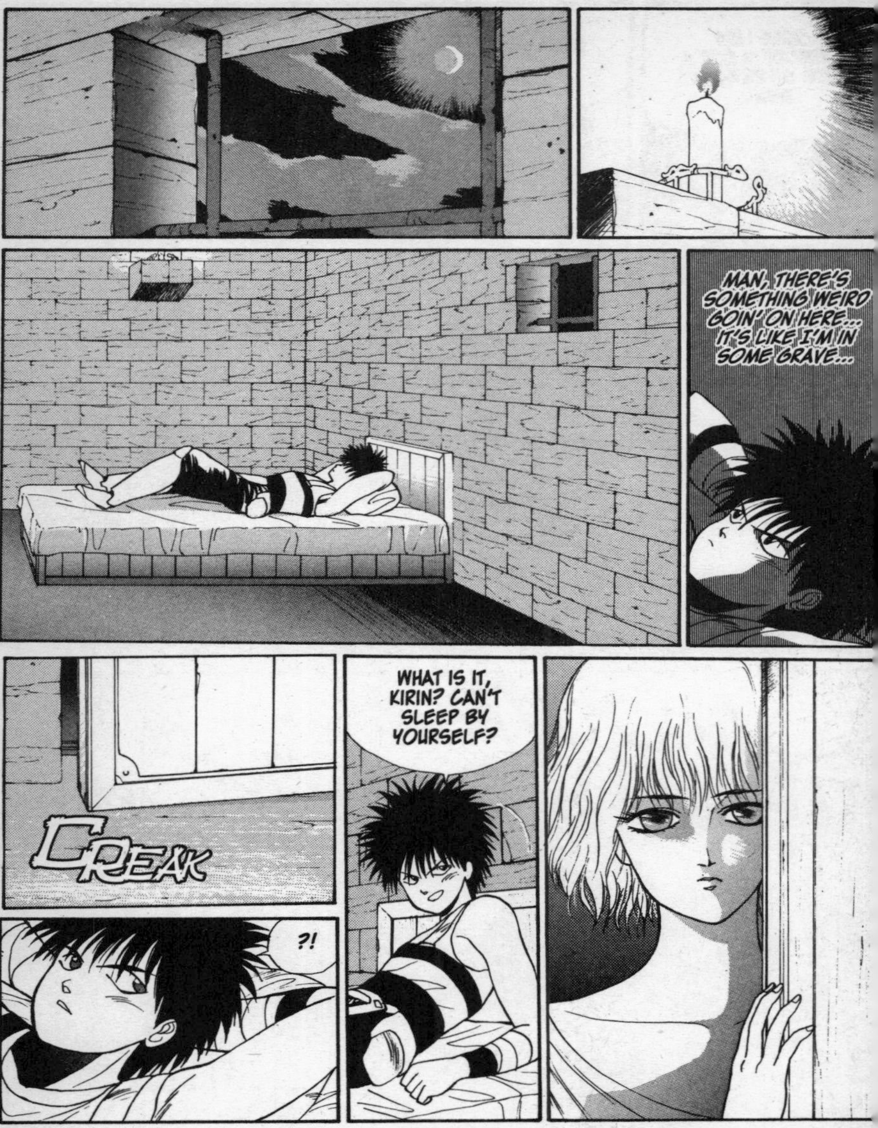
MAN, THERE'S SOMETHING WEIRD GOIN' ON HERE... IT'S LIKE I'M IN SOME GRAVE...
CREAK
WHAT IS IT, KIRIN? CAN'T SLEEP BY YOURSELF?
?!

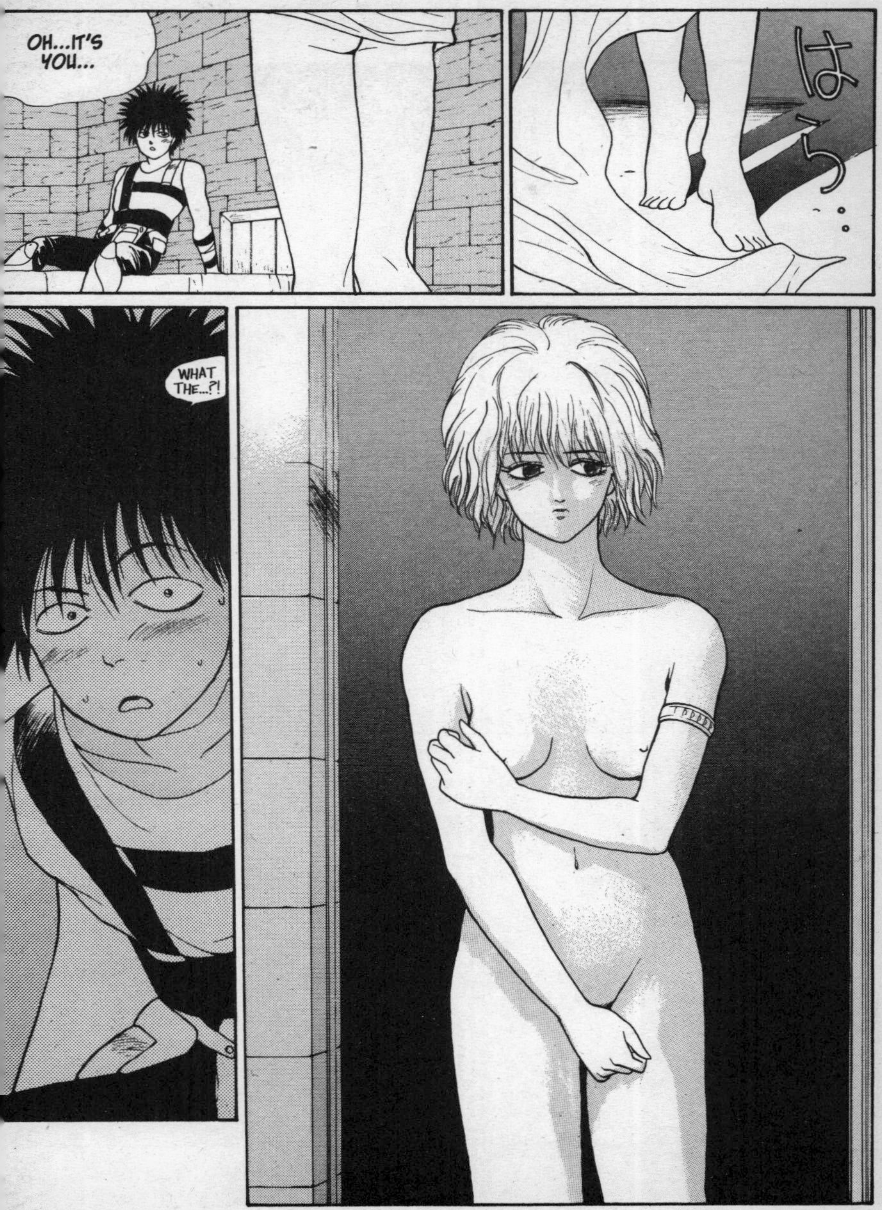

OH...IT'S YOU...
はら
WHAT THE...?!

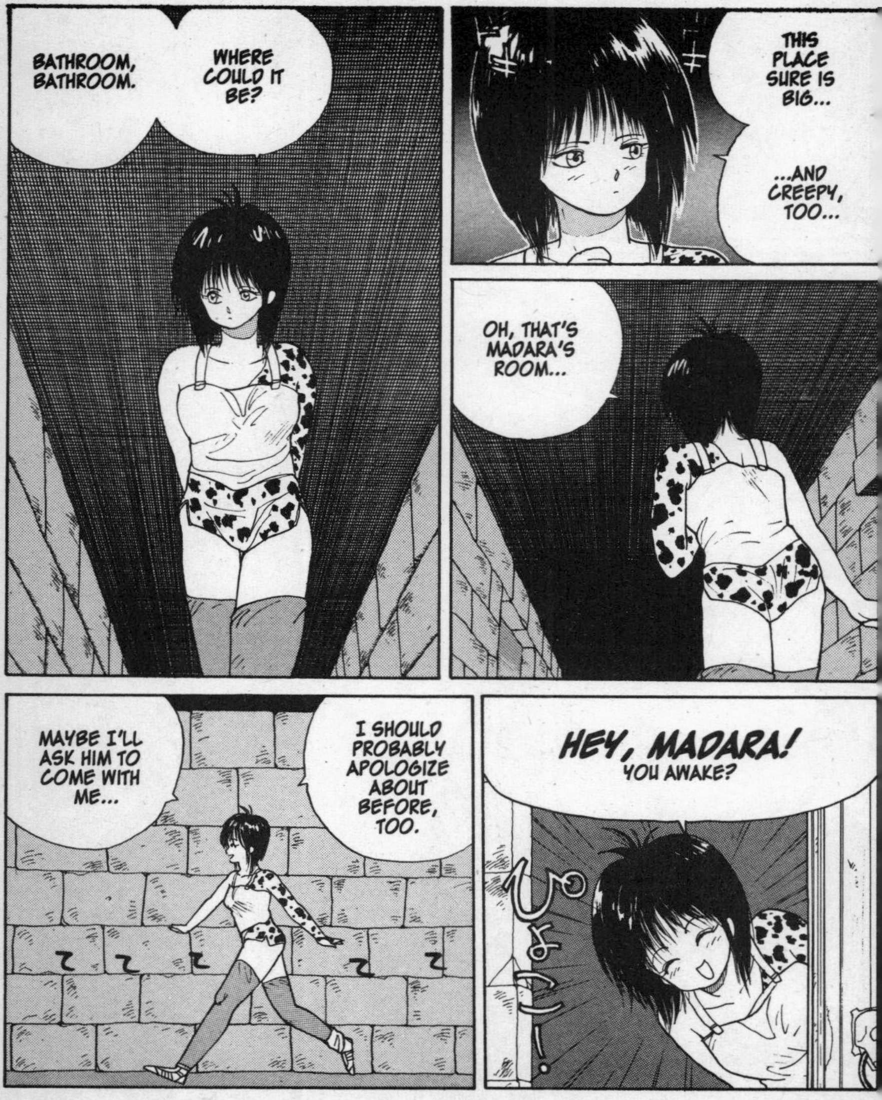
BATHROOM, BATHROOM.
WHERE COULD IT BE?
THIS PLACE SURE IS BIG...
...AND CREEPY, TOO...
OH, THAT'S MADARA'S ROOM...
MAYBE I'LL ASK HIM TO COME WITH ME...
I SHOULD PROBABLY APOLOGIZE ABOUT BEFORE, TOO.
HEY, MADARA! YOU AWAKE?
ひょこー!

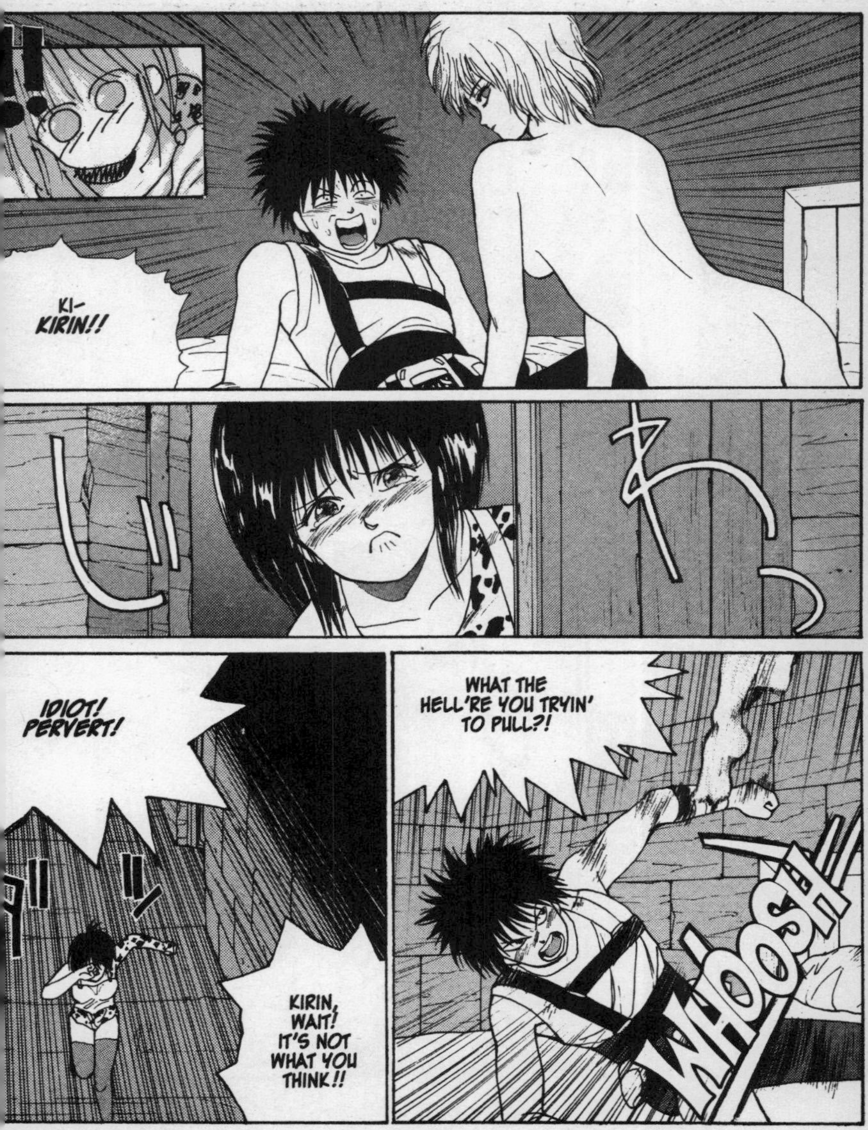
KI-
KIRIN!!
WHAT THE HELL'RE YOU TRYIN' TO PULL?!
IDIOT! PERVERT!
WHOOSH
KIRIN, WAIT! IT'S NOT WHAT YOU THINK!!

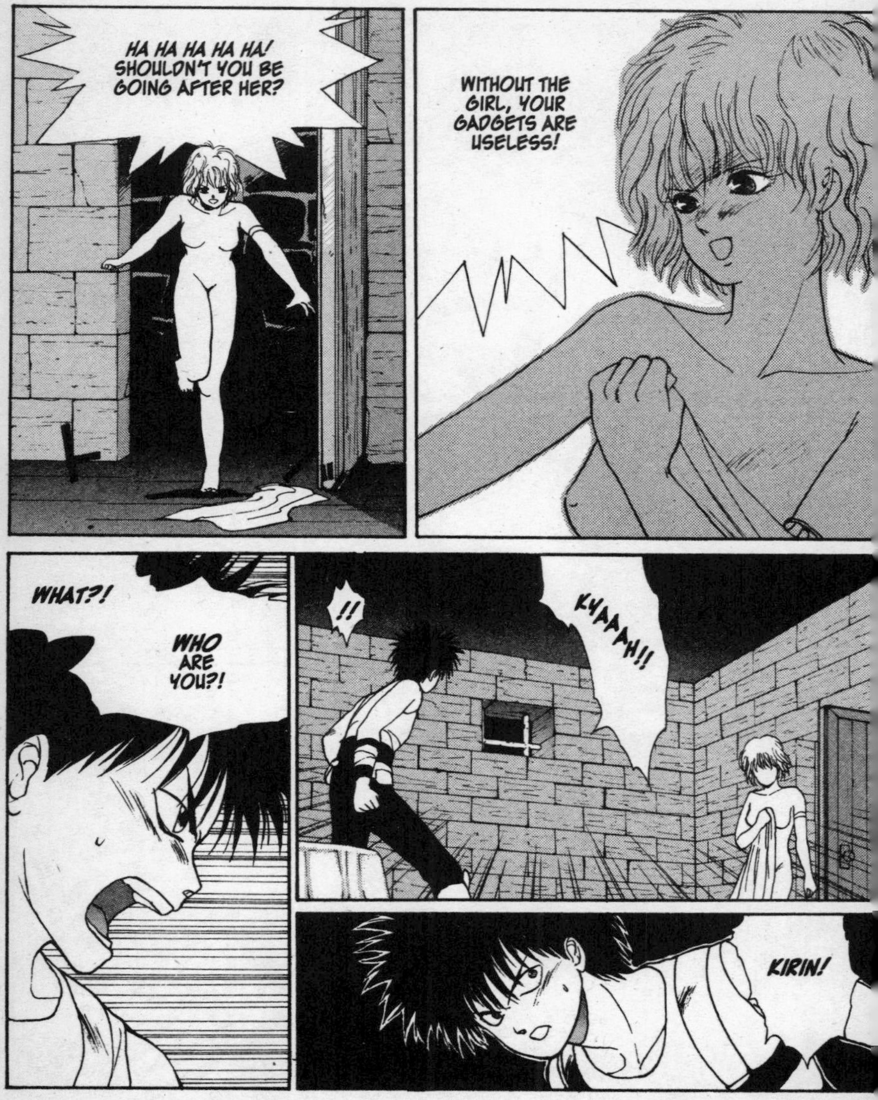
HA HA HA HA HA! SHOULDN'T YOU BE GOING AFTER HER?
WITHOUT THE GIRL, YOUR GADGETS ARE USELESS!
WHAT?!
WHO ARE YOU?!
!!
KYAAAH!!
KIRIN!

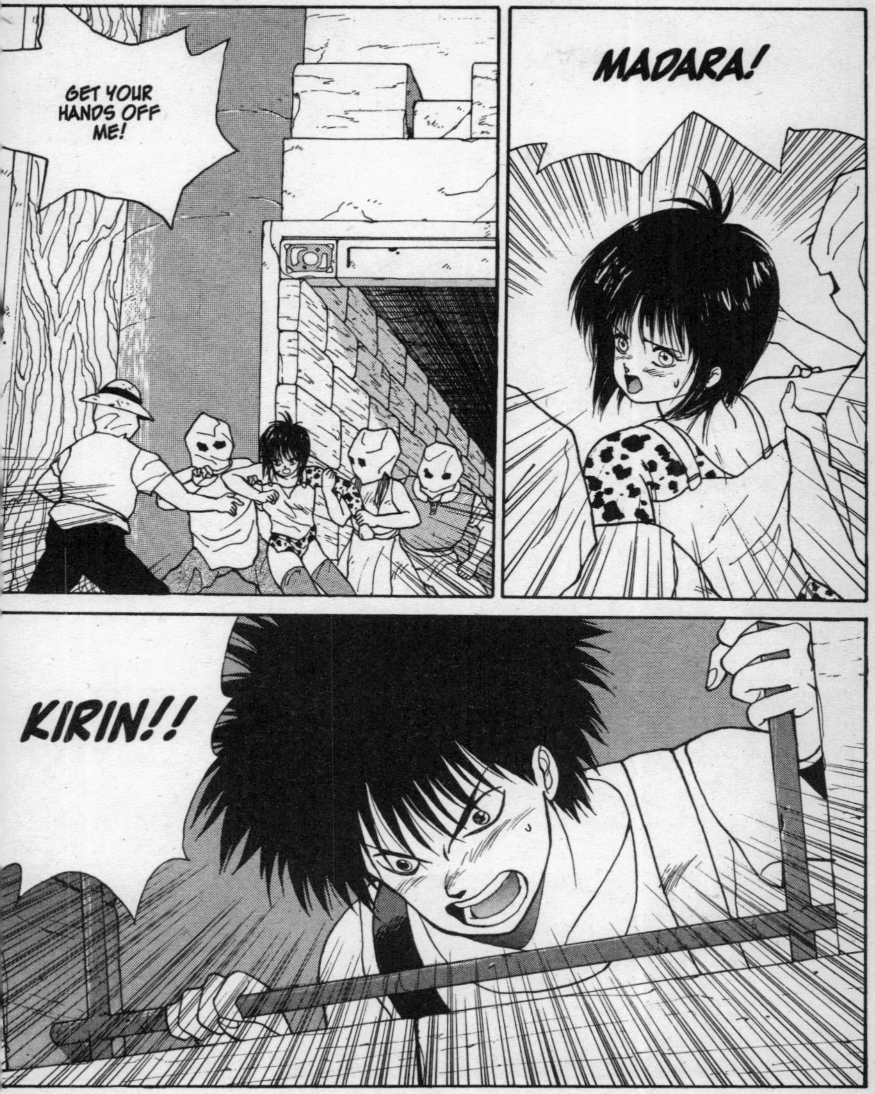
GET YOUR HANDS OFF ME!
MADARA!
KIRIN!!

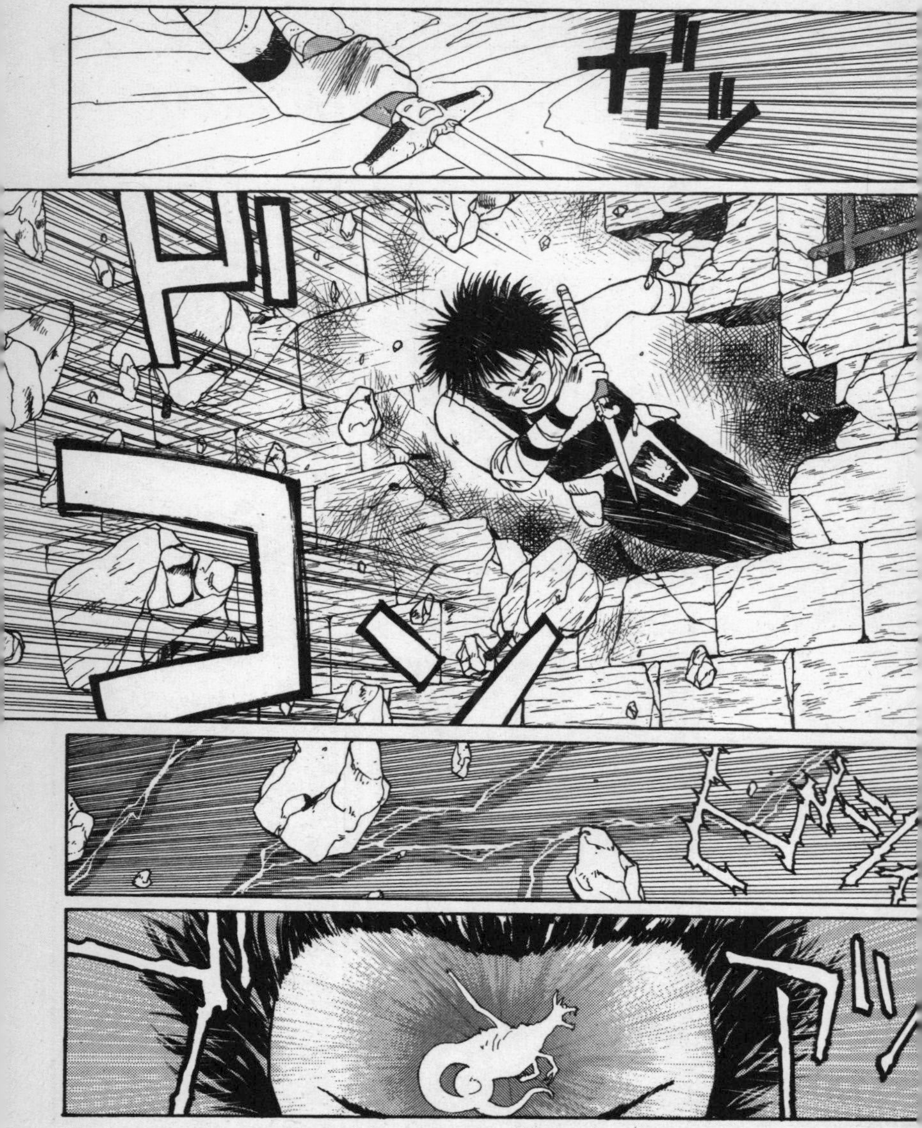

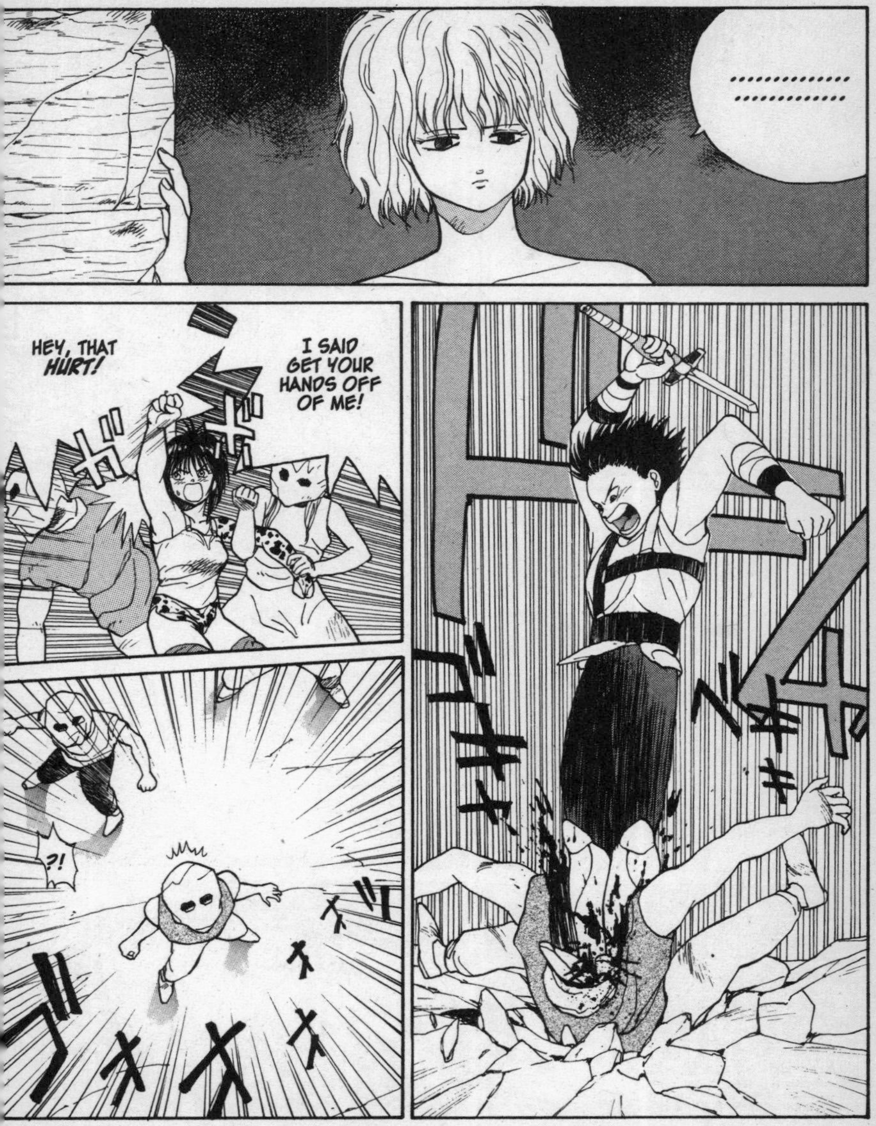

....
....
I SAID GET YOUR HANDS OFF OF ME!
HEY, THAT HURT!
?!

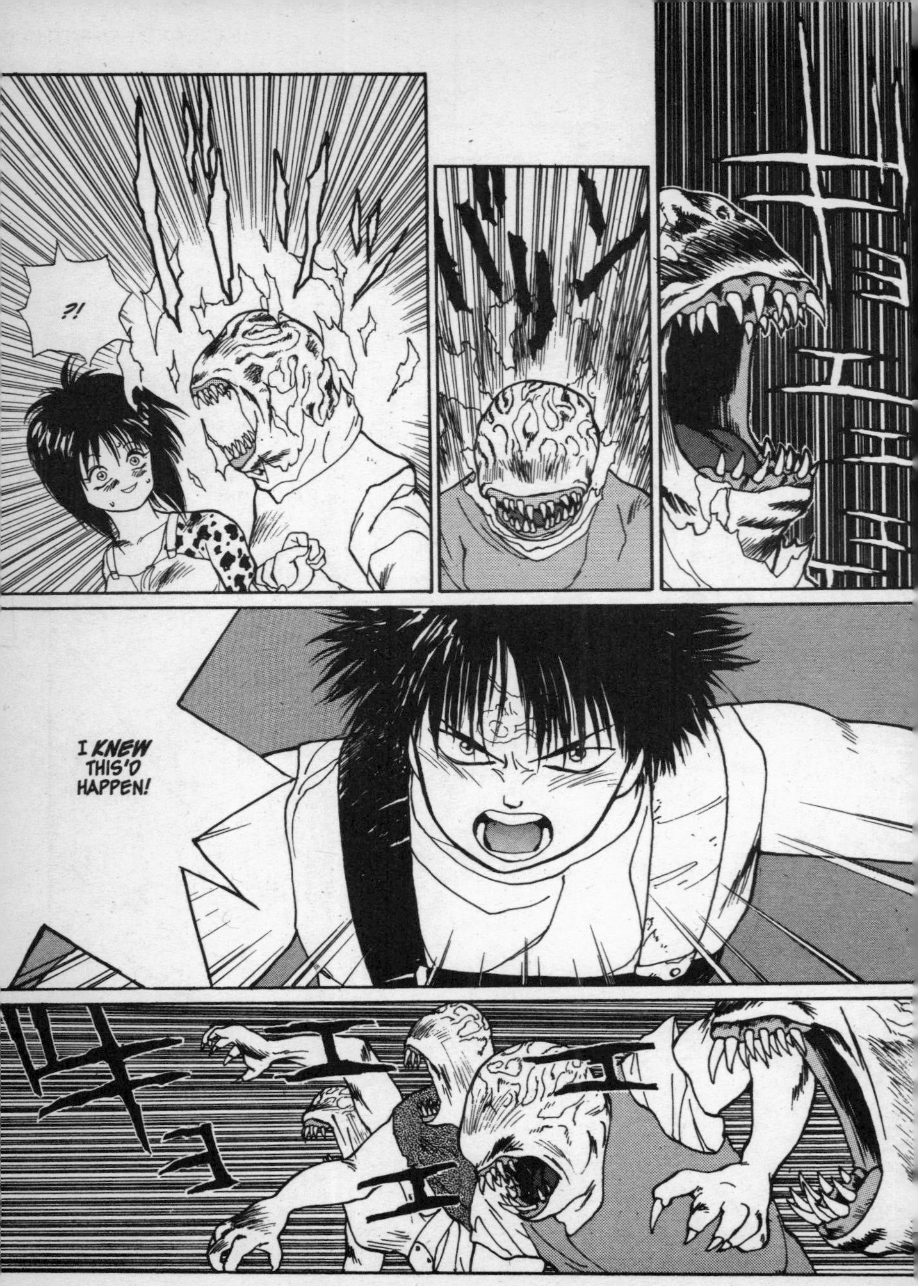
?!
I KNEW THIS'D HAPPEN!

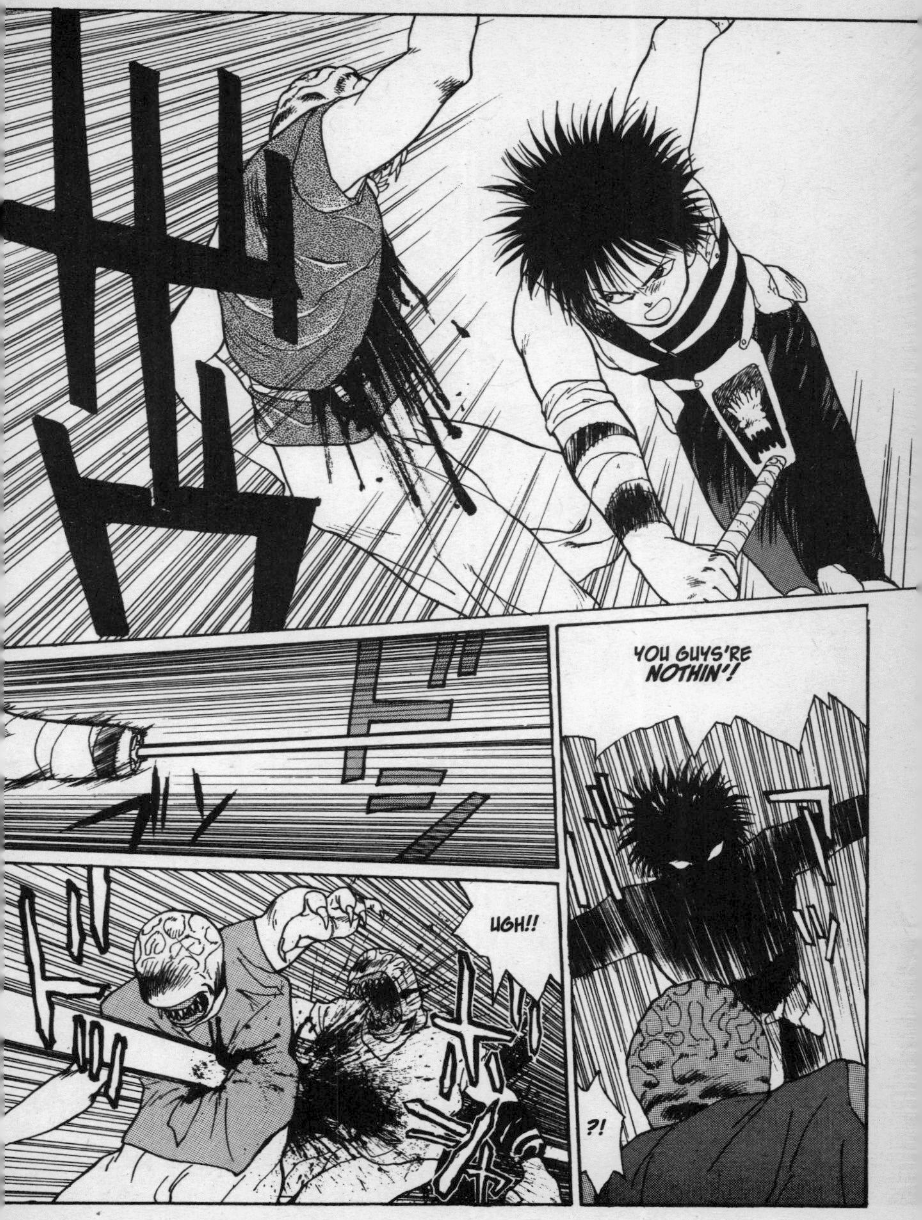

YOU GUYS'RE NOTHIN'!
UGH!!
?!

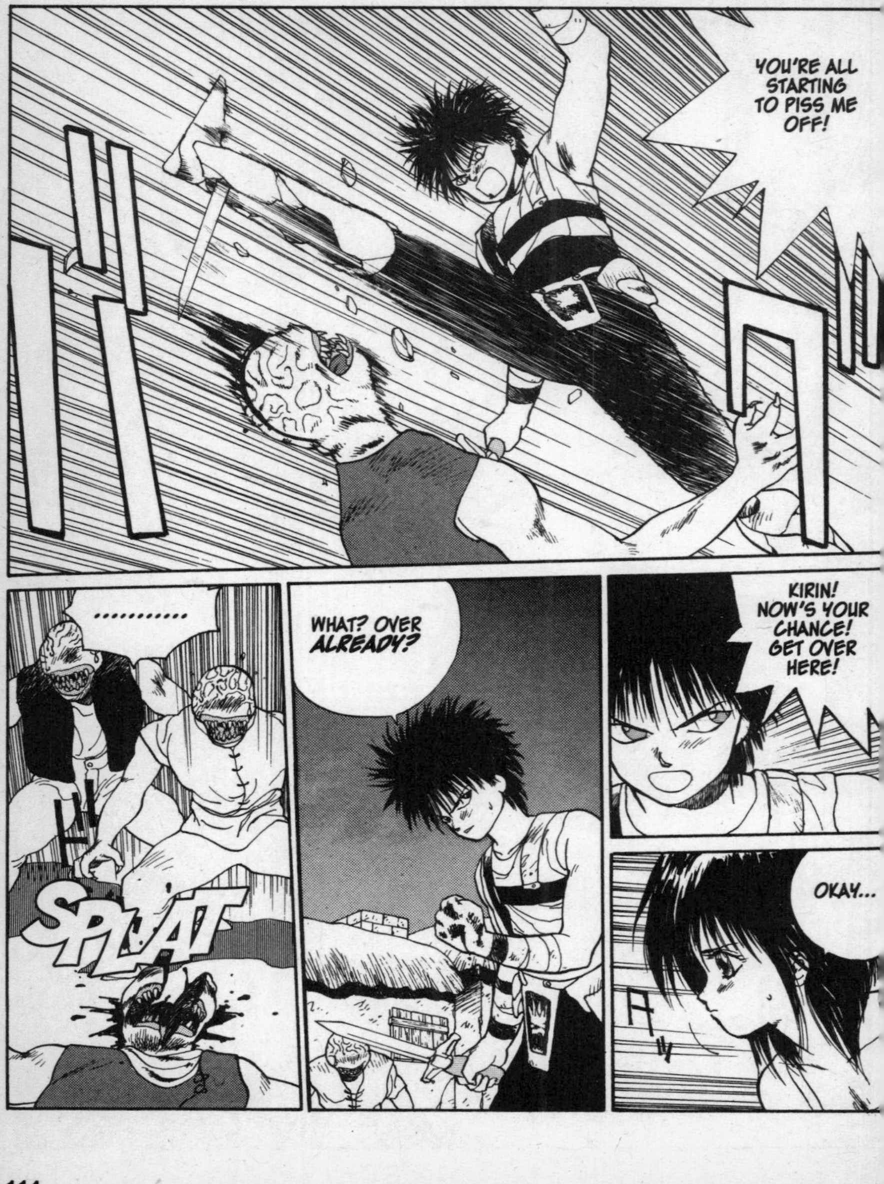
YOU'RE ALL STARTING TO PISS ME OFF!
....
SPLAT
WHAT? OVER ALREADY?
KIRIN! NOW'S YOUR CHANCE! GET OVER HERE!
OKAY...

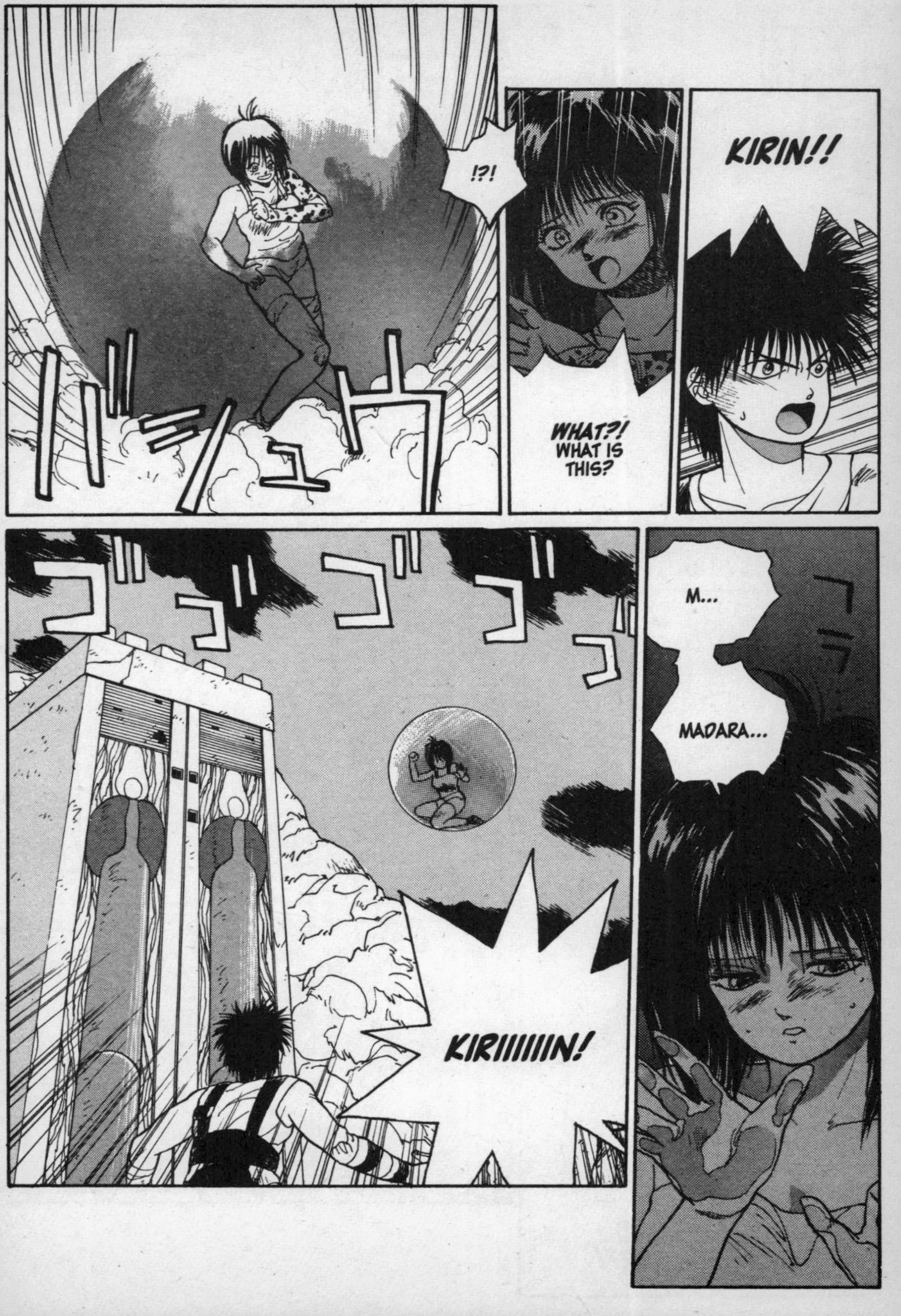
!?!
WHAT?! WHAT IS THIS?
KIRIN!!
KIRIIIIIIN!
M...
MADARA...

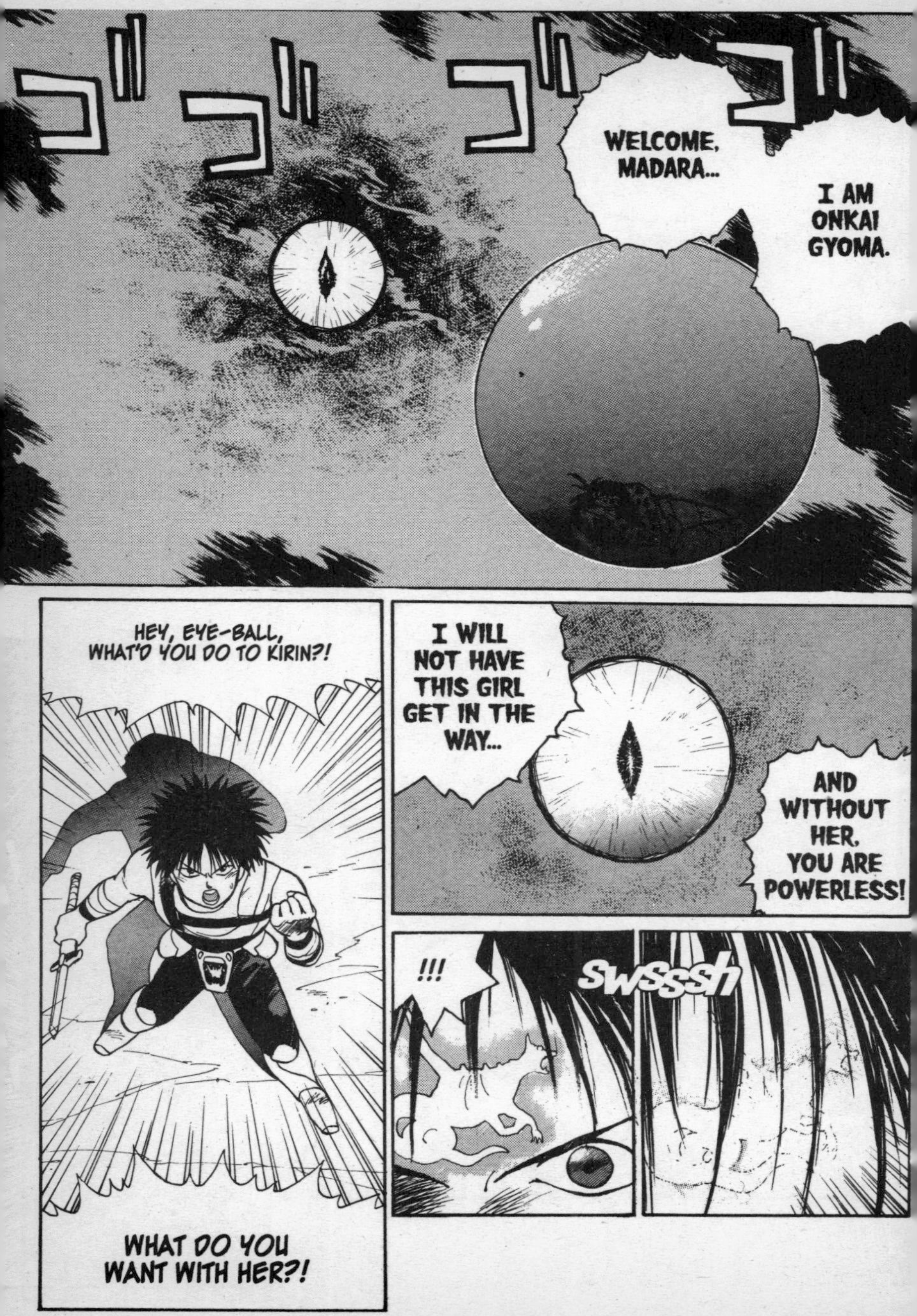
ゴゴゴゴ
WELCOME, MADARA...
I AM ONKAI GYOMA.
I WILL NOT HAVE THIS GIRL GET IN THE WAY...
AND WITHOUT HER, YOU ARE POWERLESS!
HEY, EYE-BALL, WHAT'D YOU DO TO KIRIN?!
WHAT DO YOU WANT WITH HER?!
SWSSSH
!!!

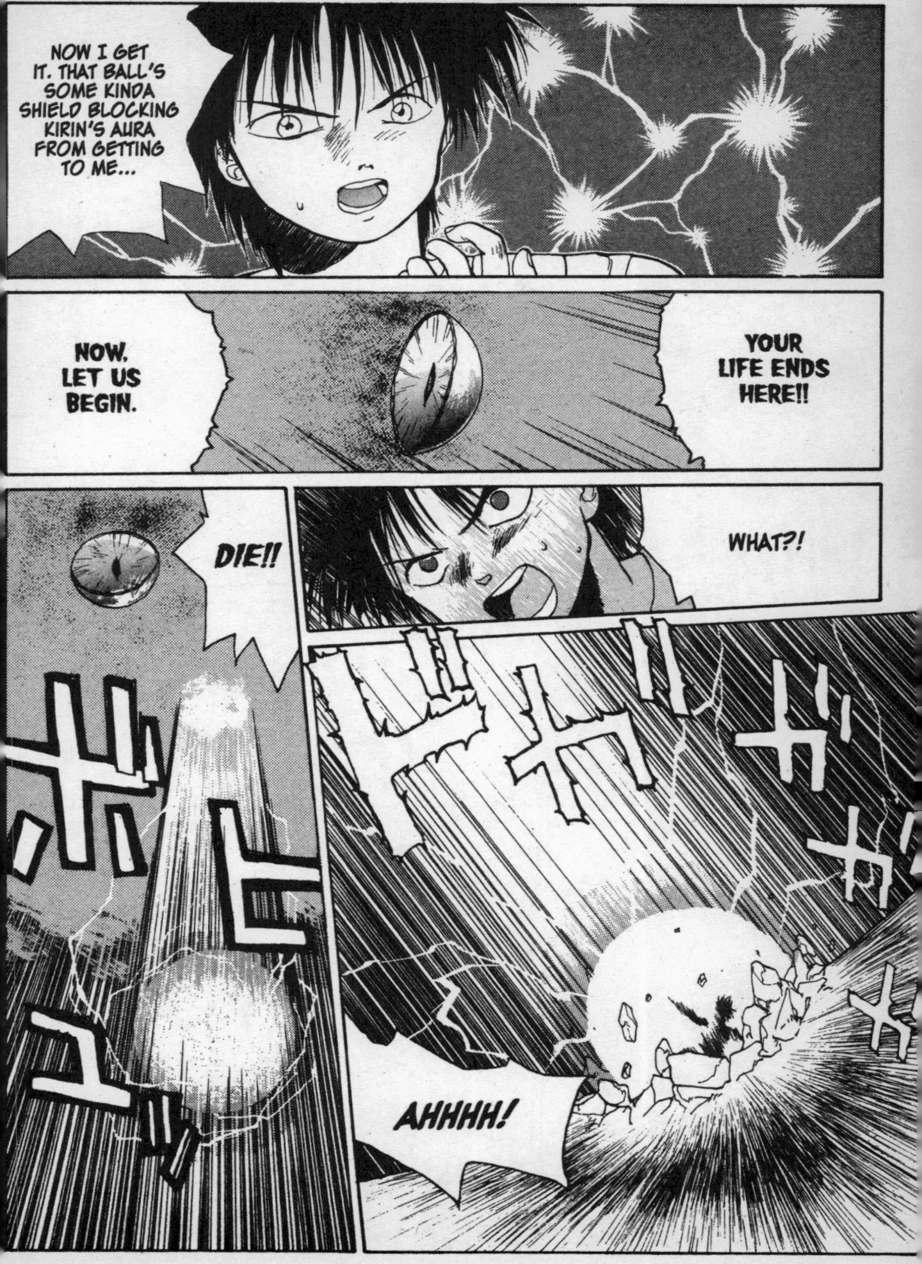
NOW I GET IT. THAT BALL'S SOME KINDA SHIELD BLOCKING KIRIN'S AURA FROM GETTING TO ME...
YOUR LIFE ENDS HERE!!
NOW, LET US BEGIN.
WHAT?!
DIE!!
AHHHH!

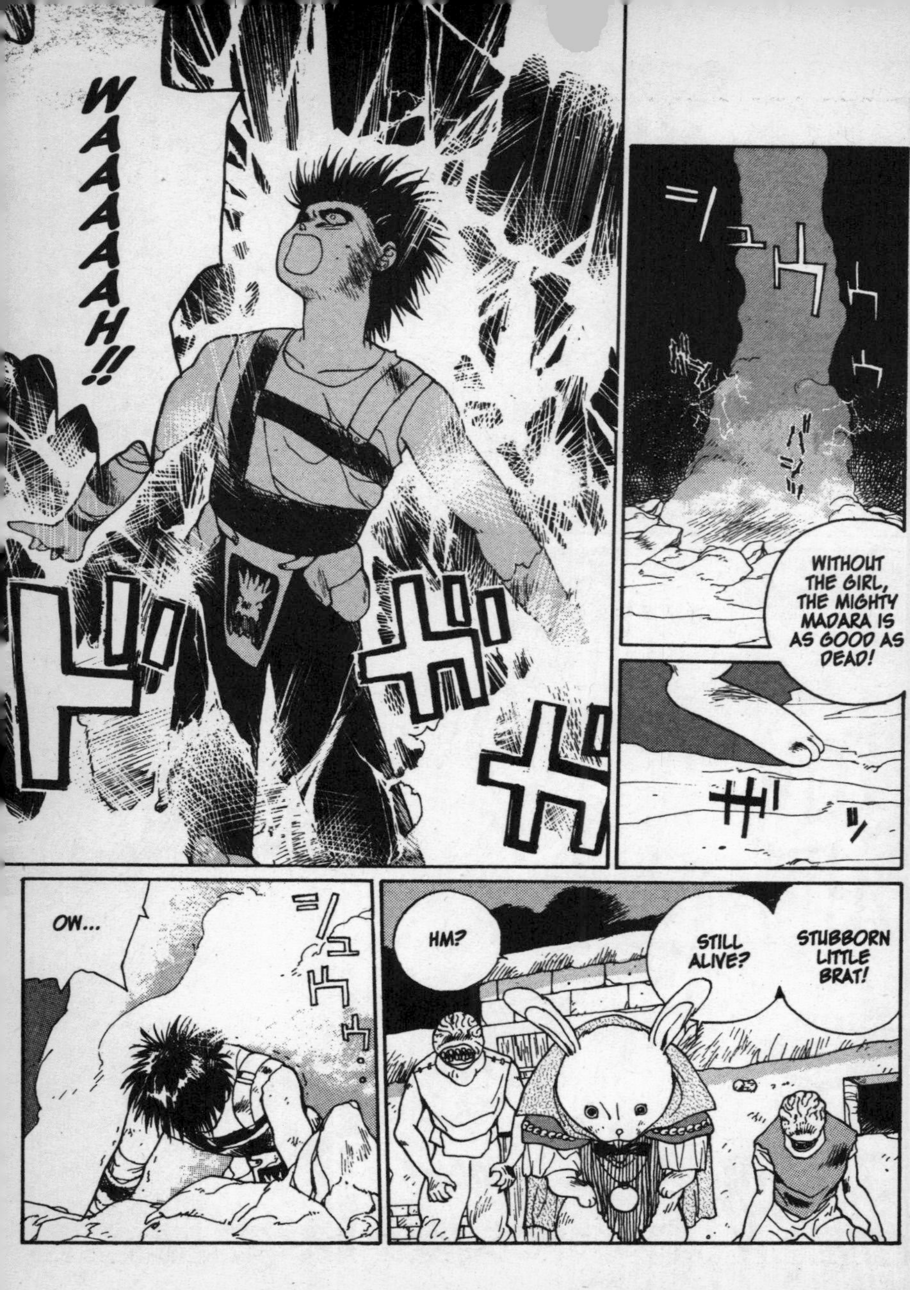
WAAAAAAAH!!
WITHOUT THE GIRL, THE MIGHTY MADARA IS AS GOOD AS DEAD!
OW...
STILL ALIVE?
STUBBORN LITTLE BRAT!
HM?

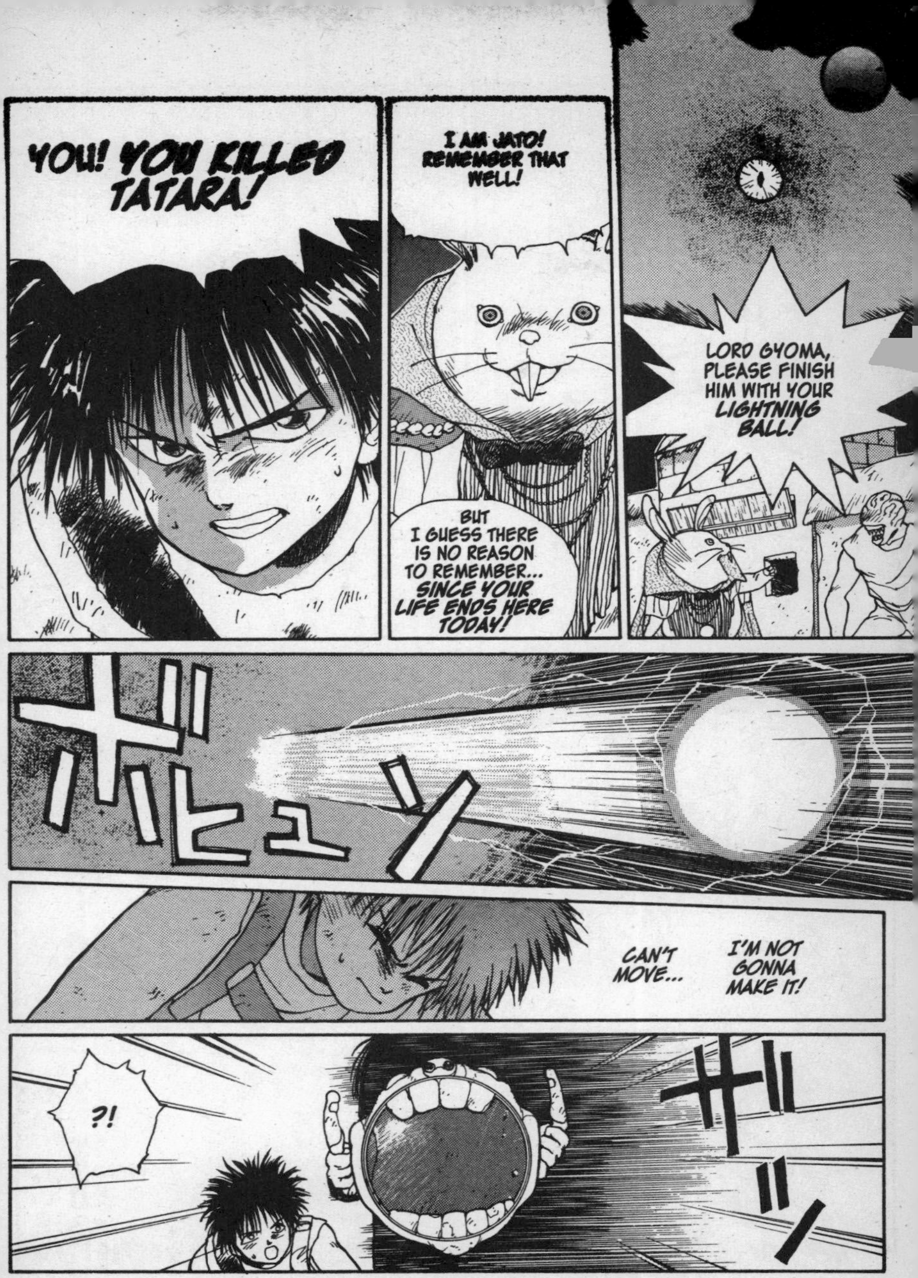
YOU! YOU KILLED TATARA!
I AM JATO! REMEMBER THAT WELL!
BUT I GUESS THERE IS NO REASON TO REMEMBER... SINCE YOUR LIFE ENDS HERE TODAY!
LORD GYOMA, PLEASE FINISH HIM WITH YOUR LIGHTNING BALL!
ボヒュッ
CAN'T MOVE...
I'M NOT GONNA MAKE IT!
?!

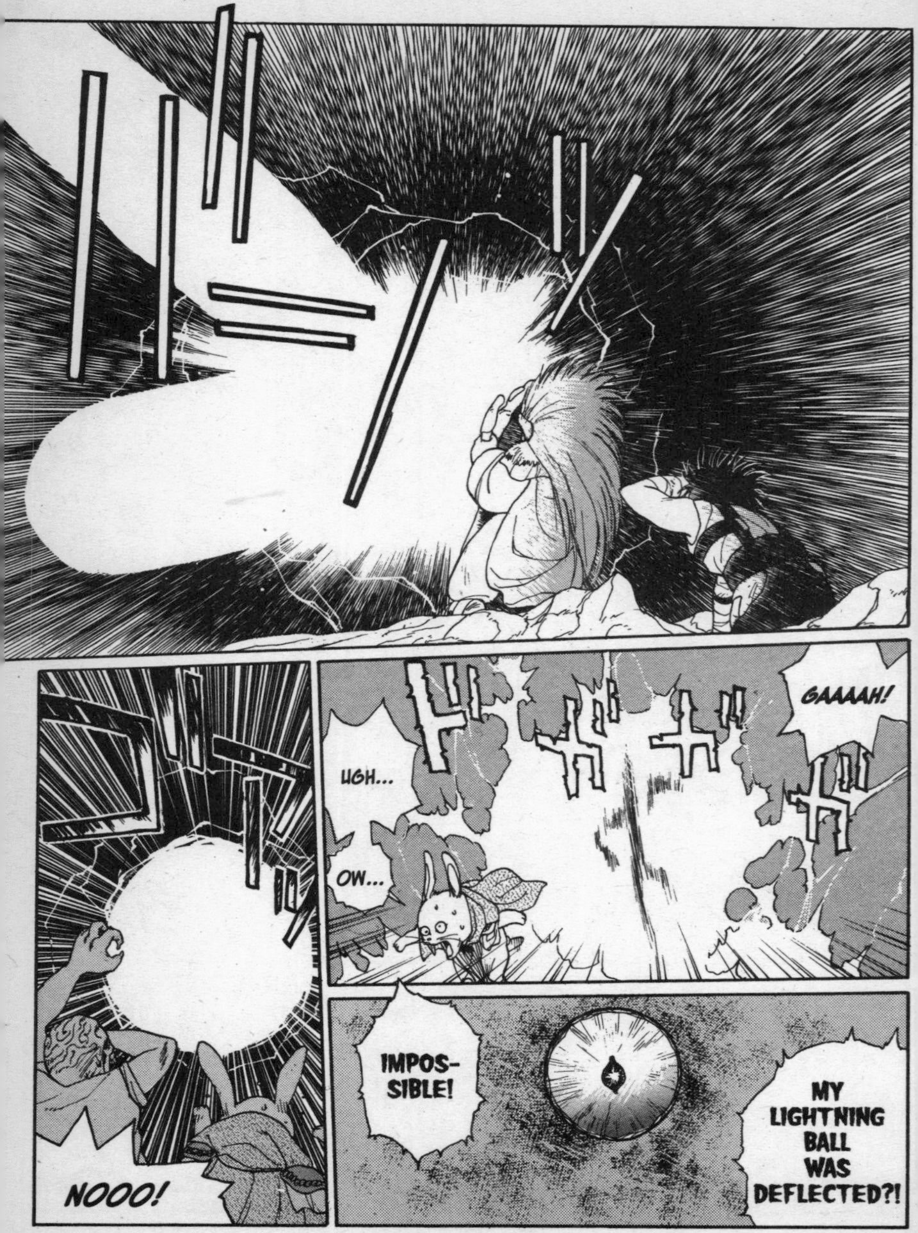
NOOO!
UGH...
OW...
GAAAAH!
IMPOS-SIBLE!
MY LIGHTNING BALL WAS DEFLECTED?!

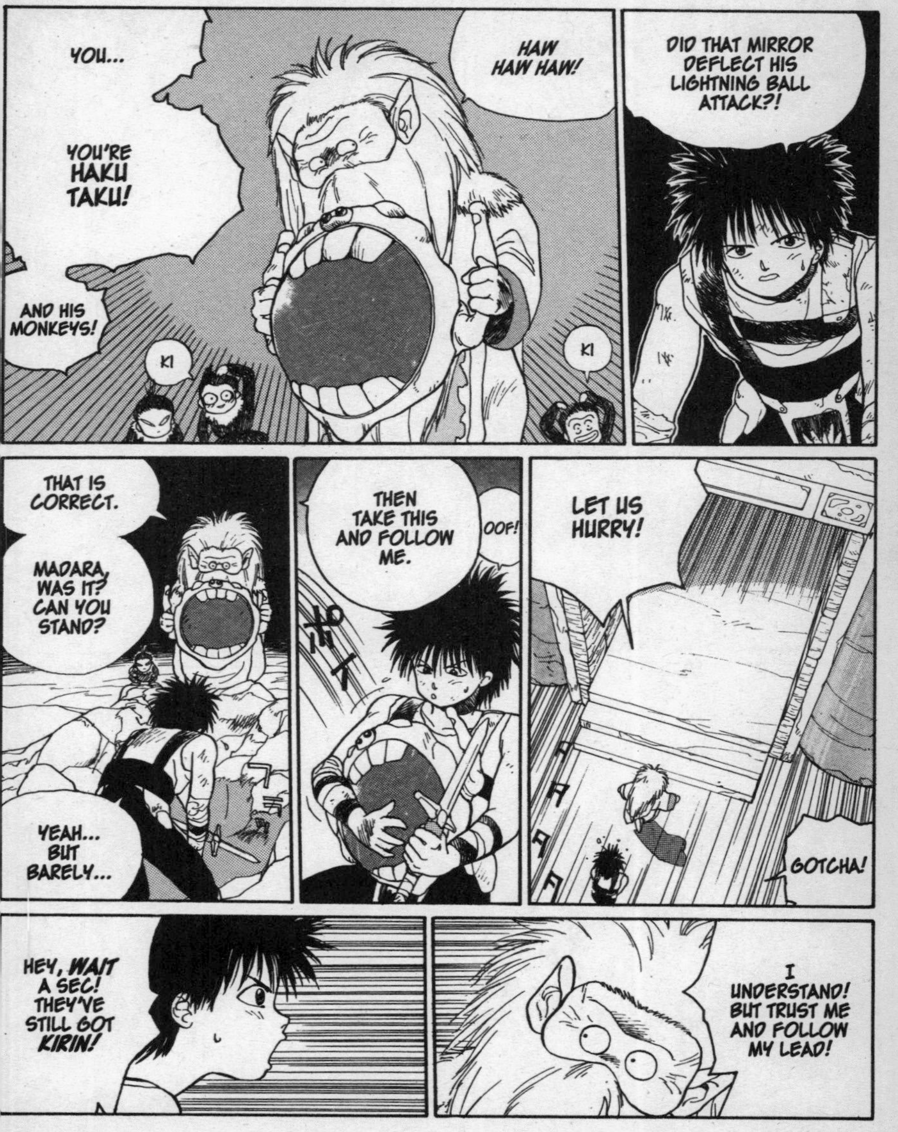
YOU...
YOU'RE HAKU TAKU!
AND HIS MONKEYS!
KI
HAW HAW HAW!
KI
DID THAT MIRROR DEFLECT HIS LIGHTNING BALL ATTACK?!
THAT IS CORRECT.
MADARA, WAS IT? CAN YOU STAND?
YEAH... BUT BARELY...
THEN TAKE THIS AND FOLLOW ME.
OOF!
LET US HURRY!
GOTCHA!
HEY, WAIT A SEC! THEY'VE STILL GOT KIRIN!
I UNDERSTAND! BUT TRUST ME AND FOLLOW MY LEAD!

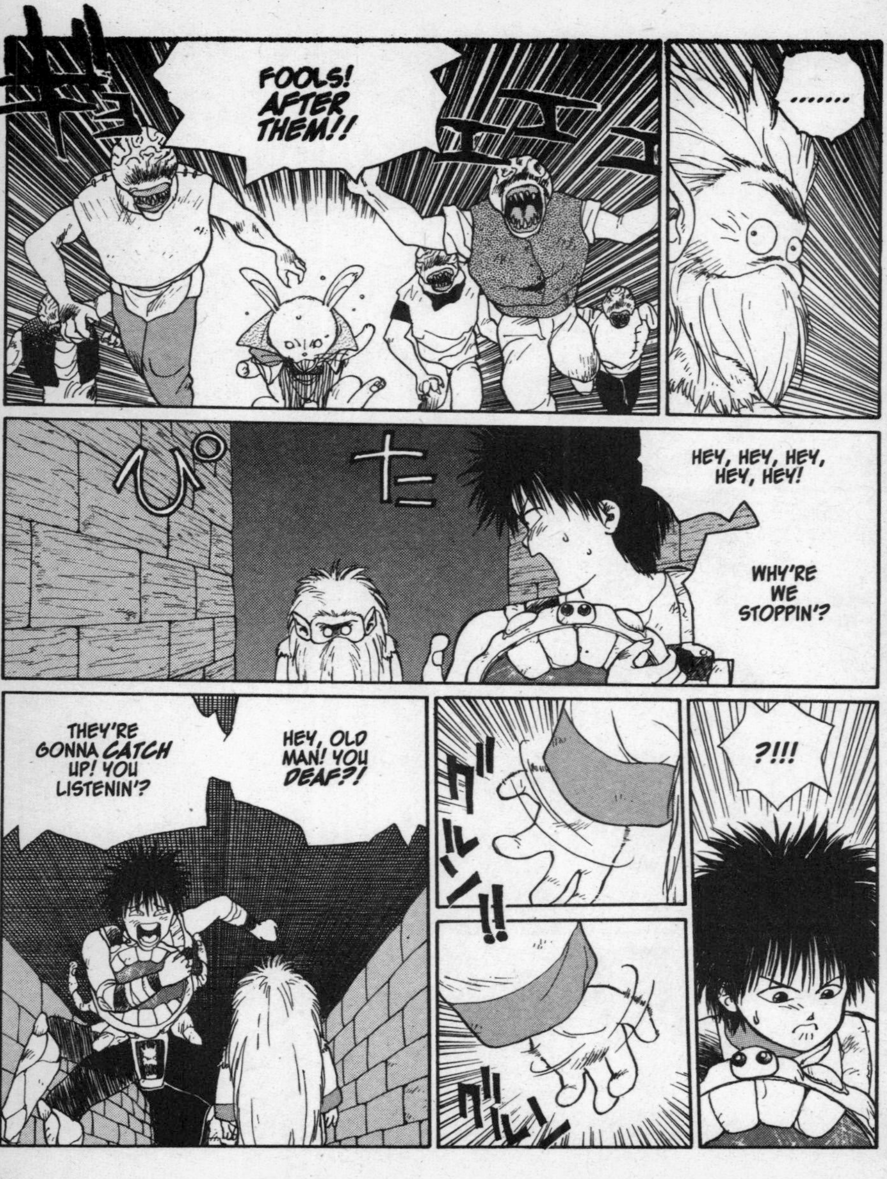
FOOLS! AFTER THEM!!
....
HEY, HEY, HEY, HEY, HEY!
WHY'RE WE STOPPIN'?
THEY'RE GONNA CATCH UP! YOU LISTENIN'?
HEY, OLD MAN! YOU DEAF?!
?!!!

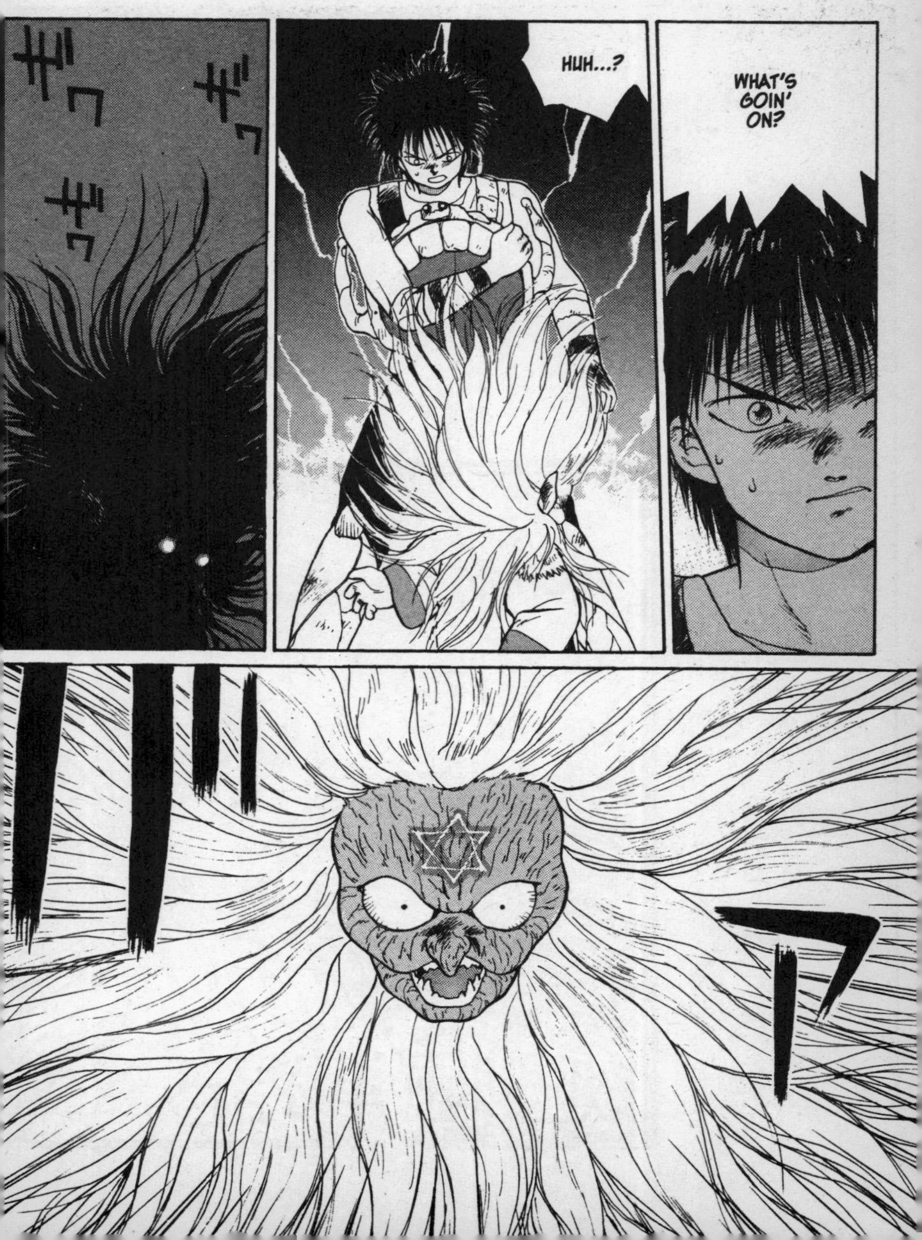
ギク
ギク
ギク
HUH...?
WHAT'S GOIN' ON?

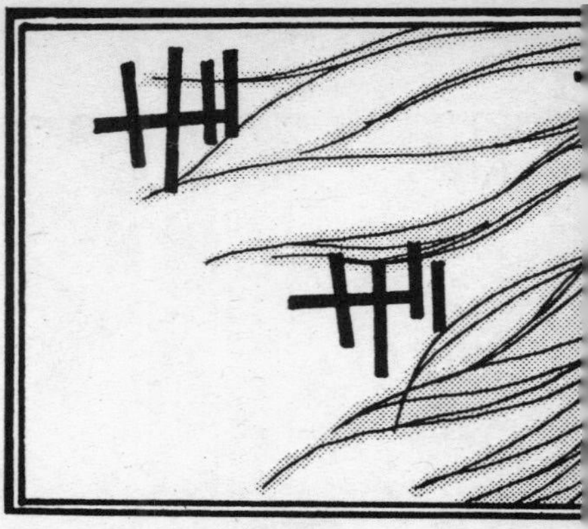
ザ
ザ

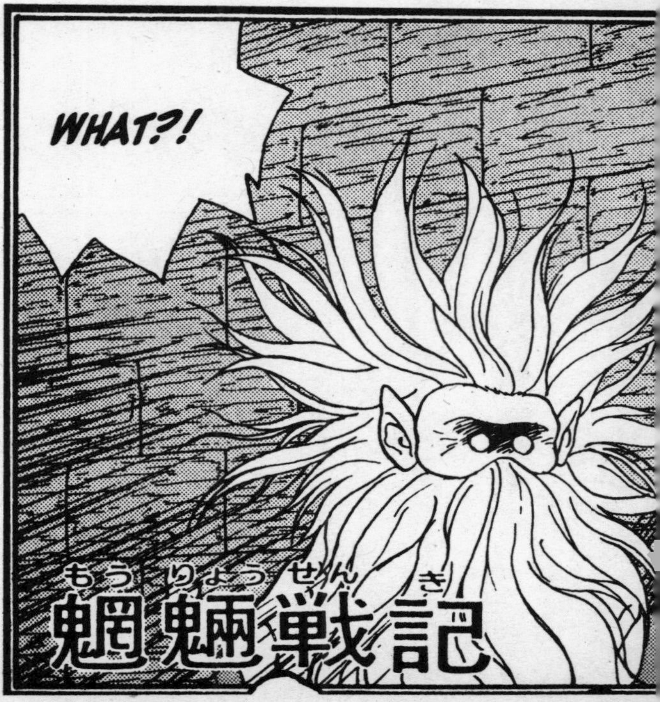
WHAT?!
魍魎戦記
もうりょうせんき

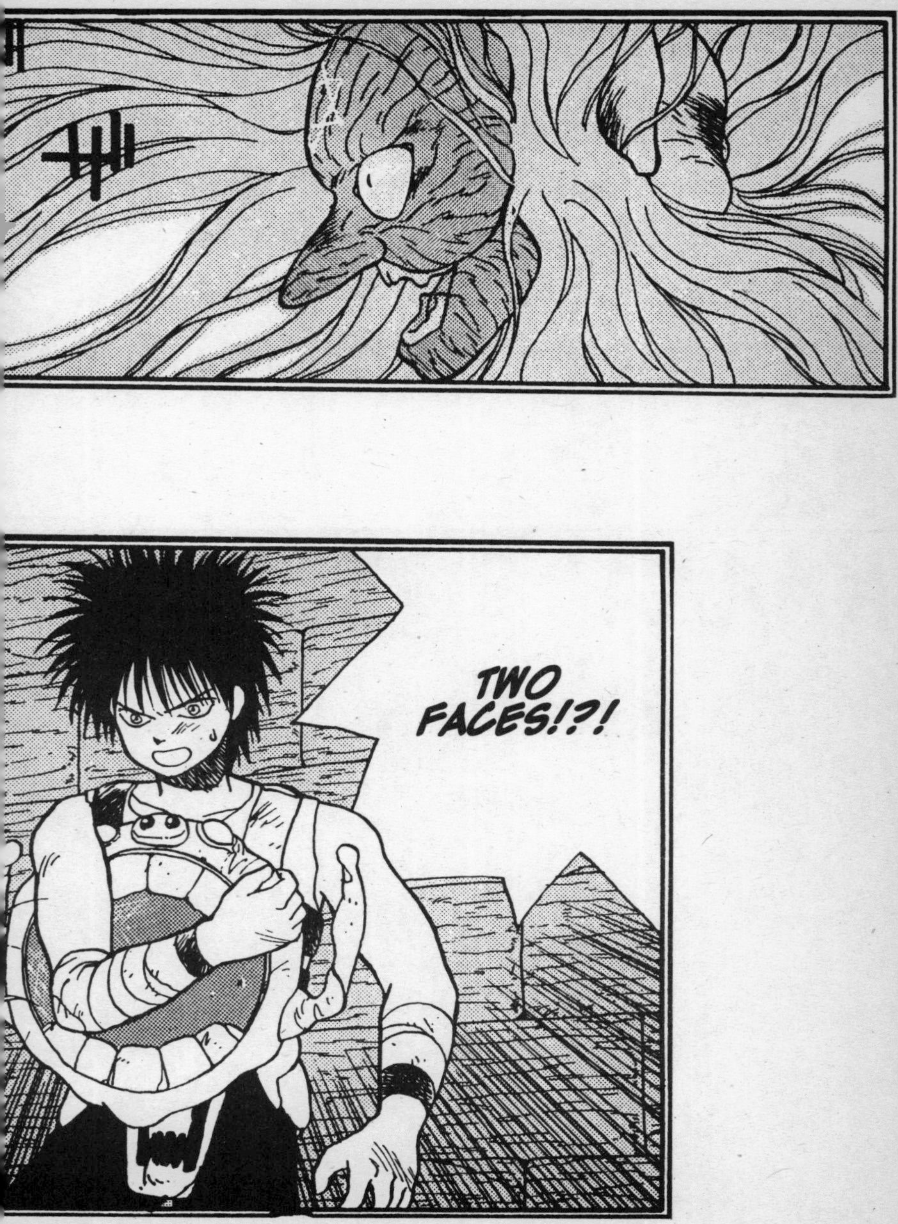
TWO FACES!?!

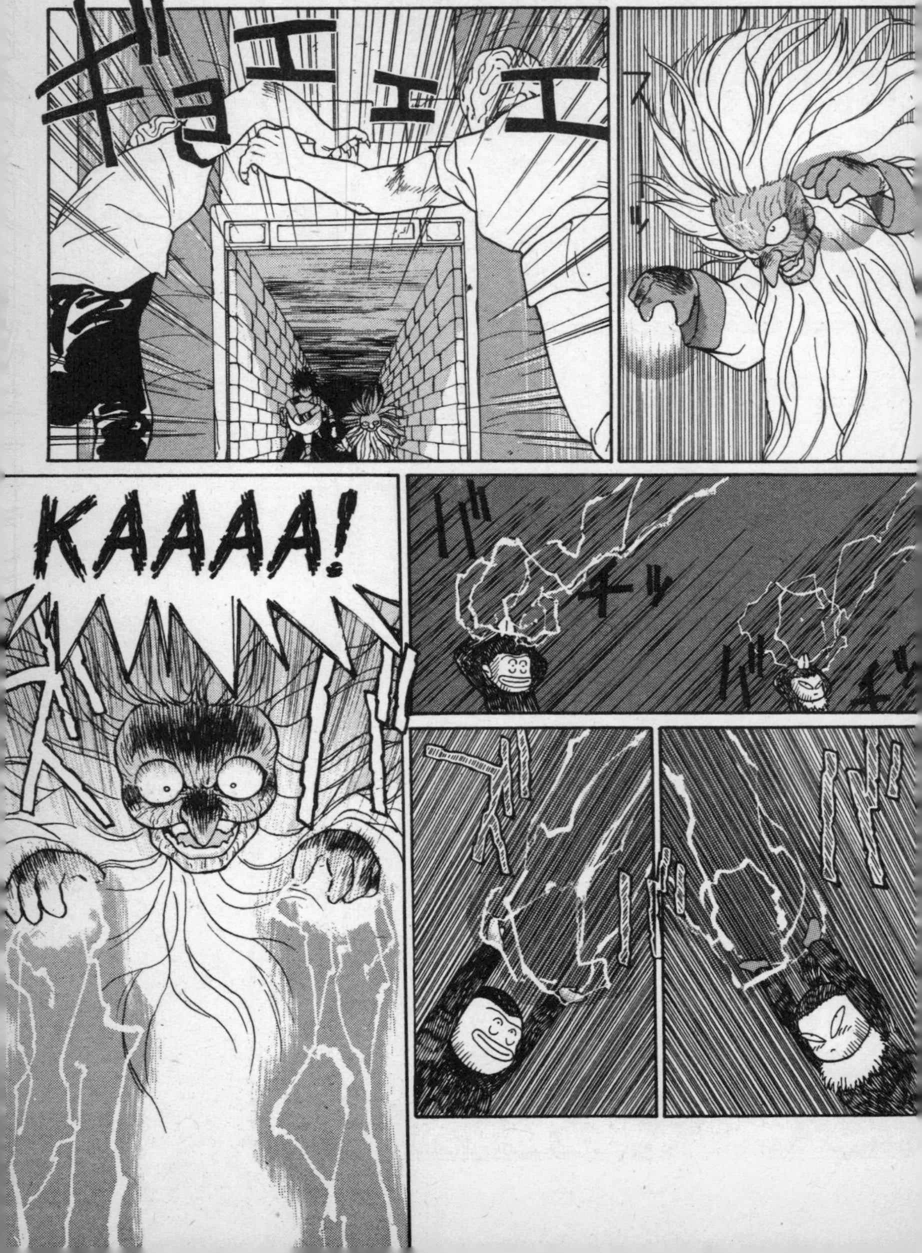
ギョエェエ
KAAAA!
バチッ
バチッ

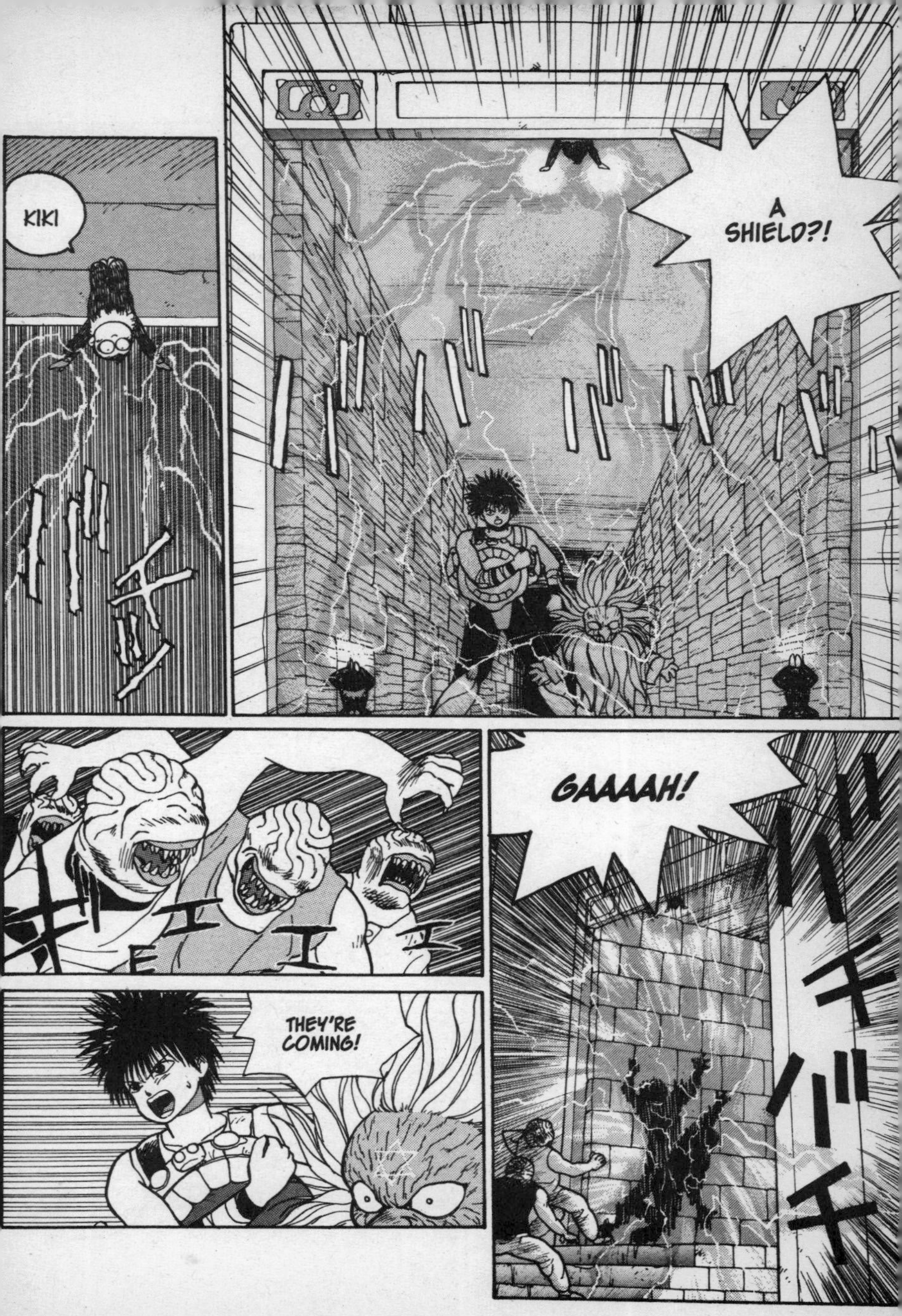
A SHIELD?!
KIKI
GAAAAH!
THEY'RE COMING!

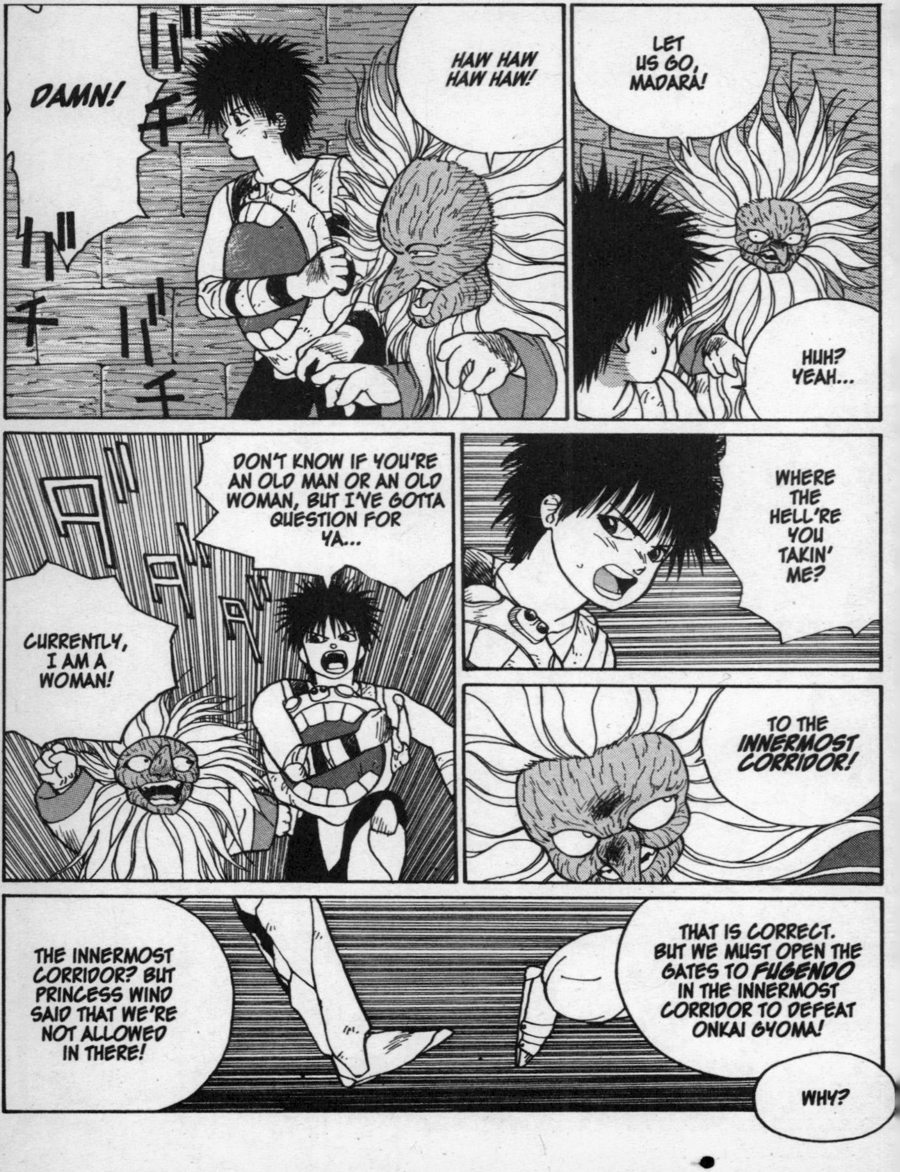
DAMN!
バチ
バチ
バチ
HAW HAW HAW HAW!
LET US GO, MADARA!
HUH? YEAH...
DON'T KNOW IF YOU'RE AN OLD MAN OR AN OLD WOMAN, BUT I'VE GOTTA QUESTION FOR YA...
CURRENTLY, I AM A WOMAN!
WHERE THE HELL'RE YOU TAKIN' ME?
TO THE *INNERMOST CORRIDOR!*
THE INNERMOST CORRIDOR? BUT PRINCESS WIND SAID THAT WE'RE NOT ALLOWED IN THERE!
THAT IS CORRECT. BUT WE MUST OPEN THE GATES TO *FUGENDO* IN THE INNERMOST CORRIDOR TO DEFEAT ONKAI GYOMA!
WHY?

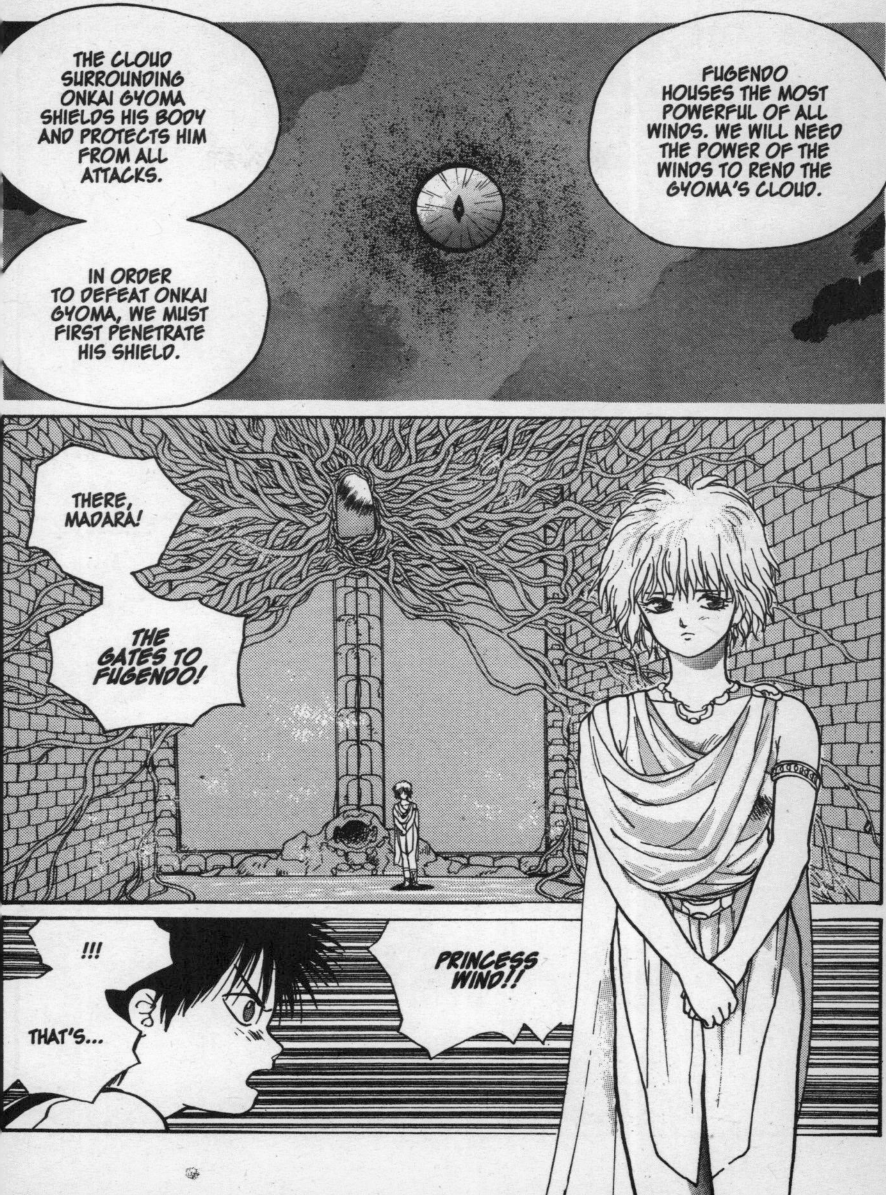
FUGENDO HOUSES THE MOST POWERFUL OF ALL WINDS. WE WILL NEED THE POWER OF THE WINDS TO REND THE GYOMA'S CLOUD.
THE CLOUD SURROUNDING ONKAI GYOMA SHIELDS HIS BODY AND PROTECTS HIM FROM ALL ATTACKS.
IN ORDER TO DEFEAT ONKAI GYOMA, WE MUST FIRST PENETRATE HIS SHIELD.
THERE, MADARA!
THE GATES TO FUGENDO!
PRINCESS WIND!!
!!!
THAT'S...

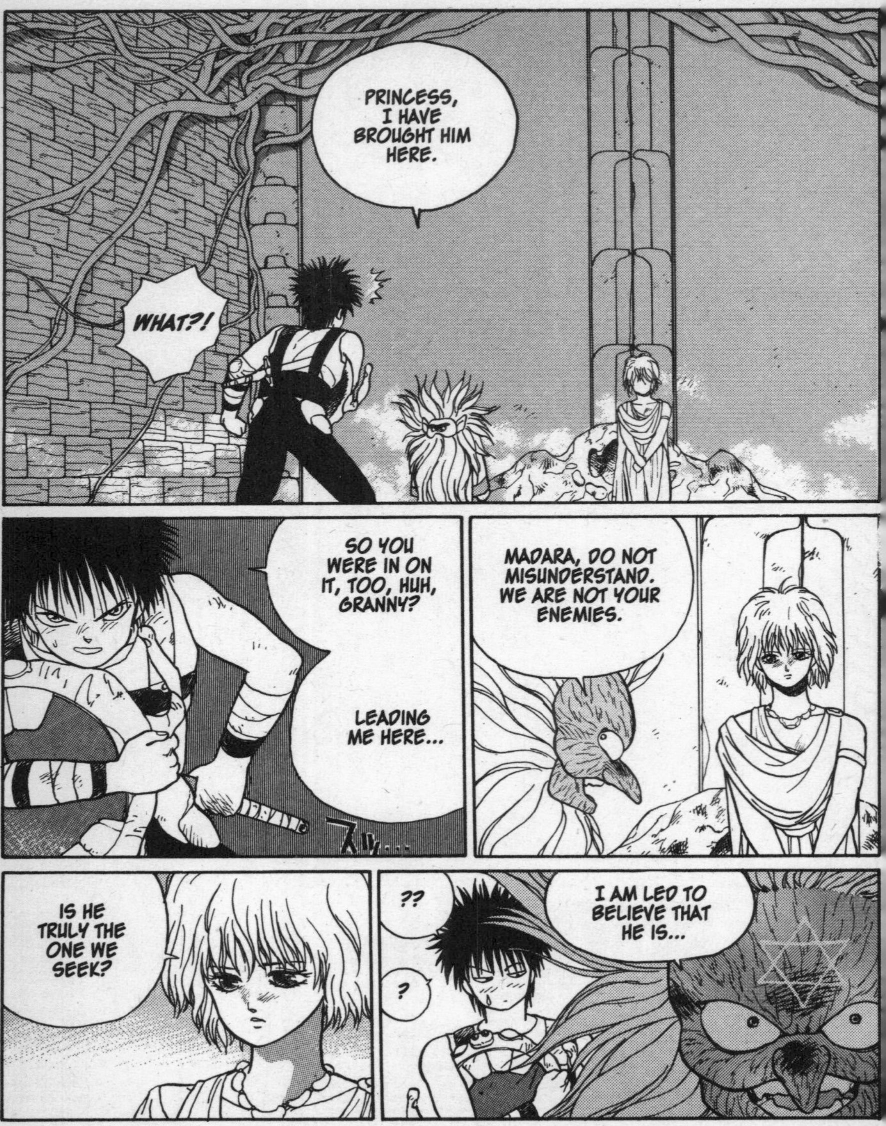
PRINCESS, I HAVE BROUGHT HIM HERE.
WHAT?!
SO YOU WERE IN ON IT, TOO, HUH, GRANNY?
LEADING ME HERE...
MADARA, DO NOT MISUNDERSTAND. WE ARE NOT YOUR ENEMIES.
IS HE TRULY THE ONE WE SEEK?
??
?
I AM LED TO BELIEVE THAT HE IS...

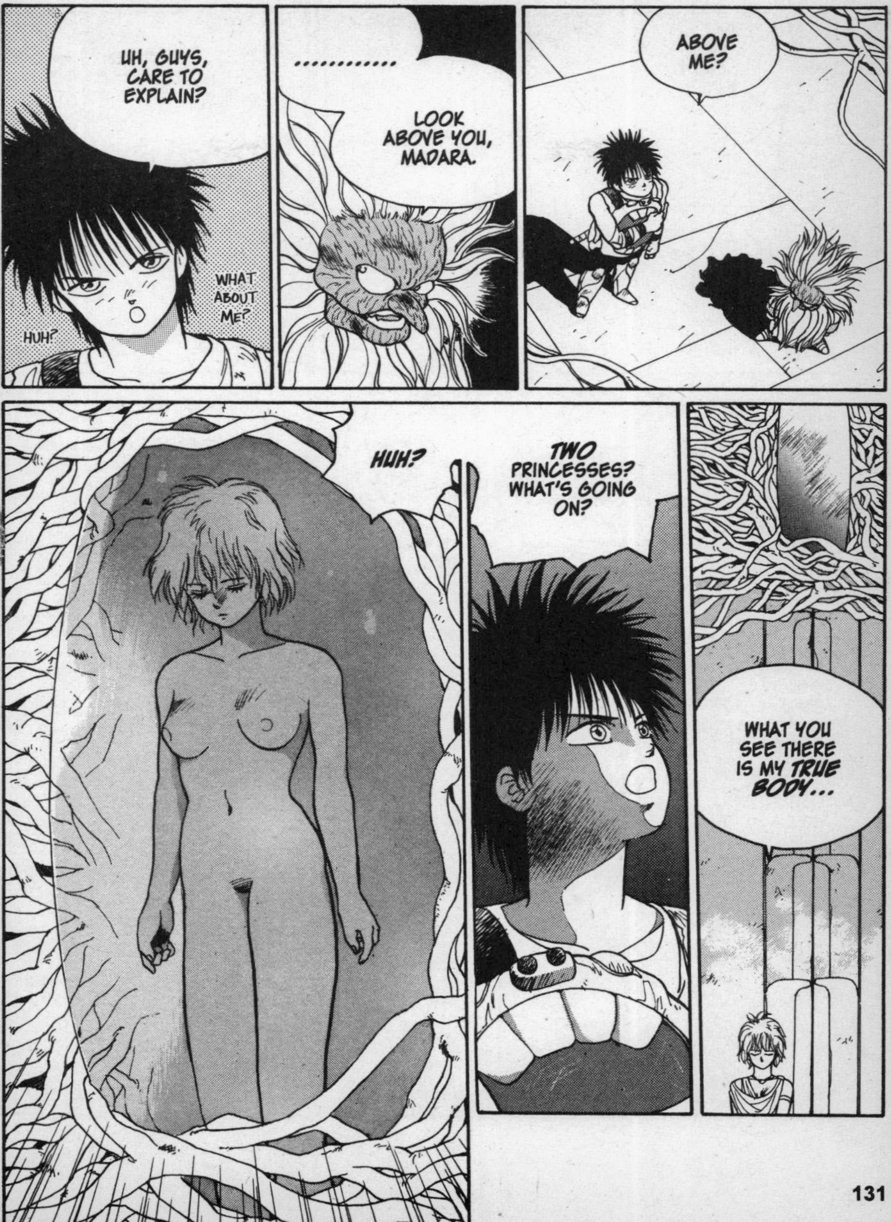
UH, GUYS, CARE TO EXPLAIN?
HUH?
WHAT ABOUT ME?
....
LOOK ABOVE YOU, MADARA.
ABOVE ME?
HUH?
TWO PRINCESSES? WHAT'S GOING ON?
WHAT YOU SEE THERE IS MY *TRUE BODY*...

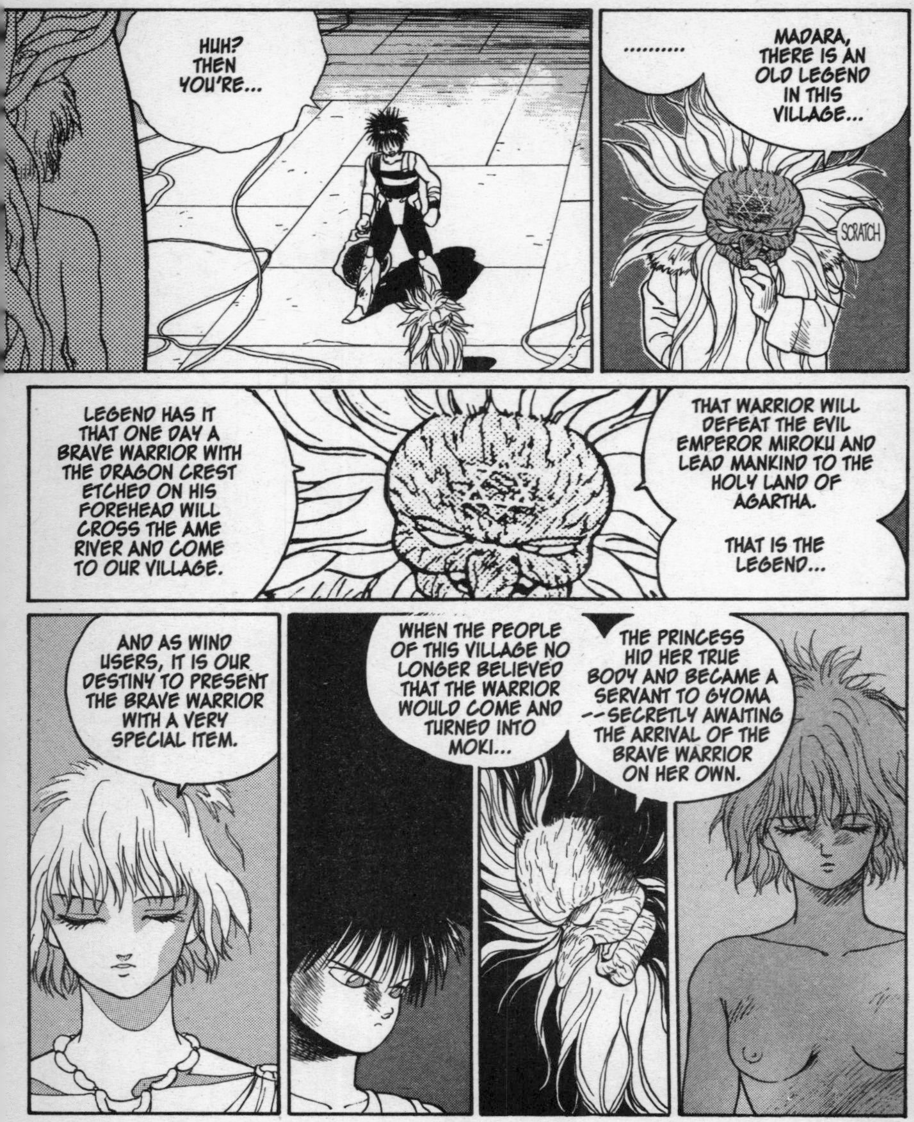
HUH? THEN YOU'RE...
....
MADARA, THERE IS AN OLD LEGEND IN THIS VILLAGE...
SCRATCH
LEGEND HAS IT THAT ONE DAY A BRAVE WARRIOR WITH THE DRAGON CREST ETCHED ON HIS FOREHEAD WILL CROSS THE AME RIVER AND COME TO OUR VILLAGE.
THAT WARRIOR WILL DEFEAT THE EVIL EMPEROR MIROKU AND LEAD MANKIND TO THE HOLY LAND OF AGARTHA.
THAT IS THE LEGEND...
AND AS WIND USERS, IT IS OUR DESTINY TO PRESENT THE BRAVE WARRIOR WITH A VERY SPECIAL ITEM.
WHEN THE PEOPLE OF THIS VILLAGE NO LONGER BELIEVED THAT THE WARRIOR WOULD COME AND TURNED INTO MOKI...
THE PRINCESS HID HER TRUE BODY AND BECAME A SERVANT TO GYOMA --SECRETLY AWAITING THE ARRIVAL OF THE BRAVE WARRIOR ON HER OWN.

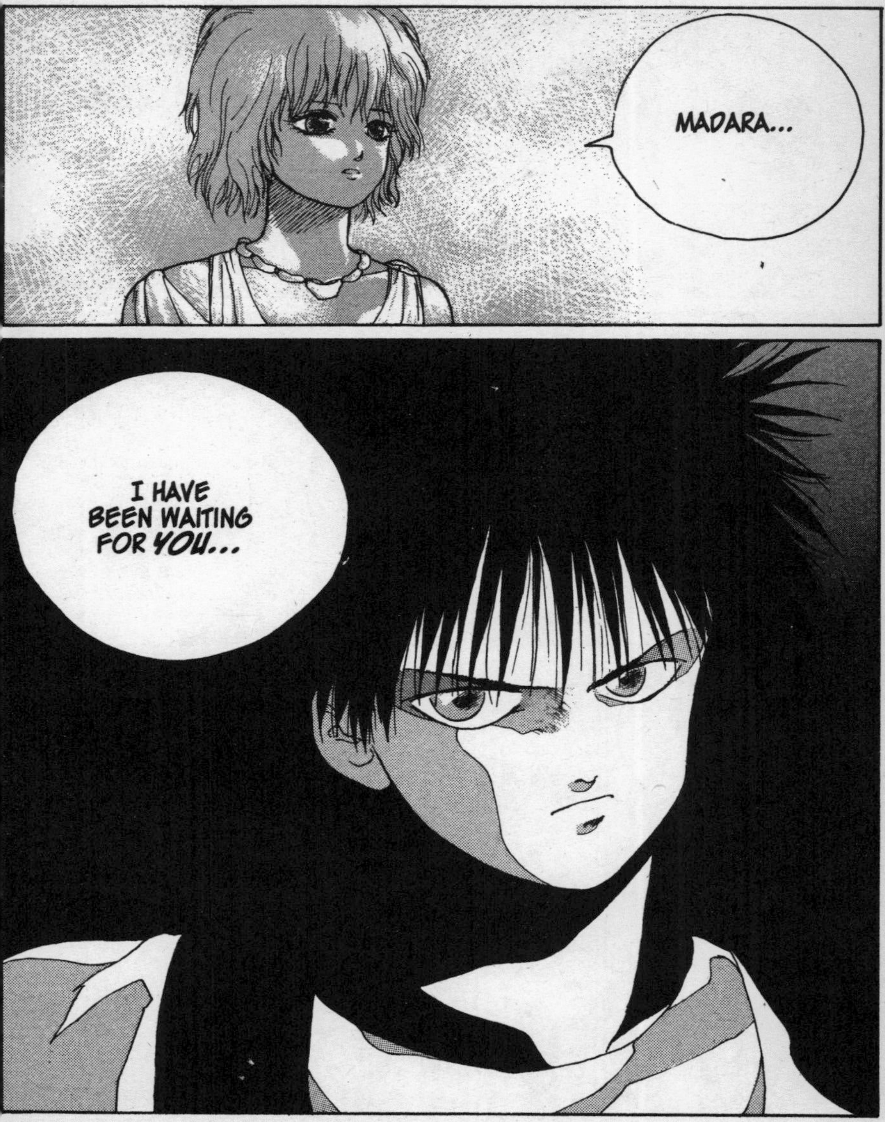
MADARA...
I HAVE BEEN WAITING FOR YOU...

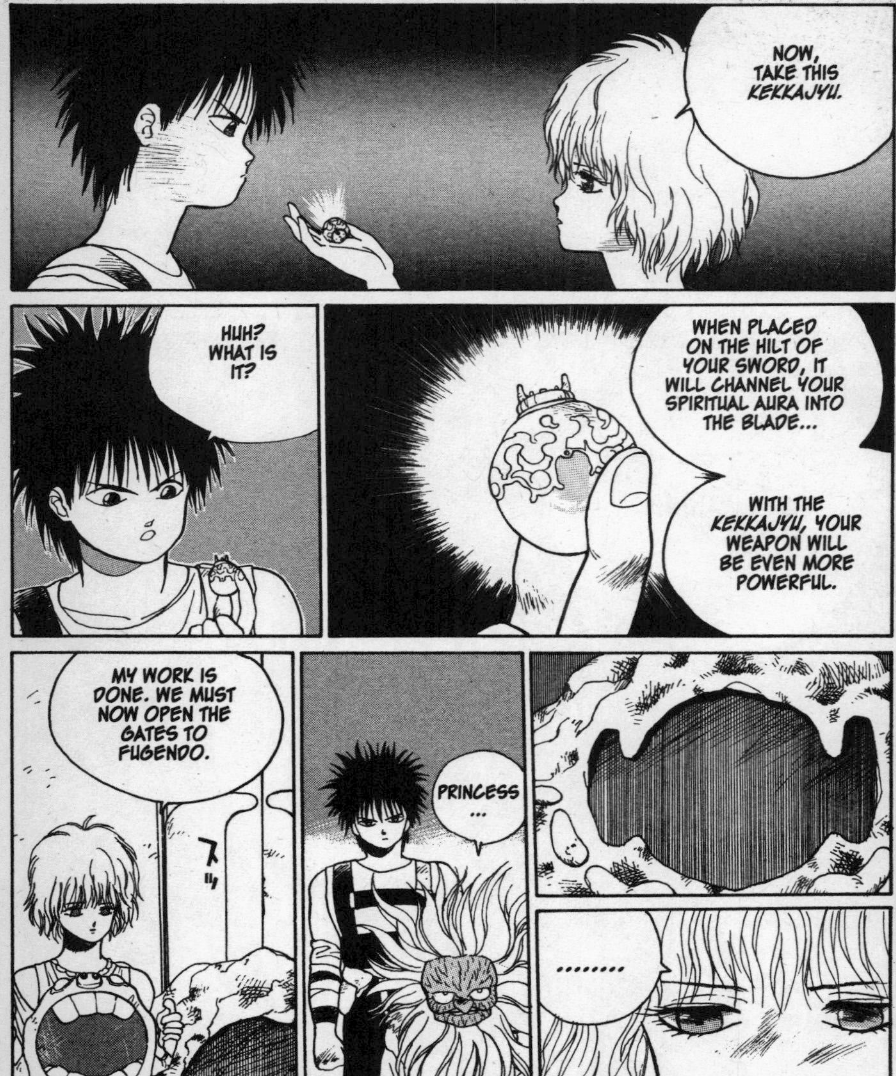
NOW, TAKE THIS KEKKAJYU.
HUH? WHAT IS IT?
WHEN PLACED ON THE HILT OF YOUR SWORD, IT WILL CHANNEL YOUR SPIRITUAL AURA INTO THE BLADE...
WITH THE KEKKAJYU, YOUR WEAPON WILL BE EVEN MORE POWERFUL.
MY WORK IS DONE. WE MUST NOW OPEN THE GATES TO FUGENDO.
PRINCESS ...
....

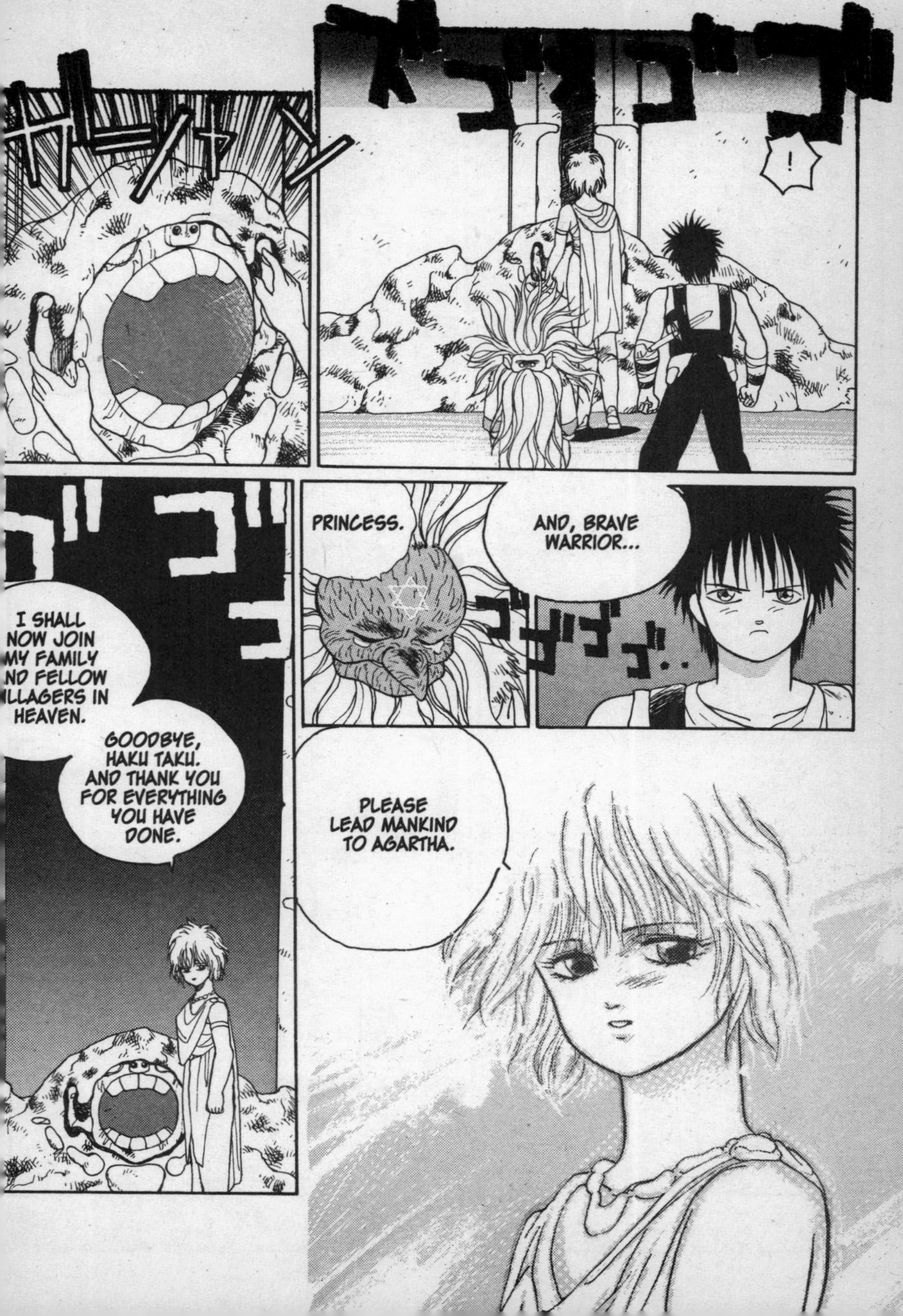
!
PRINCESS.
AND, BRAVE WARRIOR...
PLEASE LEAD MANKIND TO AGARTHA.
I SHALL NOW JOIN MY FAMILY ND FELLOW LLAGERS IN HEAVEN.
GOODBYE, HAKU TAKU. AND THANK YOU FOR EVERYTHING YOU HAVE DONE.

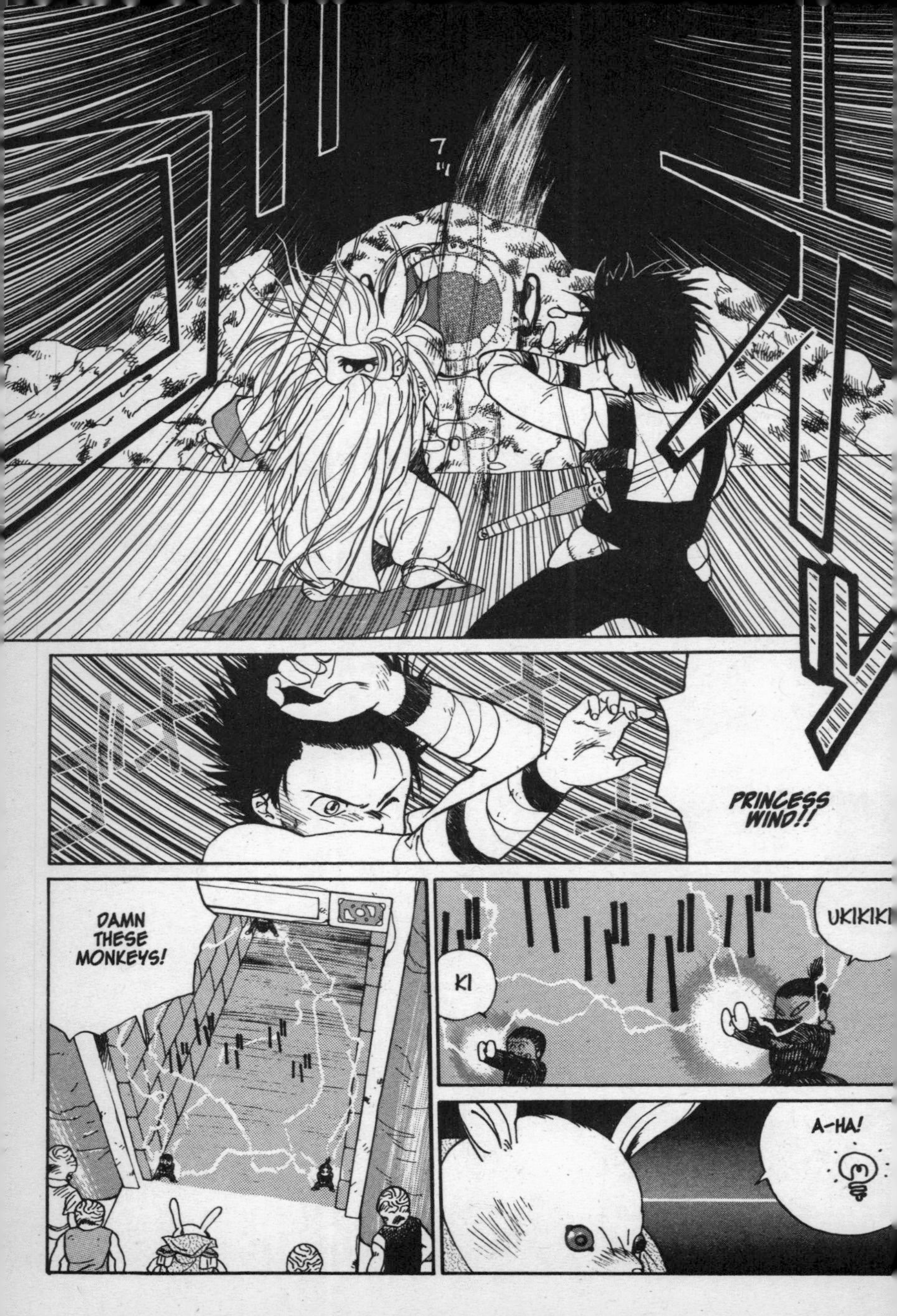
ブッ
PRINCESS WIND!!
DAMN THESE MONKEYS!
UKIKIKI
KI
A-HA!

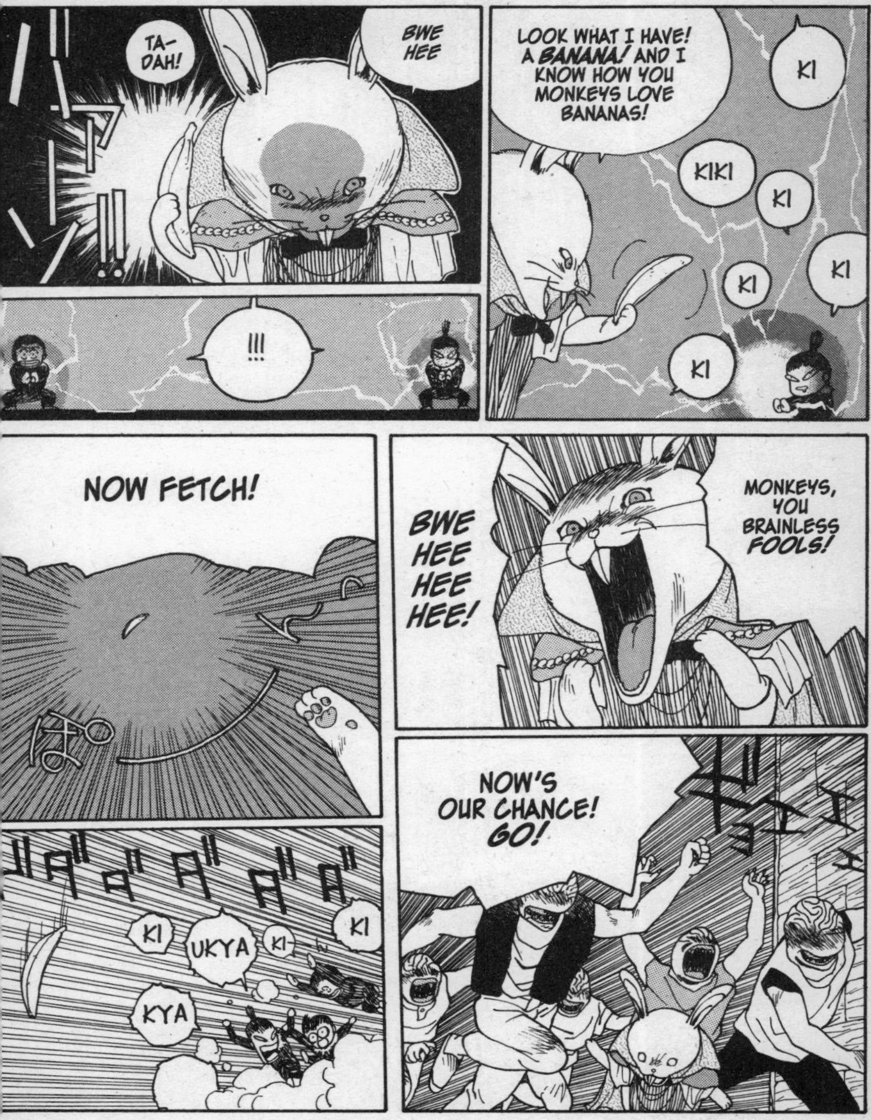
TA-DAH!
BWE HEE
LOOK WHAT I HAVE! A BANANA! AND I KNOW HOW YOU MONKEYS LOVE BANANAS!
KI
KIKI
KI
KI
KI
KI
!!!
NOW FETCH!
BWE HEE HEE HEE!
MONKEYS, YOU BRAINLESS FOOLS!
KI
UKYA
KI-
KI
KYA
NOW'S OUR CHANCE! GO!

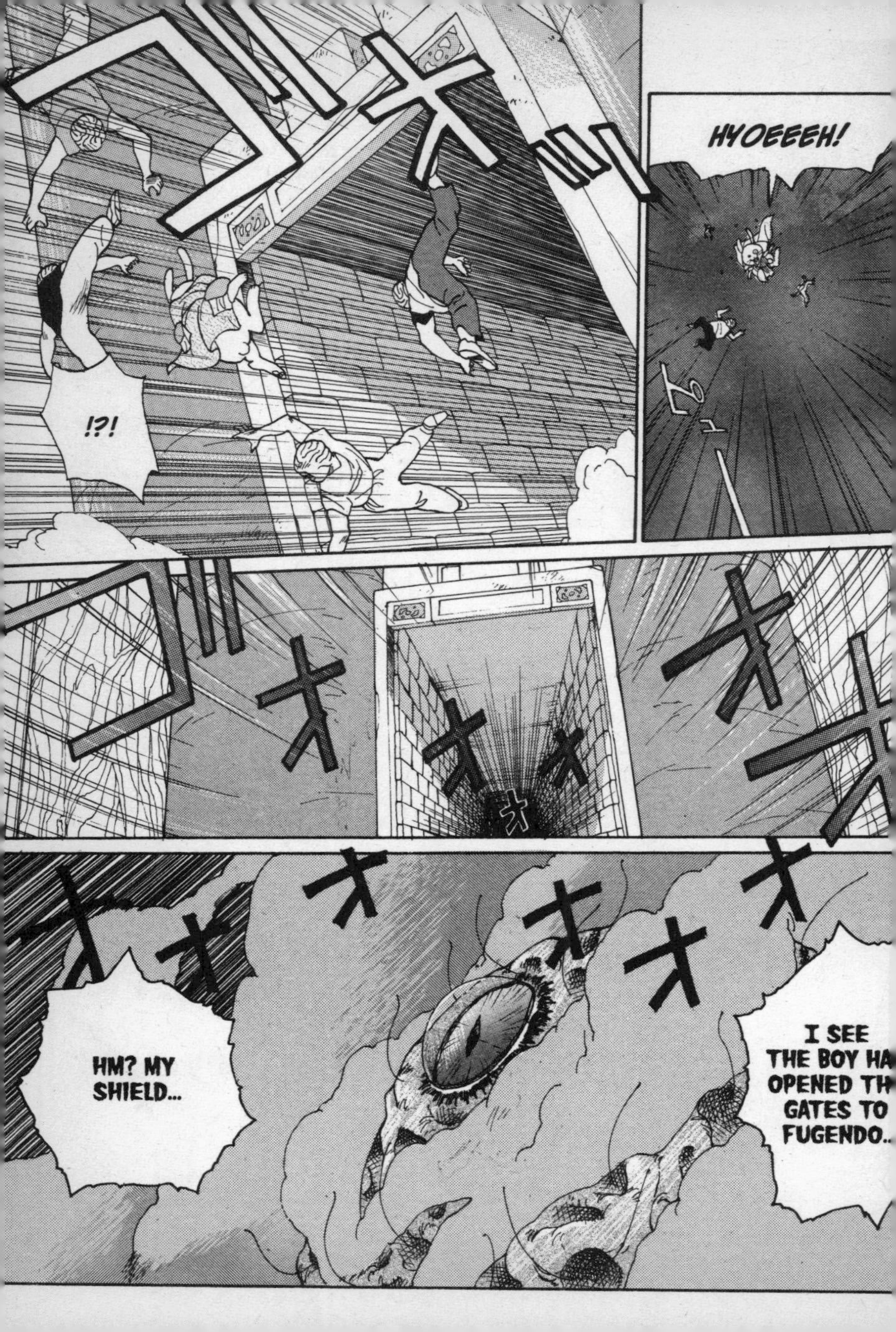

HYOEEEH!
!?!
I SEE THE BOY HA OPENED TH GATES TO FUGENDO..
HM? MY SHIELD...

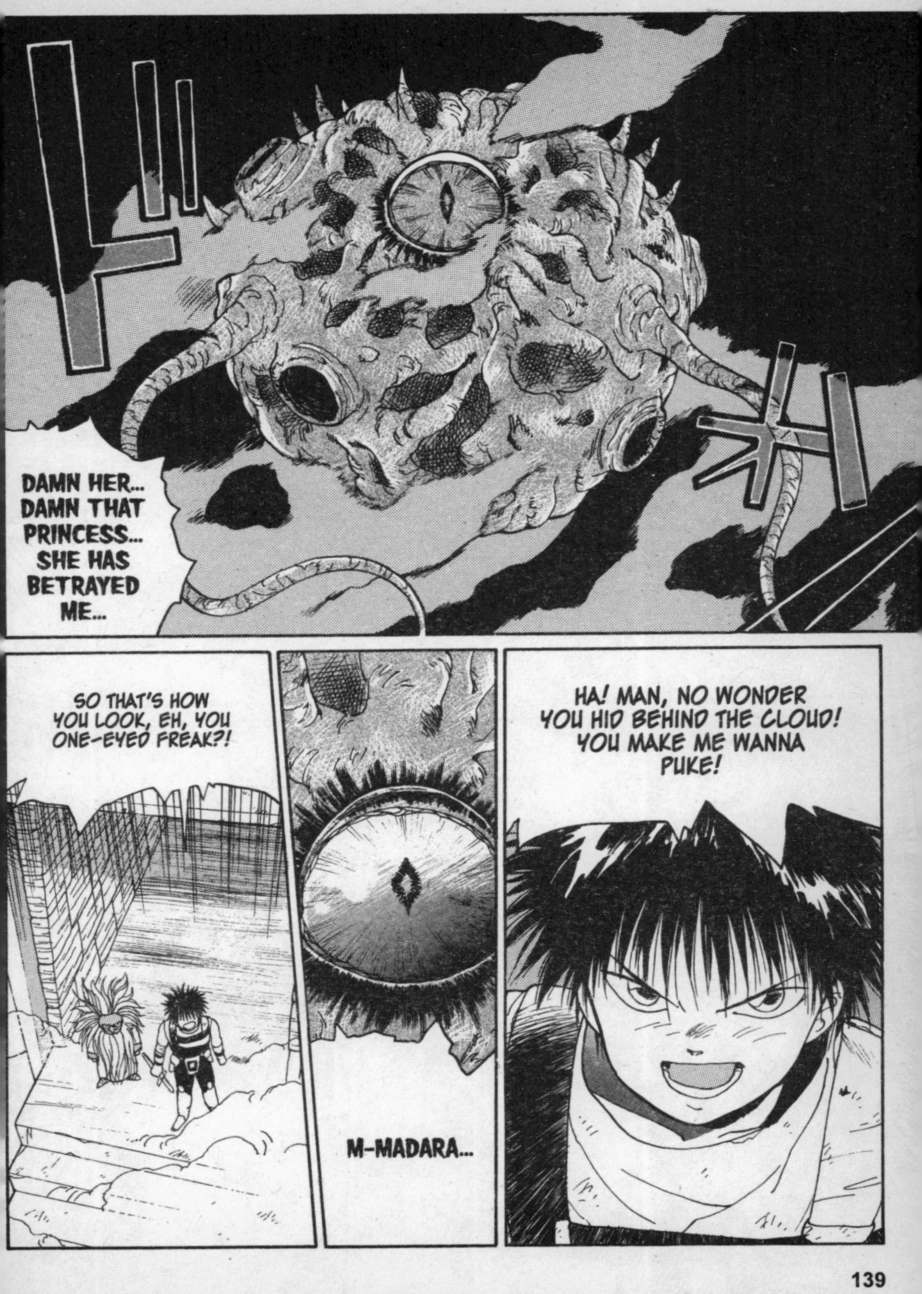
DAMN HER... DAMN THAT PRINCESS... SHE HAS BETRAYED ME...
SO THAT'S HOW YOU LOOK, EH, YOU ONE-EYED FREAK?!
M-MADARA...
HA! MAN, NO WONDER YOU HID BEHIND THE CLOUD! YOU MAKE ME WANNA PUKE!

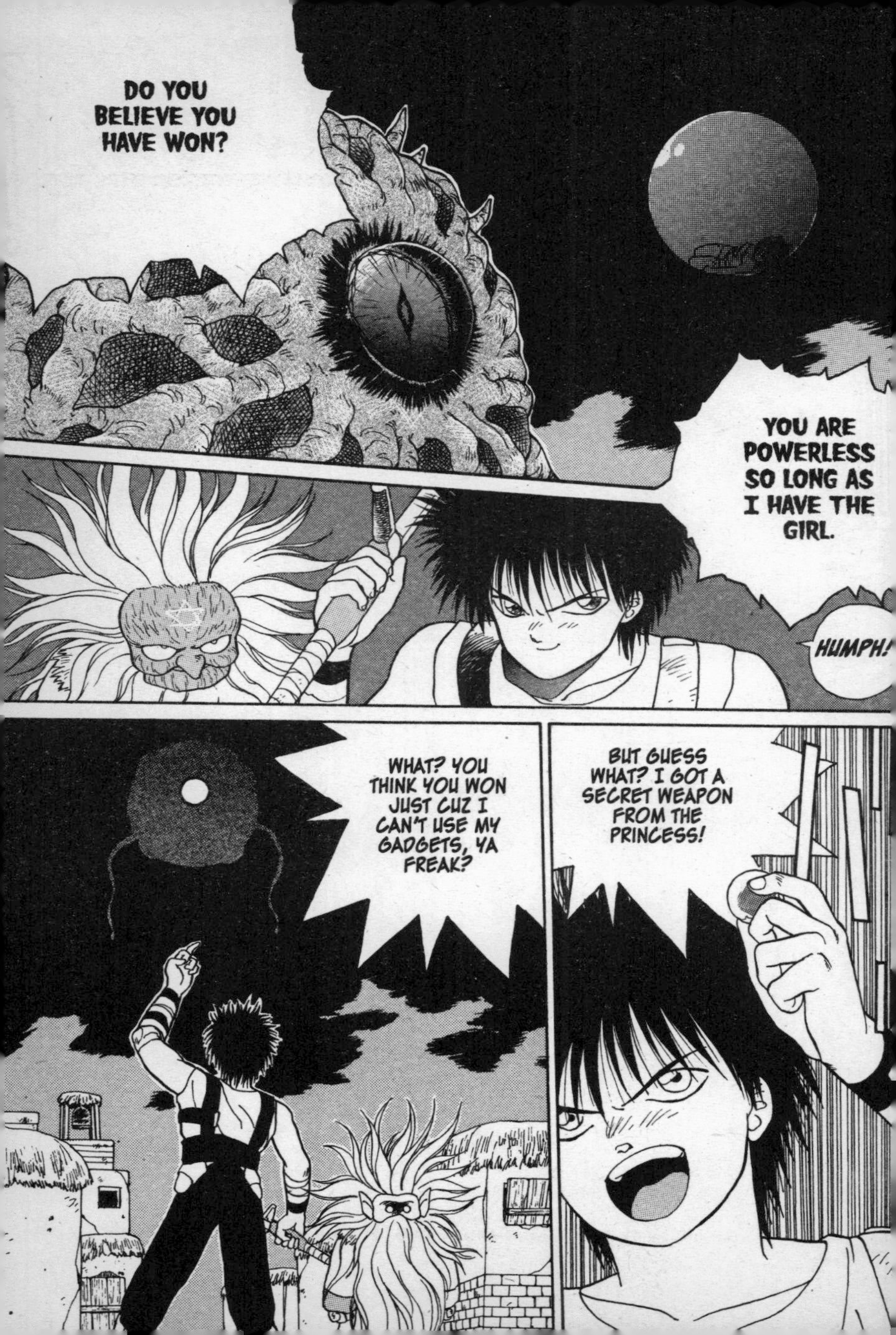

DO YOU BELIEVE YOU HAVE WON?
YOU ARE POWERLESS SO LONG AS I HAVE THE GIRL.
HUMPH!
BUT GUESS WHAT? I GOT A SECRET WEAPON FROM THE PRINCESS!
WHAT? YOU THINK YOU WON JUST CUZ I CAN'T USE MY GADGETS, YA FREAK?

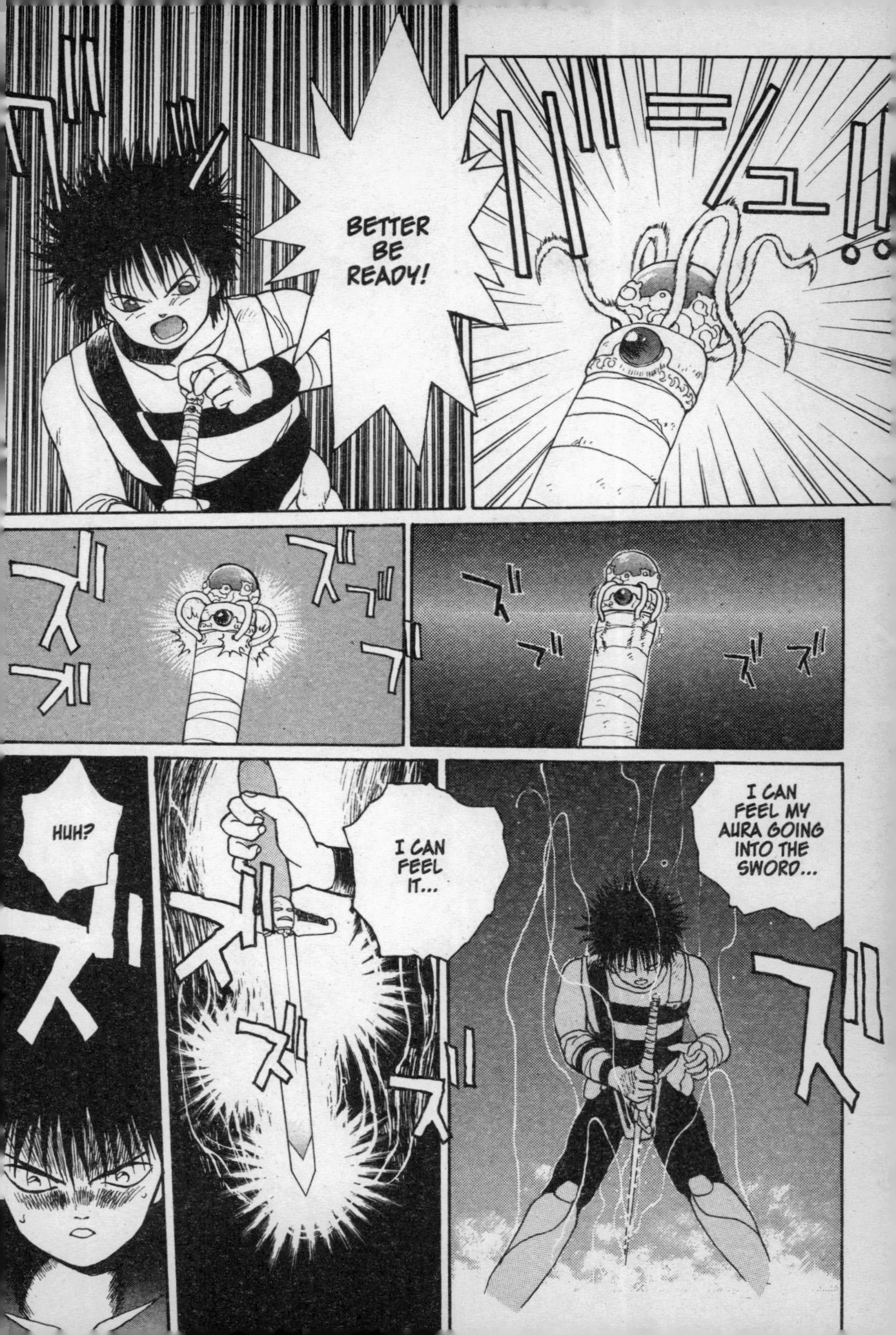

BETTER BE READY!
I CAN FEEL MY AURA GOING INTO THE SWORD...
I CAN FEEL IT...
HUH?

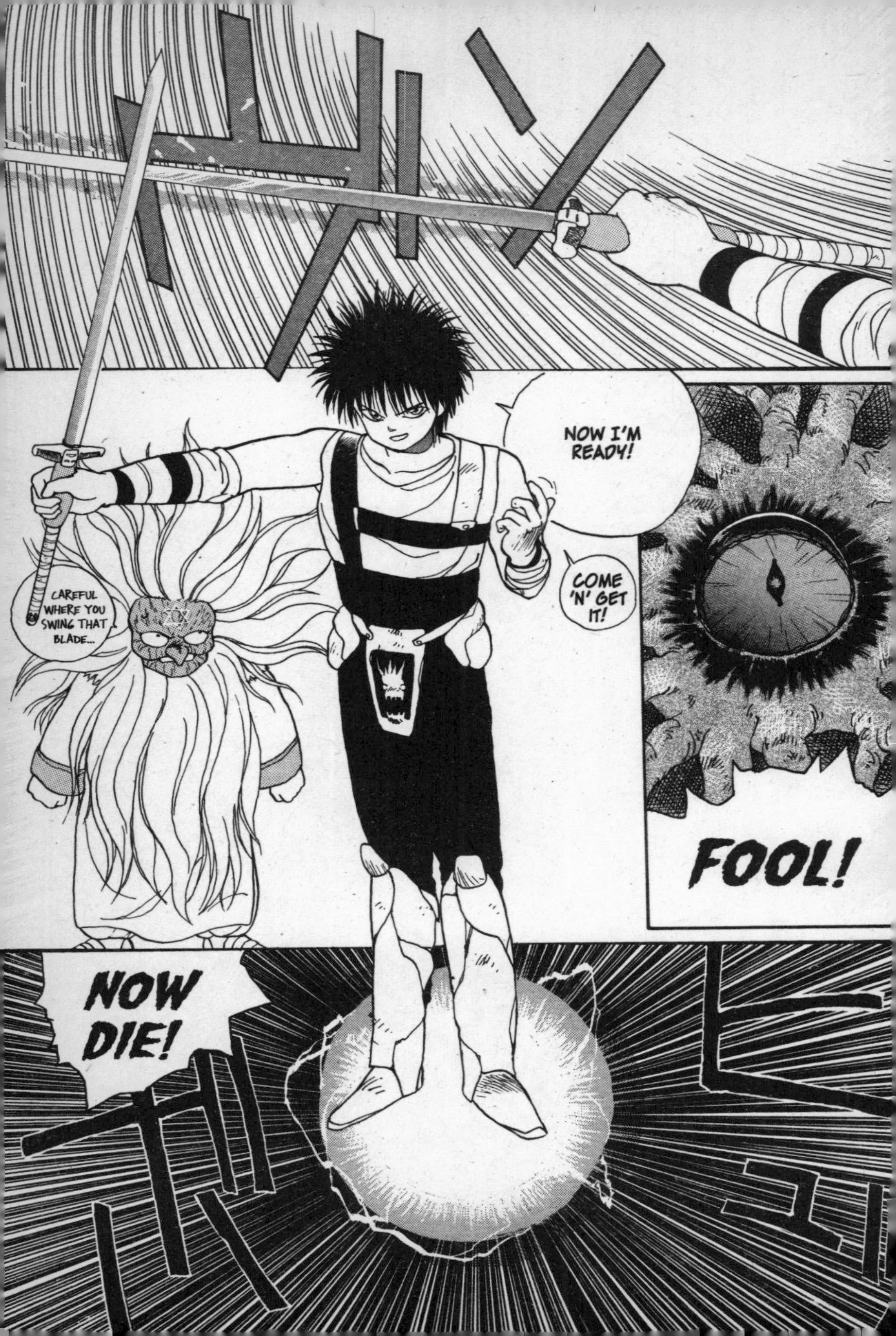
NOW I'M READY!
COME 'N' GET IT!
CAREFUL WHERE YOU SWING THAT BLADE...
FOOL!
NOW DIE!

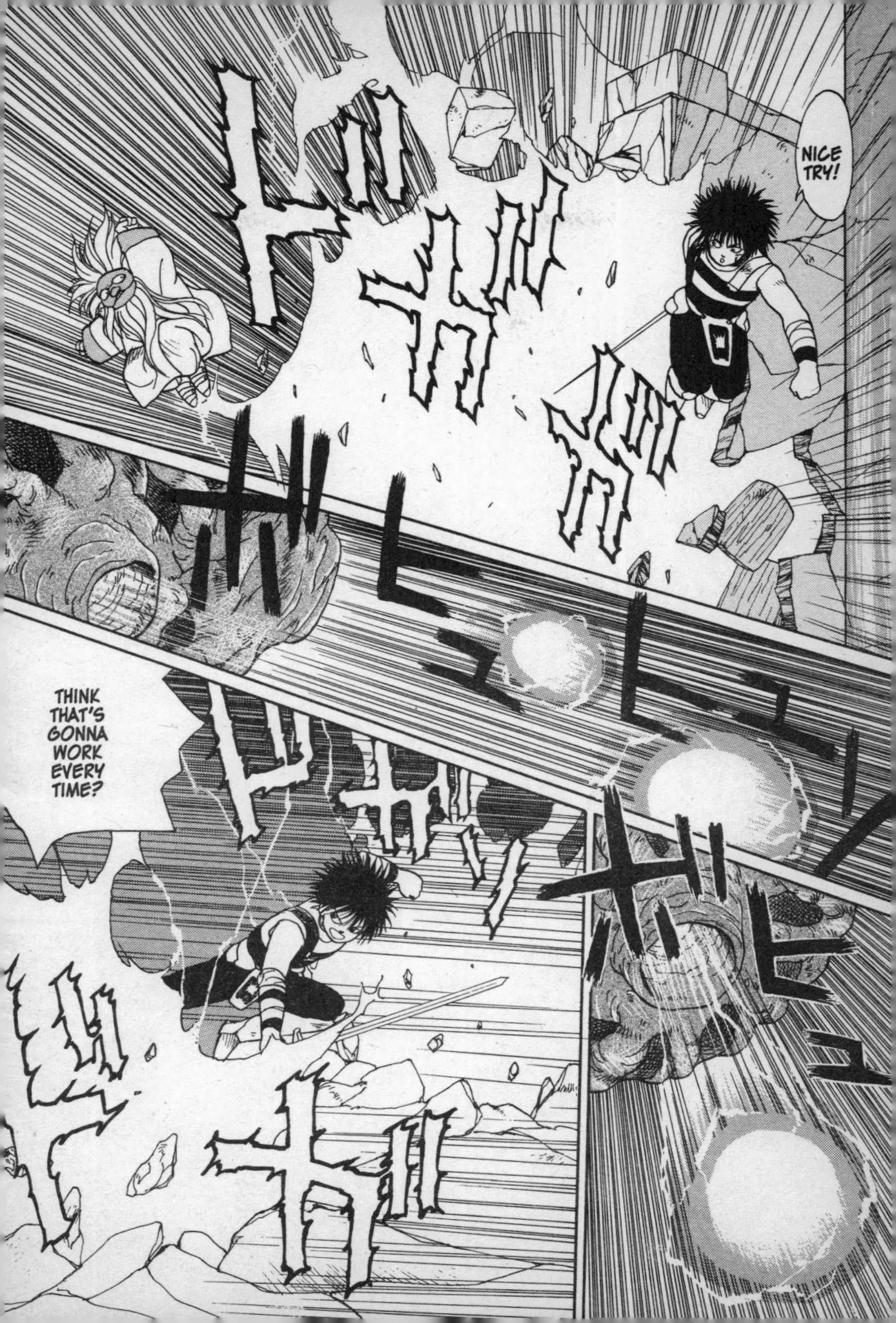
NICE TRY!
THINK THAT'S GONNA WORK EVERY TIME?

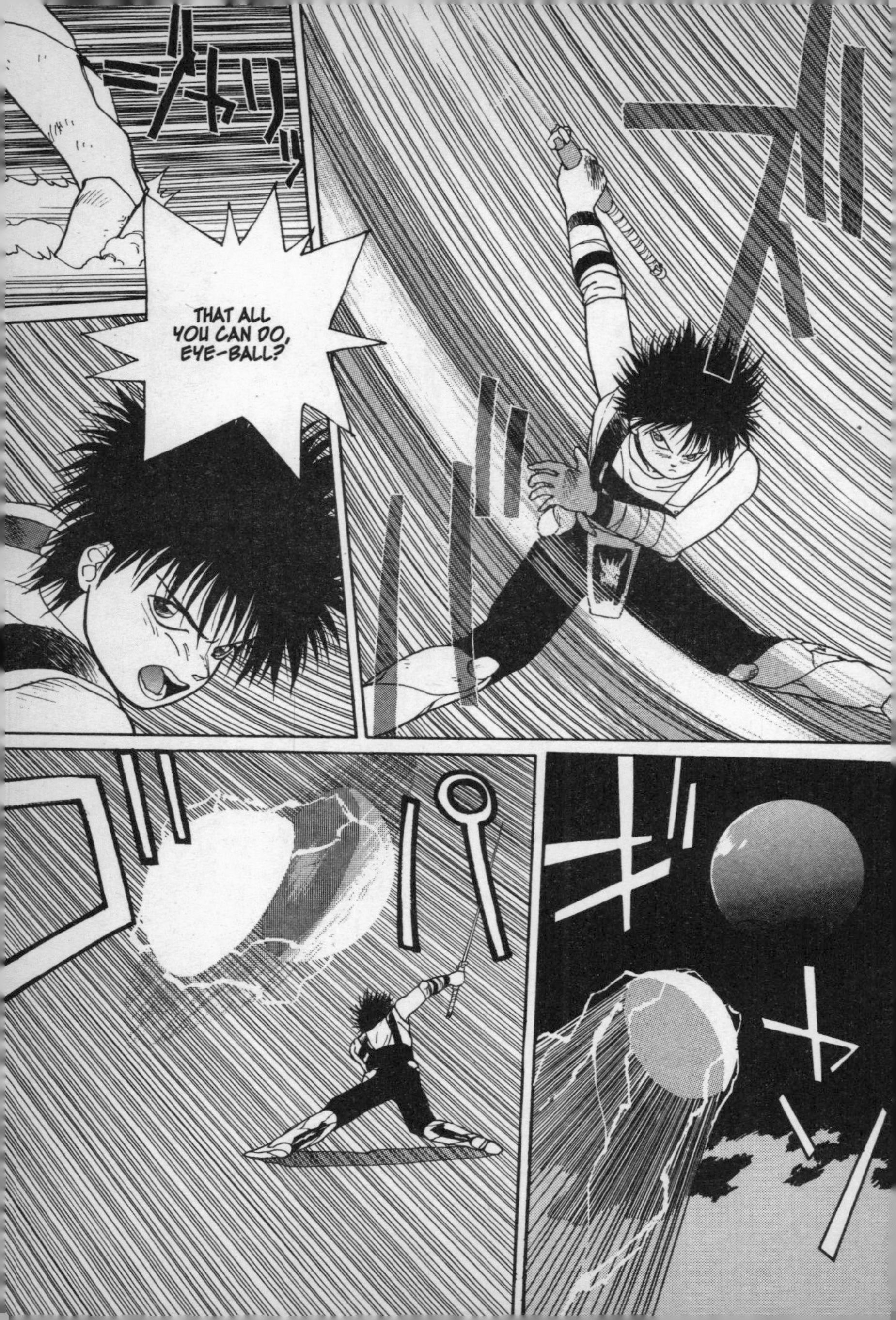

THAT ALL YOU CAN DO, EYE-BALL?

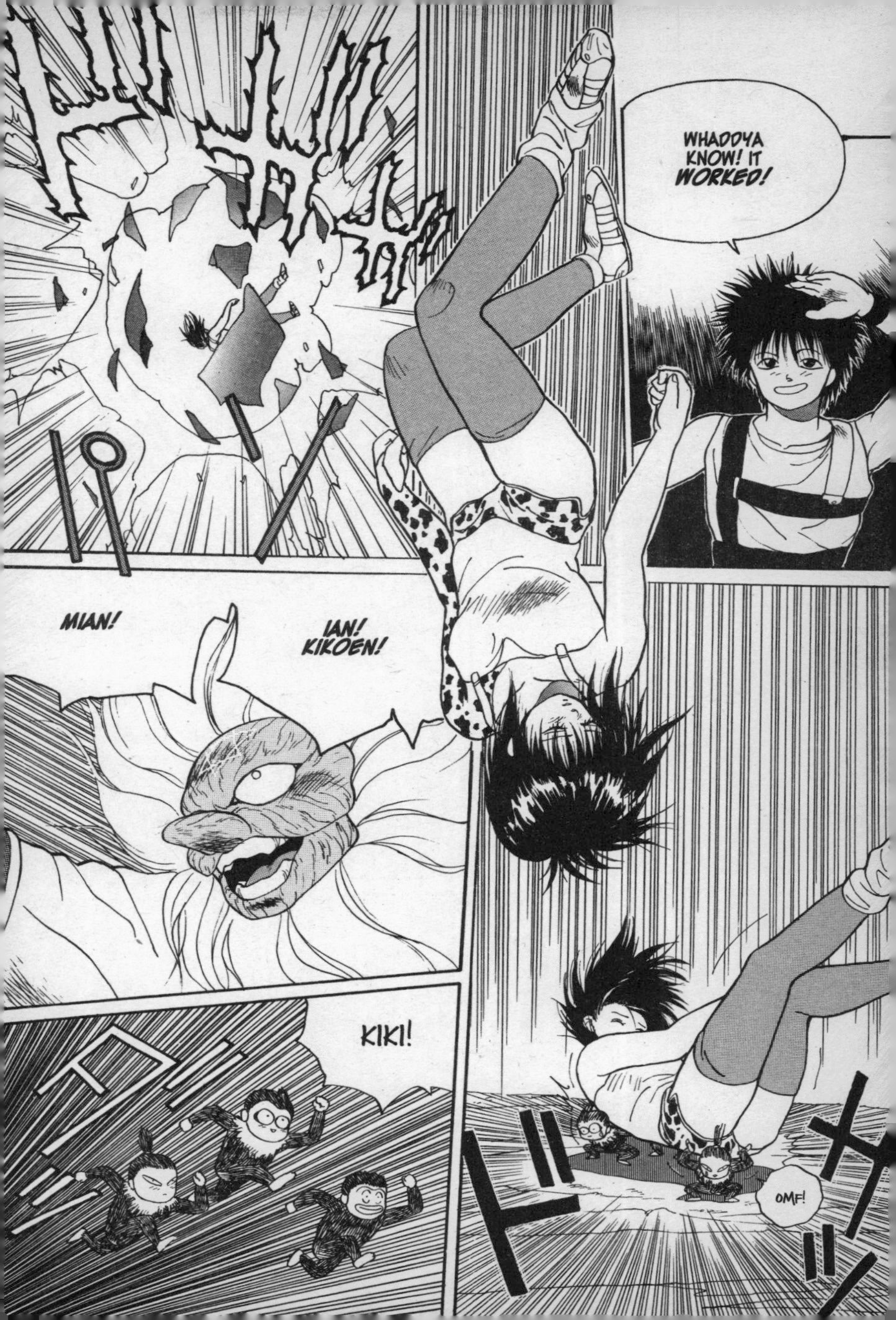
WHADDYA KNOW! IT WORKED!
MIAN!
IAN! KIKOEN!
KIKI!
OMF!

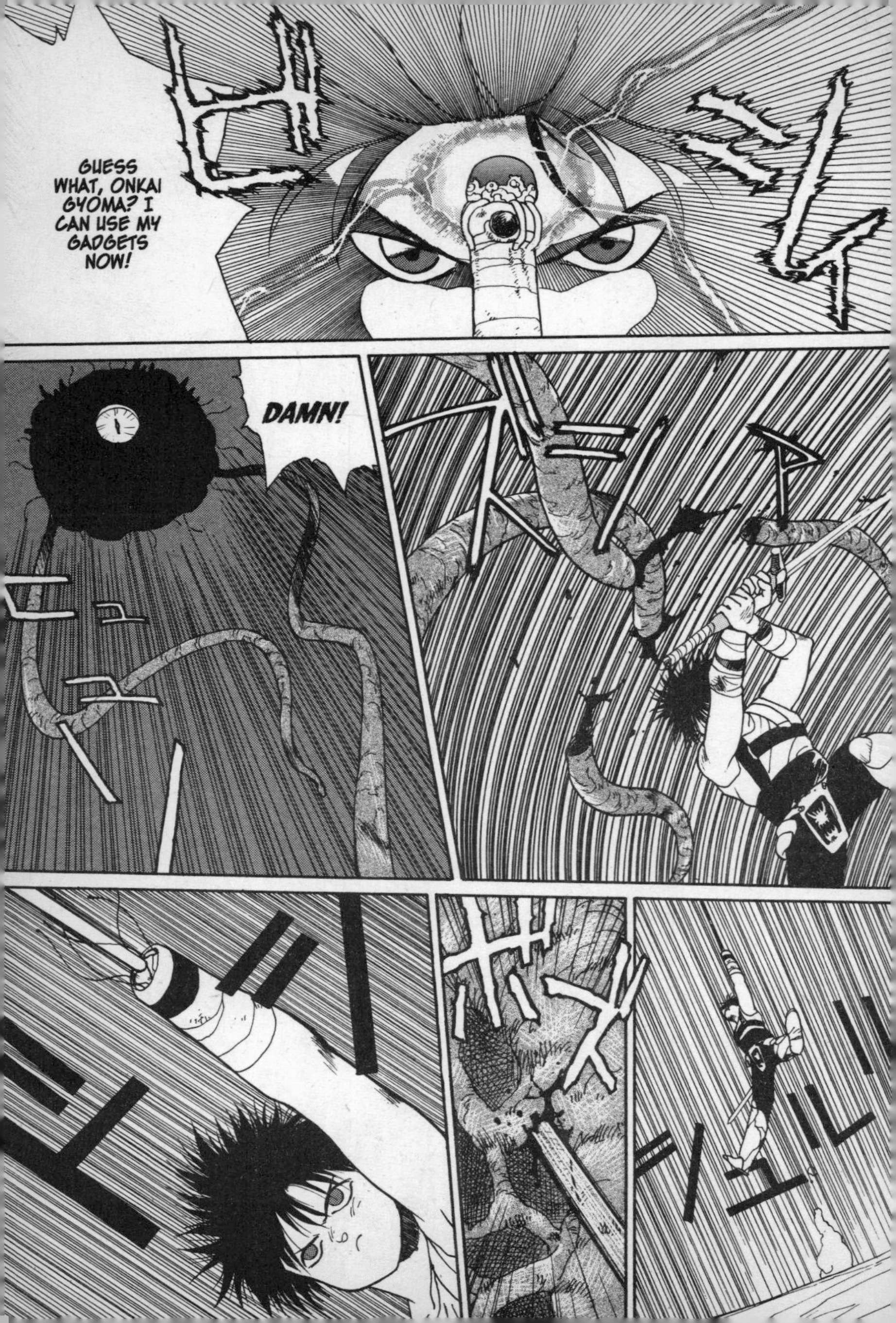
GUESS WHAT, ONKAI GYOMA? I CAN USE MY GADGETS NOW!
DAMN!

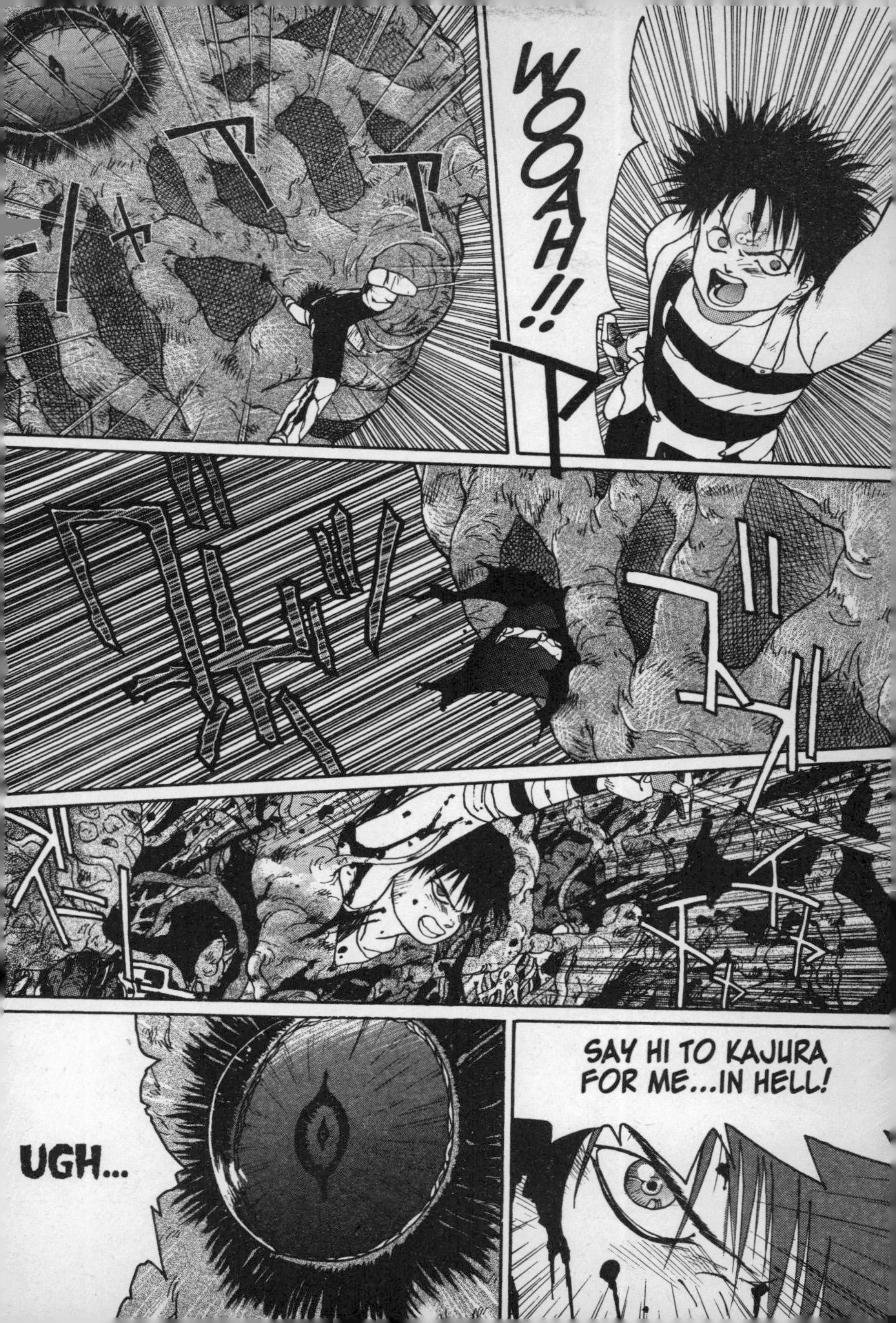
WOOAH!!
SAY HI TO KAJURA FOR ME...IN HELL!
UGH...

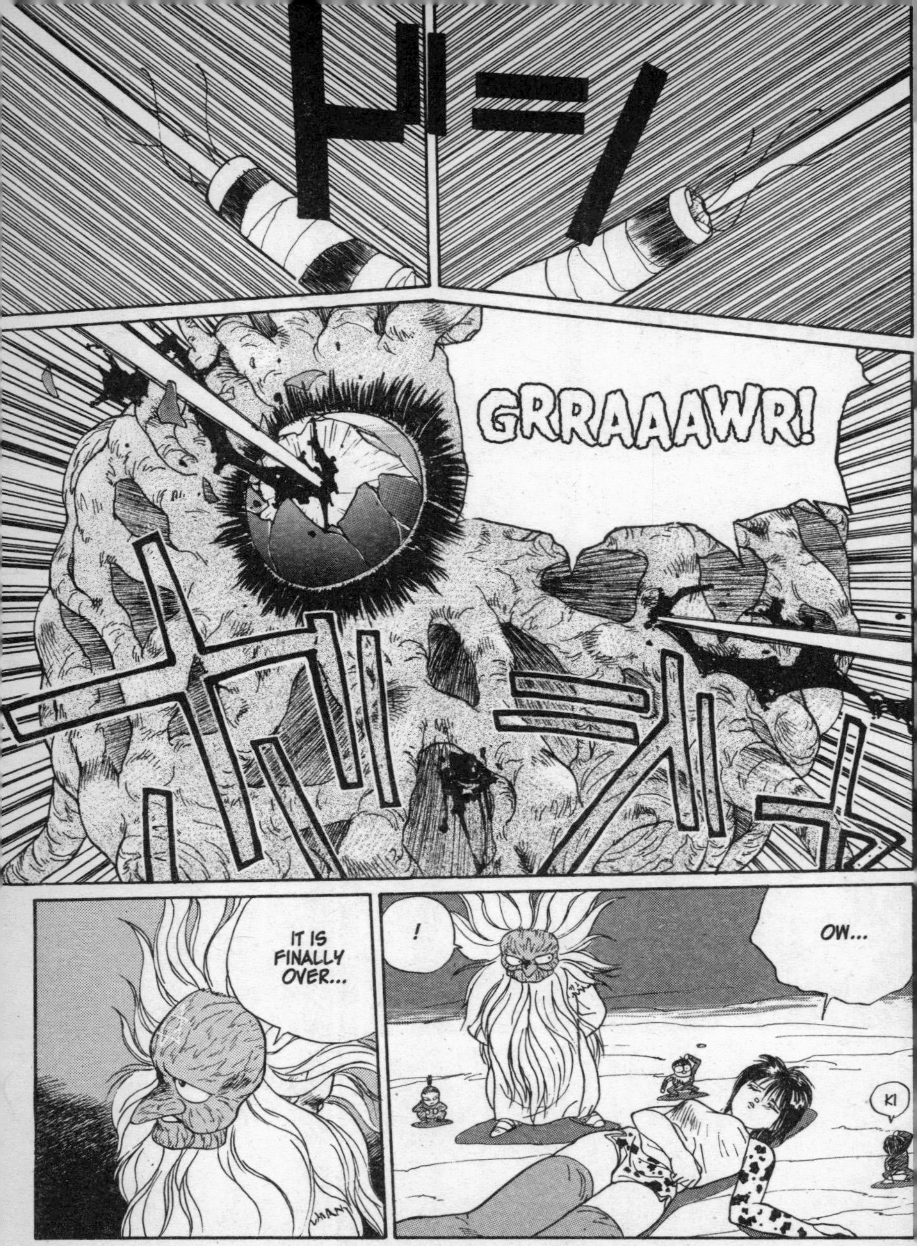
GRRAAAWR!
IT IS FINALLY OVER...
!
OW...
KI

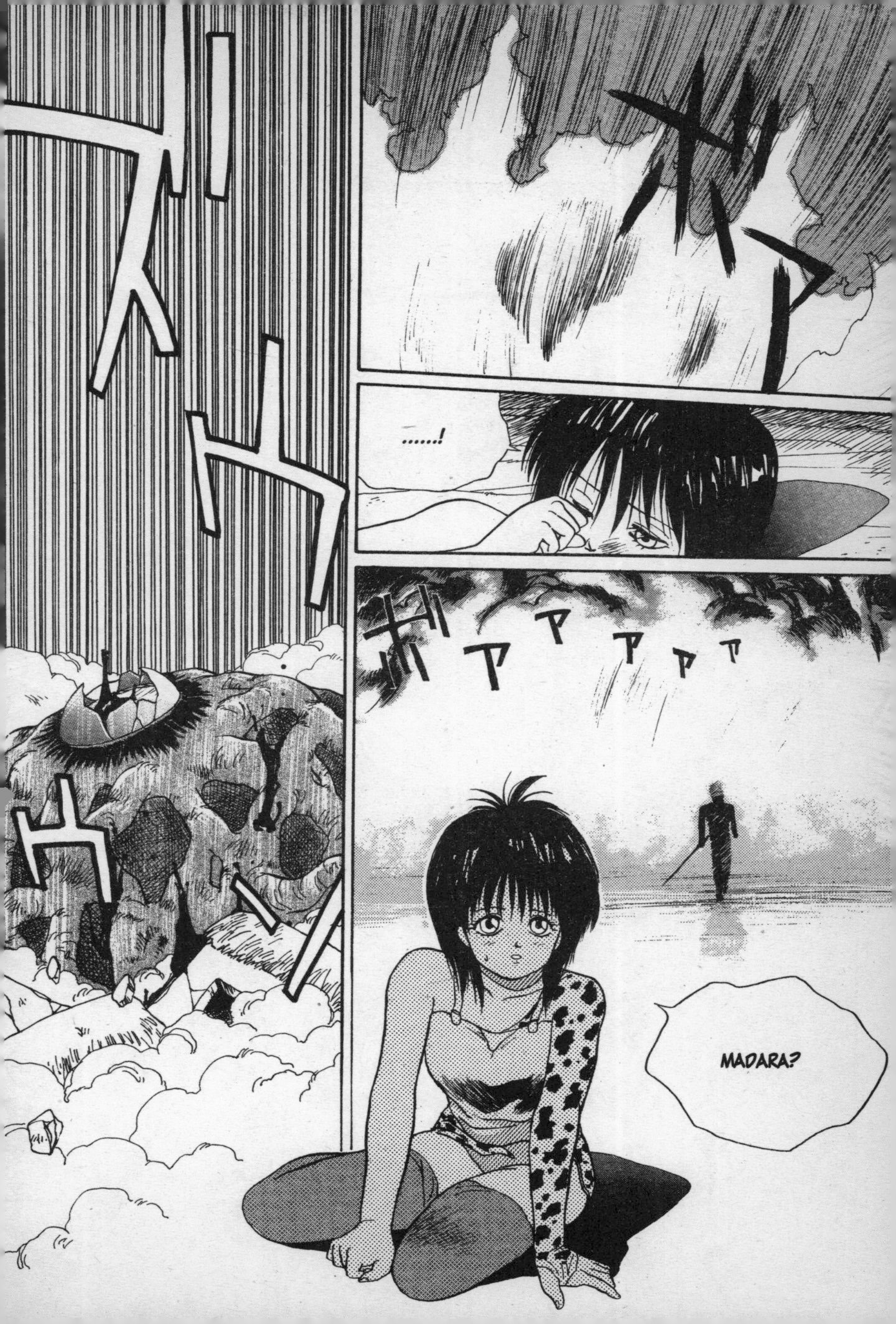
......!
MADARA?

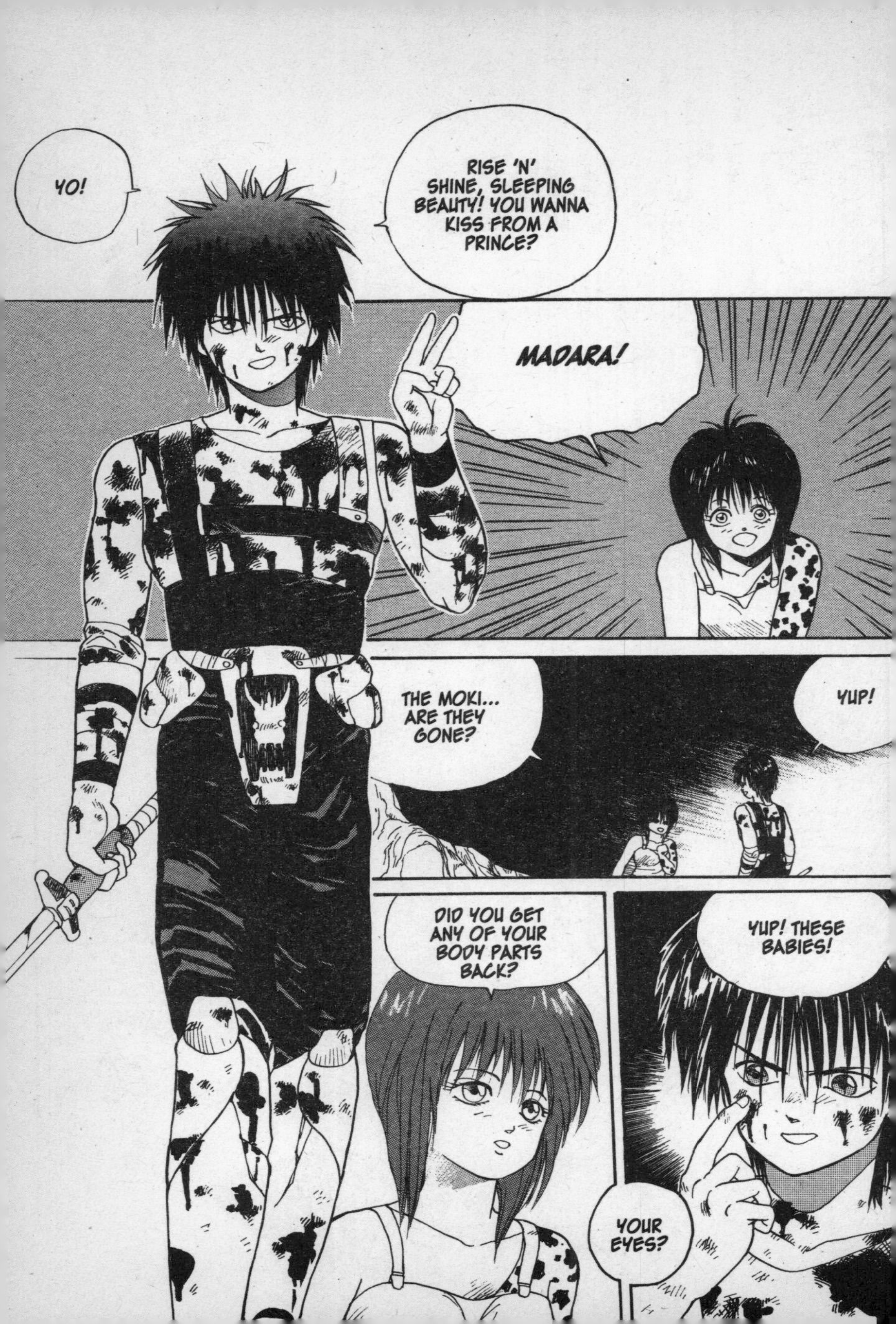
YO!
RISE 'N' SHINE, SLEEPING BEAUTY! YOU WANNA KISS FROM A PRINCE?
MADARA!
THE MOKI... ARE THEY GONE?
YUP!
DID YOU GET ANY OF YOUR BODY PARTS BACK?
YUP! THESE BABIES!
YOUR EYES?

UP 'TIL NOW I COULD ONLY SEE IN BLACK AND WHITE...

NEVER KNEW MY SKIN AND THE DIRT WERE THESE COLORS...

!

HUH!

KYAH!

HAW HAW HAW HAW!

RUB RUB

HAKU TAKU!

KI

WHEN DID YOU CHANGE BACK INTO AN OLD MAN?

JUST WHAT DO YOU THINK YOU'RE DOING, PERVERTED OLD MAN?!

YOU WANNA GET HURT?

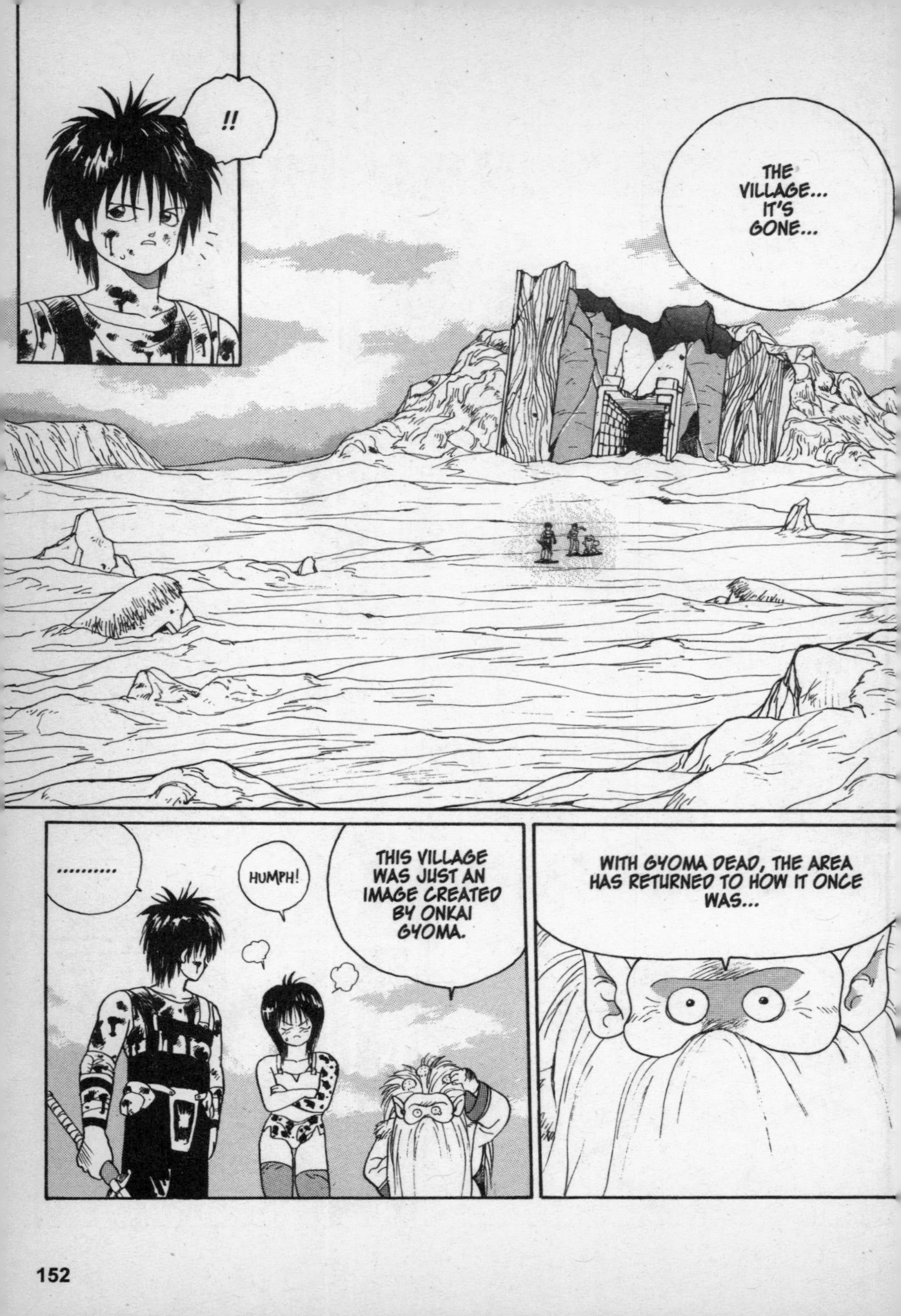
!!
THE VILLAGE... IT'S GONE...
....
HUMPH!
THIS VILLAGE WAS JUST AN IMAGE CREATED BY ONKAI GYOMA.
WITH GYOMA DEAD, THE AREA HAS RETURNED TO HOW IT ONCE WAS...

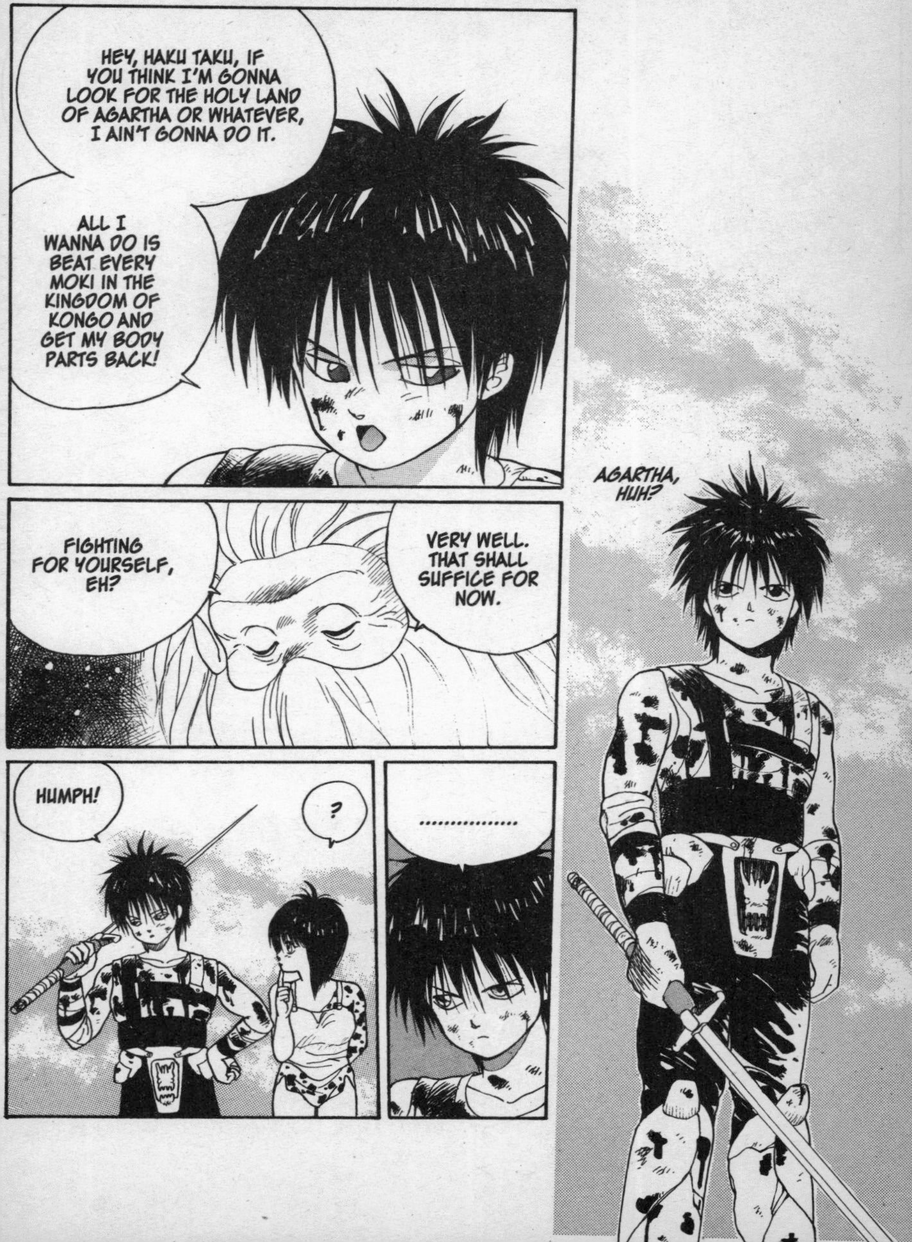

HEY, HAKU TAKU, IF YOU THINK I'M GONNA LOOK FOR THE HOLY LAND OF AGARTHA OR WHATEVER, I AIN'T GONNA DO IT.
ALL I WANNA DO IS BEAT EVERY MOKI IN THE KINGDOM OF KONGO AND GET MY BODY PARTS BACK!
VERY WELL. THAT SHALL SUFFICE FOR NOW.
FIGHTING FOR YOURSELF, EH?
AGARTHA, HUH?
....
?
HUMPH!

廃皇子譚

Chapter 2: The Tale of the Abandoned Prince

"Home of the Sleeping Gods, he who
opens the gates to the Holy Land of
Agartha shall surpass the deities, the
demons and mankind to become
the true ruler of all…"

– From the National Chronicles of Horai, Agartha Chapter

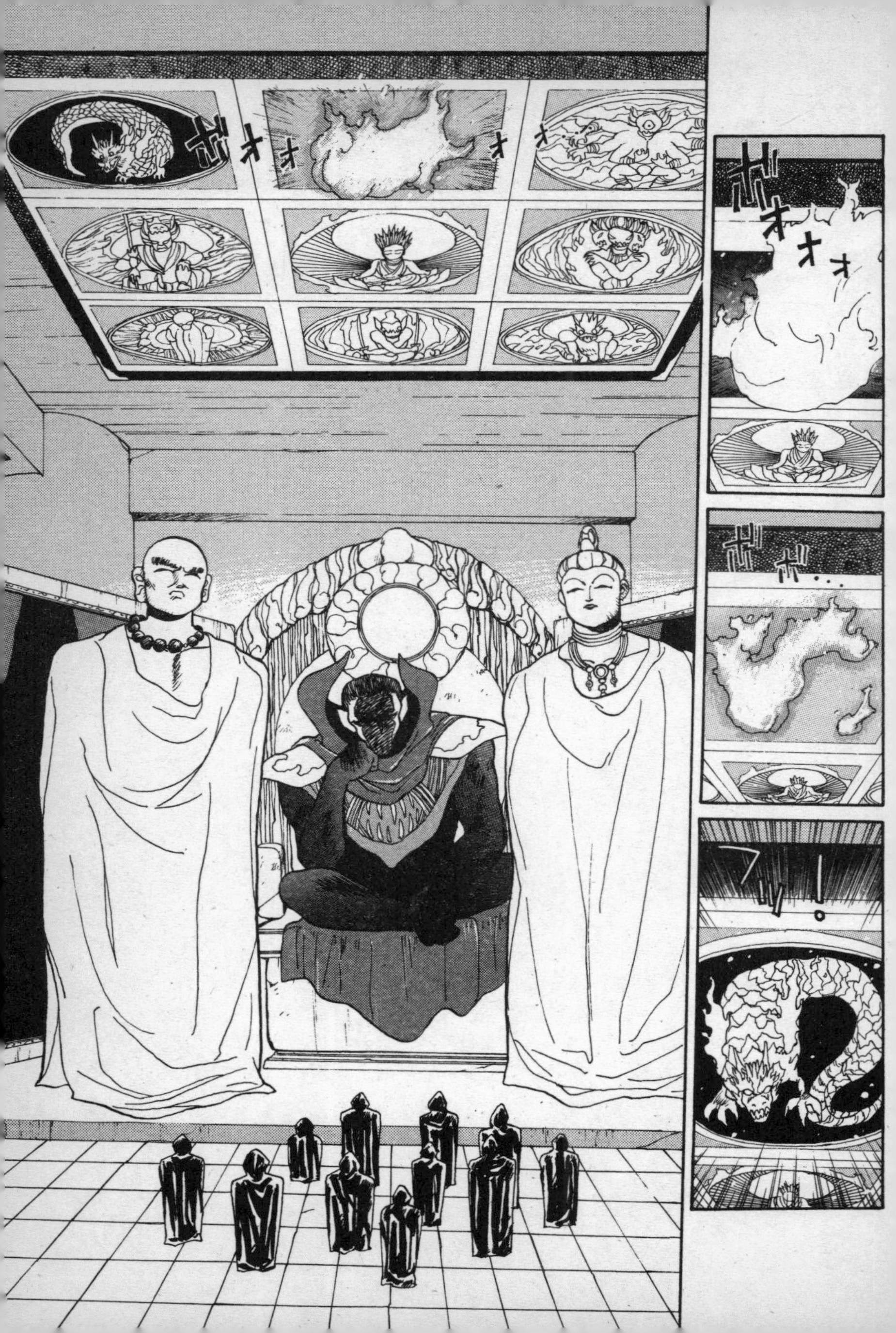

ボオオ
オオ
ボオオオオ
ボボ...
フッ!

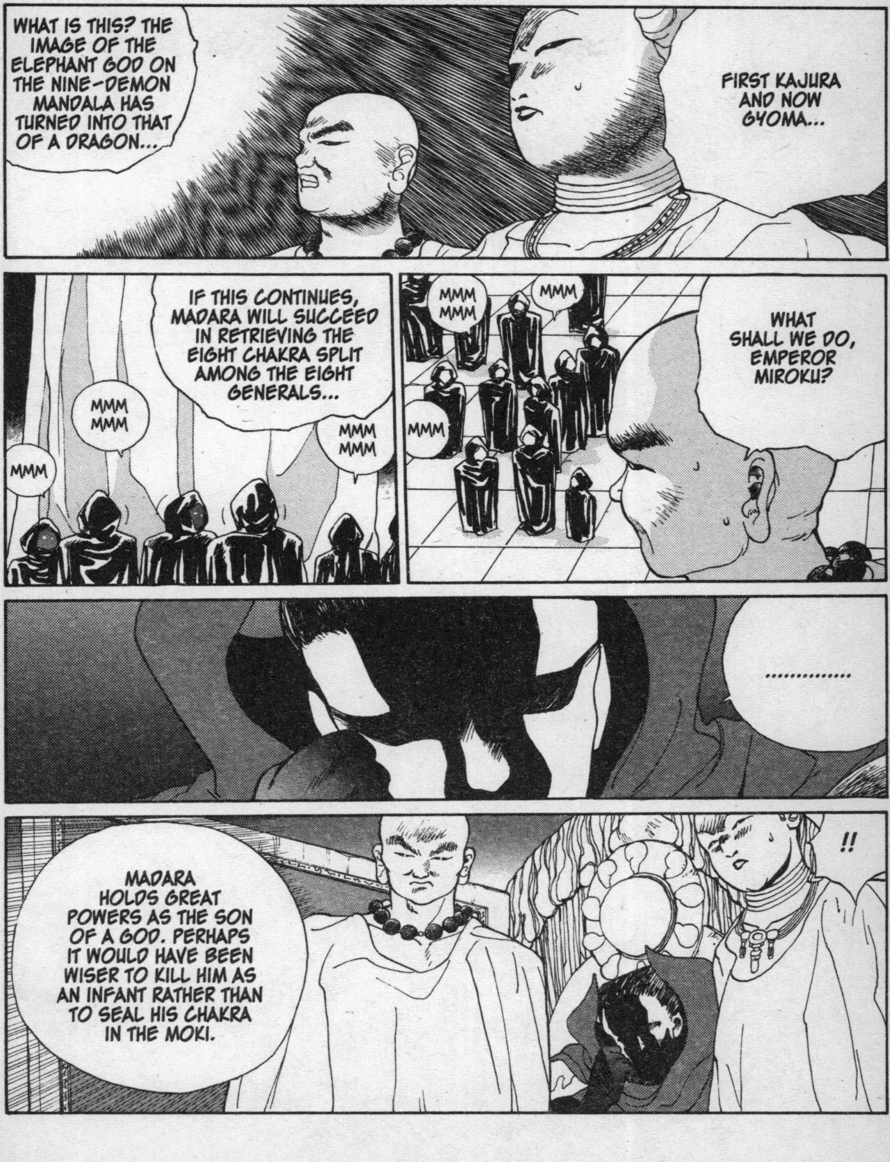
WHAT IS THIS? THE IMAGE OF THE ELEPHANT GOD ON THE NINE-DEMON MANDALA HAS TURNED INTO THAT OF A DRAGON...
FIRST KAJURA AND NOW GYOMA...
IF THIS CONTINUES, MADARA WILL SUCCEED IN RETRIEVING THE EIGHT CHAKRA SPLIT AMONG THE EIGHT GENERALS...
MMM
MMM MMM
MMM MMM
MMM MMM
MMM
MMM
WHAT SHALL WE DO, EMPEROR MIROKU?
....
MADARA HOLDS GREAT POWERS AS THE SON OF A GOD. PERHAPS IT WOULD HAVE BEEN WISER TO KILL HIM AS AN INFANT RATHER THAN TO SEAL HIS CHAKRA IN THE MOKI.
!!

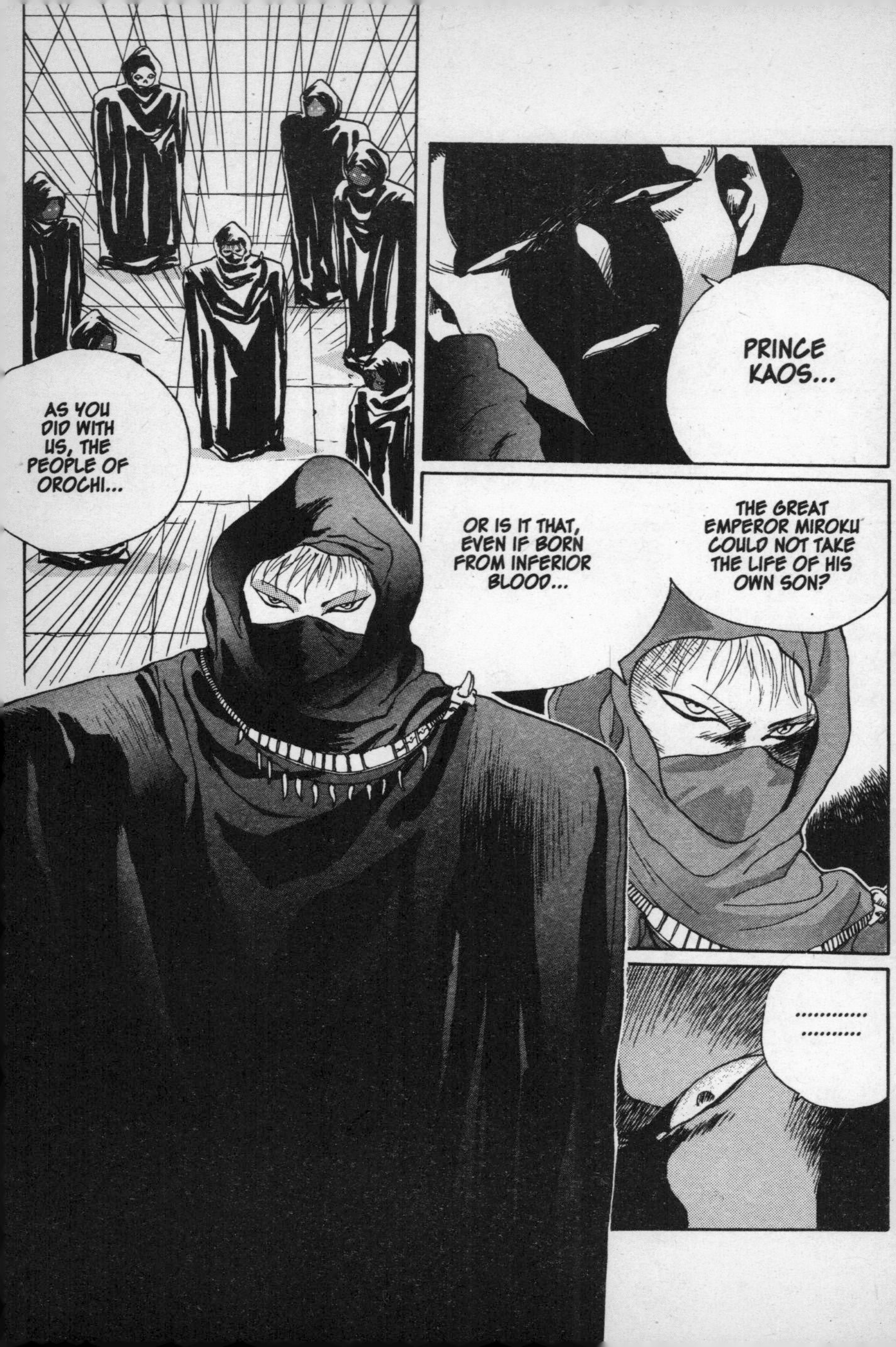

PRINCE KAOS...
AS YOU DID WITH US, THE PEOPLE OF OROCHI...
THE GREAT EMPEROR MIROKU COULD NOT TAKE THE LIFE OF HIS OWN SON?
OR IS IT THAT, EVEN IF BORN FROM INFERIOR BLOOD...
....

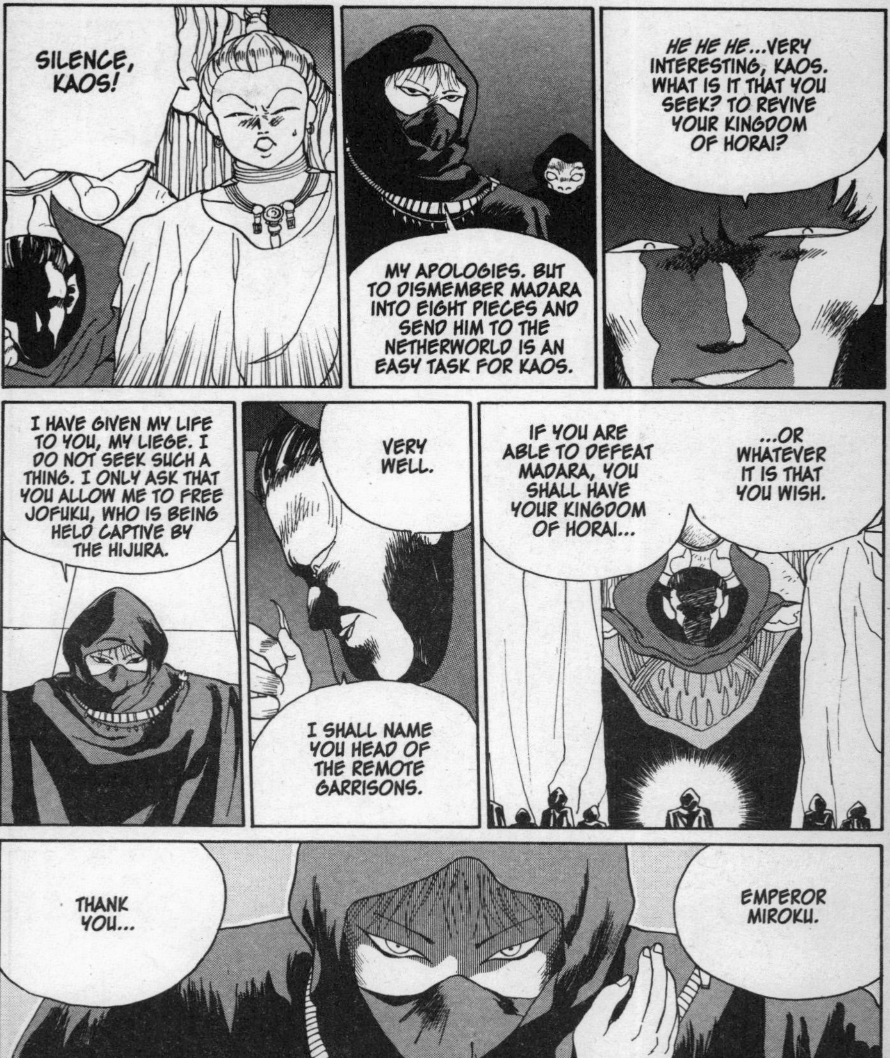
SILENCE, KAOS!
MY APOLOGIES. BUT TO DISMEMBER MADARA INTO EIGHT PIECES AND SEND HIM TO THE NETHERWORLD IS AN EASY TASK FOR KAOS.
HE HE HE...VERY INTERESTING, KAOS. WHAT IS IT THAT YOU SEEK? TO REVIVE YOUR KINGDOM OF HORAI?
I HAVE GIVEN MY LIFE TO YOU, MY LIEGE. I DO NOT SEEK SUCH A THING. I ONLY ASK THAT YOU ALLOW ME TO FREE JOFUKU, WHO IS BEING HELD CAPTIVE BY THE HIJURA.
VERY WELL.
I SHALL NAME YOU HEAD OF THE REMOTE GARRISONS.
IF YOU ARE ABLE TO DEFEAT MADARA, YOU SHALL HAVE YOUR KINGDOM OF HORAI...
...OR WHATEVER IT IS THAT YOU WISH.
THANK YOU...
EMPEROR MIROKU.

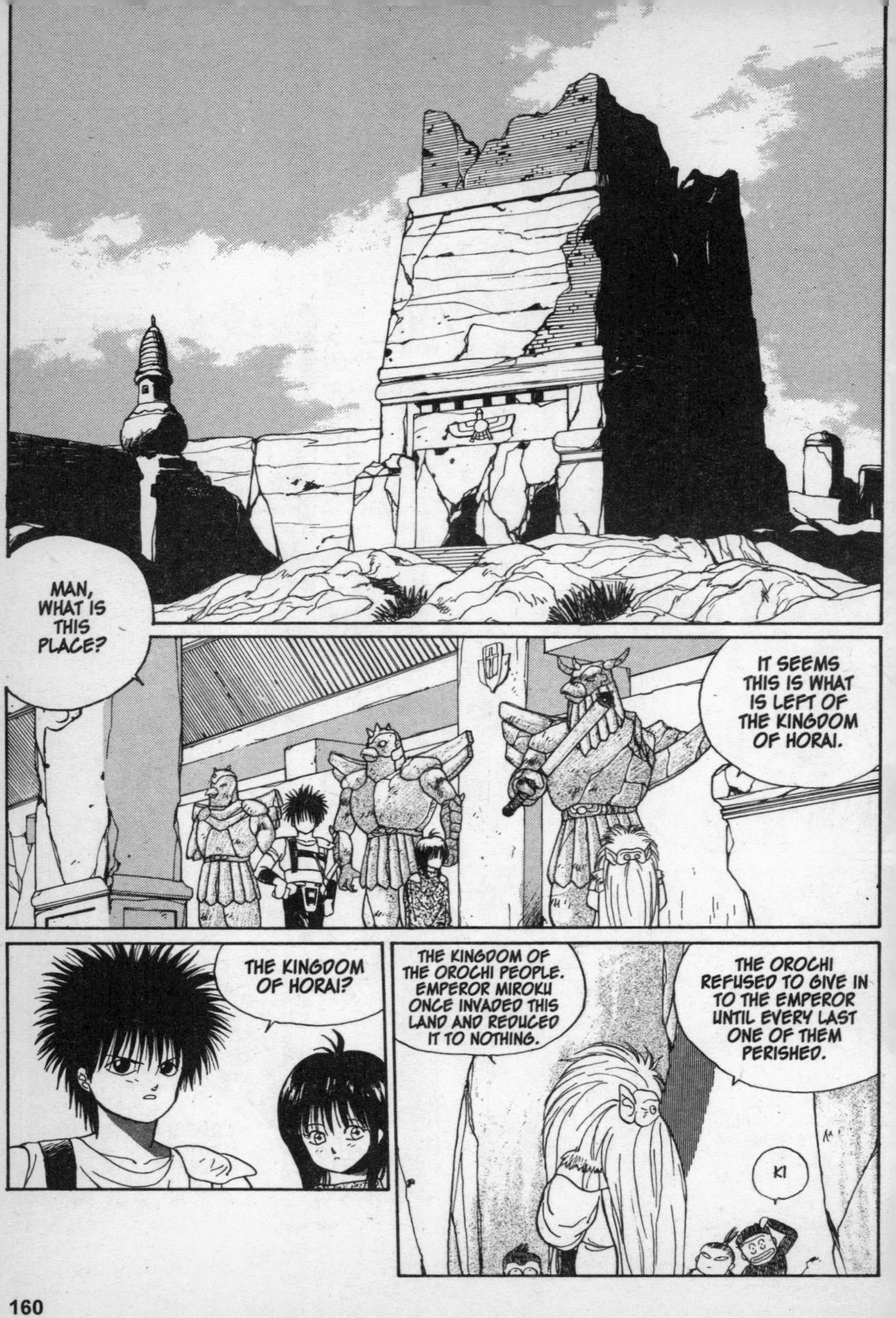
MAN, WHAT IS THIS PLACE?
IT SEEMS THIS IS WHAT IS LEFT OF THE KINGDOM OF HORAI.
THE KINGDOM OF HORAI?
THE KINGDOM OF THE OROCHI PEOPLE. EMPEROR MIROKU ONCE INVADED THIS LAND AND REDUCED IT TO NOTHING.
THE OROCHI REFUSED TO GIVE IN TO THE EMPEROR UNTIL EVERY LAST ONE OF THEM PERISHED.
KI

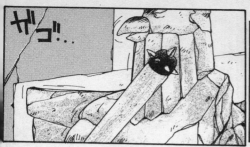

ザゴ...

!

KYAAAH! THAT STATUE JUST MOVED!

AHHHHH!

HUH?!

YOU'RE JUST SEEIN' THINGS.

N-NO... REALLY...

SEE, NOT MOVIN' AT ALL.

MAYBE BEING STUCK IN GYOMA'S BALL MADE YOU CRAZY?

THAT'S WEIRD...I SWEAR IT MOVED...

WHO ARE YOU CALLING CRAZY?

161

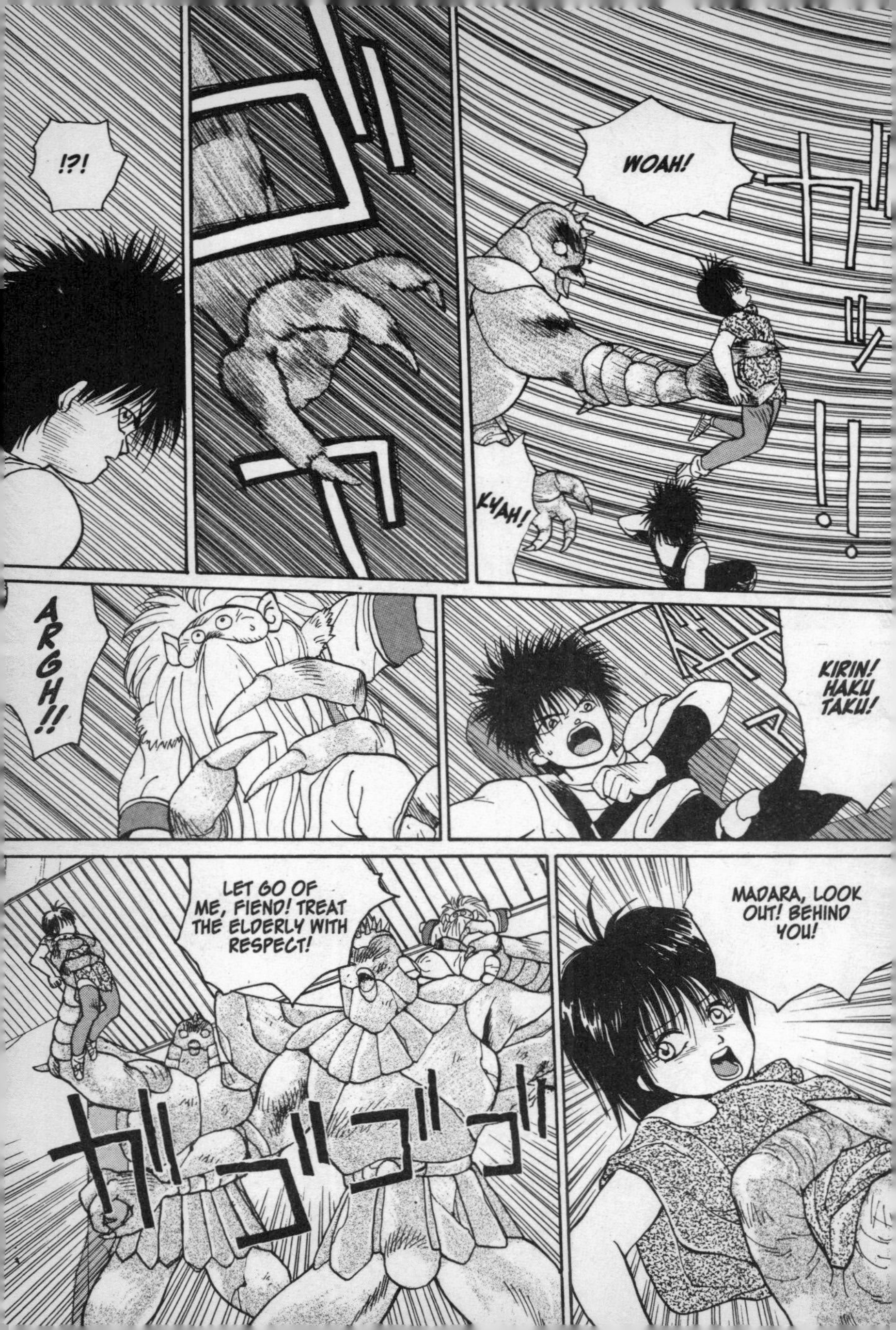

WOAH!
KYAH!
!?!
KIRIN! HAKU TAKU!
ARGH!!
MADARA, LOOK OUT! BEHIND YOU!
LET GO OF ME, FIEND! TREAT THE ELDERLY WITH RESPECT!

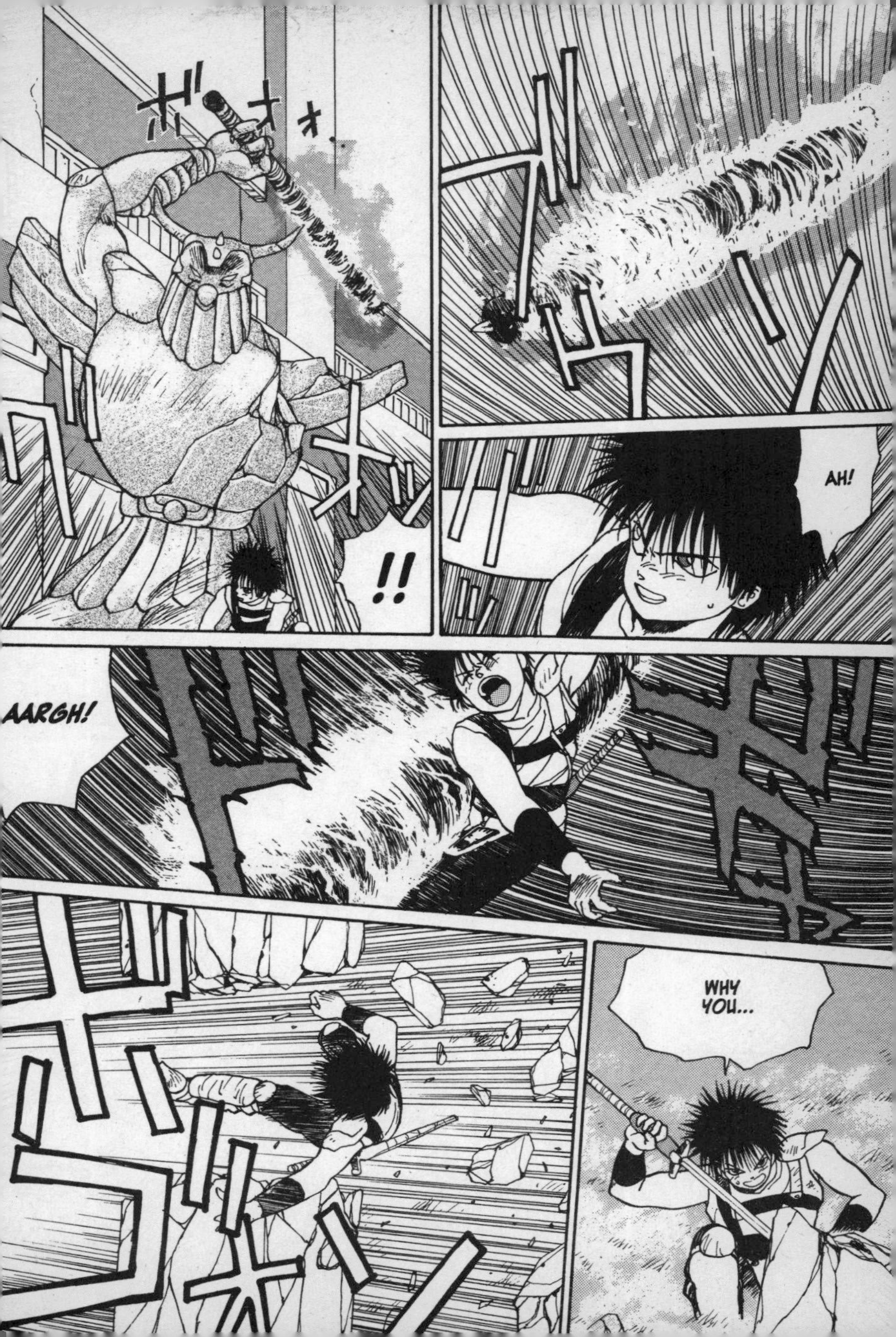
AH!
!!
AARGH!
WHY YOU...

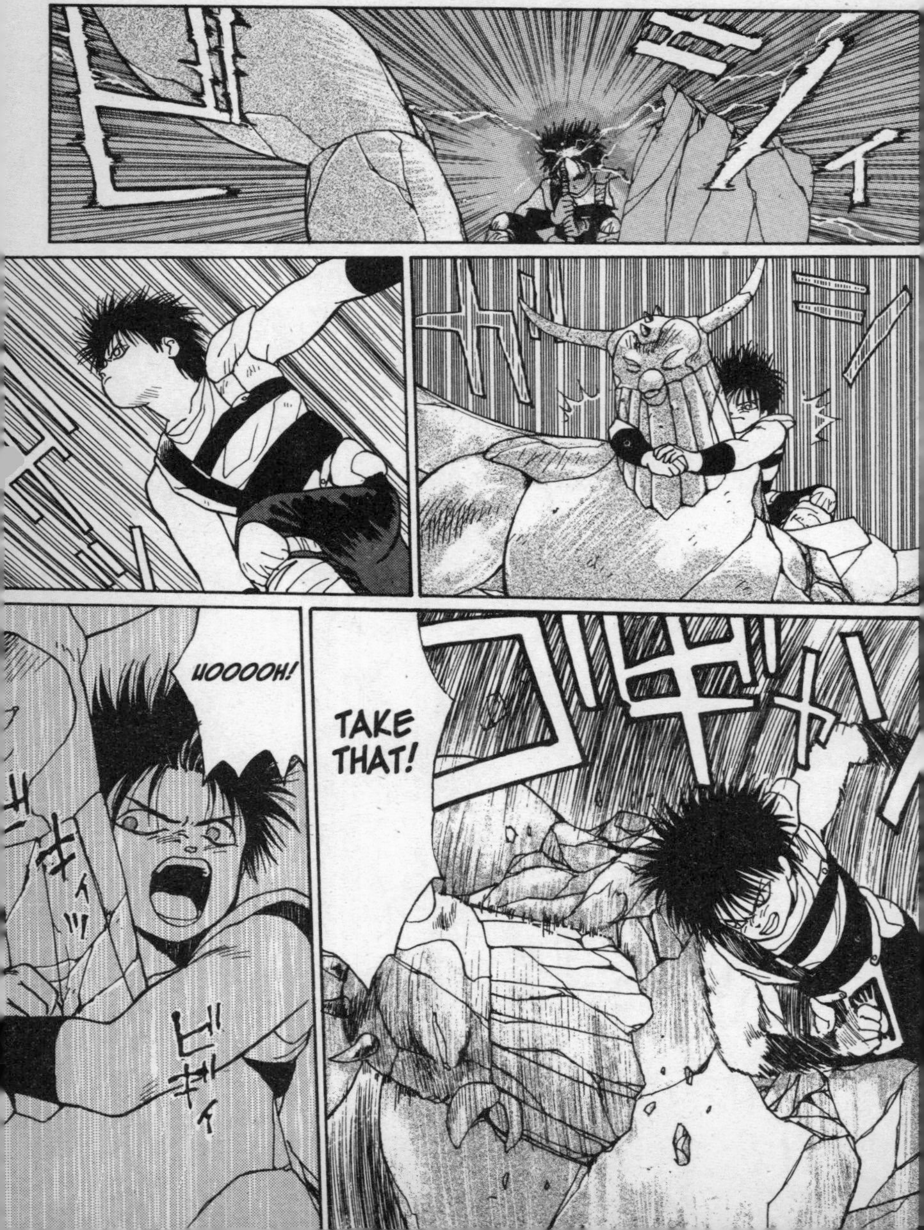
TAKE THAT!
UOOOOH!

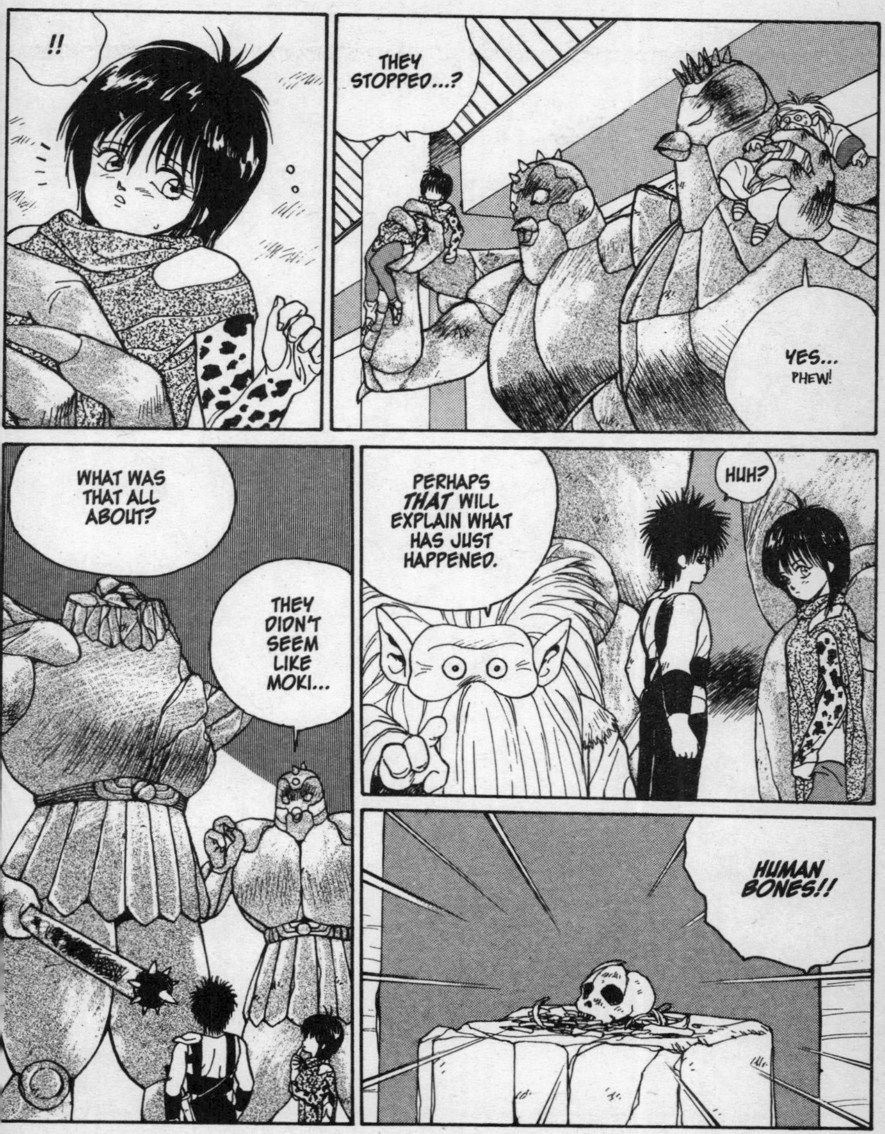
!!
THEY STOPPED...?
YES... PHEW!
WHAT WAS THAT ALL ABOUT?
THEY DIDN'T SEEM LIKE MOKI...
PERHAPS *THAT* WILL EXPLAIN WHAT HAS JUST HAPPENED.
HUH?
HUMAN BONES!!

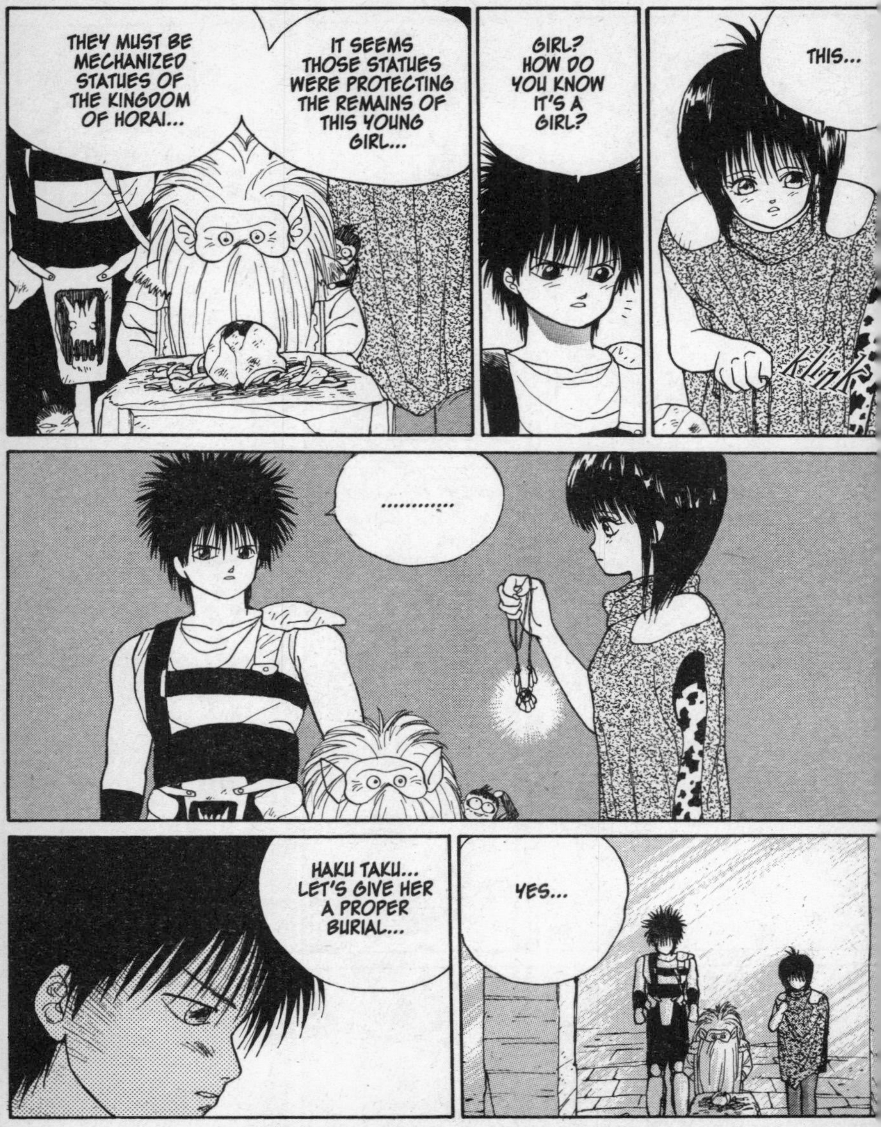
THEY MUST BE MECHANIZED STATUES OF THE KINGDOM OF HORAI...
IT SEEMS THOSE STATUES WERE PROTECTING THE REMAINS OF THIS YOUNG GIRL...
GIRL? HOW DO YOU KNOW IT'S A GIRL?
THIS...
klink
....
HAKU TAKU... LET'S GIVE HER A PROPER BURIAL...
YES...

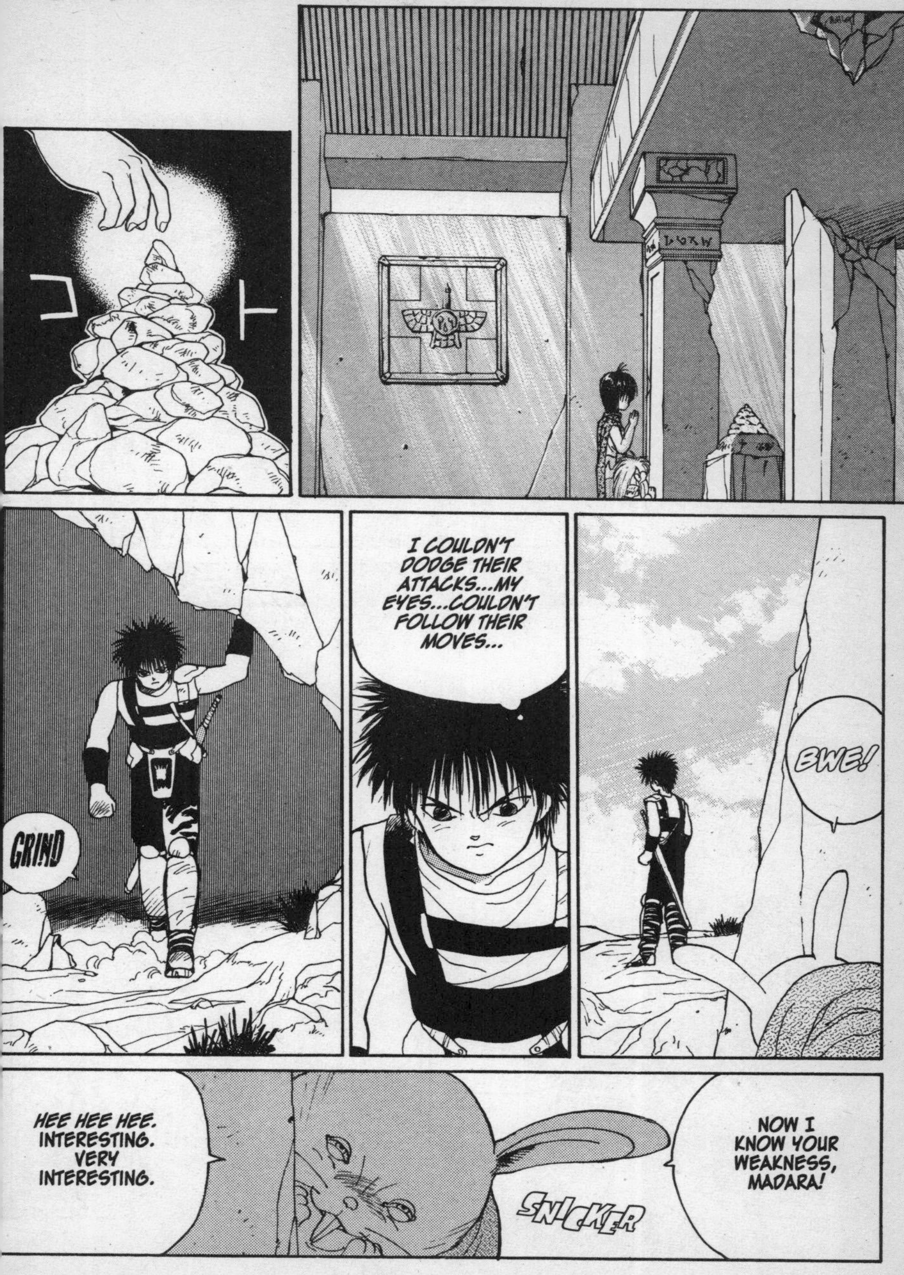

コト
GRIND
I COULDN'T DODGE THEIR ATTACKS...MY EYES...COULDN'T FOLLOW THEIR MOVES...
BWE!
HEE HEE HEE. INTERESTING. VERY INTERESTING.
SNICKER
NOW I KNOW YOUR WEAKNESS, MADARA!

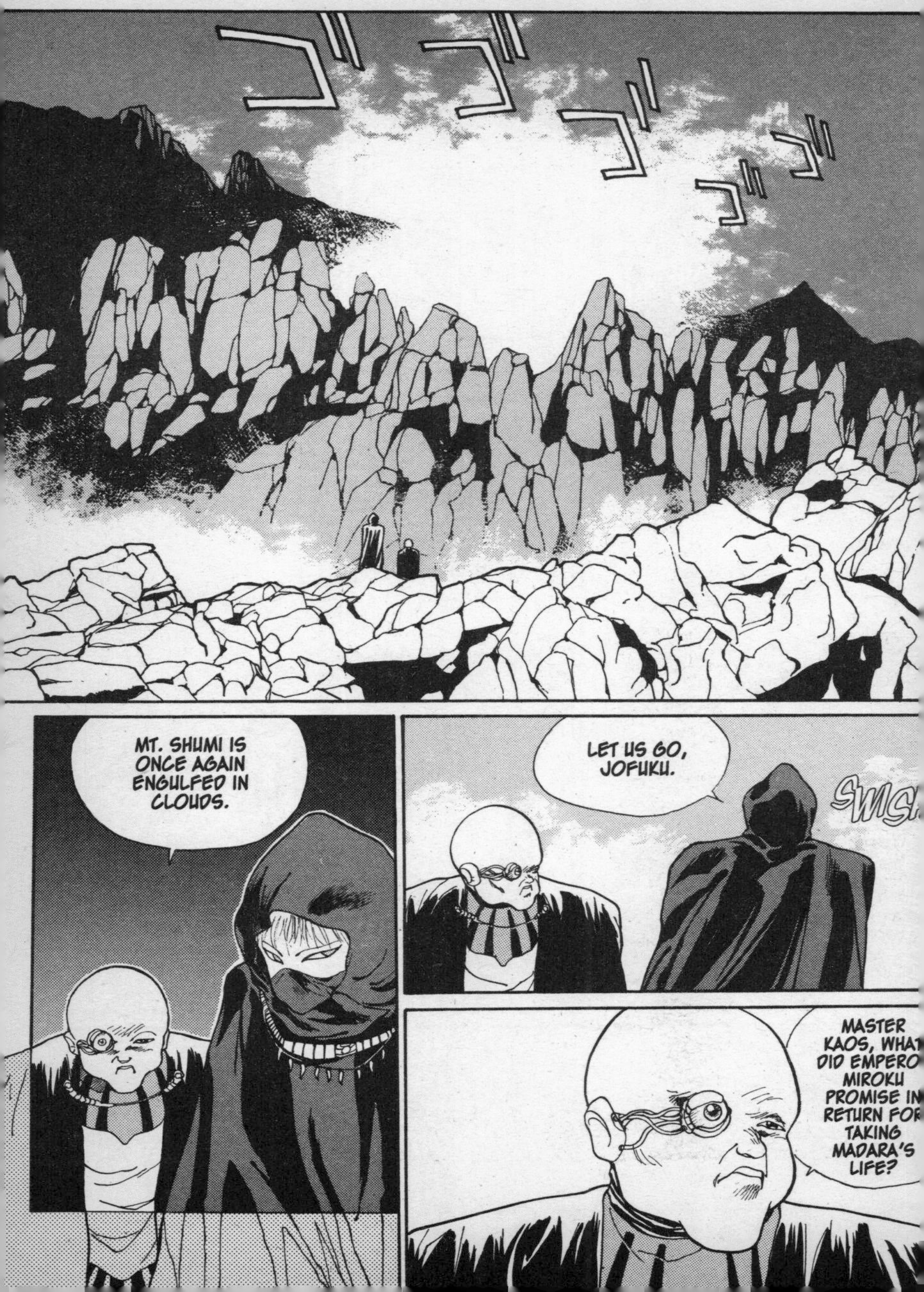

MT. SHUMI IS ONCE AGAIN ENGULFED IN CLOUDS.
LET US GO, JOFUKU.
SWISH
MASTER KAOS, WHAT DID EMPERO MIROKU PROMISE IN RETURN FOR TAKING MADARA'S LIFE?

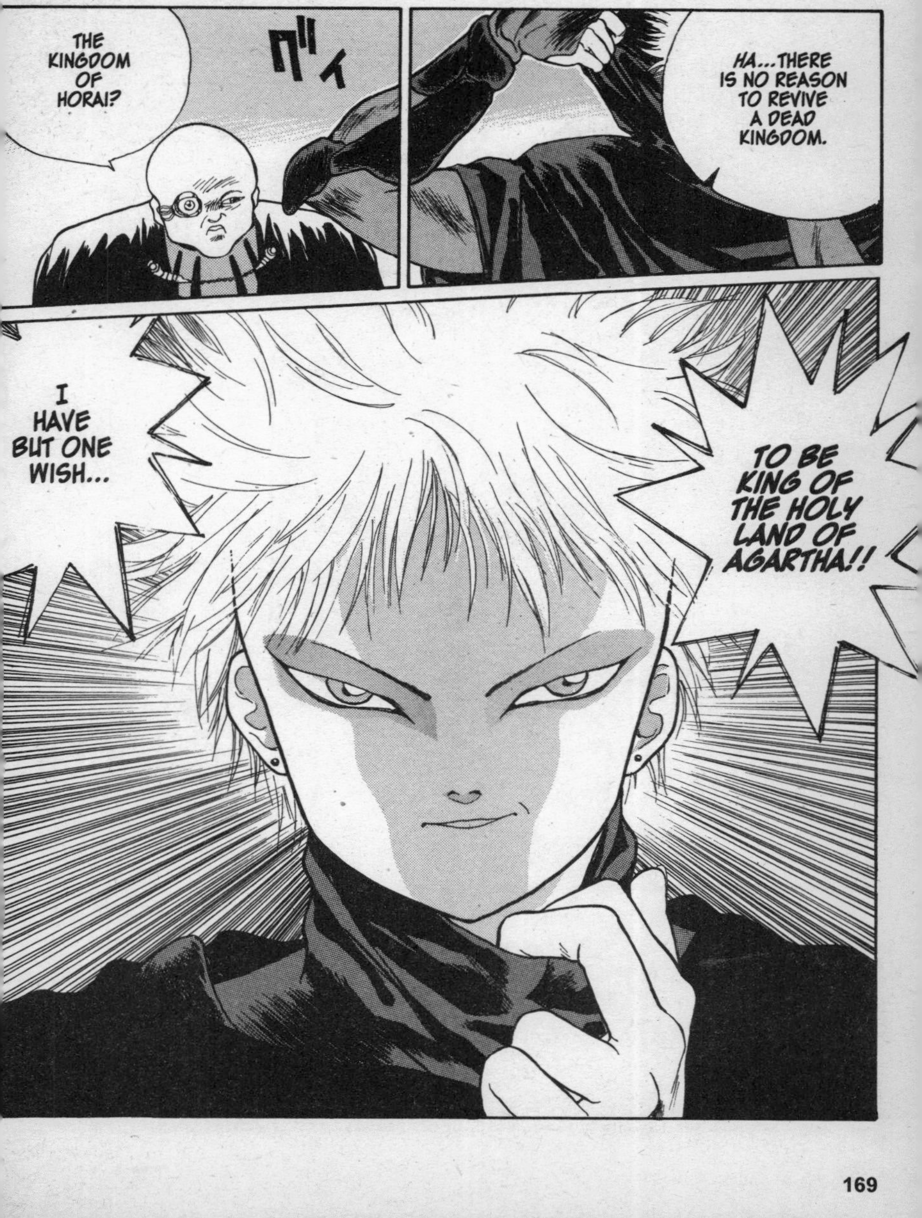
THE KINGDOM OF HORAI?
グイ
HA...THERE IS NO REASON TO REVIVE A DEAD KINGDOM.
I HAVE BUT ONE WISH...
TO BE KING OF THE HOLY LAND OF AGARTHA!!

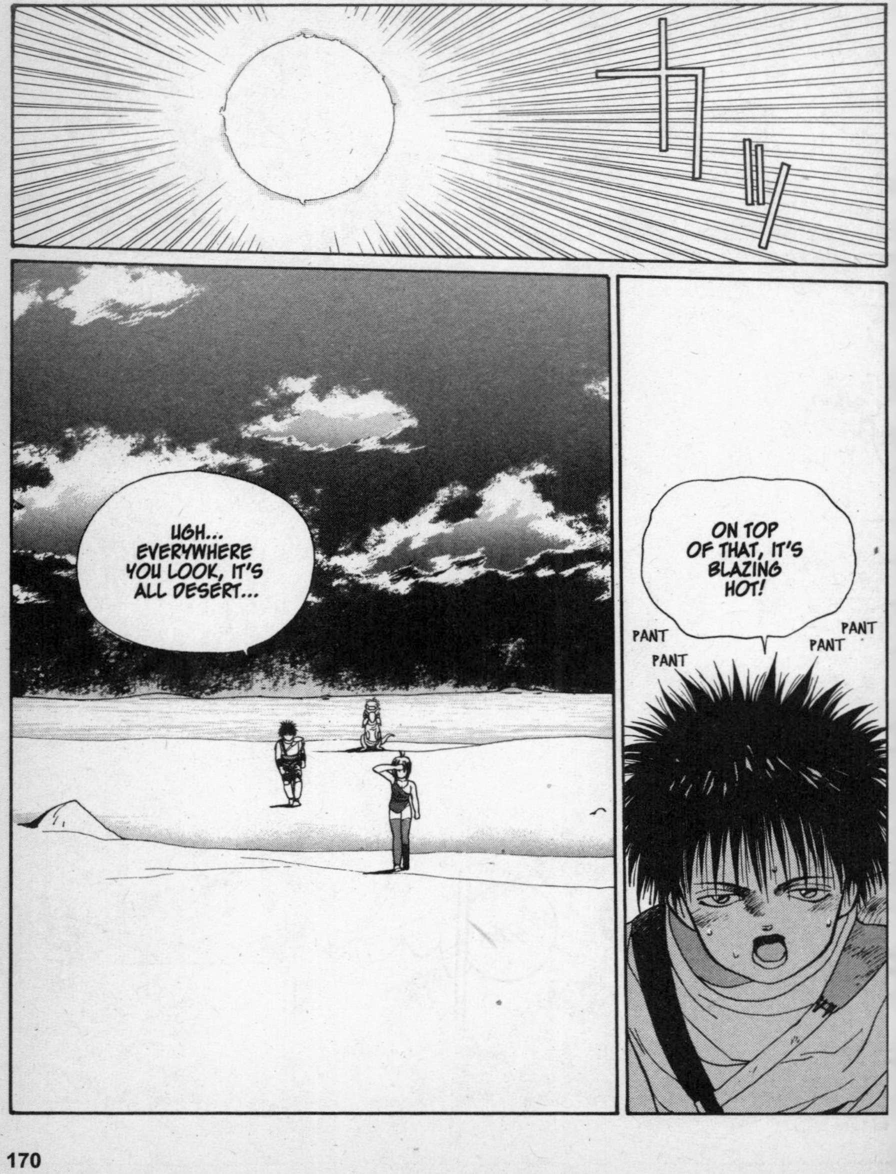
UGH... EVERYWHERE YOU LOOK, IT'S ALL DESERT...
ON TOP OF THAT, IT'S BLAZING HOT!
PANT
PANT
PANT
PANT

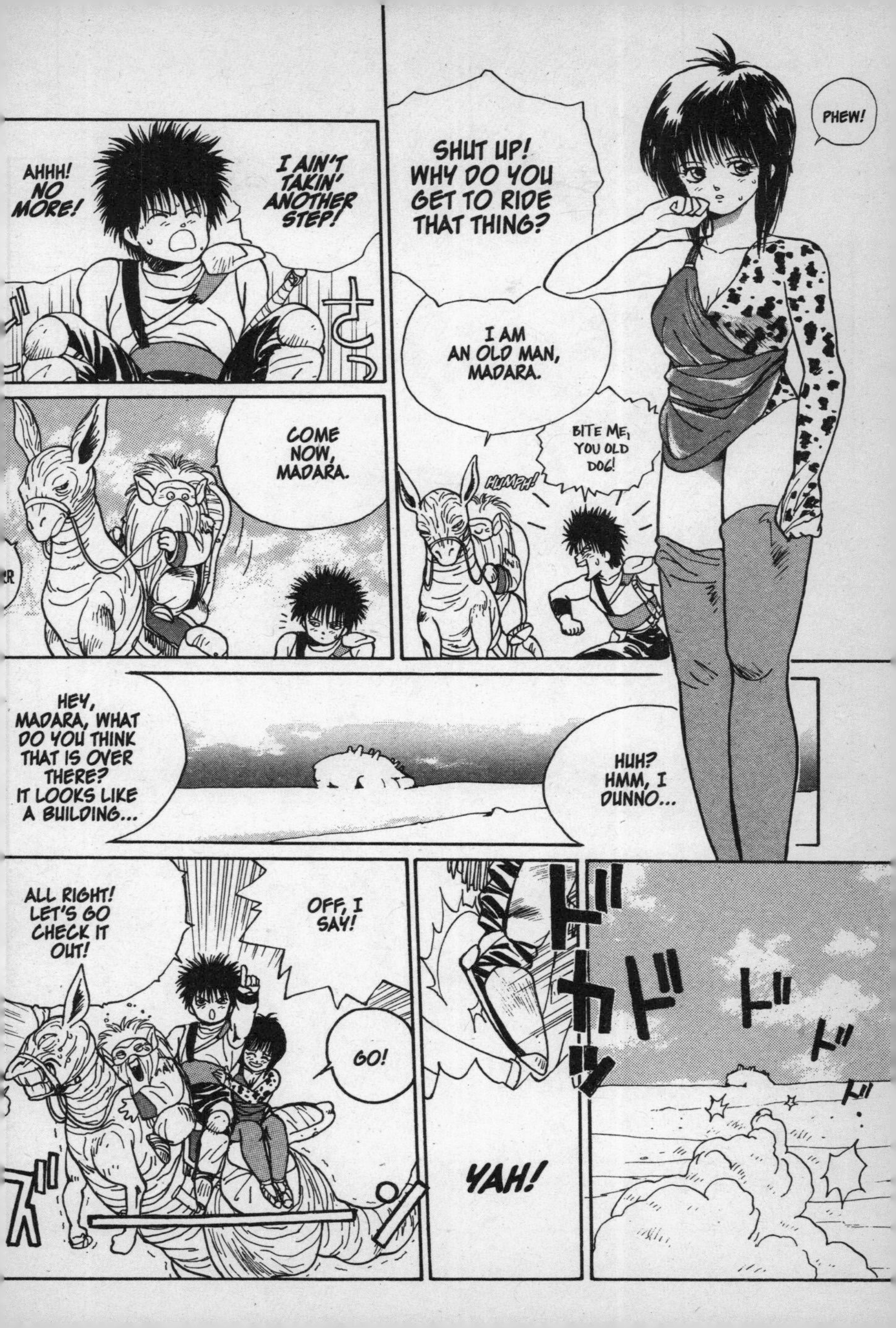

AHHH! NO MORE!
I AIN'T TAKIN' ANOTHER STEP!
COME NOW, MADARA.
SHUT UP! WHY DO YOU GET TO RIDE THAT THING?
I AM AN OLD MAN, MADARA.
HUMPH!
BITE ME, YOU OLD DOG!
PHEW!
HEY, MADARA, WHAT DO YOU THINK THAT IS OVER THERE? IT LOOKS LIKE A BUILDING...
HUH? HMM, I DUNNO...
ALL RIGHT! LET'S GO CHECK IT OUT!
OFF, I SAY!
GO!
YAH!

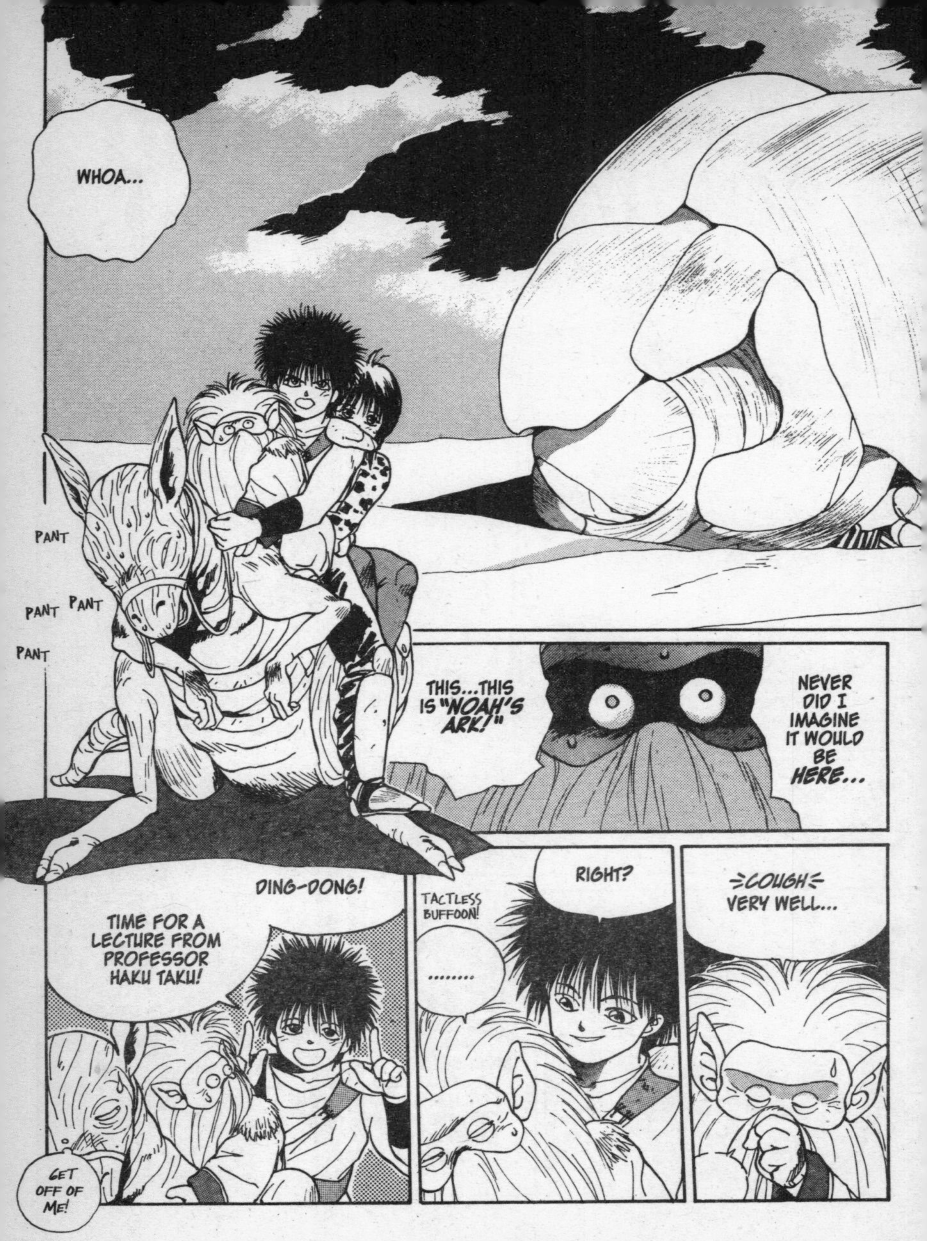
WHOA...
PANT
PANT PANT
PANT
THIS...THIS IS "NOAH'S ARK!"
NEVER DID I IMAGINE IT WOULD BE HERE...
DING-DONG!
TIME FOR A LECTURE FROM PROFESSOR HAKU TAKU!
GET OFF OF ME!
RIGHT?
TACTLESS BUFFOON!
....
COUGH
VERY WELL...

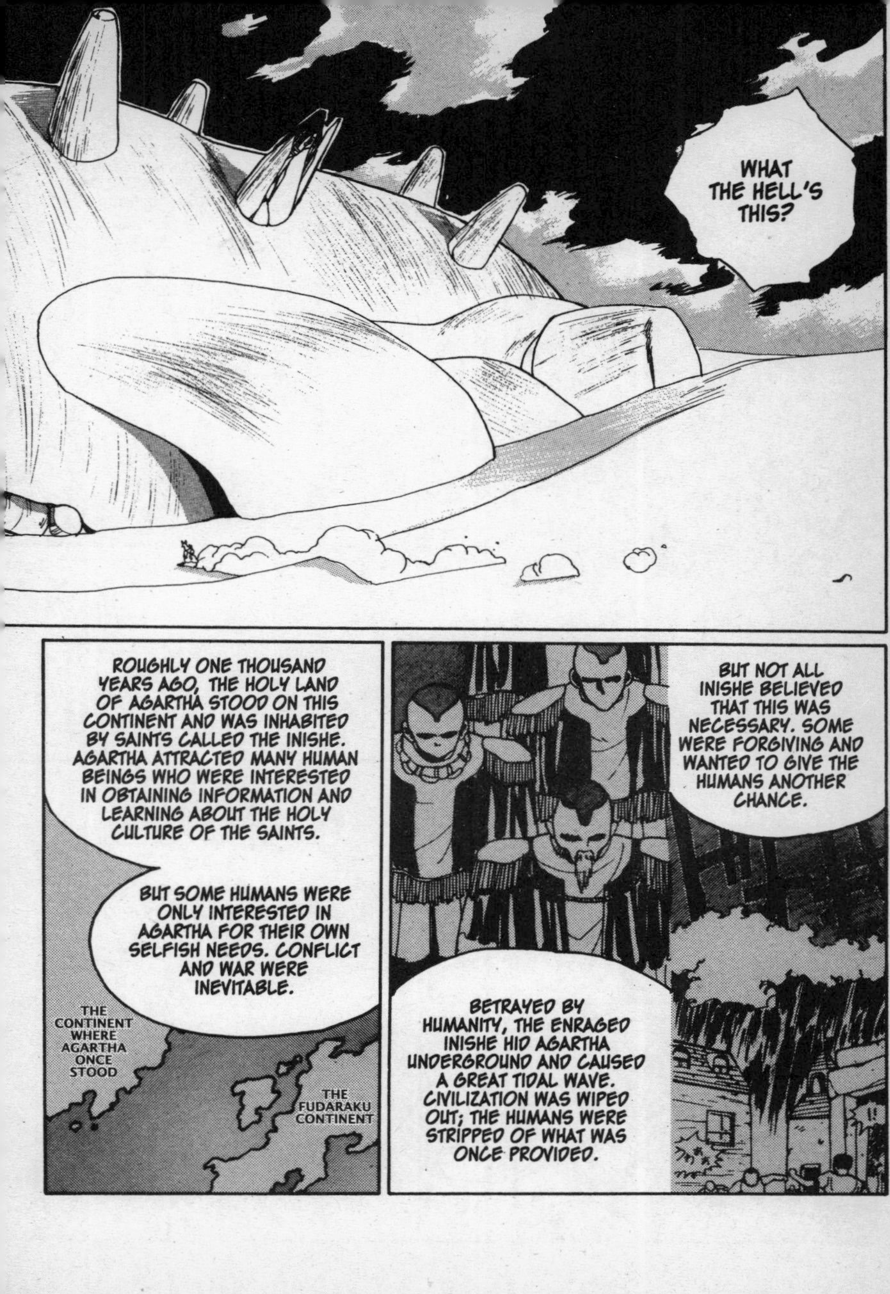
WHAT THE HELL'S THIS?
ROUGHLY ONE THOUSAND YEARS AGO, THE HOLY LAND OF AGARTHA STOOD ON THIS CONTINENT AND WAS INHABITED BY SAINTS CALLED THE INISHE. AGARTHA ATTRACTED MANY HUMAN BEINGS WHO WERE INTERESTED IN OBTAINING INFORMATION AND LEARNING ABOUT THE HOLY CULTURE OF THE SAINTS.
BUT SOME HUMANS WERE ONLY INTERESTED IN AGARTHA FOR THEIR OWN SELFISH NEEDS. CONFLICT AND WAR WERE INEVITABLE.
THE CONTINENT WHERE AGARTHA ONCE STOOD
THE FUDARAKU CONTINENT
BUT NOT ALL INISHE BELIEVED THAT THIS WAS NECESSARY. SOME WERE FORGIVING AND WANTED TO GIVE THE HUMANS ANOTHER CHANCE.
BETRAYED BY HUMANITY, THE ENRAGED INISHE HID AGARTHA UNDERGROUND AND CAUSED A GREAT TIDAL WAVE. CIVILIZATION WAS WIPED OUT; THE HUMANS WERE STRIPPED OF WHAT WAS ONCE PROVIDED.
!!

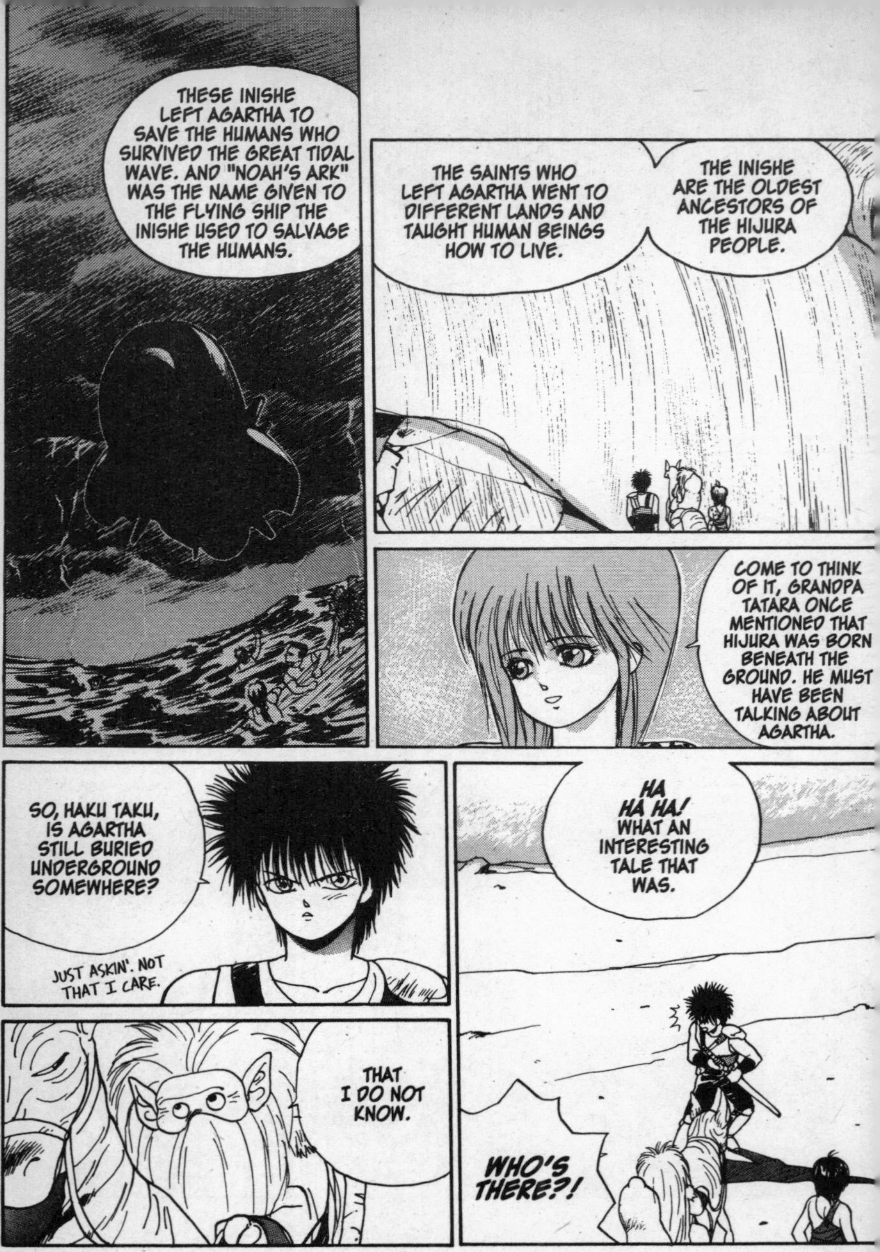

THESE INISHE LEFT AGARTHA TO SAVE THE HUMANS WHO SURVIVED THE GREAT TIDAL WAVE. AND "NOAH'S ARK" WAS THE NAME GIVEN TO THE FLYING SHIP THE INISHE USED TO SALVAGE THE HUMANS.
THE SAINTS WHO LEFT AGARTHA WENT TO DIFFERENT LANDS AND TAUGHT HUMAN BEINGS HOW TO LIVE.
THE INISHE ARE THE OLDEST ANCESTORS OF THE HIJURA PEOPLE.
COME TO THINK OF IT, GRANDPA TATARA ONCE MENTIONED THAT HIJURA WAS BORN BENEATH THE GROUND. HE MUST HAVE BEEN TALKING ABOUT AGARTHA.
SO, HAKU TAKU, IS AGARTHA STILL BURIED UNDERGROUND SOMEWHERE?
JUST ASKIN'. NOT THAT I CARE.
THAT I DO NOT KNOW.
HA HA HA! WHAT AN INTERESTING TALE THAT WAS.
WHO'S THERE?!

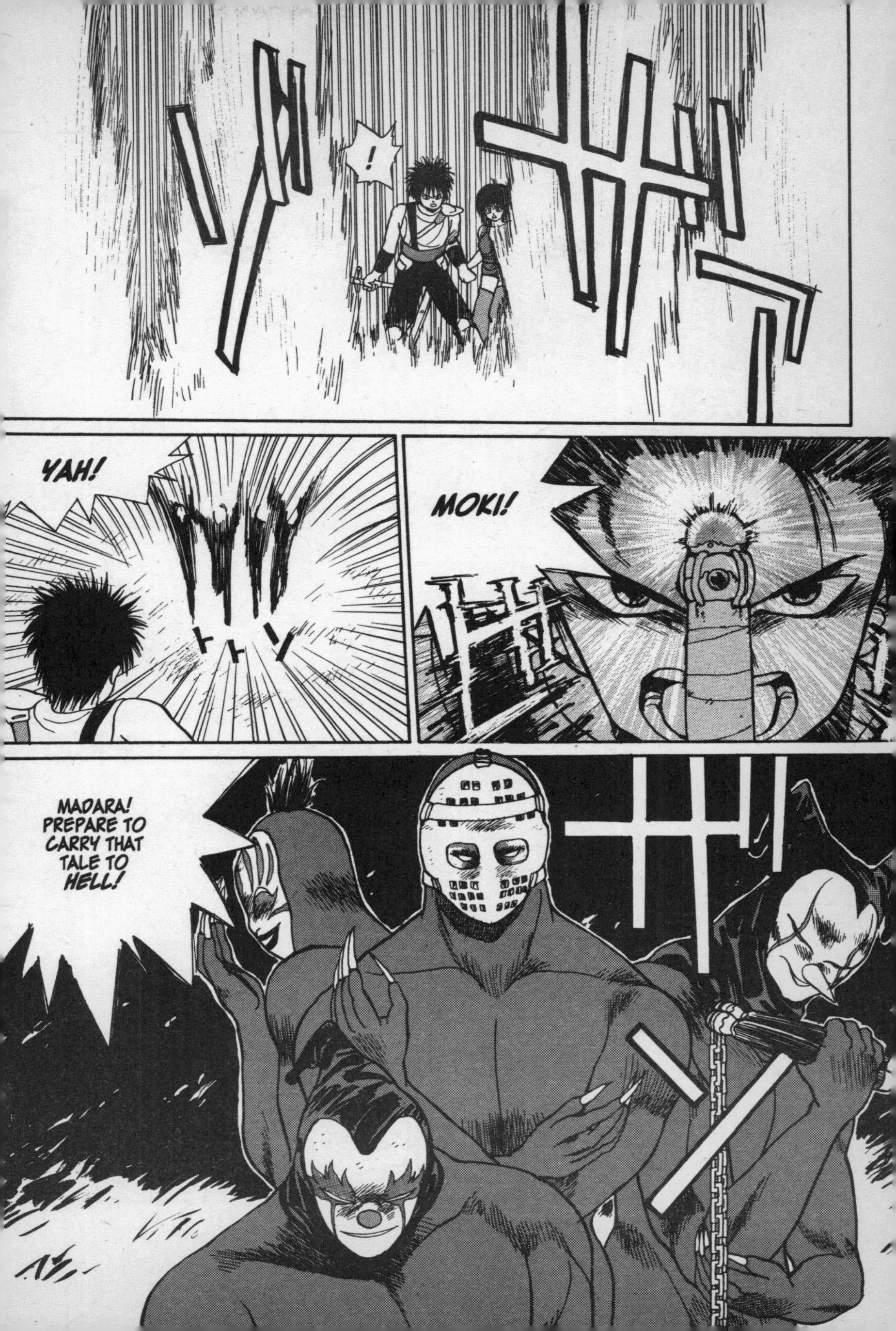
!
YAH!
MOKI!
MADARA! PREPARE TO CARRY THAT TALE TO HELL!

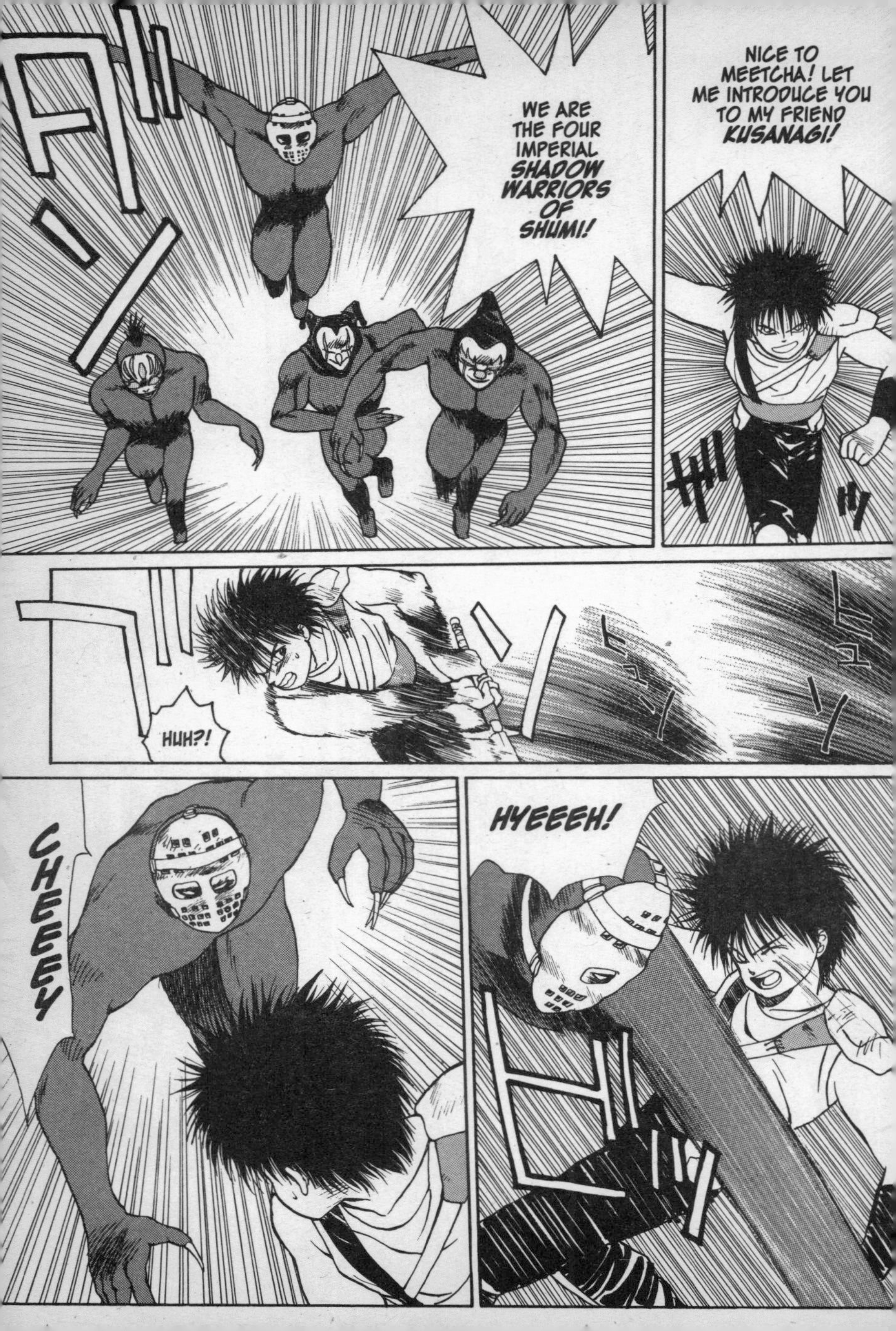

NICE TO MEETCHA! LET ME INTRODUCE YOU TO MY FRIEND KUSANAGI!
WE ARE THE FOUR IMPERIAL SHADOW WARRIORS OF SHUMI!
HUH?!
HYEEEH!
CHEEEEY

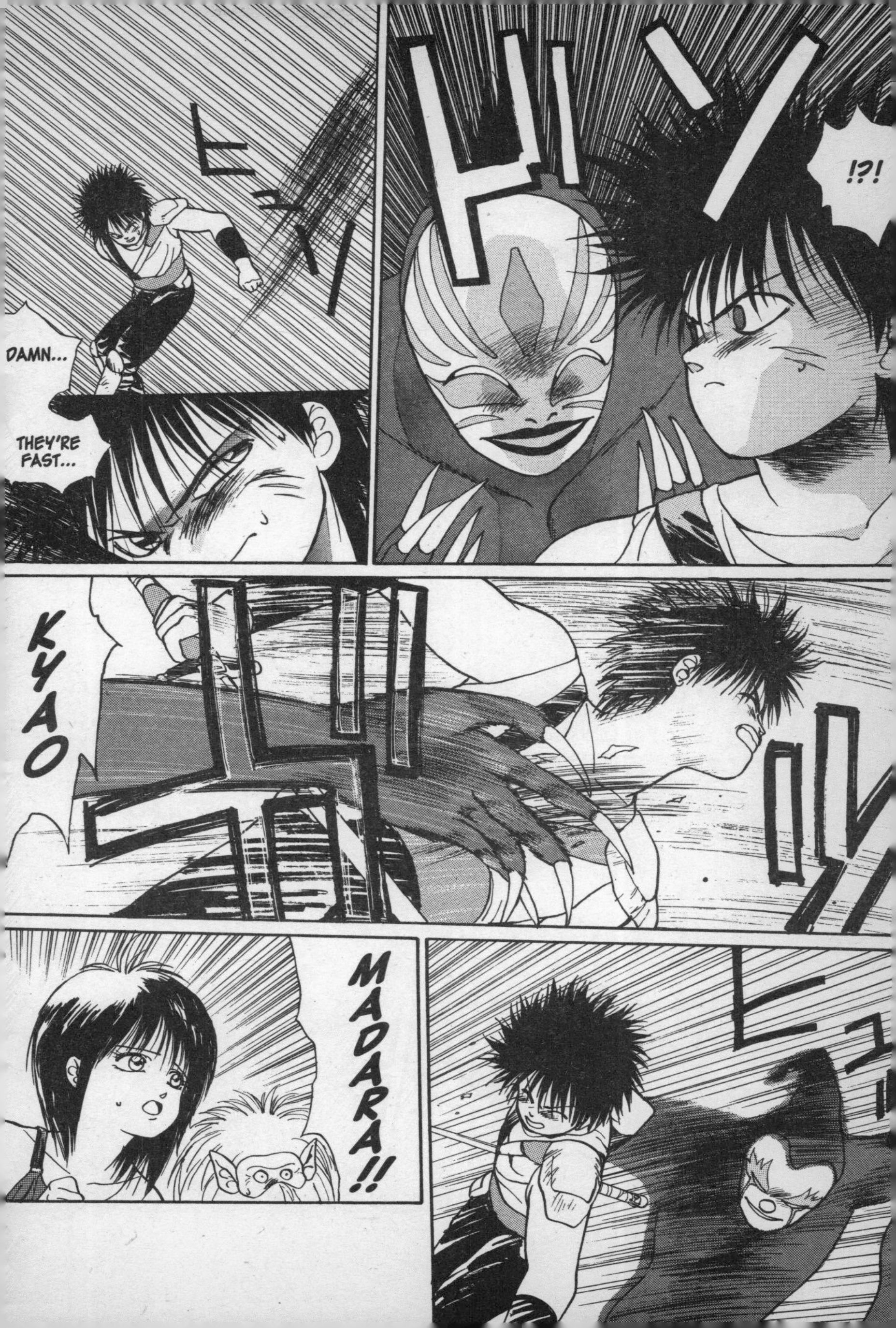
!?!
DAMN...
THEY'RE FAST...
KYAO
MADARA!!

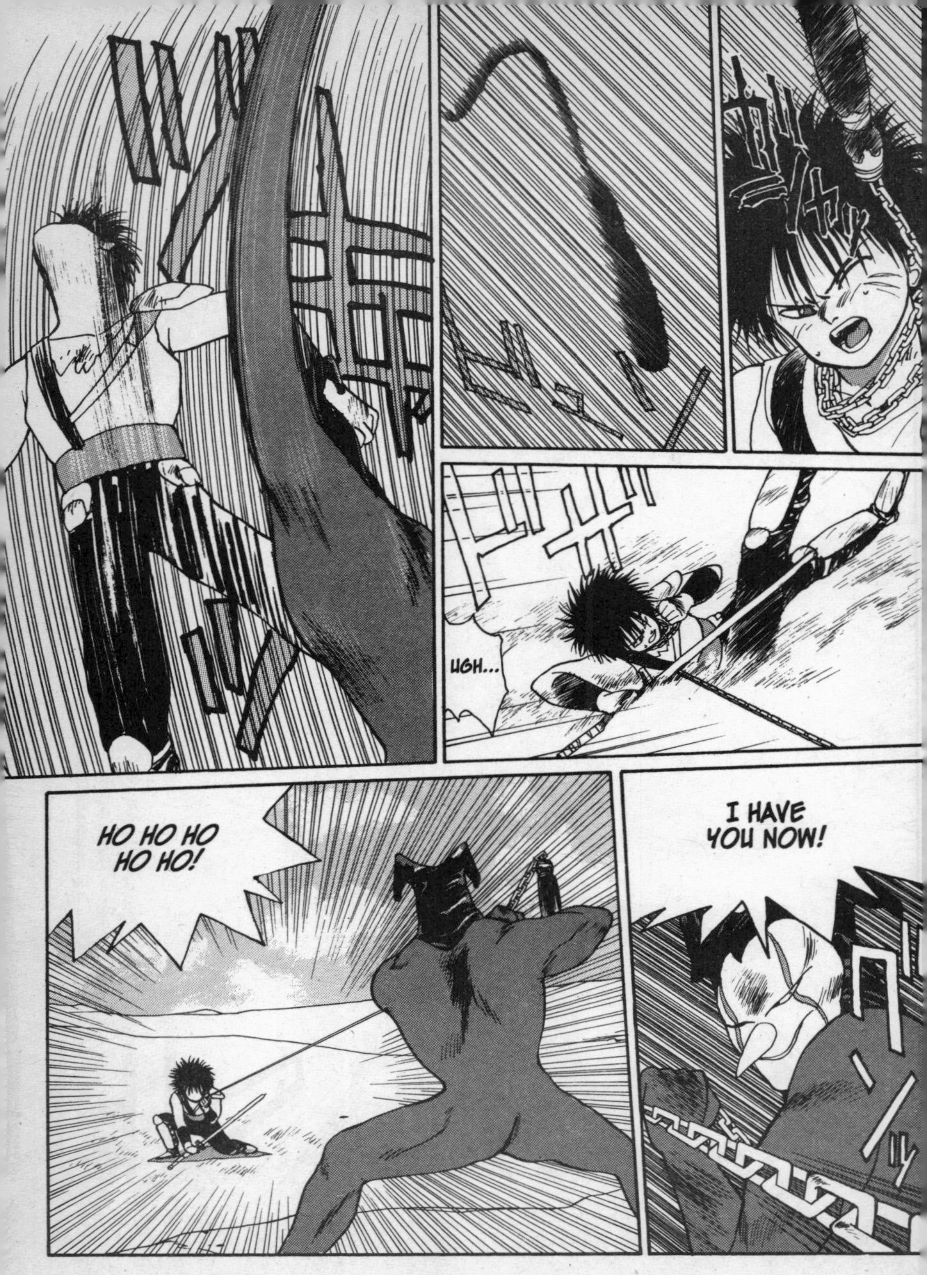
UGH...
HO HO HO
HO HO!
I HAVE
YOU NOW!

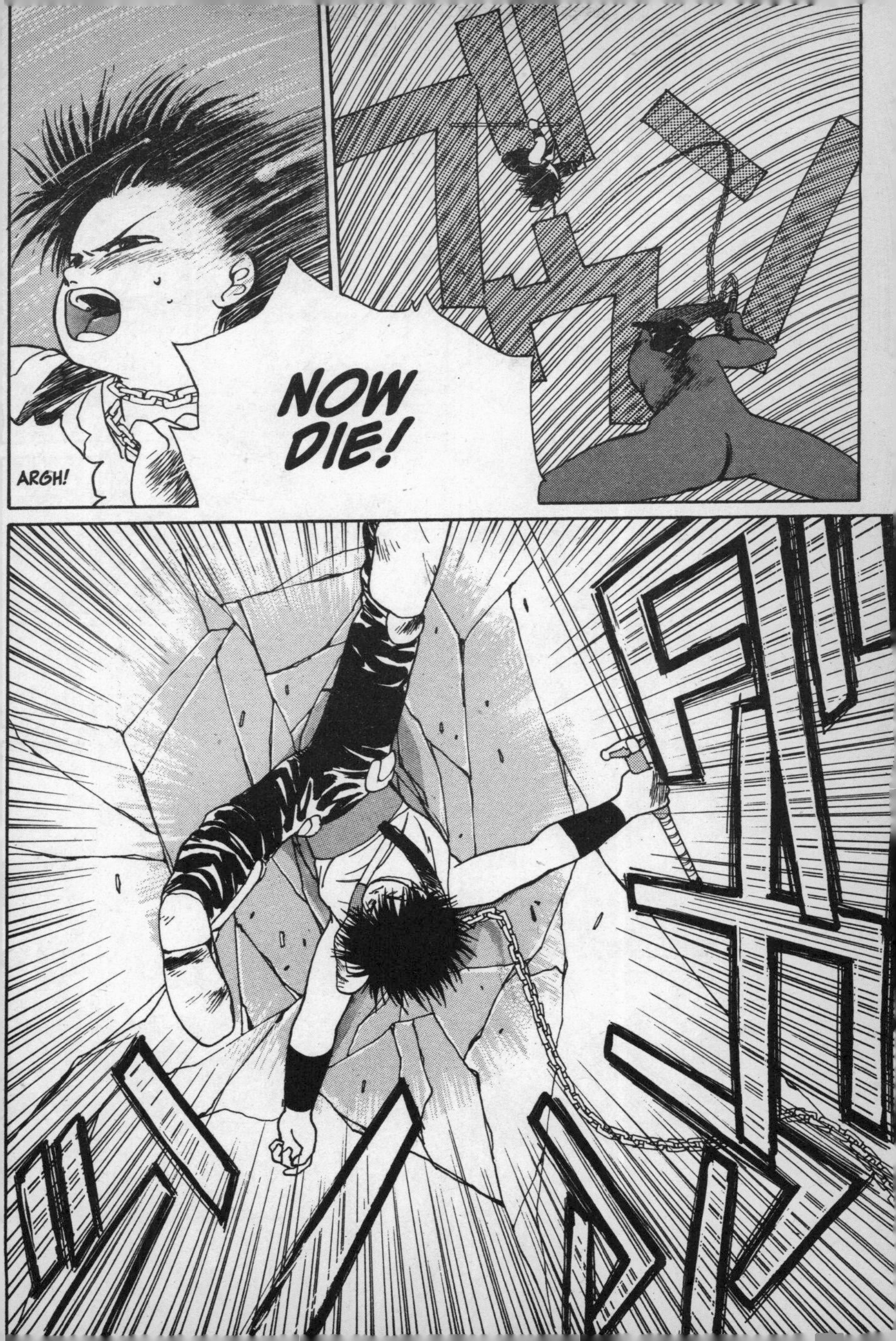
NOW DIE!
ARGH!

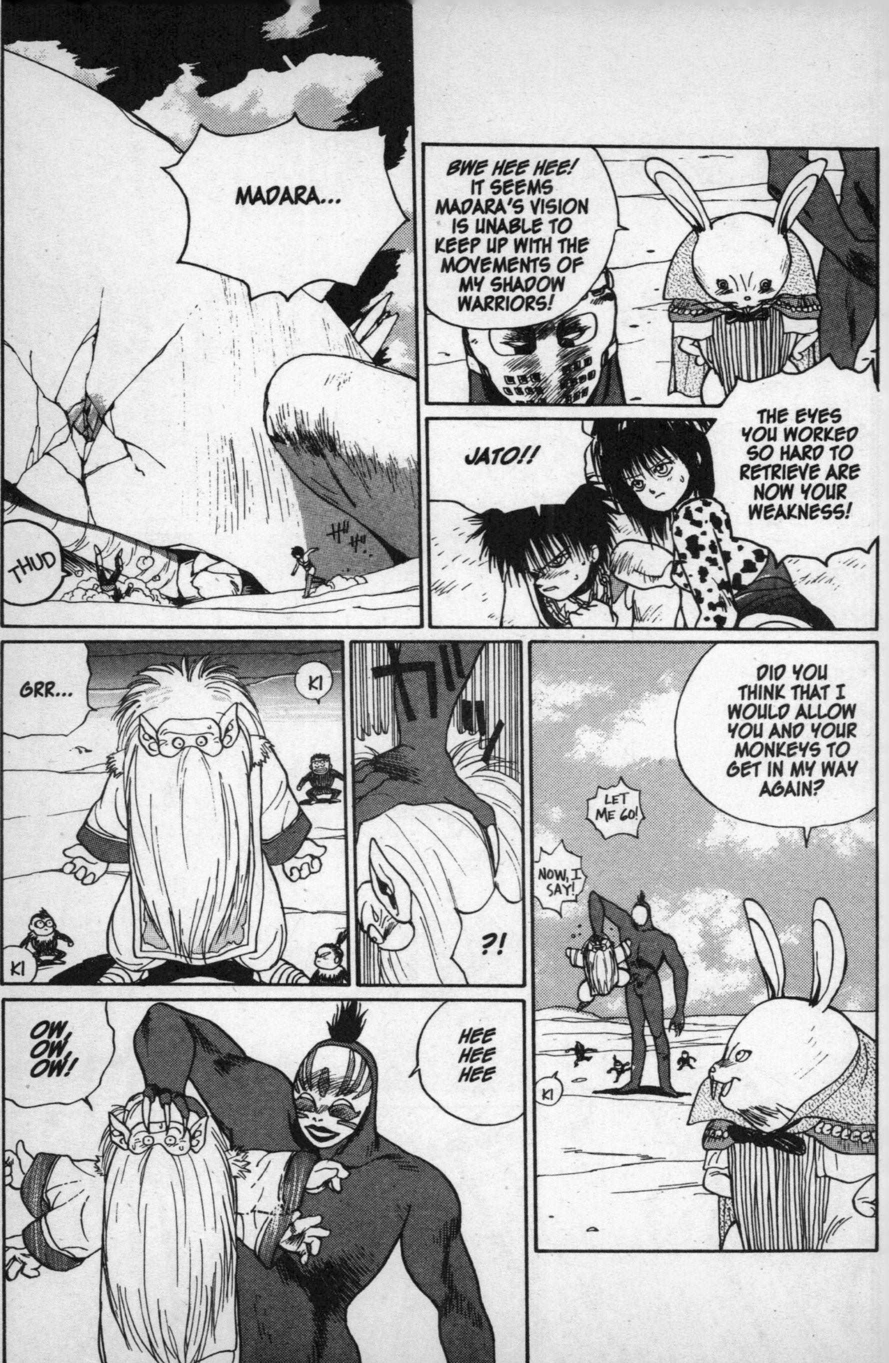
MADARA...
THUD
BWE HEE HEE! IT SEEMS MADARA'S VISION IS UNABLE TO KEEP UP WITH THE MOVEMENTS OF MY SHADOW WARRIORS!
JATO!!
THE EYES YOU WORKED SO HARD TO RETRIEVE ARE NOW YOUR WEAKNESS!
GRR...
KI
KI
?!
DID YOU THINK THAT I WOULD ALLOW YOU AND YOUR MONKEYS TO GET IN MY WAY AGAIN?
LET ME GO!
NOW, I SAY!
KI
OW, OW, OW!
HEE HEE HEE

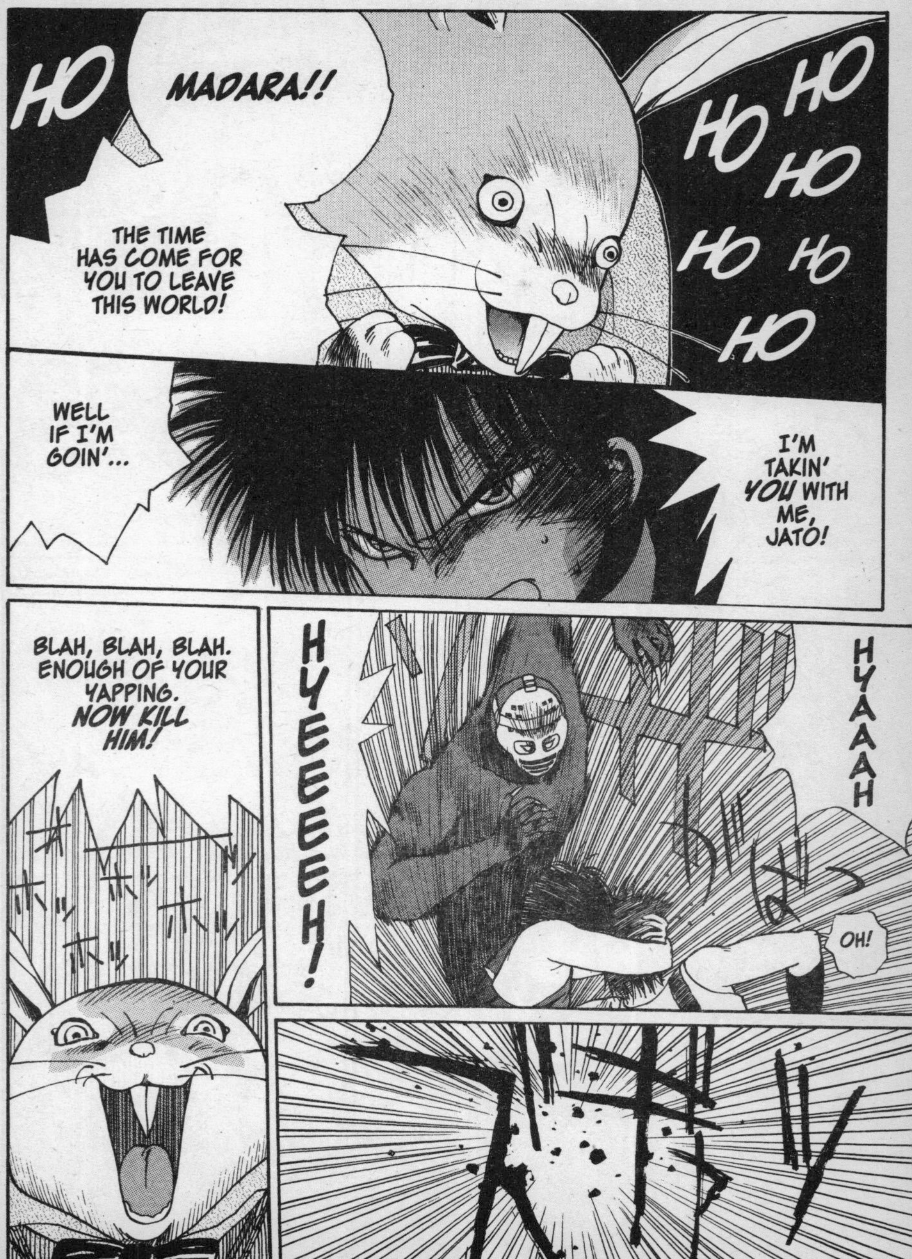
HO
MADARA!!
THE TIME HAS COME FOR YOU TO LEAVE THIS WORLD!
HO HO HO HO HO HO HO HO
WELL IF I'M GOIN'...
I'M TAKIN' YOU WITH ME, JATÓ!
BLAH, BLAH, BLAH. ENOUGH OF YOUR YAPPING. NOW KILL HIM!
HYEEEEEEH!
HYAAAH
OH!

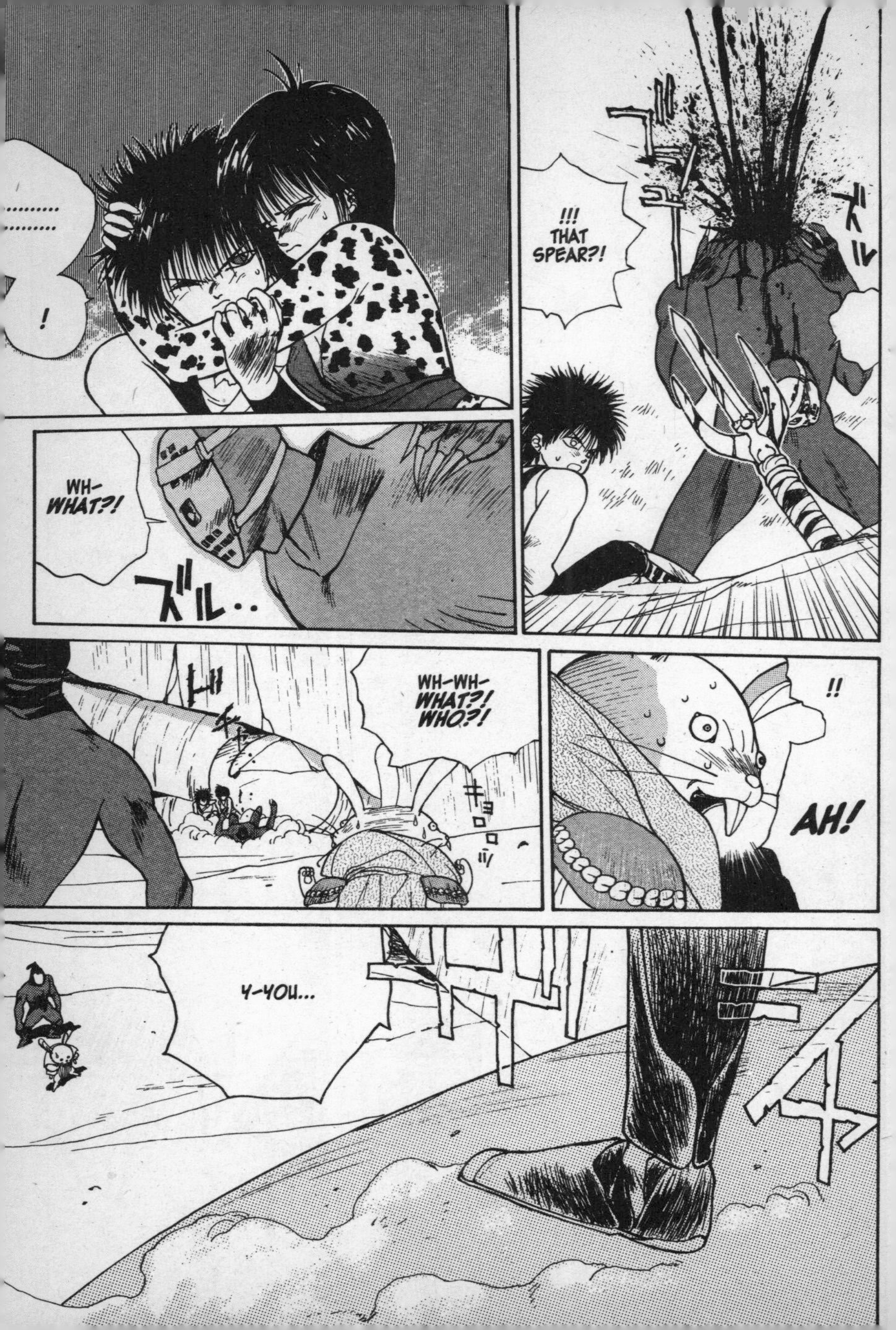
!!!
THAT SPEAR?!
ズル
....
....
!
WH-WHAT?!
ズル..
!!
AH!
WH-WH-WHAT?! WHO?!
キョロロ
Y-YOU...

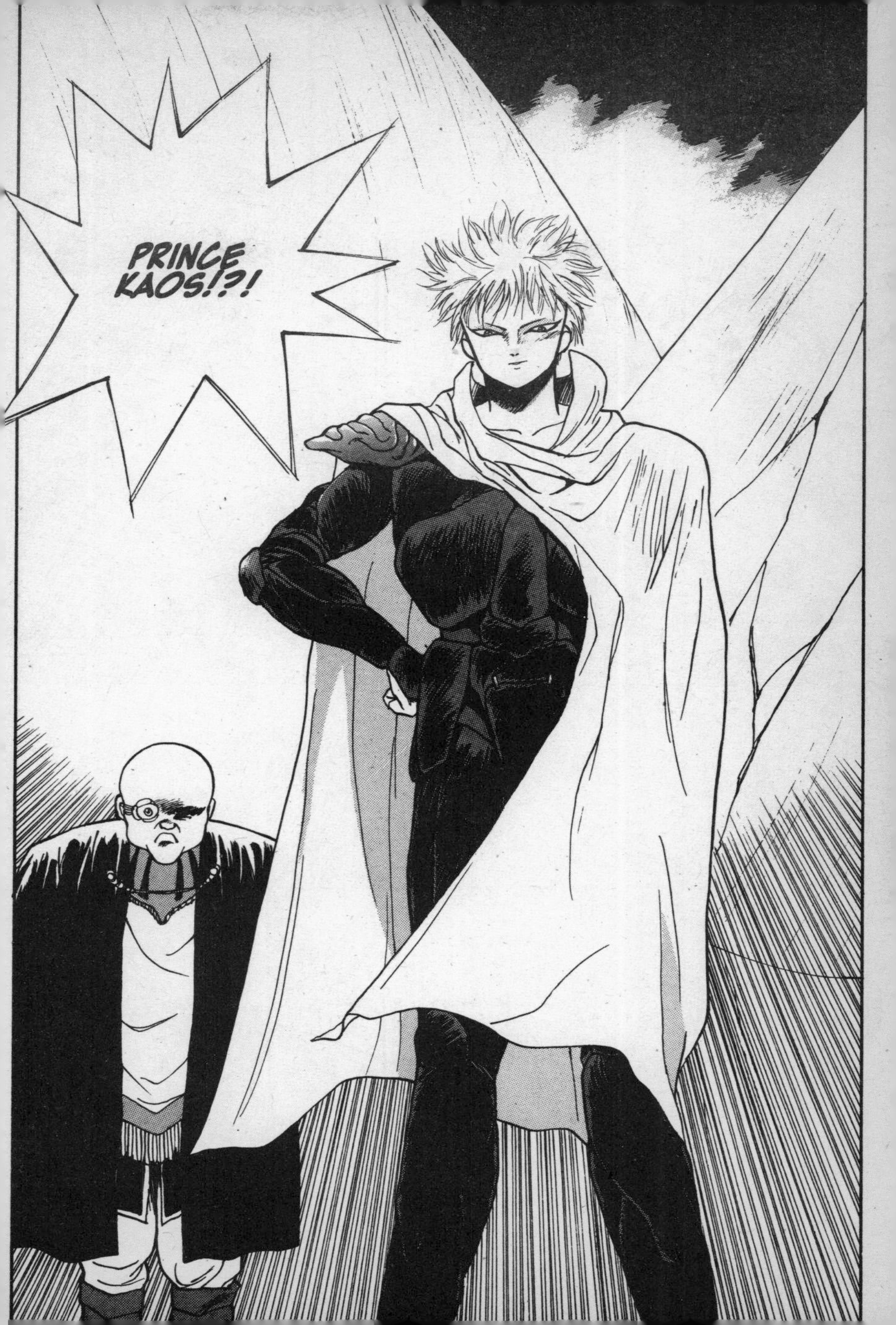
PRINCE KAOS!?!

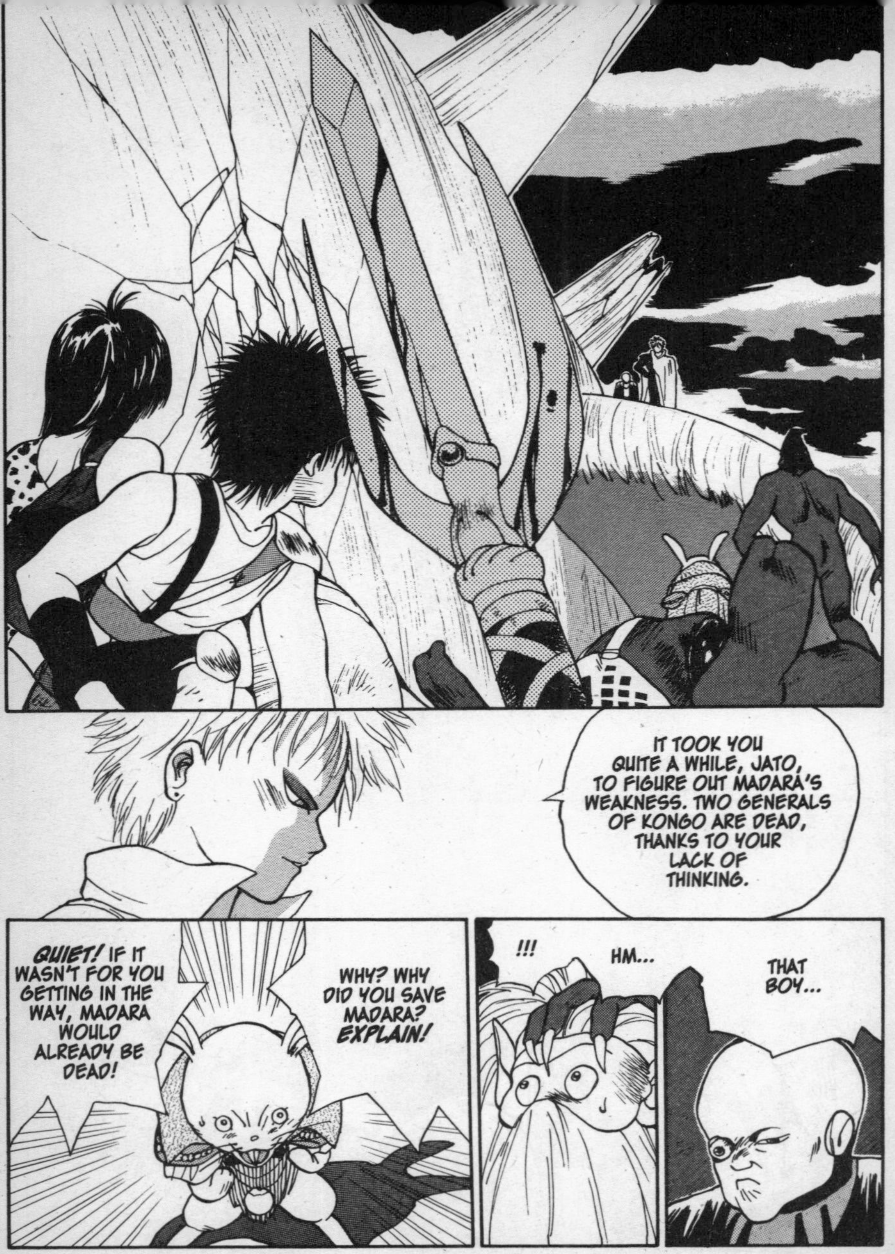
IT TOOK YOU QUITE A WHILE, JATO, TO FIGURE OUT MADARA'S WEAKNESS. TWO GENERALS OF KONGO ARE DEAD, THANKS TO YOUR LACK OF THINKING.
QUIET! IF IT WASN'T FOR YOU GETTING IN THE WAY, MADARA WOULD ALREADY BE DEAD!
WHY? WHY DID YOU SAVE MADARA? EXPLAIN!
!!!
HM...
THAT BOY...

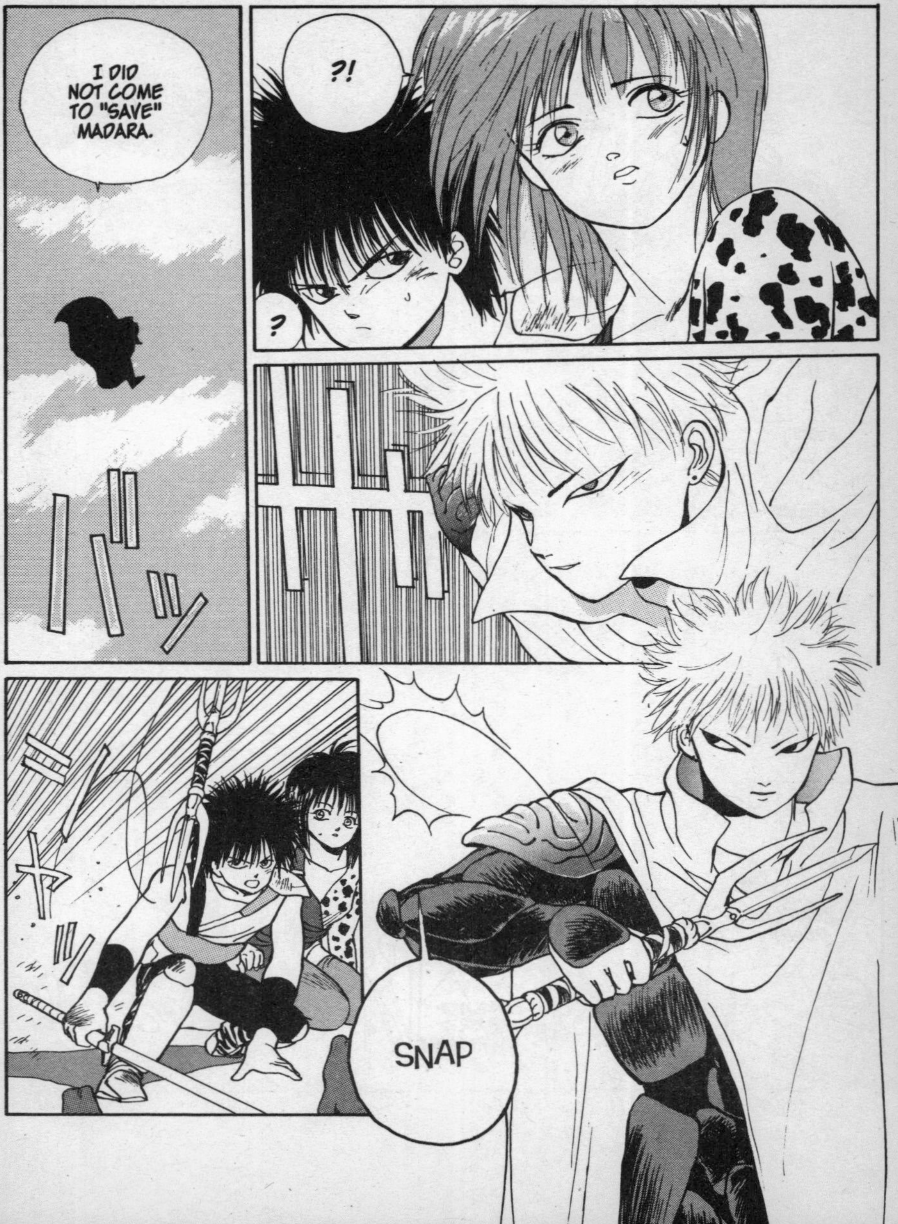

I DID NOT COME TO "SAVE" MADARA.
?!
?
SNAP

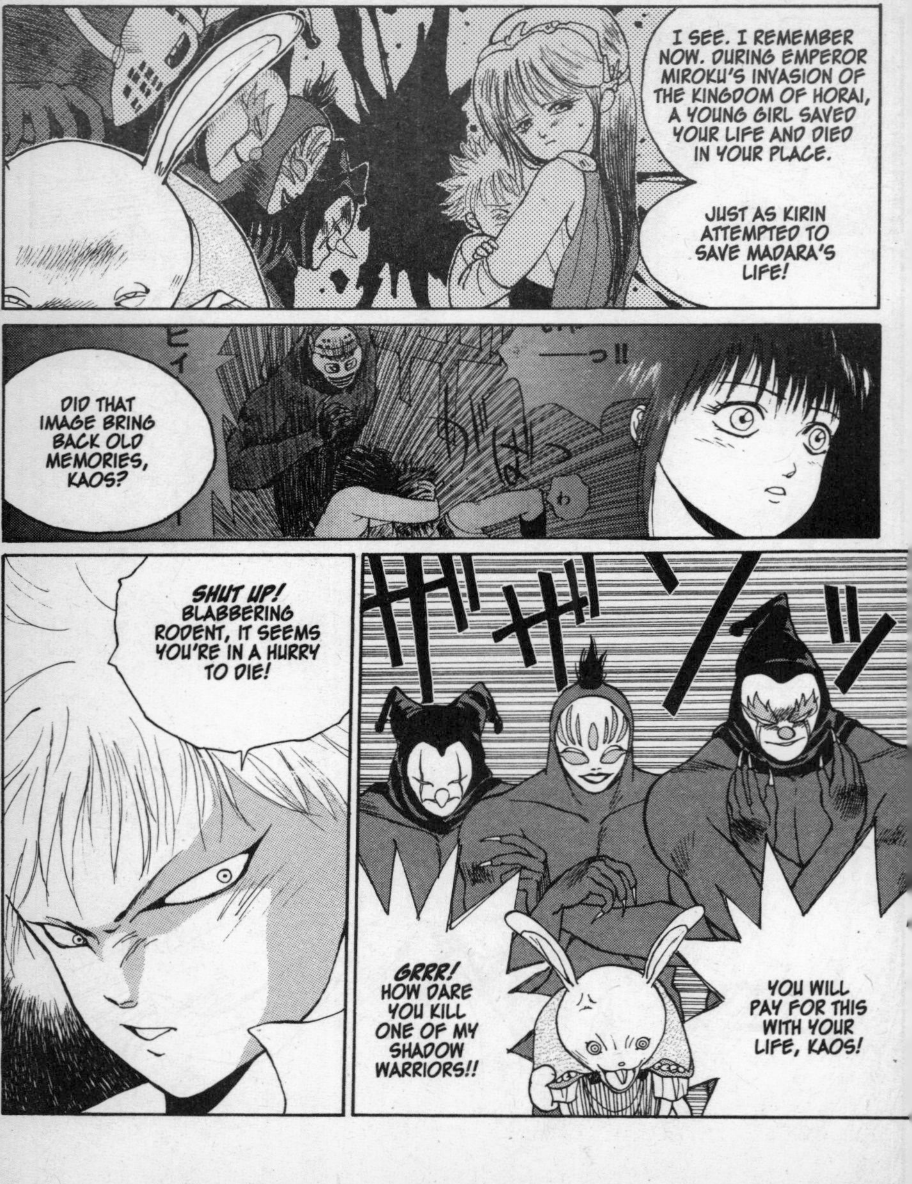
I SEE. I REMEMBER NOW. DURING EMPEROR MIROKU'S INVASION OF THE KINGDOM OF HORAI, A YOUNG GIRL SAVED YOUR LIFE AND DIED IN YOUR PLACE.
JUST AS KIRIN ATTEMPTED TO SAVE MADARA'S LIFE!
DID THAT IMAGE BRING BACK OLD MEMORIES, KAOS?
SHUT UP! BLABBERING RODENT, IT SEEMS YOU'RE IN A HURRY TO DIE!
GRRR! HOW DARE YOU KILL ONE OF MY SHADOW WARRIORS!!
YOU WILL PAY FOR THIS WITH YOUR LIFE, KAOS!

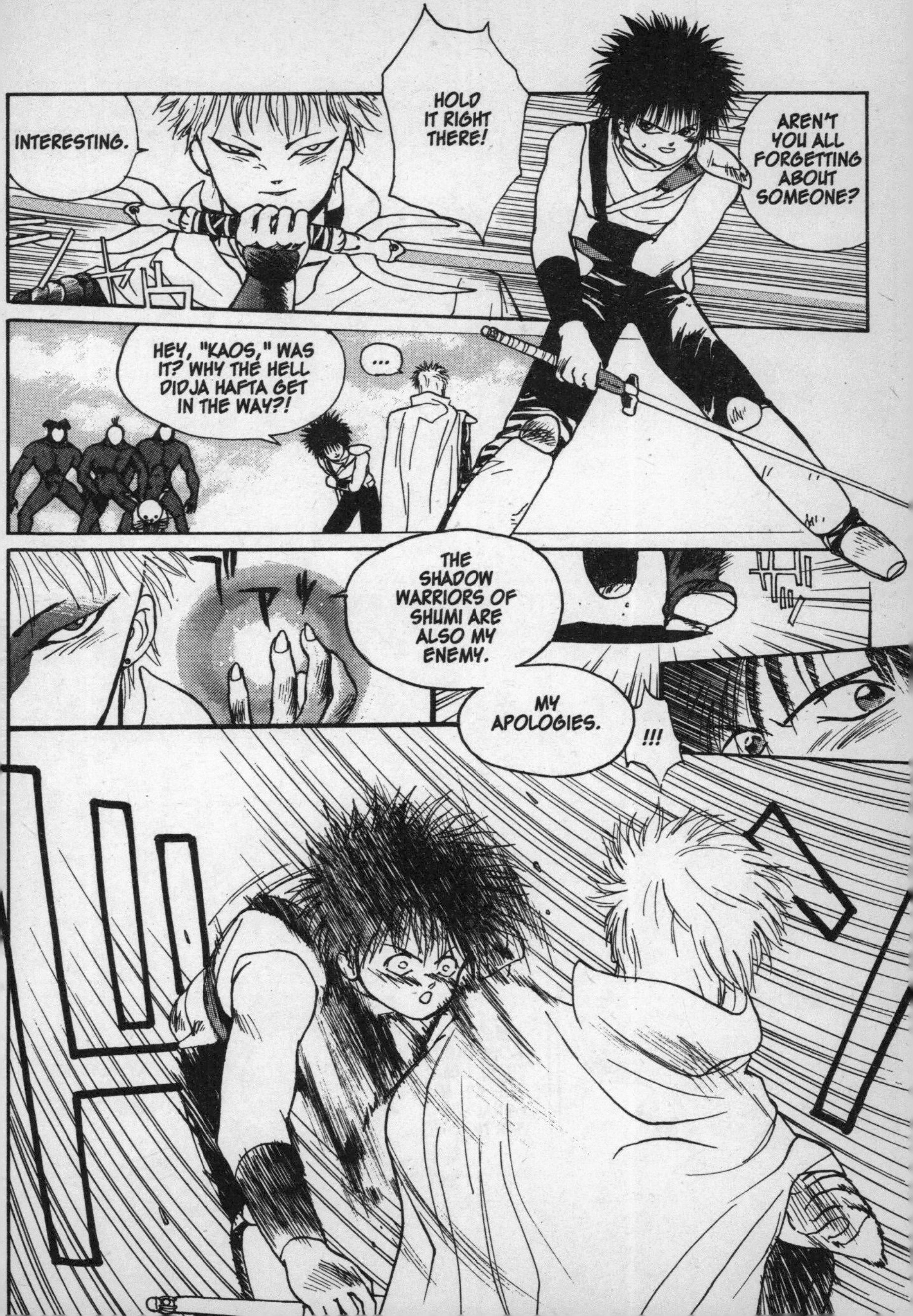
HOLD IT RIGHT THERE!
AREN'T YOU ALL FORGETTING ABOUT SOMEONE?
INTERESTING.
HEY, "KAOS," WAS IT? WHY THE HELL DIDJA HAFTA GET IN THE WAY?!
...
THE SHADOW WARRIORS OF SHUMI ARE ALSO MY ENEMY.
MY APOLOGIES.
!!!

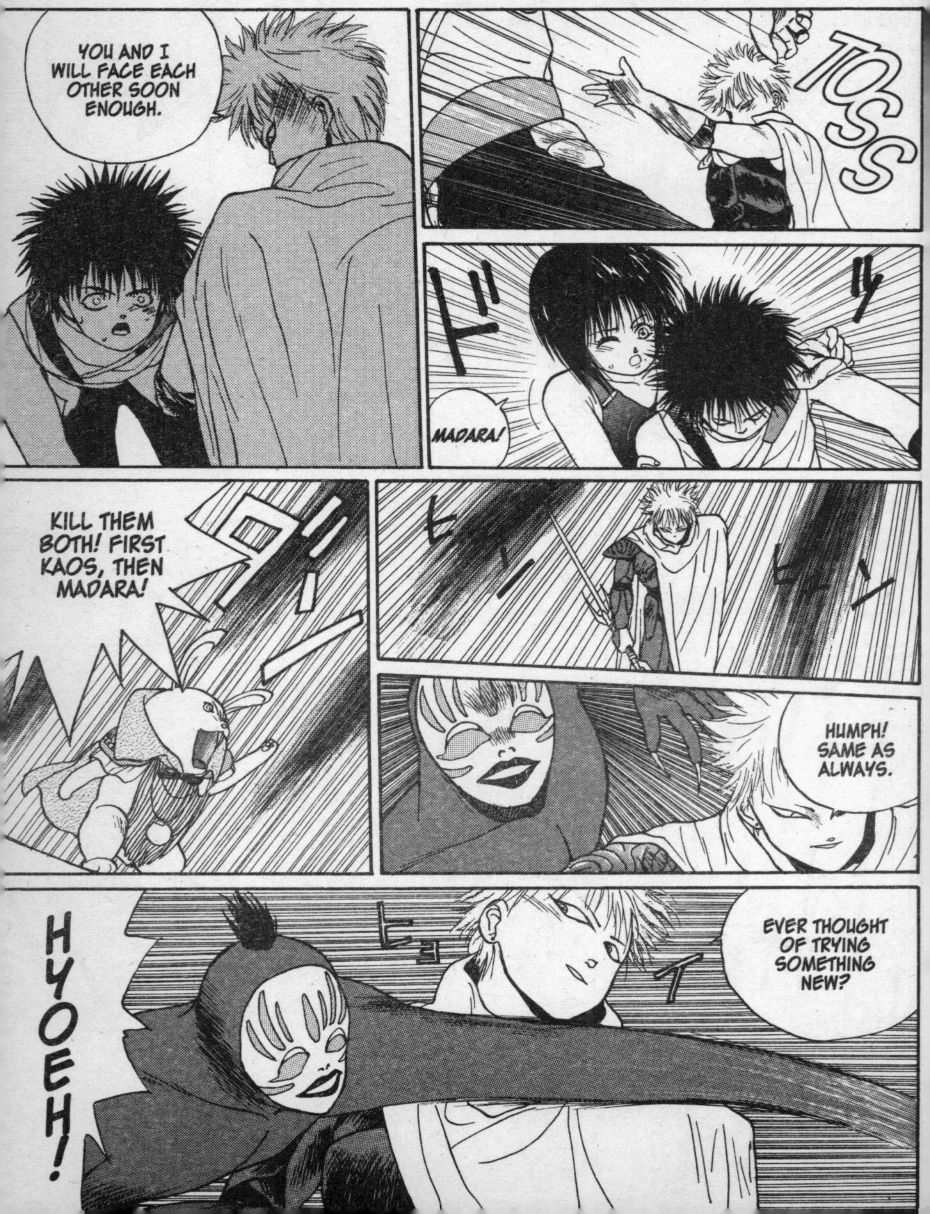
YOU AND I WILL FACE EACH OTHER SOON ENOUGH.
TOSS
MADARA!
KILL THEM BOTH! FIRST KAOS, THEN MADARA!
HUMPH! SAME AS ALWAYS.
HYOEH!
EVER THOUGHT OF TRYING SOMETHING NEW?

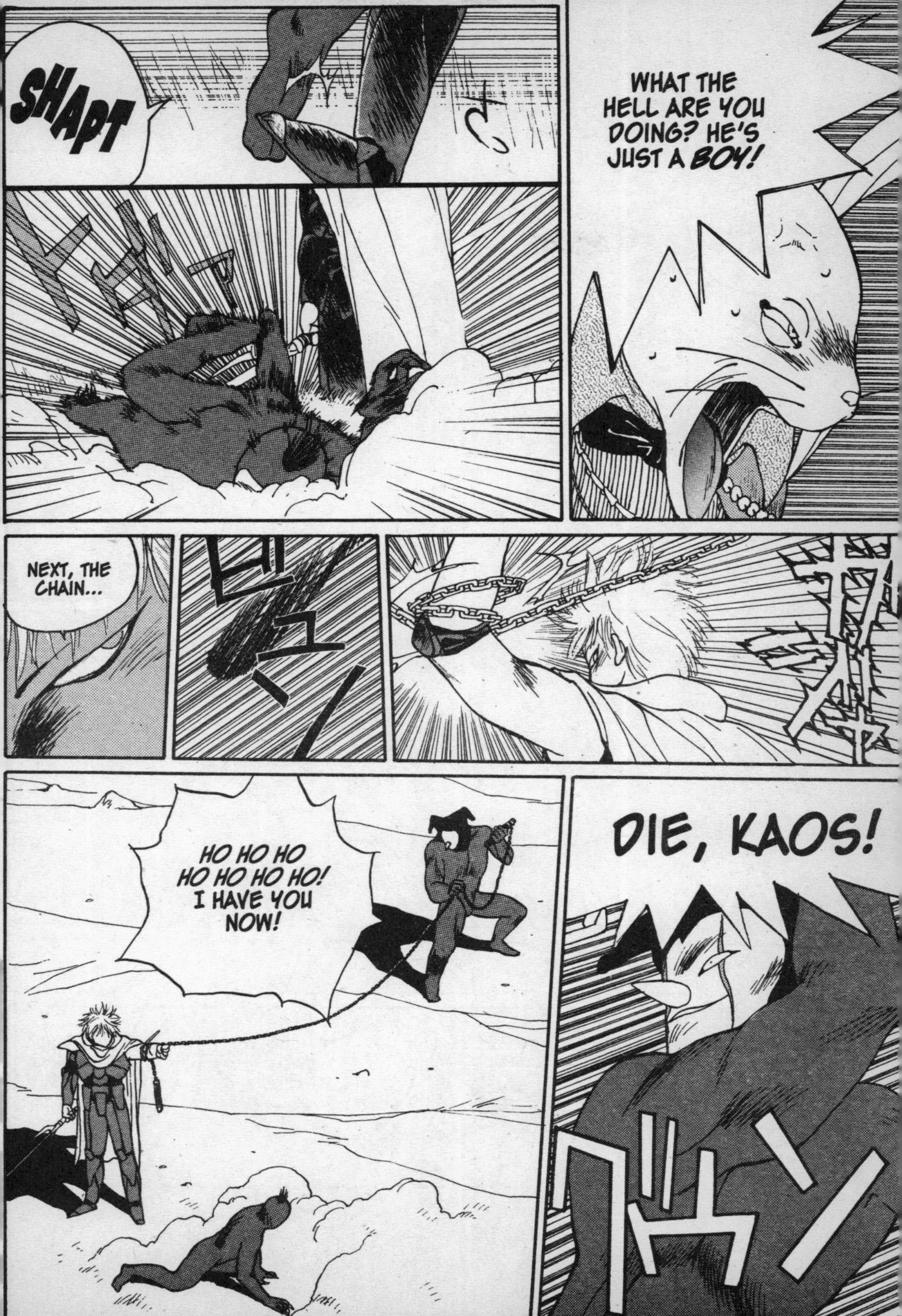
WHAT THE HELL ARE YOU DOING? HE'S JUST A BOY!
SHAPT
NEXT, THE CHAIN...
DIE, KAOS!
HO HO HO HO HO HO HO! I HAVE YOU NOW!

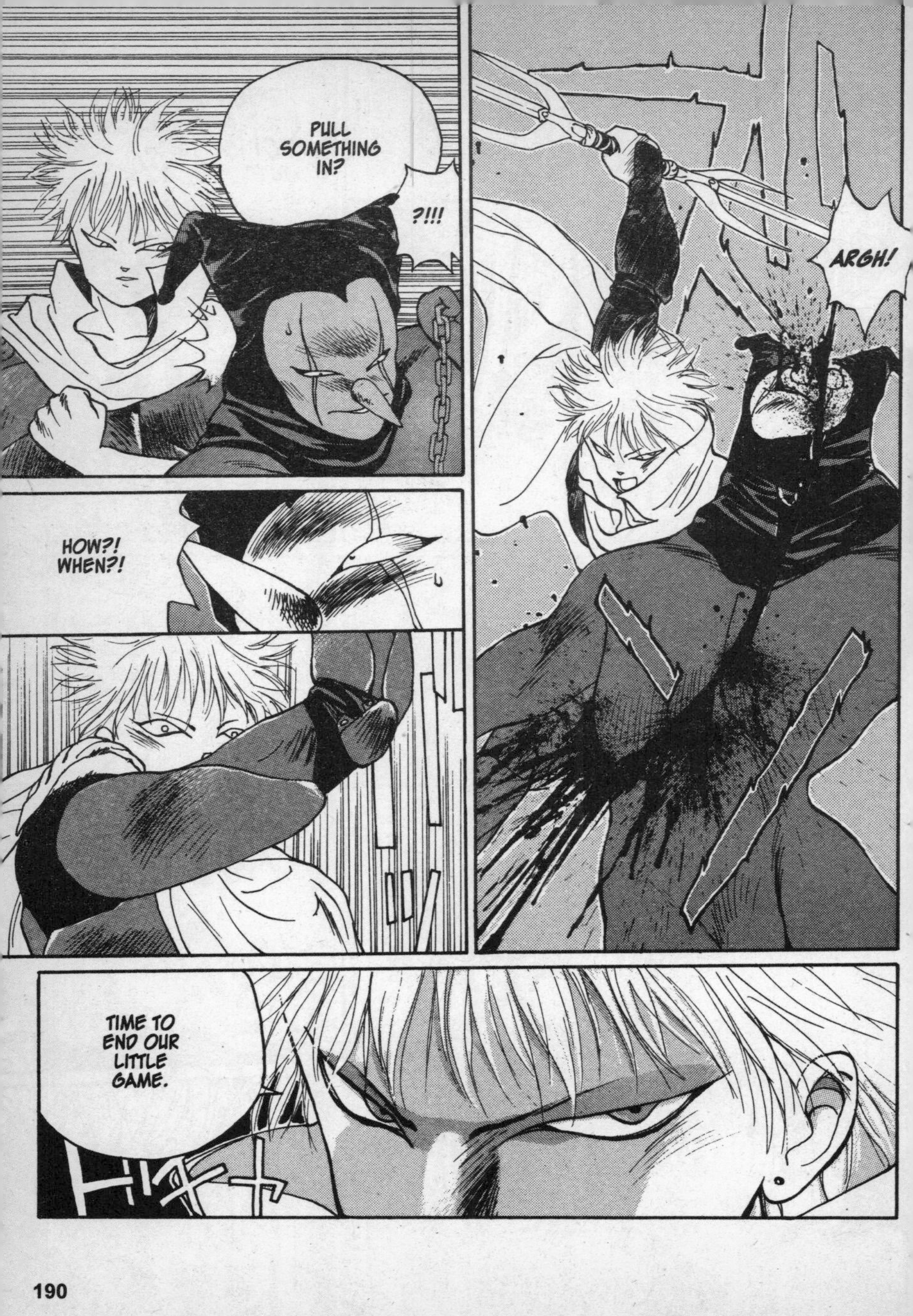
PULL SOMETHING IN?
?!!!
ARGH!
HOW?! WHEN?!
TIME TO END OUR LITTLE GAME.

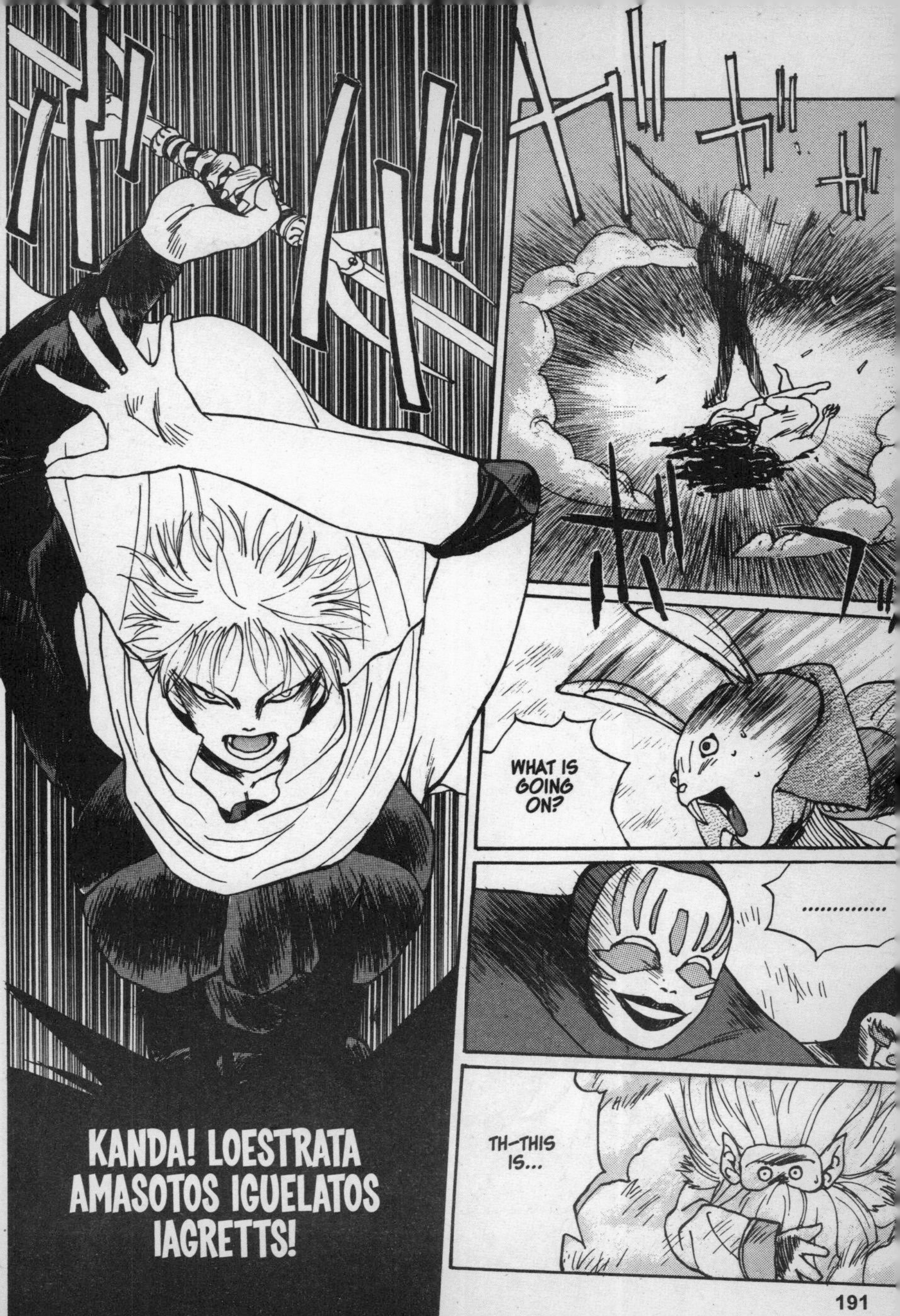
WHAT IS GOING ON?
....
TH-THIS IS...
KANDA! LOESTRATA AMASOTOS IGUELATOS IAGRETTS!

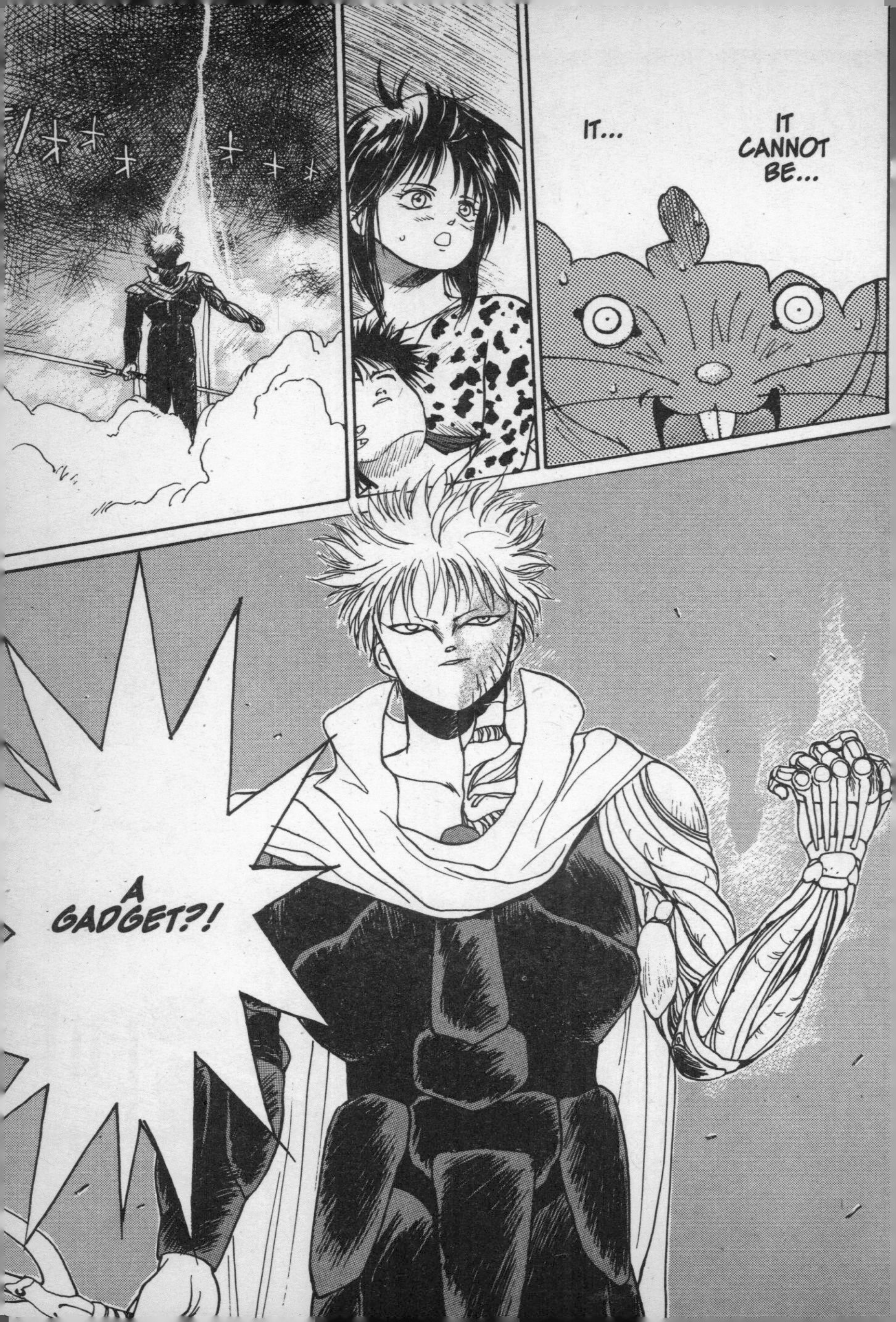
IT...
IT CANNOT BE...
A GADGET?!

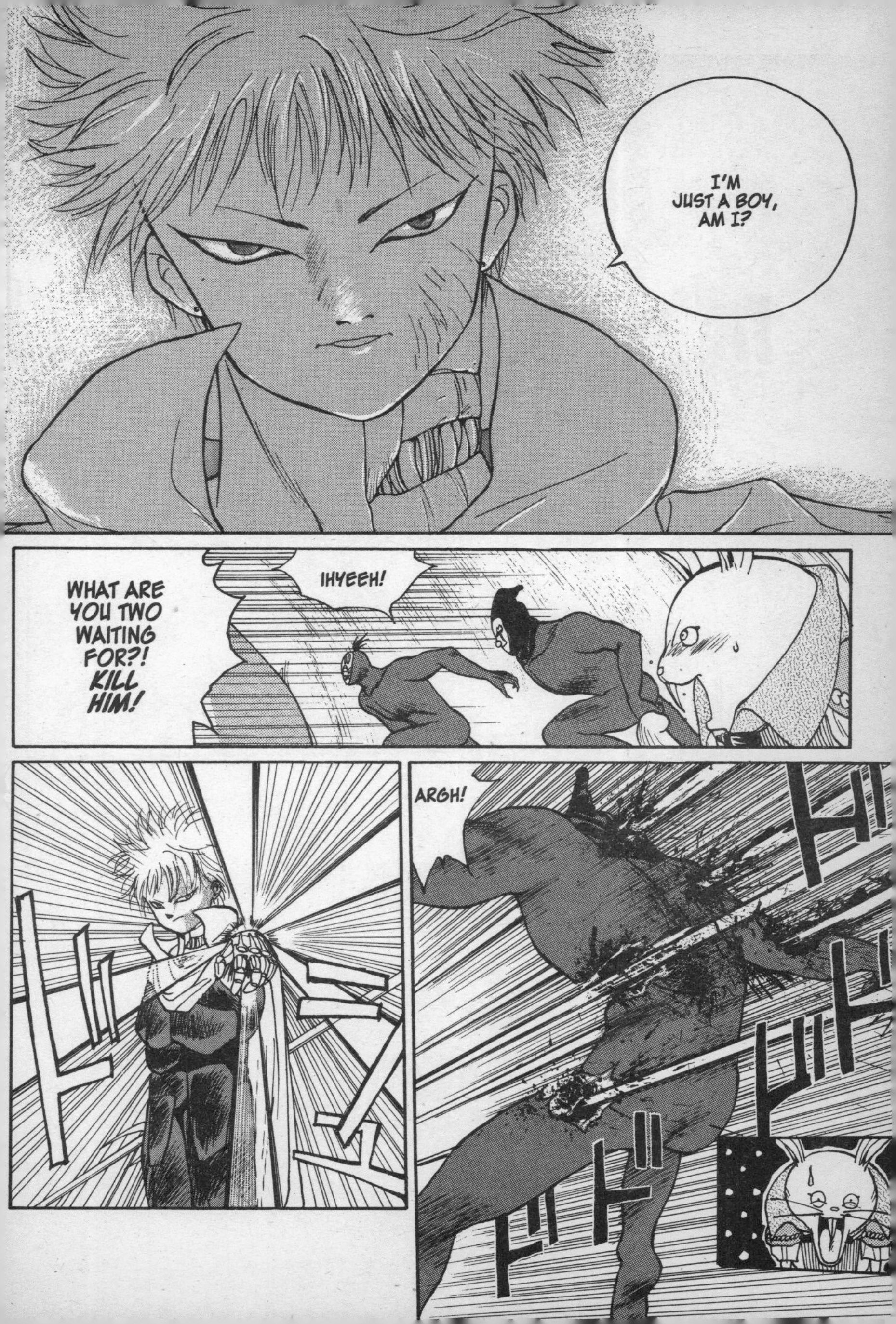
I'M JUST A BOY, AM I?
IHYEEH!
WHAT ARE YOU TWO WAITING FOR?! KILL HIM!
ARGH!

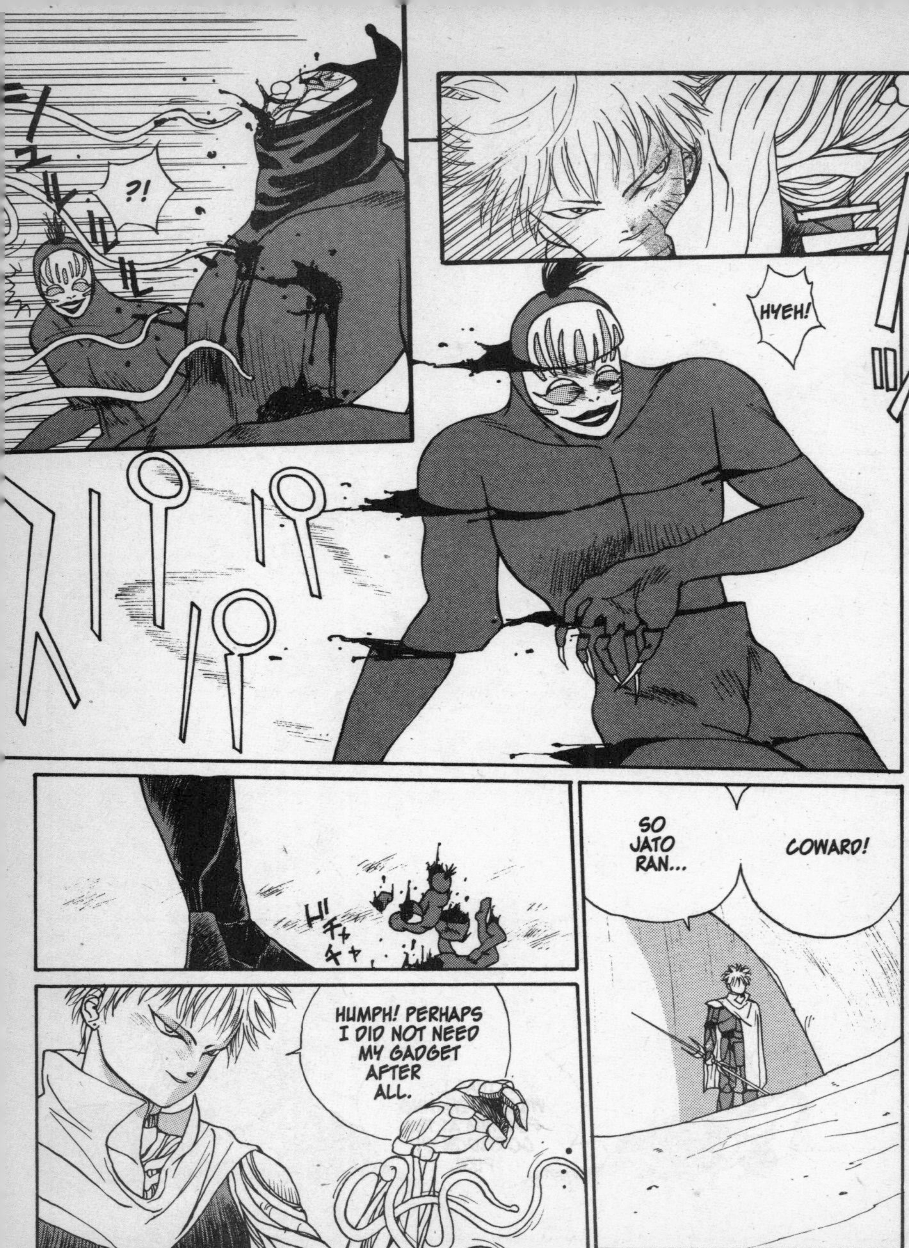
?!
HYEH!
COWARD!
SO JATO RAN...
HUMPH! PERHAPS I DID NOT NEED MY GADGET AFTER ALL.

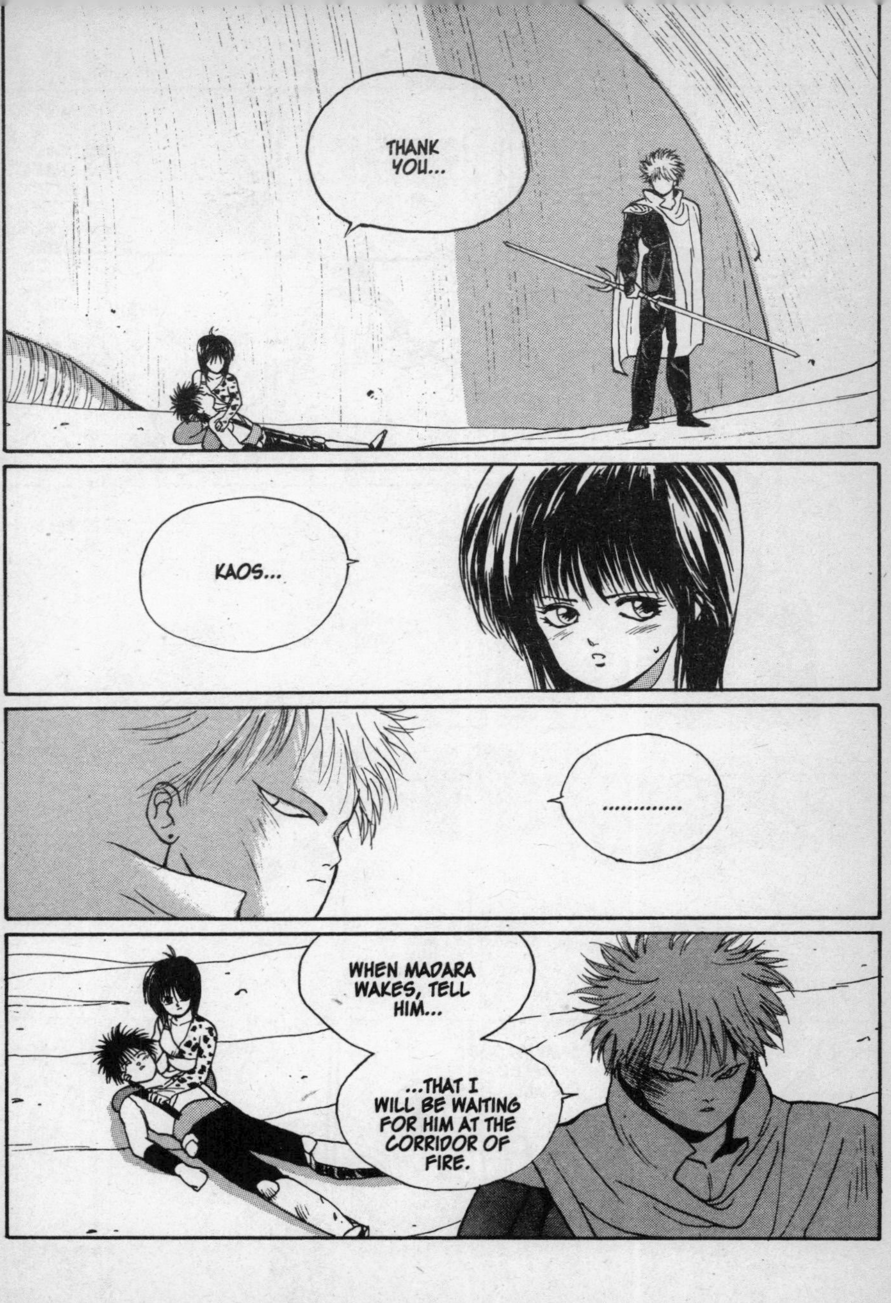
THANK YOU...
KAOS...
....
WHEN MADARA WAKES, TELL HIM...
...THAT I WILL BE WAITING FOR HIM AT THE CORRIDOR OF FIRE.

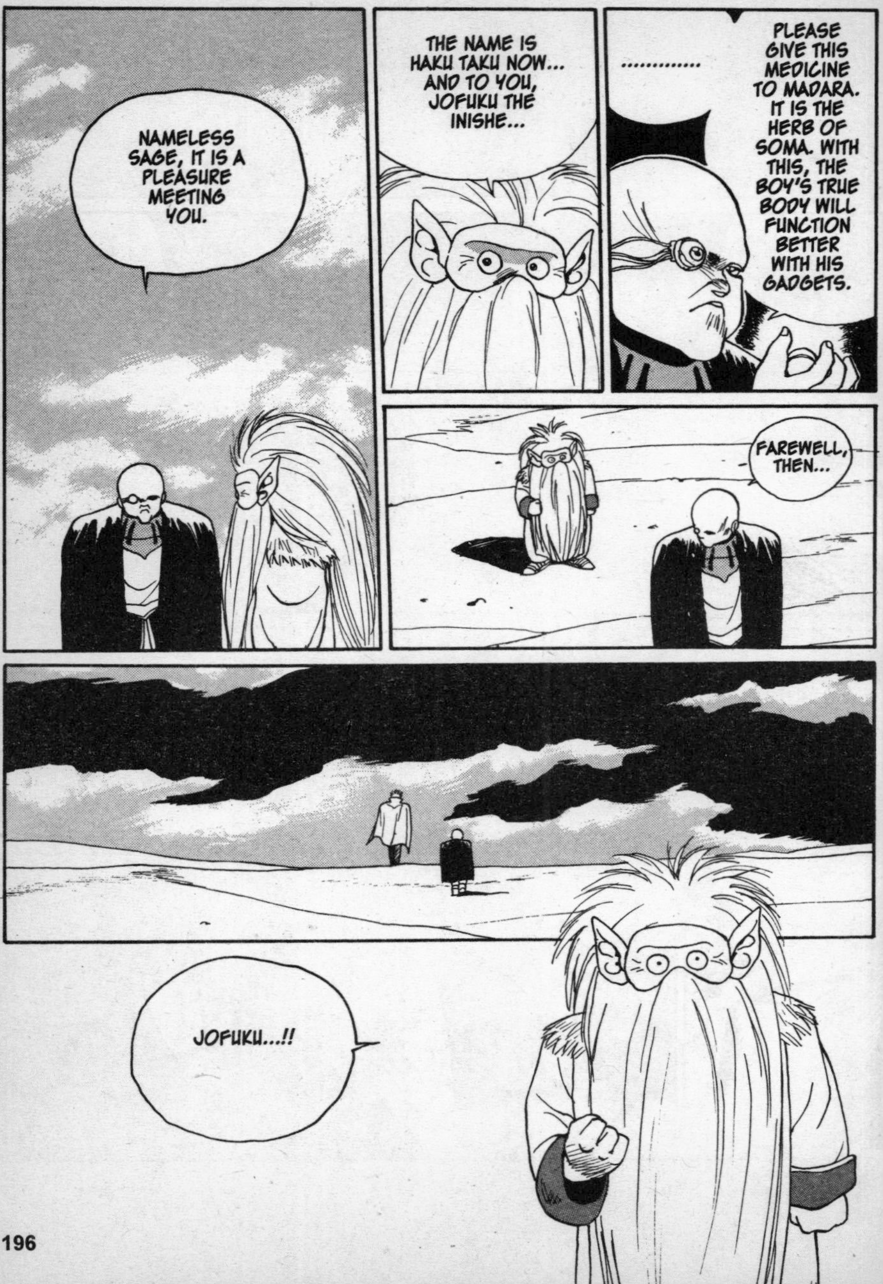
NAMELESS SAGE, IT IS A PLEASURE MEETING YOU.
THE NAME IS HAKU TAKU NOW... AND TO YOU, JOFUKU THE INISHE...
....
PLEASE GIVE THIS MEDICINE TO MADARA. IT IS THE HERB OF SOMA. WITH THIS, THE BOY'S TRUE BODY WILL FUNCTION BETTER WITH HIS GADGETS.
FAREWELL, THEN...
JOFUKU...!!

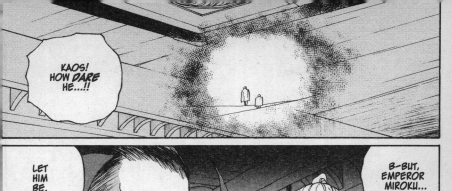

KAOS! HOW *DARE* HE...!!

LET HIM BE.

B-BUT, EMPEROR MIROKU...

IT DOES NOT MATTER WHAT KAOS DOES...JUST AS LONG AS HE KILLS MADARA.

AND...

DO NOT FORGET THAT WE HAVE WHAT HE SEEKS.

THE OTHER HALF OF HIS BODY!

To be continued...